Rethinking the Atlantic World

*Also by Manuela Albertone:*
MONETA E POLITICA IN FRANCIA: DALLA CASSA DI SCONTO AGLI ASSEGNATI (1776–1792)

IL REPUBBLICANESIMO MODERNO: L'IDEA DI REPUBBLICA NELLA RIFLESSIONE STORICA DI FRANCO VENTURI

*Also by Antonino De Francesco:*
IL GOVERNO SENZA TESTA: MOVIMENTO DEMOCRATICO E FEDERALISMO NELLA FRANCIA RIVOLUZIONARIA 1789–1795

MITO E STORIOGRAFIA DELLA 'GRANDE RIVOLUZIONE': LA RIVOLUZIONE FRANCESE NELLA CULTURA POLITICA ITALIANA DEL '900

# Rethinking the Atlantic World

## Europe and America in the Age of Democratic Revolutions

Edited by

Manuela Albertone
*Professor of Modern History, University of Turin*

and

Antonino De Francesco
*Professor of Modern History, University of Milan*

Editorial matter, selection and introduction © Manuela Albertone and Antonino De Francesco 2009. All remaining chapters © their respective authors 2009.
Softcover reprint of the hardcover 1st edition 2009 978-0-230-20678-6

All rights reserved. No reproduction, copy or transmission of this publication may be made without written permission.

No portion of this publication may be reproduced, copied or transmitted save with written permission or in accordance with the provisions of the Copyright, Designs and Patents Act 1988, or under the terms of any licence permitting limited copying issued by the Copyright Licensing Agency, Saffron House, 6-10 Kirby Street, London EC1N 8TS.

Any person who does any unauthorized act in relation to this publication may be liable to criminal prosecution and civil claims for damages.

The authors have asserted their rights to be identified as the authors of this work in accordance with the Copyright, Designs and Patents Act 1988.

First published 2009 by
PALGRAVE MACMILLAN

Palgrave Macmillan in the UK is an imprint of Macmillan Publishers Limited, registered in England, company number 785998, of Houndmills, Basingstoke, Hampshire RG21 6XS.

Palgrave Macmillan in the US is a division of St Martin's Press LLC, 175 Fifth Avenue, New York, NY 10010.

Palgrave Macmillan is the global academic imprint of the above companies and has companies and representatives throughout the world.

Palgrave® and Macmillan® are registered trademarks in the United States, the United Kingdom, Europe and other countries

ISBN 978-1-349-30244-4        ISBN 978-0-230-23380-5 (eBook)
DOI 10.1057/9780230233805

This book is printed on paper suitable for recycling and made from fully managed and sustained forest sources. Logging, pulping and manufacturing processes are expected to conform to the environmental regulations of the country of origin.

A catalogue record for this book is available from the British Library.

A catalog record for this book is available from the Library of Congress.

10  9  8  7  6  5  4  3  2  1
18 17 16 15 14 13 12 11 10 09

Transferred to Digital Printing in 2011

# Contents

*Preface* vii
*Notes on the Contributors* viii

Introduction: Beyond Atlantic History 1
*Manuela Albertone and Antonino De Francesco*

## Part I  Political Ideas and Economic Models in Eighteenth-Century Europe and America 15

1  The One and the Many: The Two Revolutions Question and the 'Consumer-Commercial' Atlantic, 1789 to the Present 17
   *Allan Potofsky*

2  Democracy and Equality in the Radical Enlightenment: Revolutionary Ideology before 1789 46
   *Jonathan Israel*

3  Between Republicanism and the Enlightenment: Turgot and Adams 61
   *Maria Luisa Pesante*

4  Nicolas Bergasse and Alexander Hamilton: The Role of the Judiciary in the Separation of Powers and Two Conceptions of Constitutional Order 80
   *Pasquale Pasquino*

5  Neutrality and Trade in the Dutch Republic (1775–1783): Preludes to a Piecemeal Revolution 100
   *Koen Stapelbroek*

## Part II  Free Trade and Democratic Revolutions in Eighteenth-Century Europe and America 121

6  Thomas Jefferson and French Economic Thought: A Mutual Exchange of Ideas 123
   *Manuela Albertone*

## vi Contents

7  The Question of Slavery in the Physiocratic Texts:
   A Rereading of an Old Debate — 147
   *Marcel Dorigny*

8  'A New Kind of Federalism': Benjamin Constant and
   Modern Europe — 163
   *Biancamaria Fontana*

9  Industry, Government and Europe: From the
   Mercantilists to Saint-Simon — 180
   *Gino Longhitano*

### Part III  The American and the French Revolutions: From Two Continents a New Political World — 201

10  France and the United States at the End of
    the Eighteenth Century — 203
    *James Roger Sharp*

11  The French and North American Revolutions in
    Comparative Perspective — 219
    *Richard Whatmore*

12  Federalist Obsession and Jacobin Conspiracy: France and
    the United States in a Time of Revolution, 1789–1794 — 239
    *Antonino De Francesco*

13  In Search of the Atlantic Republic: 1660–1776–1799
    in the Mirror — 257
    *Pierre Serna*

14  The Republican Imagination and Race: The Case of
    the Haitian Revolution — 276
    *Bernard Gainot*

*Index* — 294

# Preface

This volume is the result of a project financed by the Italian Ministry for Universities and Research (PRIN 2005) which combined the efforts of four universities (Milan, Turin, Catania and L'Orientale in Naples). It is the fruit of cooperation between scholars at an international level, who met and discussed their ideas on occasions such as the workshop entitled 'L'idea di Europa nel Settecento nella storia e nella storiografia' (Turin, 22–23 March 2007) and the international conferences 'Républiques en miroir: Le Directoire devant la révolution atlantique' (Paris Sorbonne, 25–26 January 2008) and 'Rivoluzioni democratiche e libertà economica tra Europa e America nel XVIII secolo' (Catania, 10–12 April 2008). The editors would like to thank all those who helped bring this project to completion, in particular Enrico Decleva, Rector of the University of Milan and Enrico Iachello, Dean of the Faculty of Letters at the University of Catania, for the many ways in which they freely offered their aid and support.

# Notes on the Contributors

**Manuela Albertone** is Professor of Modern History at the University of Turin. She won scholarships to the Fondazione Luigi Einaudi in Turin and the Scuola Normale Superiore in Pisa. Her works focus on eighteenth-century French and American history and the relationship between politics and economics. Her publications include *Moneta e politica in Francia: Dalla Cassa di Sconto agli assegnati (1776–1792)* (1992). She also co-edited *Political Economy and National Realities* (1994) with Alberto Masoero and edited *Fisiocrazia e proprietà terriera* (2004) and *Il repubblicanesimo moderno: L'idea di repubblica nella riflessione storica di Franco Venturi* (2006). She is currently writing a monograph on the reception of French economic thought in America in the eighteenth and nineteenth centuries.

**Antonino De Francesco** is Professor of Modern History at the University of Milan. He has published numerous articles on the French and Italian democratic movements as well as a number of books, including *Il governo senza testa: Movimento democratico e federalismo nella Francia rivoluzionaria, 1789–1795* (1992); *Vincenzo Cuoco: Una vita politica* (1997); *1799: Una storia d'Italia* (2004); and *Mito e storiografia della 'Grande Rivoluzione': La Rivoluzione francese nella cultura politica italiana del '900* (2006). He is currently working on a comparative history of the American and French Revolutions.

**Marcel Dorigny** teaches at the Department of History of the University of Paris 8 and carries out research into liberalism in the eighteenth century and during the French Revolution with special reference to the colonies and the question of slavery. He is the editor of *Dix-huitième siècle* and president of the Association pour l'étude de la colonisation européenne (1750–1850). Among his recent publications are: *La France et les Amériques au temps de Jefferson et de Miranda* (with Marie-Jeanne Rossignol) (2001); *Révoltes et révolutions en Europe et aux Amériques (1773–1802)* (2004); *Haïti, première république noire* (2004), and co-editor (with Bernard Gainot) of *Atlas des esclavages: Traites négrières, sociétés coloniales, abolition de l'Antiquité à nos jours* (2006).

Notes on the Contributors ix

**Biancamaria Fontana** studied at the universities of Milan and Cambridge. She has been a fellow of King's College, Cambridge, of the Institute for Advanced Studies of the University of Edinburgh and Jean Monnet Fellow at the European University Institute in Florence. Since 1992 she has been Professor of the History of Political Ideas at the Institut d'études politiques et internationales at the University of Lausanne. Her works focus on the history of classical liberalism and the shaping of representative government before and after the French Revolution. Her publications include: *Rethinking the Politics of Commercial Society: The Edinburgh Review, 1802–1832* (1995); *Benjamin Constant and the Post-Revolutionary Mind* (1991); and *Montaigne's Politics: Authority and Governance in the 'Essais'* (2008).

**Bernard Gainot**, *normalien*, is Directeur de recherches in Modern History at the University of Paris 1 (Paris-Sorbonne) and Associate Professor at the Écoles militaires de Saint-Cyr Coëtquidan. His works focus on the political history of the French Revolution and on the history of colonial wars and societies from 1750 to 1830. His publications include *1799, un nouveau jacobinisme?* (2001) and *Les officiers de couleur dans les armées de la Révolution et de l'Empire* (2007). Together with Marcel Dorigny, he has recently published *Atlas des esclavages* (2006) and with Jean-Luc Chappey *Atlas de l'Empire napoléonien 1799–1815* (2008).

**Jonathan Israel** has been Professor of Modern History at the Institute for Advanced Study, Princeton, since 2001. Prior to this he held the chair in Dutch History at University College London from 1985 to 2000. Among his recent books are *The Dutch Republic: Its Rise, Greatness and Fall, 1477–1806* (1995); *Radical Enlightenment: Philosophy and the Making of Modernity, 1650–1750* (2001); and *Enlightenment Contested: Philosophy, Modernity, and the Emancipation of Man 1670–1752* (2006). He is presently working on the third part of his Enlightenment trilogy, dealing with the period 1750–89.

**Gino Longhitano**, Professor of Modern History at the University of Catania, researches eighteenth- and nineteenth-century French history. His publications focus on Physiocracy and the 1848 revolution. He has edited the marquis de Mirabeau's and F. Quesnay's *Traité de la monarchie*. He is presently working on an Italian edition of François Quesnay's works.

x  Notes on the Contributors

**Pasquale Pasquino** is Global Distinguished Professor in Law and Politics at New York University and Directeur de recherche at the CNRS, Centre de théorie et analyse du droit – Paris EHESS, and works on comparative constitutional adjudication. He has published a book on *Sieyes et l'invention du constitutionnalisme en France* (1998) and numerous articles concerning European and American political and constitutional theory and history.

**Maria Luisa Pesante** teaches modern history at the Faculty of Political Sciences of the University of Turin. Her main field of research is the history of political economy, especially in eighteenth-century England. She has recently completed a book entitled *Vita da servi: Concettualizzazioni del lavoro salariato da Grozio a Hume*. Her more recent publications include: 'Contro il paradigma: Il repubblicanesimo difficile di Franco Venturi', in M. Albertone (ed.), *Il repubblicanesimo moderno: L'idea di repubblica nella riflessione storica di Franco Venturi* (2006); 'Un pensiero economico laico?', in *Il Rinascimento italiano e l'Europa*, vol. IV, F. Franceschi, R.A. Goldthwaite and R.C. Mueller (eds) *Commercio e cultura mercantile* (2007).

**Allan Potofsky** is a Maître de conférences habilité (associate professor), at the University of Paris-VIII. The essay in this volume represents a historiographical overview of a book, a contribution to Atlantic History, whose tentative title is 'Credit, Debt, and Political Economy in the Atlantic, 1763–1809'. He is also the author of *Constructing the Capital in the Age of Revolution: The Builders of Paris, from the Old Regime to the Empire* (forthcoming). This is a history of one of the largest sectors of the French economy, and a crucible of urban renewal, capitalist practices and labour protest.

**Pierre Serna** is Director of the Institut d'histoire de la Révolution française at Paris Sorbonne and of UMS 622 at CNRS. His works focus on the political history of elites in the eighteenth century. Among his works are *Antonelle: Aristocrate révolutionnaire, 1747–1817* (1997) and *La république des girouettes: Une anomalie politique: La France de l'extrême centre, 1789–1815* (2005). He has recently edited *Républiques en miroir: Le Directoire devant la Révolution atlantique: Modélisations, confrontations, interréciprocité des républiques naissantes* (2009) and he is presently working on a comparison of the republican systems at the end of the eighteenth century.

**James Roger Sharp** is a Professor of History at the Maxwell School at Syracuse University. He is the author of *American Politics in the Early Republic: The New Nation in Crisis* (1993 and 1995) and *The Jacksonians Versus the Banks: Politics in the States after the Panic of 1837* (1970) as well as numerous articles. Together with Nancy Weatherly Sharp, he co-edited *American Legislative Leaders, 1911–1994* (1997) in 4 volumes. He is currently completing *The Election of 1800* for the University Press of Kansas series on American presidential elections.

**Koen Stapelbroek** is a Dutch Academy researcher and lecturer at the Erasmus University in Rotterdam and visiting fellow of the Helsinki Collegium for Advanced Studies. He received his PhD from the University of Cambridge and has since published *Love, Self-Deceit and Money: Commerce and Morality in the Early Neapolitan Enlightenment* (2008). He is currently completing a monograph on Dutch economic reform debate in the second half of the eighteenth century.

**Richard Whatmore** is Reader in Intellectual History and Associate Director of the Sussex Centre for Intellectual History. He is the author of *Republicanism and the French Revolution* (2000) and together with Brian Young edited *Palgrave Advances in Intellectual History* (2006) and, with Brian Young and Stefan Collini, *Economy, Polity, and Society* (2000) and *History, Religion, and Culture* (2000). Together with Béla Kapossy he has published a new edition of Emer de Vattel's *Droit des gens* (2008). Whatmore is currently working on Genevan politics, political economy and religion in the long eighteenth century.

# Introduction: Beyond Atlantic History

Manuela Albertone and Antonino De Francesco

In recent years, the most important contributions to the New Atlantic History have come from British and American historians, and have revolved especially around the history of the British Atlantic Empire.[1] Even taking into account histories of the Atlantic-based empires of Spain, Portugal and France, continental Europe has thus remained very much on the sidelines.[2] From the point of view of intellectual history, too, historical studies of the Atlantic world of the eighteenth century have been rather 'Anglocentric'. This is because the success of the Atlantic republican tradition has led to the idea that Anglo-American political thought in the modern age is very much of a unity; consequently scant regard has been granted to the contributions made in this field by continental Europe.[3]

This volume, however, develops a different point of view. Its aim is to go beyond an analysis of one specific area of the Atlantic world and question the central importance given to the area ruled over by Britain and America, taking into account once more the intellectual history of the democratic revolutions that took place at the end of the eighteenth century. It brings our attention back to the role continental Europe played and the connections between the different national cultures, which have a sense of unity about them despite their apparent variety. It shows how ideas rebounded across the Atlantic and how events had a knock-on effect on the other side of the ocean, how these came together and were received, and how these gave rise to new ideas and courses of action. On the one hand, this approach allows us to overcome the practice of simplistically linking the American and French Revolutions, demonstrating that the history of the intellectual life of the eighteenth century, spanning the Atlantic, was more than simply an exchange of ideas between Great Britain and North America. On the other hand, and as a direct consequence of this, it places the French Revolution firmly at the heart of Atlantic History, but from a point of view which goes beyond the ideological limits laid down by historical debate in the twentieth century.

An approach such as this cannot help but take into account the discussions that are currently taking place regarding national histories and global history and recent thought about the ideas of Europe and modernity. This project is also, in fact, a response to calls to rethink the ways that national histories and area studies interact, to follow the way ideas and economic and political movements spread from country to country, and to practise global history which helps also to take into account the differences between nations.[4] The aim of this work, then, in line with these ideas, is to go beyond a simple history of the Atlantic by examining anew the connections between America and Europe in the cosmopolitan eighteenth century.

For the most part, the authors of the essays contained in this volume are European – from Italy, France, Holland or England – or else are Americans interested in the history of the French Revolution and European culture. This allows for a different point of view than the mainly Anglo-American one from which much of the recent New Atlantic History has been written, and this in turn enriches historical debate taking place about this period. Even though our attention has been centred on the single nations, the intention is to place Europe at the heart of historical debate about the age of democratic revolutions on both sides of the Atlantic. In this sense, post-national history offers ideas which have been developed in a number of ways[5] – by taking into account the global context, the interconnections between national histories, the transnational nature of the same, and by re-establishing the links between history and geography. All this within the context of a highly permeable century such as the eighteenth which is reconstructed through an intellectual history whose aim is to continually correlate ideas and action.[6]

Certain choices have been made in terms of methodology and content, and these are reflected both in the intentions of the editors and in the essays themselves. They have led to a concentration on themes related to economic ideas and policies, vindicating the importance of these in a historical framework characterized by differences and in terms of a global history which by its very nature does not move in a single direction. In this way, an attempt has been made to place Europe in a context which does not gloss over its own very special characteristics and the controversial contributions of European thought (dealt with here, for example, in the discussion of events in Haiti and the slavery debates) or the translation of ideas and processes.

Recent historiographical approaches have not only led to a critical re-evaluation of the problems surrounding 'European time'; they have also aroused historians' suspicions about the modern political world and the historicist approach linked to both of these.[7] We feel that the themes dealt with here help contribute to the debates surrounding these areas. The idea of modernity that arose in the eighteenth century coincided with the period in which Europe became the leading player in history. It is also true that the complex nature of the *ancien régime* offers us a privileged position from which to observe the non-linear character of modernity and the way conservatism and innovation interact. In more than one of the essays collected here, the European frameworks of the ideas of equality and liberty have been reconstructed, ideas that influenced the way the concept of the nation state was formed, moving out beyond the continent and triggering off violence both inside and outside Europe. In the global, multicultural context of the contemporary world, and in a political context which, after the fall of the Berlin Wall, has led us to redefine our ideas of what Europe is, the historical thought that emerges from the pages of this volume is aimed at recuperating a historical role for the Old World through an examination of the different meanings that it was given in the eighteenth century.[8]

Centred on the intellectual history of the age of democratic revolutions at the end of the eighteenth century, the themes investigated by the essays in this volume also make a contribution to the history of republican thought, with particular attention being paid to the connections between countries and the transmission of republican ideas, namely the Radical Enlightenment, the separation of powers, centralism and federalism, protectionism and free trade, and politics and economics. The essays link up with one another in many ways, bringing together the different areas of expertise of each of the authors.

The essays in Part I, 'Political Ideas and Economic Models in Eighteenth-Century Europe and America', bring France and the French Revolution back to the heart of Atlantic History. Jonathan Israel's powerful thesis questions the idea that revolutionary thought was the gift of the American and French Revolutions, identifying a 'revolution of the mind' which was already at work in France in the 1770s and 1780s, the elaboration of an ideology based on equality and liberty and the foundation of democratic republicanism on both sides of the Atlantic, which pre-dates the events of the revolutions themselves. Critical of interpreting conservative republicanism from a purely British perspective, he reconstructs – in line with the idea of the Radical Enlightenment in his recent important work – the European and continental genealogy of materialist thought, which counter-posed Reason to tradition and found its origins in Spinozistic thought, which spread out from the United Provinces to France, England, Italy, Germany and America. In opposition to Hobbes, Montesquieu and the English model of a mixed monarchy, Israel also cites the English Unitarians. The attack on the churches and traditional religion and critical thought aimed at the Catholic Church, expressed in the shape of Deism and materialism, was the product specifically of the European Enlightenment, as opposed to the religious debate in America, which, as Richard Whatmore demonstrates in his essay, became the vehicle for political protest. The democratic ideology expressed by the representative democracy of Condorcet and Jefferson is thus opposed to a tradition of moderation and the English concept of liberty. In terms of Atlantic History, then, Jonathan Israel's democratic republicanism can without doubt be seen as an alternative to the classical British republicanism investigated by Anglo-Saxon historiography.

The theme of the relationship between republicanism and Enlightenment thought is also dealt with in Maria Luisa Pesante's essay, which proposes an analytical method based on a fertile comparison of history and historiography. Two different approaches to the idea of the republic, the meaning of the Enlightenment and the way in which the Atlantic world is to be perceived in the modern age can be found in the work of two historians, Franco Venturi and John Pocock, who have greatly influenced historical studies. Venturi was a scholar of eighteenth-century Europe – including Russia – who examined the ideas of a modern republic and the Enlightenment,[9] whose ideas were circulating in Europe and across the Atlantic, in terms of the ways these developed at a national level, reconstructed through the many volumes of *Settecento riformatore* from an especially Italian point of view.[10] The latter is representative of an Anglocentric interpretation of political culture in the seventeenth and eighteenth centuries, of republicanism set in a classical type of framework, and the idea of different Enlightenments, one form of which is the religious, conservative English Enlightenment, the specific nature of which Pocock attempts to reconstruct.[11] Stimulated by the interpretations and research methods of both these scholars, the author examines their different approach to their subject, with special reference to their different interpretations of a key passage in the development of the discussion in the eighteenth century concerning the nature of the American Revolution: the debate that took place at a distance between Turgot, with his *Lettre au docteur Price* and John Adams in his *Defence of the Constitutions and Government of the United States of America*. Pesante then goes on to offer her own analysis of Turgot's thought, discovering points of contact between French and English constitutional thought regarding the separation of powers, thus bringing Turgot closer to Harrington. The result is an interpretation which invites us to reconsider the connections between republicanism and the Enlightenment.

Pasquale Pasquino approaches the question of the separation of powers from a different angle. He identifies two distinct doctrines in America and France regarding this question, which is at the heart of modern constitutional theory and the most recent historical thought.[12] He does this by looking at the role of the judiciary, which highlights on the one hand the English origins of the separation of powers in America, based on the idea of checks and balances between opposing interest groups, and, on the other, French political rationalism, which saw power as indivisible but articulated according to a series of specialized functions. His analysis is based on an examination of the positions of two leading lights of constitutional debate during the American and French Revolutions: Alexander Hamilton and Nicolas Bergasse. According to Bergasse, judges should be subject to the law and thus dependent on the nation as an expression of the will of the body politic. According to Hamilton, judges should play an active role in guaranteeing constitutional balance and be independent of the people's control. Step by step, Pasquino follows the arguments of the two authors, each an expression of two different traditions of constitutional thought, which made judges in France simply the instruments through which the law was applied, while in America they became the guardians of the law itself.

Koen Stapelbroek's essay is an original contribution to the debate, lying as it does between Atlantic History and national history, between Europe and America, between economics and politics. He re-examines revolutionary developments in the United Provinces between 1780 and 1848, offering an interpretation of the patriotic movement there which pre-dates 1787 and concentrates on the political implications of the debate on free trade, which was triggered off in the declining republic by the outbreak of the American Revolution. This essay is part of the recent move in historical debate to take into account the international dimension in the eighteenth century when discussing economic thought, which was aimed at overcoming jealousy between nations.[13] Dutch merchants were sympathetic to what was taking place in America and hoped for an economic policy founded on free trade, an idea for which the colonies were becoming the spokesmen. This pushed the United Provinces towards an abandonment of its traditional policy of neutrality, a policy which linked the House of Orange to England, and towards more friendly relations with France, which was lined up on the side of the American rebels. This can be seen as an attempt to restore the fortunes of Dutch trade and the role of the republic, realigning the international balance of trade and undermining the English monarchy in the name of the economic freedom proclaimed by the Americans, partly as a way of speeding up recognition of the newly fledged republic. On the other hand, however, the critics of this hoped-for new international balance of trade were aware of the uncertainty and danger posed by America, a huge country with all the potential of becoming a new commercial power. The distinction between small state and large state as an alternative way of interpreting the opposition between monarchies and republics, proposed in Richard Whatmore's essay, seems to be confirmed by Stapelbroek's. He shows how the supporters of the House of Orange felt that England would react to the course of events by setting itself up as champion of the small states within a modern political and economic framework that went well beyond the Atlantic and within which both the United Provinces and America were busy reinventing or inventing a role for themselves.

Allan Potofsky's historiographical essay opens this volume. He concludes by outlining how the end of the Cold War and the end of opposition between Marxist historians and the school of François Furet have allowed historians of the two revolutions to turn their attention once again to the economic aspects of the events that took place, rather than concentrating on the politics of the period, as they have done for so long. In this way, as Potofsky underlines, it has become clear that Atlantic History cannot be reduced to the histories of national empires, separate and impregnable, and this encourages us to examine in depth the relationship of cause and effect between the consumer revolution that took place in the eighteenth century and the political revolutions of the same period. At the same time, recent studies have questioned the existence of a single, global Atlantic economy, given the socio-economic system based on local economies which was still in place. This highlights all the ideological weight behind eighteenth-century political economy, which was a stimulus for governments to create a form of commercial republicanism more perceived than real.

Alongside the most recent readings of eighteenth-century political economy as a way of interpreting the unity of the Enlightenment,[14] the essays collected here thus also have the aim of highlighting the political implications of economic ideas in the age of the democratic revolutions. The relationship between economics and politics and the role that economics as a science was assuming as a new form of political language in the eighteenth century are the subjects dealt with in the second part of the volume, 'Free Trade and Democratic Revolutions in Eighteenth-Century Europe and America'.

In Part II, Manuela Albertone reconstructs the role played by French economic thought, and the Physiocratic tradition in particular, in the way Thomas Jefferson and his Republicans elaborated the idea of an American national identity and their own agrarian ideology, as opposed to the ideas of Hamilton's Federalists and the economic and political model of England. At the basis of this essay is a political interpretation of Physiocracy, the result of more than a decade of research by a number of historians,[15] and the idea of using the Physiocratic tradition, over and above its status as a body of fixed, immutable principles, as a means of describing all the ways in which the link between economics and politics changed, a link which characterizes French economic thought from Quesnay to Jean-Baptiste Say. Economic science first took shape in the form of Physiocratic theory, which supported the idea of economic development based on agriculture, and it was Phyisocracy which supplied Jefferson with a legitimate theoretical basis for agrarianism and a tool which could be used in his fight for the construction of the new state. Through his contacts with Condorcet, Du Pont de Nemours, Destutt de Tracy and Say, contacts which spanned fifty years, it is possible to follow the ways in which this idea, centred on the connection between property, political representation and the republic, moved back and forth across the Atlantic, from France to America and then back to France again, enriched by the experience of the two revolutions, thereby ensuring that political economy was to lie at the very foundations of the idea of representative democracy.

An unusual interpretation of Phyisocracy is offered by Marcel Dorigny. Though they do not figure very largely in studies on anti-slavery theories, all the Physiocrats, from the marquis de Mirabeau through to Baudeau and Du Pont de Nemours, with the interesting exception of Le Mercier de La Rivière, developed solid economic arguments proving that slavery was both unjust and unproductive. They denounced slavery as a basic violation of the rights of the individual and personal liberty, ideas which are at the basis of Physiocratic economic theory, and attacked it as an economically inefficient means of production because it violated the laws of labour demand and supply. This is yet another example of the liberal implications of Phyisocratic thought. Dorigny, too, presents us with an analysis of Phyisocracy which goes beyond the direct influence their principles had to deal with, a question which is the example par excellence of the relationship between economics and politics. As the author clearly states, the Phyisocrats did not take up arms themselves

8  *Manuela Albertone and Antonino De Francesco*

in the fight against slavery, but many of the ideas they proposed were later adopted by the abolitionists. The first among many was Condorcet, as ever close to the Physiocrats' ideas. The contribution made by the colonies to European culture has long been passed over, as recent historians have pointed out, and Bernard Gainot's essay, in Part III, examines precisely this question in great depth by focusing on the revolution in Haiti. The way ideas moved between Europe and its American colonies, and the contribution made by both to events in the other, are clearly shown by the way Dorigny's and Gainot's essays relate to one another.

Biancamaria Fontana's piece makes an interesting contribution to historical debate about the nature of empires in the modern age by offering us the different viewpoint of a continental empire and the unique relationship between economics and politics characteristic of modern Europe immediately after the caesura caused by the French Revolution. Napoleon's empire and the uniformity he imposed on Europe through conquest were, in the eyes of Benjamin Constant, in apparent contrast with the unifying force of the economy. Confronted with the bad uniformity of the empire and the good uniformity of the market, the complexity and contradictions inherent in Constant's analysis, which are reconstructed for us here, pose for us the problem of how the French economy managed to prosper so well under the aegis of the Napoleonic Empire. The author also touches on another question, which then as now is at the heart of European reconstruction: the sense of unity through diversity. The author deals with this theme by analysing the area of political representation, an area which recent French historians have helped to reconstruct.[16] Constant responded to the problem of governance in large states with the creation of a plan for a confederation of European states. However, this in itself posed the complex question of how to set up a modern system of political representation capable of respecting the different positions of rulers and citizens.

The ability of the market to pacify states is a point which is touched on in a number of the essays in this collection, and it is one which Gino Longhitano also deals with by looking at the way Saint-Simon and Augustin Thierry reacted to the creation of the Napoleonic Empire, the onset of war and the Continental Blockade. Once again, these writers responded to the problems posed by proposing the creation of a European Confederation led by France and England, a confederation which would have united the continent on the basis of liberal principles agreed upon by both countries. After the French Revolution, however, these unifying principles could no longer be based on the political interests of the states themselves. Rather, they would have to be based on the peoples' interests, and the cement which would hold these together would be *industrie*, that is, the capacity for work, initiative and the relationships that held people together, based on the exchange of labour and of goods. Longhitano reconstructs the way that this new vision of the relationship between politics and economics developed. To be sure, it was a vision which took from the culture of the eighteenth century, but at the same time it went beyond it. The industrial model of Saint-Simon and Thierry, who also looked to the new republic of the United States as an example of what they meant, was in fact clearly different not only from the older mercantilist policies of intervention that viewed the wealth of nations in terms of the conflicting power politics of the states, but also from Physiocratic liberalism, which did not recognize any other valid means of production outside agriculture. And it was this industrial model which was eventually to lay the foundation for modern Europe, a model which would guarantee that the economy would function on the basis of cooperation, not conflict, at both a national and an international level.

This represented one possible way of bringing France (and Europe) out of the revolutionary period, which, along with the disastrous results of the Napoleonic era, was now seen as a complete failure; and, once again not by chance, it was a viewpoint which looked across the Atlantic to the example of America. For continental Europe, it was the beginning of a new political and cultural era, an era in which the Anglo-American models would once again become the main point of reference. Naturally enough, these models would now prefer to see the connections between 1776 and 1789 in terms of differences between the two revolutions, if not of open opposition with one another. Yet things did not always turn out this way, partly because in the years of the Revolution on both sides of the Atlantic there was clearly no lack of evidence that the two countries were in fact travelling in the same direction, evidence which only nineteenth-century historians would attempt to deny. It is precisely this idea – the comparison of America and France during the years of the revolutions – which is the theme of the third and final part of this volume, 'The American and the French Revolutions: From Two Continents a New Political World'.

In Chapter 1, Allan Potofsky's careful historiographical reconstruction of the ways in which the revolutions of 1776 and 1789 have been compared demonstrates how Robert Palmer's well-known thesis of the democratic revolutions[17] represents more the end point of research into this question after World War I than the basis for a more thoughtful and detailed consideration of the links between the revolutions that took place on either side of the Atlantic. Furthermore, Potofsky shows how each of the interpretations of this theme was underpinned by a political and cultural bias of one kind or another, and concludes by showing how in recent years – and certainly not by chance – the question of the relationship between the 1776 and 1789 revolutions seems to have exhausted itself. This lack of attention towards any real attempt at a comparative history of the two revolutions is itself a direct consequence of a lack of interest in Palmer's thesis, which even now obliges anyone interested in examining reactions in America to the 1789 revolution to refer back to studies completed in the 1920s.

The essays in Part III are no less dissatisfied with this state of affairs, beginning with James Sharp's piece. Sharp takes up a strong stand in favour of an interpretative approach aimed at underlining just how important events in France were for the balance of political power in the United States at the end of the eighteenth century. His careful reconstruction of the relationship between American and French politics suggests that there are indeed remarkable similarities between the two republics in the way they both constructed a political system based on the mutual recognition of political parties. This essay, which analyses relations between France and America right up to the advent of Bonapartism in France and the Jeffersonian political revolution in the United States, clears the ground of any facile opposition between the American Revolution, whose success was so rapid, and the French, which failed so quickly. Rather it insists, as suggested some time ago by David B. Davis and Lloyd Kramer, that the 1789 revolution was of clear importance for the construction of the American political system.[18] This is a point of view which reintroduces the idea of reciprocal relations to the history of the Atlantic revolutions as defined by Palmer and Jacques Godechot and, at the same time, is at the basis of Richard Whatmore's essay. He interprets the revolutionary events in the two countries through a reconstruction of the debate between individual political figures, which was both self-interested and, often, predatory.

The pages of Whatmore's essay, in fact, make it clear how the 'Anglocentrism' of the American Revolution was due to hostility towards the figure of Paine, and how this would soon lead many opinion leaders, on both sides of the Atlantic, to underline the fact that the two sets of revolutionary events were not only essentially different from one another, but also that they had influenced one another hardly at all. Much was made of the many ways in which the two revolutions differed from one another, and no little stress was placed on the fact that the ideological roots of the American Revolution were clearly British in origin.

Thus not only does Whatmore focus our attention once more on the debate which took place about the revolutions at the end of the eighteenth century on both sides of the Atlantic, paying great attention in particular to Great Britain; he also gives us a clear indication of what it means to be American, and great importance is given – in line with recent developments in historiography[19] – to the Protestant ethic and the relationship between religion and revolutionary political discourse. It helps to define the impact of the political battle taking place in both America and Great Britain and formed the basis upon which the revolution of 1776 came to be seen as unique in and of itself. It is certainly not by chance that the nineteenth century, with the difficult progress towards liberalism that was taking place in France itself, was to take it upon itself to inflate this point of view to such a point that all traces of the similarity between the two revolutions were eventually to be lost altogether.

The essays that follow insist on this point. Their aim essentially is to strip away the presuppositions that the political debate and the specific characteristics of respective national cultures have imposed upon the relationship between the revolutions of 1776 and 1789. The first, the work of Antonino De Francesco, goes against a broadly accepted interpretation of events by demonstrating how the American model of the constitution remained a point of reference for revolutionary France right up to 1792, and how the events of that year, resulting in the establishment of the republic, were the result of a political confrontation between Jacobin democrats, broadly inspired by the political discourses of Paine and Madison, and the liberal Feuillants, who based all their ideas on a two-chamber system and the politics of Hamilton as a way of bringing stability to the new political order that had emerged in 1789. De Francesco's essay shows how the political battle taking place in both America and France throughout the last decade of the eighteenth century reflected what the one and the other knew of events that had taken place in the other continent, suggesting that we need to interpret any relationship between the two not only in terms of the ideological choices that were being made, but also in the rather more concrete terms of practical politics. Looking at the way the Jacobins and the Republicans behaved on the one hand and the Feuillants and the Federalists behaved on the other, it allows us to take a fresh look at the question of why, in 1793, the political development of the two nations suddenly parted ways, soon turning into that competitiveness which the Directory was to make so much of.

Pierre Serna's essay re-examines the way that America came to be viewed in France, first under the Directory and later under the Consulate.

It does much to undermine the commonplace belief that the two republics were clearly opposed to one another. Rather, it suggests a different way of interpreting events according to which the two countries were continually attentive to, and interested in, developments taking place on the other side of the Atlantic. Through a refined study of French political journalism during the years of the Directory and the Consulate, Serna says a great deal about the way both politicians and opinion leaders in France looked both at Europe's past history and at the extraordinarily original model of America for ways of constructing a new republican model for their country. Despite the differences of opinion, there are traits that are common to all. It is particularly interesting to notice how Serna is able to re-establish the importance of the English republic for French thinkers of the time. They considered it a negative example, in part because of the dramatic conclusion to the republic in 1660, but one which republican France, along with America, was required to come to terms with. The pages of Serna's essay also suggest how the search for a new republican model bringing together the best of the previous republican traditions of the modern age, was soon to spill over onto the Atlantic stage and become even more important with the birth of the black republic of Haiti, which – not by chance – was to combine the experience of the French Revolution with the ideological appeal of the American.

This is also what Bernard Gainot proposes in his more detailed essay on the revolution in Haiti. Gainot attempts to measure just how much impact revolutionary events in France and America had on this dramatic episode in the history of the Caribbean island. He underlines how the equal status of the island before the law and enjoyment of the same level of political representation collided with a sense of *patriotisme américain* which was influenced greatly by the War of Independence in 1776, and transforms the events that took place on Saint-Domingue into an extremely violent political laboratory in which a range of different forms of revolutionary activity and republicanism took shape. Given its specifically colonial nature and the strength of the revolutionary ideologies behind it, the Haitian Revolution is clearly of a different type when compared to the French Revolution, because, however transitory and experimental it was, it became real proof of how the New World was to take shape as a result of the way political events and ideas in both Europe and America influenced one another. In this sense, the central importance of the theme of property, which was soon seen as the element that could bring together in the name of republicanism ideas that derived from a range of different political models, is brilliant confirmation of how, melding economics and ideology in the context of original political practice, it is possible to reinterpret in a fruitful fashion the meaning of the democratic revolutions that took place at the end of the eighteenth century.

Taken together, then, the essays in this collection present us with a new point of view that goes beyond Atlantic History, not least by taking up the suggestion made by an American historian of the standing of Robert Palmer to examine the democratic revolutions that took place at the end of the eighteenth century together,[20] placing them, however, in a radically new context. Naturally enough, there are differences between the approach adopted here and that used by Palmer so many years ago, and they are the fruit both of a historiographical sensibility which in the meantime has changed and the special attention given here to the links between economics and politics. What is most likely to arouse the interest of the historian in this volume, in fact, are the interconnections and interactions which favoured an ongoing dialogue between the Old World and the New and the birth of new forms of republicanism on the American continent, which is the most important witness to this dialogue. Yet it is also essential to point out how this new perspective has only become possible thanks to renewed interest in the American and French Revolutions – an interest expressed in terms of an ever more careful study of the ways in which these revolutions influenced one another. In this sense, we feel that the need to bring together the cultural and ideological processes which led to the growth of political practices destined to influence modern republicanism so deeply and the need to give back to France and continental Europe their own special roles, which for too long have been sacrificed to the 'Anglocentric' point of view that has dominated Atlantic History, are ones which now demand to be met.

## Notes

1. D. Armitage and M.J. Braddick (eds) (2002) *The British Atlantic World, 1500–1800* (London: Palgrave Macmillan); B. Bailyn (2005) *Atlantic History Concept and Contours* (Cambridge, Mass.: Harvard University Press).
2. N. Canny and A. Pagden (eds) (1987) *Colonial Identity in the Atlantic World, 1500–1800* (Princeton: Princeton University Press); A. Pagden (1995) *Lords of All the World: Ideologies of Empire in Spain, Britain and France c.1500–c.1800* (New Haven and London: Yale University Press); J.H. Elliott (2006) *Empires of the Atlantic World: Britain and Spain in America 1492–1830* (New Haven and London: Yale University Press).
3. J.G.A. Pocock (1975) *The Machiavellian Moment: Florentine Political Thought and the Atlantic Republican Tradition* (Princeton: Princeton University Press).

4. Cf. C.A. Bayly (2004) *The Birth of the Modern World 1780–1914* (Malden and Oxford: Blackwell).
5. Th. Bender (2006) *A Nation among Nations: America's Place in World History* (New York: Hill and Wang).
6. Cf. J. Israel (2006) *Enlightenment Contested: Philosophy, Modernity, and Emancipation of Man, 1670–1752* (Oxford: Oxford University Press).
7. D. Chakrabarty (2000) *Provincializing Europe, Postcolonial Thought and Historical Difference* (Princeton and Oxford: Princeton University Press); B. Fuchs and D.J. Baker (2004) 'The Postcolonial Past', *Modern Language Quarterly*, LXV, 3, 329–40.
8. Cf. M. Albertone (ed.) (2008) 'The Eighteenth Century Idea of Europe in History and Historiography', special part issue of *History of European Ideas*.
9. Cf. M. Albertone (ed.) (2006) *Il repubblicanesimo moderno: L'idea di repubblica nella riflessione storica di Franco Venturi* (Naples: Bibliopolis).
10. F. Venturi (1969–90) *Settecento riformatore*, 5 vols (Turin: Einaudi) (Engl. tr. of vols III and IV *The End of the Old Regime in Europe*, 3 vols (Princeton: Princeton University Press, 1989–91)).
11. J.G.A. Pocock (1999–2003) *Barbarism and Religion*. vol. I, *The Enlightenment of Edward Gibbon, 1737–1764*, vol. II, *Narratives of Civil Government*, vol. III, *The First Decline and Fall* (Cambridge: Cambridge University Press).
12. S. Baume and B. Fontana (eds) (2008) *Les usages de la séparation des pouvoirs / The Uses of the Separation of Powers* (Paris: M. Houdiard).
13. I. Hont (2005) *Jealousy of Trade: International Competition and the Nation-state in Historical Perspective* (Cambridge, Mass. and London: Belknap Press of Harvard University Press).
14. J. Robertson (2005) *The Case for the Enlightenment: Scotland and Naples, 1680–1760* (Cambridge: Cambridge University Press).
15. C. Larrère (1992) *L'invention de l'économie au XVIIIe siècle: Du droit naturel à la physiocratie* (Paris: Presses universitaires de France); Ph. Steiner (1998) *La 'science nouvelle' de l'économie politique* (Paris: Presses universitaires de France); M. Albertone (ed.) (2004) 'Fisiocrazia e proprietà terriera', special issue of *Studi settecenteschi* (Naples: Bibliopolis).
16. P. Serna (1997) *Antonelle: Aristocrate révolutionnaire 1747–1817* (Paris: Éditions du Félin); B. Gainot (2001) *1799, un nouveau Jacobinisme? La démocratie représentative, une alternative à brumaire* (Paris: CTHS); P. Brunet (2004) *Vouloir pour la nation: Le concept de représentation dans la théorie de l'État* (Paris: LGDJ).
17. Robert R. Palmer (1959–64) *The Age of Democratic Revolution: A Political History of Europe and America, 1760–1800*, 2 vols (Princeton: Princeton University Press).
18. D.B. Davis (1990) *Revolutions: Reflections on American Equality and Foreign Liberations* (Cambridge, Mass.: Harvard University Press); L.S. Kramer (2002) 'The French Revolution and the Creation of American Political Culture', in J. Klaits and M.H. Haltzel (eds), *The Global Ramifications of the French Revolution* (Cambridge: Cambridge University Press).
19. M. Sonenscher (2007) *Before the Deluge: Public Debt, Inequality, and the Intellectual Origins of the French Revolution* (Princeton and Oxford: Princeton University Press).
20. Cf. E. Tortarolo (2008) 'Atlantic History Old and New', special part issue of *History of European Ideas*, XXIV, 4.

# Part I
# Political Ideas and Economic Models in Eighteenth-Century Europe and America

# 1
# The One and the Many: The Two Revolutions Question and the 'Consumer-Commercial' Atlantic, 1789 to the Present

*Allan Potofsky*

Who was the first American to link the American and French Revolutions with a historical analysis of their common origins? Tom Paine clearly has a claim to the mantle of the first political Atlantic historian of the 'two revolutions question', explicitly linking the origins of the French Revolution to the events in the United States. Paine dedicated a good part of his life and writings in the 1790s to amplify the impact of the American Revolution upon the events in France. He also unwittingly launched what is now a 220-year-old interpretive, historiographical and methodological controversy.[1]

Paine's *Rights of Man*, first published in March 1791, was a polemic against Edmund Burke's counter-revolutionary pamphlet, *Reflections on the Revolution in France*, of November 1790. Paine attacked both Burke's substantive argument and his method, rejecting in particular Burke's assertion that there had been a continuous denigration of the political order from the Enlightenment to Revolution. Burke had indeed reserved perhaps his most heated condemnation for the abstract and corrosive reasoning of revolutionaries: mere 'theorists', 'speculationists' and 'metaphysicians'.

But to Paine, philosophy alone does not provoke revolutions. None of the great *philosophes* enjoyed the influence claimed by Burke – not Montesquieu ('his mind often appears under a veil'), not Voltaire ('both the flatterer and satirist of despotism'), not Rousseau or Raynal (they 'leave the mind in love with an object, without describing the means of possessing it'). Having dismissed the argument that an Enlightenment critique radicalized public opinion and turned it against a properly hierarchical order, Paine broadened his argument to include the Physiocrats,

Quesnay, Turgot 'and their friends', brushing aside their reformist impulses ('directed to economize the administration of government, [rather] than the government itself').[2]

Elaborating on a more down-to-earth causality from that of Enlightenment political culture, Paine outlined a 'chain of circumstances' centred on actions and not ideas. He celebrates the material origins that the American struggle shared with that of Europe in a broader continuum of a movement towards liberty and democracy. Tracing the various diplomatic and geopolitical negotiations of Vergennes, Benjamin Franklin and the marquis de Lafayette, Paine suggested that the return of the thousands of French soldiers and officers after the American War of Independence was responsible for 'a vast reinforcement to the cause of liberty [that] spread itself over France'. 'The French officers and soldiers who... went to America, were eventually placed in the school of freedom, and learned the practice as well as the principles by heart.'[3] (The second book of *Rights of Man*, published a year later, was dedicated to the most prestigious member of the French contingent, Lafayette.) Underscoring the central place of what historians now call human agency, Paine concludes that 'knowledge of the practice was then joined to the theory'. He then turns to the question of the national debt, the calling of the Estates General and the mobilization of the revolutionary crowd in 1789 as precisely this revolutionary opportunity that ultimately 'joined' theory and practice.[4]

Paine sketched out the first revolutionary history to put the French Revolution squarely in an Atlantic perspective, based on the 'diffusion' of America's example to France. There was no underlying ideological continuity in its structure, no force of necessity, no question of ideological continuity, or a 'script', that played out in the logic of radicalization and regeneration from 1789. Writing well before the Terror, Paine's 'chain of circumstances' suggested another causality altogether: the Revolution was contingent and *événementielle*, not determined by the force of ideas and ideologies.[5] Of course, Paine became disillusioned by the events in France after a ten-month imprisonment during the Terror, with possible connivance by the federalist plenipotentiary minister Gouverneur Morris. But, leaving aside this subsequent story, he helped to launch the problem of the relationship of the two revolutions with this circumstantial-based 'diffusion' thesis.[6]

The argument developed by Paine was, above all, a profoundly political reading of the question of the American and French Revolutions. The traversal of revolutionary ideas across the Atlantic was a moment of alignment in which both nations were simultaneously engaged in the struggle against monarchy. The challenges that unified the two nations were precisely the same entrenched political order, monarchy, which could only be overcome by republicanism. For the following two centuries, Paine's exclusive focus on politics created the very terms of a long historical genealogy of the two revolutions question.[7]

## The problem of the two revolutions: the one and the many

After Paine, the political history of the American and French Revolutions is dominated by the problem of the one and the many. Were the American and French Revolutions part of a single movement that historians have conceptualized as the revolutionary Atlantic or were they uniquely national events? Those who emphasize the many – the plurality of national revolutions and thus the uniqueness of each – privileged the French Revolution as a singular expression of legal, corporate, religious and natural rights traditions. The French Revolution was the favoured terrain of a tradition of right- and left-wing patriotic historians, who focus on the events' nearly transcendental distinctiveness. They have contributed to making the event a subject of rich ideological, methodological and interpretive contestation, whose stakes were nothing less than the making of modern Europe, not to say modernity itself.[8] But the historians' perspective centred on the uniqueness of the Revolution also divorced events within the French *métropole* from an international context – to the point where, until recently, French Revolution scholars rarely included the colonies and the empire in their narrative of the incomparable events in France.

The origins of the American Revolution were different but, seen through an exceptionalist optic, every bit as unique. Advocates of the radicalism of the event – 'as radical and social as any revolution in history', in Gordon Wood's terms – speak of it as rooted in civic humanism, republicanism and the tradition of the freeborn Englishman. While its roots were English, exceptionalist historians also promoted the event's singularity. James Madison's *Federalist* 14 most vividly summarized this position: the Americans had 'accomplished a revolution which has no parallel in the annals of human society'.[9]

When Madison wrote these words, the term 'revolution', defined as a clean break with the past, was indeed unique to the Anglo-American world. The concept elsewhere had many meanings, but it often connoted disorders, agitations and shocks suggesting political upheaval and not a definitive, transformative rupture. Before 1789, *révolution* had meant a return to a purer and original state of things.[10] But as Madison formulated the concept two years earlier, the Americans had not created another cycle in an eternal return but rather had created a new institutional reality, a new nation of revolutionary principles. Eventually the 'exceptional' thesis of the French and American Revolutions exalted the uniqueness of the founding moment of both nations.

The alternative position to French and American national exceptionalism is a Paineite narrative of continuity – of the one rather than the many. The revolutionary Atlantic was a broad movement of democracy, protest and representative institutions that grew out of independence and protest movements spanning the ocean. These continuity historians point not only to the American Revolution but to the less familiar Swiss, Dutch, Corsican, Polish and Belgian revolts, as well as the Haitian Revolution and the Latin American revolutionary movements led by Simon Bolivar and Francisco de Miranda. In the 1950s, in particular, Jacques Godechot and R.R. Palmer spearheaded this continuity paradigm – as we will see. Most recently, historians such as Annie Jourdain, Jean-Louis Harouel and Bailey Stone have revived the question of expansionism by placing the problem of the revolution abroad at the heart of the revolutionary problematic. Above all, international relations and the demands of war, as Stone demonstrates, forced the crown and revolutionaries, first fiscally, and then internationally, to broaden the global ambitions of revolutionary France.[11]

Whether advocates of continuity or exceptionalism, of the one or the many, historians who have examined relationships, influences, impacts or analogies between the two revolutions have focused largely on the political sphere. Political ideas and institutions, beginning with the translation of the state constitutions in French in 1783, was the most outstanding dynamic between the two events.[12] Furthermore, the political sphere of the two revolutions most clearly fitted into canonical understandings of comparative history. In a famous founding statement, Marc Bloch demonstrated that comparative history is often contrastive history. His method emphasized parallel studies of historical epochs which share common origins. Warning against comparing events so widely disconnected in time and space that neither mutual influence nor common origins can explain their similarities, Bloch argued for a greater understanding of 'analogies' between different times and places. Rather than looking only for similarities, the comparative historian must also seek differences:

> First of all, what in our field of interest is there to compare? Without a doubt, to compare is to make a choice within one or several social

milieus of at least two phenomena that appear, at first glance, to suggest certain analogies. Also, it is to describe their evolutionary curves and to establish their similarities and differences and, when possible, to explain these various factors.[13]

Clearly, America and France at the end of the eighteenth century qualify for these 'analogies', for their revolutions stemmed from similar causes. The demand for no taxation without representation, for example, was a mobilizing factor on both sides of the Atlantic. But, within divergent contexts – the colonies on the one hand, a nearly bankrupt absolutist state on the other hand – the very meaning of taxation was entirely different in the two revolutions.[14]

'The value-free study of revolutions is a logical impossibility for those who live in the real world,' as John Dunn has demonstrated.[15] Indeed, a historiographical genealogy of the two revolutions question demonstrates how political contexts favoured certain interpretations up to the present day. The shifting pressures to emphasize Atlantic alliances and the equal and opposite pressures to underscore national exceptionalisms, forged interpretations across the Atlantic. They confirm the tenacity of political explanations, whereby the two revolutions question became an inquiry into comparative ideas, constitutions, institutions, state policies and diplomatic relations.

This historiographical genealogy will also pose the question of how and why the classical narrative of a political Atlantic reached a dead end. The two revolutions question has increasingly moved into domains once reserved for economic histories. The expansion of the two revolutions question into Atlantic History – and thus to issues of colonization, slavery, native peoples and non-imperial perspectives in general – opened the field of inquiry to mercantile, fiscal and commercial connections. Finally, this interpretation will point to several as yet unresolved problems, difficulties and challenges resistant to scholarly inquiry of the revolutionary Atlantic.

## From Tocqueville to *Paris en Amérique* in the nineteenth century . . .

The nineteenth century, marked by the emergence of many forms of nationalisms, was not necessarily a good one for cosmopolitan historiographies accentuating international influences between nations. European historiography of the nineteenth century stressed the specific qualities of each nation to distinguish their particular genius. It was as if Europeans had put into practice a century late David Hume's argument that 'moral causes' and not environmental influences gave each nation its national character, rendering each profoundly dissimilar to each other.[16]

In the period of the July Monarchy, Tocqueville's insights highlighted deep differences between the two national traditions. He held that the American Revolution was the more democratic, for it was fought in the name of political liberty, while the French Revolution was more tragically 'social', for it was about 'equality'. Ultimately, the fixation with 'la destruction du privilège' and the role of the 'multitudes', Tocqueville wrote, subverted the goals of 1789.[17] In Third Republic France, the United States was discussed in such neo-Tocquevillian categories, emphasizing the rights of individuals and a rich heritage of associative life. But rather than practitioners of the historian's craft, it was French writers, sociologists, economists and men of the law who were most deeply interested in American things. And rather than the Revolution, the subject of predilection was contemporary American civilization. One of the most widely sold bestsellers of the nineteenth century was *Paris en Amérique* by the republican lawyer Edouard Laboulaye. This book was republished twenty-one times between 1872 and 1887, and defended American decentralization, political pluralism, an independent judiciary and popular education.[18] All the same, 'a neo-Tocquevillian "américanisme" remained marginal', as Françoise Mélonio concludes *à propos* of the rejection at the end of the nineteenth century of the liberal American model.[19] In sum, the history of the United States was not a well-developed discipline in France, and was in fact often a pretext for essentialist generalizations about an American model, one that neatly served the political ambition of French defenders of liberalism such as Laboulaye.[20]

## ... To a twentieth-century historical cosmopolitanism?

The end of World War I featured a historians' revolt against narrow-minded nationalism and intellectual conventionality – and, in turn, a rejection of the schools of exceptionalism and nationalist distinctiveness in the historical profession. One result of this new historical cosmopolitanism was the development, on both sides of the Atlantic, of Franco-American histories that revived the thesis of a Francophile–Americanophile eighteenth century. As a way of countering the chauvinist sentiments of the First World War, French and American historians launched separate and interrelated projects to restore an international dimension to history missing from national narratives.[21]

Writing in 1919, a group of French and American historians took stock of the poverty of transatlantic studies in each nation with a collection of *mea culpas*. These were collected in Henri Berr's prestigious *Revue de Synthèse Historique*. For D. Pasquet, nothing of consequence had been published on the United States for nearly a century in France. 'Since the long-ago period when Tocqueville published *Démocratie en Amérique*, the history and institutions of the United States have not received in France the attention they deserved.' The American historian Frederick Morrow Fling also regretted the utter poverty of serious historical research engaged by his compatriots, concluding that 'no complete and scholarly study of the Revolution or Empire has come from the pen of an American academic'. This paradoxical situation – popular interest, scholarly dearth – would soon be partially rectified. Pasquet and Fling accurately predicted that the recent war would force change upon the insularity of French and American historians.[22]

True to the spirit of this call, members of the American Historical Association supported a proposal by French scholars in 1925 for an 'international journal of comparative cultural history'. The members of the French contingent – Lucien Febvre and Marc Bloch – were, in fact, proposing to their American colleagues to join forces in what would become *les Annales* in 1929. The founding charter of this project promised to study 'those social, economic, and moral factors in history which transcend all political boundaries and demonstrate the essential solidarity of mankind'.[23] While Febvre and Bloch ultimately relied on French national resources to found *les Annales*, the venture was inspired by the dominant cosmopolitanism and, specifically, Atlanticism in the 1920s.[24]

In France during the same epoch, a cosmopolitan Atlanticism was reflected in the work of Alphonse Aulard and Philippe Sagnac, the first two tenured nominees of the Sorbonne Chair in the French Revolution. They published significant studies on the impact of the American Revolution in France. Aulard's immense output should not be reduced to his work on the two revolutions question, but he was among the first to open up the category of Atlantic revolutionary 'influence' beyond that of Benjamin Franklin, Thomas Jefferson and Lafayette. Aulard's research on the treatment of the United States' debt to France, accrued during the War of Independence, was a rigorous and sensitive treatment that stands up well to scrutiny. Seeing in the debt question a problem of practice and circumstances, rather than ideological 'solidarity', he set forth a research agenda involving the complex of financial ties, intrigue and politics. He blazed the path opened by Tom Paine, in focusing on the 'chain of circumstances' that influenced both the causes and trajectory of the Revolution, but unlike the Anglo-American revolutionary, Aulard scrupulously avoided exalted judgements.[25]

Aulard's replacement, Philippe Sagnac, spent the war years at the new School for Social Research in New York. Sagnac was criticized as an uninspired choice for the Sorbonne Chair after the more dynamic, if controversial, Robespierrist Albert Mathiez – not nominated to the Sorbonne, despite his immense scholarship – was passed over. Less partisan than Mathiez, Sagnac was a sensitive craftsman of political history. His doctoral dissertation partially focused on the significance of the American Revolution in inspiring the principles of 1789. In particular, he paid great attention to the diffusion of the Declaration of Independence in Paris and the provinces. His originality was to insist that the American influence upon French writers was much greater than the impact of the *philosophes* on Americans: the American influence 'fortified and sometimes modified the principles that the philosophes and economists had already laid down'. Also, decades before R.R. Palmer, Sagnac compared the constitutions and constitutional debates of the two revolutionary nations, finding many parallels.[26] We note here the surprising fact that none of the subsequent holders of the chair in the History of the French Revolution, founded in 1889, treated international topics of the Revolution – no original research on the Atlantic, colonies, slavery, diplomacy or expansionism was published by the Sorbonne historian after Sagnac.[27]

Gilbert Chinard in the 1920s and 1930s also drew attention to the indebtedness of the French Revolution to America. His greatest contributions lie not in his historical interpretations – many of his publications were popularizations – but rather in his rigorous original editions of Thomas Jefferson's correspondence with French revolutionaries. Well before the papers of Jefferson were properly assembled and published in systematic fashion, Chinard assembled the core documentary history of the two revolutions. His volumes of correspondence between Jefferson and Lafayette, Volney, Cabanis, J.-B. Say, Auguste Comte and Dupont de Nemours, published between the 1920s and 1940s, remain pillars of the scholarship on the two revolutions to this day.[28]

Bernard Faÿ, on the other hand, is a much more difficult figure to grasp. His doctoral thesis, *L'esprit révolutionnaire en France et aux États-Unis à la fin du XVIIIe siècle*, was published in 1923, along with the bibliography. Professor of American Civilization at the vaunted Collège de France from 1932 to 1944, Faÿ was nominated by the Vichy government as Administrateur général de la Bibliothèque nationale (1940–44), replacing the Jewish director, Julien Cain, in office since 1930 and who would survive a 1944 deportation to Buchenwald. Faÿ's major project as directeur de la Bibliothèque nationale was to write a positively chilling report in 1943 to align the BN with the Maréchal's ambitions of the *Révolution Nationale*. He also created a *fichier maçonnique*, 60,000 names to proscribe from the French public service. Having applied Vichy laws meticulously, having banned Jewish readers and suspended Jewish personnel employed at the BN, Faÿ was condemned to life imprisonment with hard labour at the Liberation, as well as the confiscation of all his property and 'national degradation'. He escaped from a prison hospital in 1951, and settled in Switzerland. Faÿ was eventually pardoned in 1959.[29]

The paradox of Faÿ's career was to have written an innovative thesis on the two revolutions question that focused on cultural, rather than political, influences. In 1927, it was even translated and published in the United States by a popular press.[30] In this piece he reined in his right-wing political views. His understanding of 'influence' is also attentive to other sources besides that of the *philosophes*. His chapter 'Union Spirituelle, 1789–1794' is an astute exercise on the spread of French-language education, theatre representations of French melodramas, and European history and philosophy in American universities in the federalist era. He mastered American literary sources and American poems and novels concerning the French Revolution, discussed in the context of federalist and republican newspaper articles about France. Finally, the chronological breadth extends from 1770 to 'le grand schisme' of 1798 in an epoch of increasingly specialized studies on the Revolution. Faÿ also consulted manuscripts in the United States National Archives and Library of Congress collections – a rare cosmopolitan research agenda.[31]

Was it at all significant that the holder of the Chair in American Civilization at the Collège de France from 1932 to 1945 would later be condemned as a Vichy criminal? To this author's knowledge, the question of Faÿ's possible nefarious impact on American studies in France, and more globally on the two revolutions question, has not been discussed outside informal forums. It is clearly beyond the scope of this essay to enter into an issue much too easily open to speculation. Nevertheless, Faÿ may have contributed to the idea that Franco-American studies were necessarily conservative, a tendency reinforced later by the Cold War. Yet, despite a tendency to project present-day *Américanophilie* to a right-wing pro-Americanism, there was, in fact, rarely an automatic conservative-Atlanticist component in attraction to the United States. As Michel Cordillot has demonstrated, the US has attracted French exiled radicals throughout its history, from Condorcet to the Utopian Étienne Cabet to the Socialist Victor Drury to the Fouriérist Victor Considerant.[32]

## The emergence of an 'American school' of revolutionary history, the 1930s–1940s

The 1930s and 1940s was the era of a growing American fascination with sensational and popular biographies about revolutionaries – no doubt an effect of the dominating anti-democratic figures emerging in Europe.[33] At the same time, American scholars began to leave a mark on French revolutionary studies. In 1935, the Harvard historian Donald Greer published a groundbreaking work quantifying the Terror. Against all expectations, Greer demonstrated that a majority of condemned victims issued from the sans-culotte and labouring classes rather than elite circles. Greer's conclusions are still widely cited today, as is his richly quantified study on the émigrés two decades later.[34] His major contributions helped turn American students away from the French Revolution as morality play, featuring bloodthirsty tyrants guillotining hapless victims, cheered on by *les tricoteuses*.[35] The specific question of the relationship of the two revolutions was also re-examined by a commanding figure, Louis Gottschalk, at the University of Chicago, who trained under Albert Mathiez. Gottschalk spearheaded a revival of Lafayette with two biographies celebrating Franco-American solidarities for general audiences. The synthetic *The Place of the American Revolution in the Causal Pattern of the French Revolution* (1941) treated the question of 'influence' in a rigorous manner that sought to apply the philosopher Wilhelm Dilthey's methodology to the revolutions by emphasizing common 'lived experiences' of Americans and French.

On the eve of America's entry into the Second World War, Robert R. Palmer's first major book, *Twelve Who Ruled: The Year of the Terror in the French Revolution* (1941), was also the first widely read American study on the French Revolution. It merited a translation during the bicentenary celebrations forty-eight years afterward and is perhaps the only book on the French Revolution, on either side of the Atlantic, to have remained in print since publication. This study of the Committee of Public Safety from the perspective of each of its members rejected the ideological Robespierrist-'totalitarian' paradigm in depicting the Terror as a set of circumstances born of war, popular movements, as well as political blunders. Without apologizing for its excesses, Palmer keenly analysed the political mechanisms of Terror, focusing on the Committee as a war cabinet with absolute powers. A scholarly detachment and rigorous analysis – for the Terror was morally repugnant *and* politically necessary in Palmer's rendering – showed that the moment had arrived where American historians began to contribute to 'Revolutionary' scholarship on equal footing with French colleagues just as war would delay that moment's fruition.[36]

## 'Taming' the American Revolution, radicalizing the French Revolution: the 1950s

By contrast, the 1950s was the era of moderating the American Revolution, meaning, for American historians, it was also the moment to radicalize the French Revolution. Louis Hartz, Edmund Morgan, Robert Brown, John P. Roche, Richard Hofstadter and Benjamin Wright were only a few names associated with distinguishing the American from both the French and Russian Revolutions, but without the apparatus of comparative political science that inspired Crane Brinton's simplistic *The Anatomy of Revolution* in 1939. The American Revolution was superior because it was never tempted by utopianism.[37]

The background of the Cold War had stigmatized the very concept of revolution, of course, and thus Hofstadter commented that 'the American Revolution has to be tamed and naturalized, distinguished from other, more mischievous revolutions'.[38] And, so, the great myth of the peaceful, democratic American Revolution, that contrasted with other, more extreme and violent revolutions, was reborn. The question of precisely for whom it was peaceful and democratic would not be posed until a decade later with the rise of social history in the United States academia.

The primary historical source material for these consensus historians, or what Jack Greene would later call neo-Whigs, were not the favoured ones of comparative historians. The neo-Whigs turned away from the Declaration of Independence and the state and federal constitutions, so deftly treated by two revolutions historians such as Aulard, Sagnac and Chinard, who traced their commonalities to the founding documents of the French Revolution. The 1950s and 1960s witnessed a return to other sources as the vital documents of the making of America. This was the era that rediscovered and reinterpreted Crèvecoeur's 1782 *Letters from an American Farmer* – and most particularly his third essay, 'What is an American?' Also, the *Federalist Papers* achieved canonical status by their post-war entry into the Great Books courses of many

American universities and colleges. Four distinct editions appeared in 1961 alone. 'The one product of the American mind that is rightly counted among the classics of political theory', as Clinton Rossiter wrote in his introduction to an edition first published in 1961 and in print ever since.[39]

Indeed, *Federalist* 51, by James Madison, is a concise digest of the way in which a liberal pluralism in a greater republic is nourished by political debate: 'Ambition must be made to counteract ambition ... It may be a reflection on human nature that such devices should be necessary to control the abuses of government. But what is government itself but the greatest of all reflections of human nature?'[40] By emphasizing the balance of power at the heart of the American Revolution's accomplishments, the historians of the 1950s and 1960s also underscored that compromise was the leitmotif of America's 'greatest' philosophical document. *Federalist* 51 also interpreted bicameralism as essential to the division of powers at the heart of the US constitution, and that differentiated the United States from a Jacobin and unicameral France.[41]

The divergences between the two revolutions were also brought out by an emphasis on the Englishness of the American Revolution, portraying the Founding Fathers as more a Whig reform caucus than a group of radicals. By emphasizing the founders' Lockean fibre, the neo-Whigs also created the grounds for a great intellectual debate that posited a British-centred moderate and intellectualized Atlantic. Shortly afterward, an Ideological-Constitutional school of intellectual history both affirmed the American Revolution's English roots while rehabilitating its radicality by tracing those roots to seventeenth-century Commonwealth origins. The classical republican paradigm, beyond the scope of this essay, was successfully elaborated by Bernard Bailyn, Gordon Wood and J.G.A. Pocock in the 1960s and 1970s. It remains perhaps the dominant historical thesis on the intellectual origins of the American Revolution. Also, it marginalized the Franco-American Atlantic revolutionary tradition.[42]

## The democratic-revolution paradigm of Godechot and Palmer

In the mid-1950s, Jacques Godechot and Robert R. Palmer responded to both the neo-Whigs and to the classical republican paradigm in revolutionary studies by developing the thesis of a democratic Atlantic Revolution. The two scholars advanced arguments to challenge the specificity of the American and French Revolutions, reinterpreting them as the foundation moments of a much larger process. Although not specialists in the American Revolution, they inscribed an argument of continuity between the two shores of the Atlantic.[43]

Despite subsequent insistence on Godechot's and Palmer's fruitful collaboration, deep methodological differences guided their approaches to the Atlantic. While Godechot and Palmer will forever be mentioned in the same breath, in fact, upon a comparative rereading, one becomes aware of several incompatibilities. Godechot's approach was more deeply structural than the approach of Palmer.[44] He viewed the revolutions as of a piece with the demographic and social changes in the Atlantic world over the seventeenth and eighteenth centuries. These inspired economic grievances politicized later in the revolutions. Godechot's training, in particular his doctoral thesis at the Sorbonne with Mathiez and Lefebvre on *Les commissiaires aux armies sous le Directoire*, had him pursuing French, Belgian, Dutch, German, Swiss and Italian archives. This kept him much more focused on Europe around the Atlantic rim than the Atlantic space, properly speaking. He was also more anchored in a materialist interpretation of the French Revolution and by the Annales school of historical structuralism.[45]

By contrast, Palmer's reading in *The Age of the Democratic Revolution: A Political History of Europe and America, 1760–1800* (2 vols, 1959 and 1964) was essentially a political history. It begins with a narrative of the Seven Years War, which unleashed a series of conflicts, and the old European order, which was progressively shaken by a series of internal conflicts whose fundamental dynamic was the democratization of society. The fiscal and constitutional struggles pitted eighteenth-century monarchies, desperately seeking new sources of income, against their own constituent bodies. These included assemblies, the British parliament, American Houses of Burgesses, the French *parlements*, the Dutch States General and even independent clubs including the Freemasons. These constituent bodies – for Palmer, the key democratic structures of the Atlantic Revolution – were the locus of powerful criticism of royal absolutism as the opponent of fiscal independence for the monarchy. A rare narrative coherence systematizes Palmer's vast panorama. The history of how these constituent bodies surpassed their parochial defence of traditional privileges propelled them inevitably towards a universalist defence of the rights of man.[46]

Well before Jürgen Habermas conceptualized the opening of a 'public sphere' in the opposition politics to Louis XV in the 1770s, Palmer argued about the opening of a 'political space' where disparate groups and individuals found their voice in opposition to the principles of hereditary rule and royal and aristocratic privilege.[47] Particularly compelling in

Palmer's reading of the revolutionary Atlantic is the study of revolutionary legacies. To Palmer, episodes of revolutionary transformation – even necessarily violent ones – were a necessary and sufficient condition for Western democracy. Palmer also conceptualized Atlantic influence based on 'interconnections' between societies that shared the same socio-economic level of development and the same Enlightenment ideas. The Enlightenment, in turn, had a deep impact not as a primary cause, but rather as the political articulation of generalized ferment.[48]

Palmer astutely kept off-balance those who looked for a national bias in the text. In comparing the American idea of democracy with that of Europe, he concludes, 'certain ideas of the Age of the Enlightenment, found on both sides of the Atlantic – ideas of constitutionalism, individual liberty, or legal equality – were more fully incorporated and less disputed in America than in Europe'. Also, that the American Revolution enjoyed a broader suffrage, and he concludes: 'The truth seems to be that America was a good deal more democratic than Europe in the 1790s.' But, simultaneously, the Convention was 'one of the most remarkable bodies in the history of the world' and Robespierre was 'a great figure of democracy'. As for the radical turn after September 1792: 'If these events prove anything, it is perhaps that no purely middle class or "bourgeois" revolution could succeed.'[49]

Having spanned over the American colonies, Britain, Ireland, the Low Countries, Italy, Poland, Russia and several east-central European states (with several pages devoted to South Africa), having displayed a reading knowledge of Dutch, French, German and Italian (graduate students helped with reading Polish and Russian sources), it seems almost churlish that many readers now only take away from the book its end point in 1799. This meant, of course, that Palmer neglected the 1804 Haitian Revolution. One American participant in the 2005 conference marking the ten-year anniversary of Harvard University's International Seminar on the History of the Atlantic World, announced that Palmer had 'notoriously ignored the island's Revolution'. In fact, in several pages, Palmer analyses the Saint-Domingue slave revolts as inspiring similar uprisings in the United States and Brazil. Above all, Palmer's selective comments were perhaps a reflection of the state of primary research in the period, for he confesses that while it is known that the number of slave revolts swelled in the 1790s, 'it is hard to estimate the effects in the United States of the revolution in Haiti'. Indeed, only a few pages are devoted to Saint-Domingue and to the slave insurrections that shook the Atlantic world – but Palmer's vivid language makes it clear he considers the coming Haitian Revolution further proof of his democratic revolution thesis.[50]

Jacques Godechot had reservations about some of the broader conclusions drawn by Palmer, especially the audacious fashion in which Palmer dissolved the French Revolution in international currents. For all his programmatic boldness, Godechot, in fact, practised Atlantic History as essentially concerning Atlantic coastal towns in their social, diplomatic and economic interconnections.[51] Palmer, on a vaster canvas, saw an Atlantic political culture through which ideas about the nature of liberty circulated.

A somewhat neglected third member of the Atlantic Revolution historical school was Durand Echeverria, the author of several Atlantic works, and, especially, the co-editor of an exhaustive, invaluable catalogue on French-language publications regarding the United States.[52] His secondary status is no doubt due to the fact that, as a literature professor at Brown University, he was without the same 'legitimacy' as the historians Godechot and Palmer. In his 1957 book, Echeverria demonstrated ways the discovery of America brought to the fore the problem of civilization for the French Enlightenment. America offered a place where peoples could live without government or with a minimum of government – the ideal nation. Spanning through the entire last half of the eighteenth century, Echeverria synthesized a wealth of material, including songs and poems, to demonstrate the twin sentiments of *Américanophilie* and *Francophilie*, as well as the opposite phobias these engendered, and on both sides of the Atlantic. His lyrical and congenial study, graced with many epigramic insights and beautifully written, was ultimately focused on stereotypes, caricatures and simplistic descriptions of life in America or politics in France. Retelling some of the anecdotes, such as Raynal's famous quips about Americans' lack of ability to concentrate or reflect for long, were ends in themselves. But lacking a systematic problematic or thesis, save that of a 'distant mirage', Echeverria comes up short conceptually, for example in a comparison with the subtle analysis of racist and differentialist language of Michèle Duchet, a decade later.[53]

Atlantic History, forged in the historical literature from the 1950s to the 1970s, and, in particular by Jacques Godechot and R.R. Palmer, contributed immensely to opening up historical imaginations and research agendas. Yet, upon rereading, these syntheses of the age of the democratic revolution bear the unmistakable trace of a certain Cold War a priori: the solidarity between the world's democracies was taken to be in the natural order of things; hence rupture could only be based on misunderstandings (the French critique of American bicameralism, stressed by Echeverria and Godechot) and/or specific circumstances (the start of the revolutionary wars as underscored by Palmer). Historians' accounts of the end of the age of the democratic revolution did not question whether the two revolutions were separated by divergent views of democracy or, for that matter, by economic interests and political economy. Hence, this approach reprised without critical distance the project of certain 'cosmopolitan' Enlightenment figures, such as Crèvecoeur, Jefferson, Brissot and Clavière in France, on the essential necessity of ties between the two nations.

Yet, in creating the scholarly opportunity for Atlantic History, these historians successfully restored the central place of revolutions in the history of the Western world. In America and France, previous exceptionalist and nationalist historians, on the left and right, tended to emphasize the making of their respective modern nations. The forward-looking 'foundation/construction' phase of these new orders, however, obscured the critical and radical nature of these revolutions. The two revolutions, after all, raised fundamental challenges for an older imperial order that only began to be dismantled at the end of the eighteenth century. The confrontation with the British Empire has always been a part of understanding the American Revolution. But the French Revolution also created the dynamic for Haitian liberation and Spanish American independence movements, as well as lessons for all other revolutions since 1800. If the dynamic of future revolutions flowed from other causes, their immediate origins must be found in the same 'sense of inequality or injustice' as well as the promise of universal human rights.[54]

The new perspective presented by the democratic revolution paradigm established the universality of eighteenth-century revolutionary movements. Neither the American nor the French Revolution, in this optic, was uniquely, compulsively, vitally, 'exceptional'. They were rather interdependent moments of a worldwide movement. The breakthrough of Atlantic History was to demonstrate the oneness of the democratic revolutionary political tradition, rather than its many and diverse national manifestations. It also called for an ambitious, cosmopolitan and anti-exceptionalist perspective in the future study of revolutions. A century and a half after *Rights of Man*, Paine's approach was vindicated once again.

## From the political to the sociological, the 1970s and the 1980s

The social interpretation of the French Revolution, and the influence of Annales school specialization upon historians of the American and French Revolutions, complicated the challenges of Atlantic History for the generation following Godechot and Palmer. The hegemonic paradigm of the new social history turned historians towards exhaustive research of forgotten peoples, social groups, ethnic and religious minorities and vital economic sectors. How, then, to use the insights of Godechot and Palmer in studying Atlantic revolutionary history? For one, the researcher, engaged, say, in studying commerce in the Atlantic, would be obliged to work on a variety of sources, in many different places and with a panoply of languages. Perhaps the very ambition of the Atlantic paradigm, along with the rise of social history, led to a return to a more circumscribed research agenda among Palmer's own students at Princeton. Isser Woloch, Melvin Edelstein, David Bien and Jeffrey Kaplow were and remained, first and foremost, national historians of the French Revolution. (Although Kaplow, in 1970, converted to teaching American Civilization and taught for nearly two decades at the Université Paris-VIII, first in Vincennes and then at Saint-Denis.)[55]

Comparative revolutionary history came to mean comparative studies of another sort, however. In 1961, Hannah Arendt wrote a study of political theory, *On Revolution*, that theorized the success of the American Revolution and the failure of the French Revolution. Her central argument was Tocquevillian, that is, she focused on the radicalizing factor in France of 'the social question'. The pressing obligation to address what Arendt meant by 'the predicament of poverty' radicalized the French Revolution. The French erred by pretending they could ameliorate the lives of the 'masses of the poor, this overwhelming majority of all men, whom the French Revolution called *les malheureux*, whom it transformed into *les enragés*, only to desert them and let them fall back into the state of *les misérables*'. The Americans, by contrast, 'were not driven by want', and were guided by 'the realistic views of human nature of the Founding Fathers with regard to the shortcomings of human nature'.[56] Different historical and institutional logics therefore structured the two revolutions: Americans accepted a constitutional compromise that excluded discussion of social issues, and the French applied radical solutions to eradicate inequality.[57]

From the 1960s to the 1980s, to speak of comparative revolutions was generally to evoke the *démarche* of political scientists following Arendt. It also often meant reviving Crane Brinton's comparative morphologies of revolutions. Brinton had argued for the necessary appearance of a liberal phase, of revolutionary extremism and the inevitability of a radical Terror, a reactionary Thermidor and an authoritarian Bonapartism.[58] Such medical 'stages' were well suited to an American audience that viewed revolutions as pathologies. But while Arendt avoided such an ahistorical approach, she was also decisively *presentiste*. Her condemnation of French revolutionary violence as the antithesis of American moderation was also an implicitly 'exceptionalist' argument. Once again, a pluralist and multiparty democracy was seen as not only different but superior to a Rousseauiste France.

After Arendt, the politologues and sociologists Arendt, Theda Skocpol, Charles Tilly, Barrington Moore and Immanuel Wallerstein effectively confiscated the entire question of comparative revolutions from historians. Perhaps the most ambitious was Theda Skocpol, who, in 1979, argued for a 'structuralist' analysis of revolutions. She examined France, Russia and China, with scattered comments on the English and American Revolutions as well. Skocpol argued for the primacy of the revolutionary state over the importance of social revolution. The state is 'potentially autonomous from (though of course conditioned by) socioeconomic interests and structures', and is 'geared to maintain control of home territories and populations and to undertake actual or potential military competition with other states in the international system'. To Skocpol, all revolutions are fundamentally about restructuring the state to meet challenges of evolving world orders. The post-revolutionary state was prepared for global conflicts and competitions to come. Such functionalism repudiated the notion of democratic revolutions on the one hand and a retooled capitalist economy forged by class struggle on the other hand. Her Hegelian, state-centred study provided a mechanistic method for studying revolutions, freed from encumbering ideological or cultural influences or, we might add, from human agency as well.[59]

## The consumer-commercial Atlantic 'turn': the end of the two revolutions question?

In 1993, the American historians Stanley Eltkins and Erick McKitrick complained: 'In the case of our relations with the French, unlike those with the English, there has somehow been nothing very cumulative. One finds strikingly little in the way of interpenetration and growth, even down to the present time.'[60] The disillusionment of Eltkins and McKitrick regarding Franco-American history reflects, perhaps, a general sense that the two revolutions question had reached a dead end. Their own political narrative of the impact of the French Revolution in America, in fact, refers almost exclusively to a historiography that had not evolved from a schema recognizable to Gilbert Chinard and Bernard Faÿ in the 1920s: Franco-American solidarity in 1778 to Divorce and the Quasi-War from 1798 to 1800.

In a certain sense, the weariness betrayed by these authors reflects the staleness of a century of nearly exclusive attention on the political moment of the two revolutions. The exclusive insistence on this intellectual and politico-diplomatic Atlantic affirmed, and in turn was strengthened by, larger tendencies within French and American historiography. The historical convergence between the classic treatment of the two revolutions and the dominant position of a neo-Tocquevellian interpretation of the French Revolution was assured by François Furet and his students and followers Patrice Gueniffey, Ran Halevy, Mona Ozouf, Marcel Gauchet, as well as American 'Furetians', such as the intellectual historian Keith Michael Baker. They shared institutional connections to the École des hautes études en sciences sociales and the Institut Raymond Aron, and later the University of Chicago. They participated in elaborating a core analysis: ideological rather than class determinants had caused the French Revolution and moulded its development.[61] In *A Critical Dictionary of the French Revolution* (1989), they forged a relentless critique of the trajectory towards radicalization, in particular the condemnation of the fateful decisions of French revolutionaries to refuse to contain absolute sovereignty of the National Assembly and Convention with Anglo-American-style checks and balances. In the most extreme argument, Keith Michael Baker explicitly argued that the National Assembly was 'opting for the Terror' by its constitutional decisions as early as in 1789, when it vilified any opposition as factional.[62]

'Furetian' methods and arguments found a growing audience in the United States in the 1980s and 1990s. As an explicit reaction to materialism, it seemed the future of all revolutionary scholarship would follow the disciplinary and interpretive model of political history. American 'revisionism' – as it came to be called in opposition to Marxist 'orthodoxy' – put into practice the mantra of George Taylor, who, as early as 1967, declared that France had experienced 'a political revolution with social consequences and not a social revolution with political consequences'.[63] This elegant formula helped to unify the causes and origins of the American and French Revolutions in a single political lens – only without the solidarities implied in the Atlantic democratic revolutions thesis. It became the clarion call, as well, for French historians in the US to reject the methods of social history that reigned as the primary explanatory model at the Sorbonne and at the journal *les Annales*.

By the end of the Cold War, the struggle between Tocquevillian political narratives and Marxist social explanations was already moving to other topics, with other methodological and thematic problems. Economic Atlantic History alternately eclipsed and complemented political

Atlantic History. In particular, economic questions compelled historians to look beyond political discourse. Regarding the two revolutions question, Jacques Godechot had already posed the good question over fifty years ago: 'Was it bad commercial relations that chilled diplomatic relations or the other way around?', in underscoring the depth of the interrelated crises across the Atlantic in the federalist period. As we have seen, historians writing in Godechot's lifetime privileged the primacy of intellectual and politico-diplomatic relations. The essentially political Atlantic reviewed above was propitious to stressing ideas and diplomacy as vital causal factors. But, more recently, that question has increasingly suggested commerce as the accurate response to Godechot's question.[64]

Economic histories and histories of material culture have looked more and more carefully at commodity production and circulation, and have turned more towards the consumer revolution in the eighteenth century. The increasing demand by popular classes for sugar, coffee, tea, chocolate – but also for rubber umbrellas, silk laces, furs, leather goods, the so-called populuxe goods – drove international and domestic commerce in the last years of the old regime. Popular dependency on some New World products was indeed profound. Simple rumours that slave rebellions in faraway Saint-Domingue had driven up the cost of sugar and coffee, already staple items in the diets of urban artisans in France, provoked several uprisings of the French Revolution between 1791 and 1793.[65]

Histories of material culture have traced the circuitous routes of Virginia tobacco to France, rice from the Carolinas to the Mediterranean rim, Madeira wine to Barbados and Boston, Irish beef to the Antilles, and sugar to most everywhere.[66] These commodities are treated in close relationship to the agents that facilitated their circulation, as well as the consumers who created the original demand for these products. Also, the history of the Atlantic economy that focuses on 'les boulevards de la fraude' has opened up to the study of modern smugglers, illicit and illegal traders, pirates and maroon renegades.[67]

Jean Tarrade's *Le commerce colonial de la France à la fin de l'ancien régime* (1972) forcefully dictated a future research agenda of the economic French Atlantic. He demonstrated that the Colbertist *Exclusif* – the mercantilist policies that all colonial trade be pursued by French ships and hands – became unworkable after 1763. Tarrade argued that an 'exclusif mitigé' was put in place in the years leading up to the Revolution. He underscored the clash between what he called French 'lobbies', the Chambers of Commerce, seaport merchants, shippers and bankers, on the one hand, and the functionaries and ministerial officials on the other, charged with carrying out trade policies from Versailles and Paris. It was no longer sufficient to speak of imperial economic policies as carved out by statesmen as if they were applied 'on the ground'.[68]

The implications for Franco-American commerce were brought out perhaps even more imaginatively by Jacob Price in 1973, who explored the triangular conflicts between London, Paris and Philadelphia concerning Maryland tobacco in the eighteenth century. Price suggested that imperial Atlantics, rather than divided tidily into empires, were systematically violated by cunning profiteers such as Robert Morris who played the French *fermiers-généraux* against Russian, English and Spanish merchants anxious to participate in one of the most lucrative commodity exchanges of the eighteenth century.[69] Price anticipated by twenty-five years a problematic only recently explored in a forum in the April 2007 edition of the *American Historical Review*, 'Entangled Empires'. The contributors, focusing on the cross-fertilization between the French, Spanish and British Atlantics, reaffirm Price's argument that the Atlantic space is not reducible into separate and distinct hermetically sealed national empires.[70]

Peter Hill's 1988 study of the dense consular networks in the American confederation and republic proposes another approach. Hill traced the application of policies, covering whale oil, lumber, tobacco, cod, dried fish and other foodstuffs, from Versailles and Paris to the consuls in Philadelphia, Boston and New York. As an American historian, Hill was particularly sensitive to the reception of these policies in America. As the title of a separate article suggests, Hill was also most deeply interested in 'the road to the Quasi-War'.[71] His interpretation was slanted by the teleology of war – that is, Hill was perhaps somewhat insensitive to the symbolic, diplomatic, intellectual and political depth of Franco-American ties, summarized powerfully by the swearing in of George Washington as president in April 1789 as the *états généraux* were being convoked.[72]

The insights of Tarrade, Price and Hill pointed to the need for a greater focus on the economic Atlantic. They also demonstrated the limits of certain a prioris of the politico-diplomatic French Atlantic. But they prefigured two separate challenges for the two revolutions question. First, one of the fundamental difficulties with the revolutionary Atlantic is how to articulate the relationship between political revolutions and the material culture circulating over the seas. Often, there is a rather forced dualism between the visible hand of empire and the invisible hand of market forces. Either the visible hand of the fiscal-military state structured the Atlantic, so that the Atlantic system was embedded in hermetically sealed empires, except of course when war obliged contact with other empires. Visible-hand readings emphasized state interventionism and the military mechanisms of the state which sought to organize, or in historical terminology, to 'police' the economic lives of subjects. In this narrative, the absolutist state collapsed under the weight of fiscal-military repressiveness.[73] Or the precise opposite took place: the invisible hand of supply and demand trumped imperial pretensions at directing commerce. The tenants of invisible-hand interpretation accentuated the primacy of market forces in upsetting the established imperial orders of the end of the eighteenth century.[74]

But the visible or invisible hand is a false dichotomy, for often the primacy of one or the other depended on chronology. Periods of war and commercial restrictions, particularly during Napoleon's Continental Blockade and Jefferson's Embargo, are the moments where an Atlantic system clearly existed. Peaceful interludes, such as after the Seven Years War, often benefited merchants, entrepreneurs and privateers. Future projects on the Atlantic consumer revolution and on material culture should step back from the cycles of production, diffusion and reception of commodities to ask: what were the implications, beyond questions of political economy, in the availability of these objects in a revolutionary Atlantic? More elusive still, the vital questions remain: are the origins of capitalism, the consumer revolution and the political revolutions of the eighteenth century interrelated or discrete phenomena?[75]

The second problem is the question of whether or not a real system of Atlantic exchanges existed before the contemporary period. A purely materialist overview of the Atlantic demonstrates limitations of the historical shortcut: the Atlantic system. Economic historians lead us to a certain Atlanto-scepticism, the poorer cousin of Euro-scepticism, in its claim to the primacy of the nation state and its domestic economy.

Perhaps the most provocative of such Atlanto-sceptic voices is Pieter Emmer. He argues that all other nations except for Portugal and the Dutch republic drew well under 10 per cent of their overall trade from exchanges during the period of the fifteenth to the eighteenth centuries. No continent on the Atlantic rim saw its Atlantic commerce approach even 2 per cent of GDP in this period. Outside the Anglo-American plantation system, there was no real socio-economic consolidation.[76] Buttressing Emmer's point, calculations by economists deny the existence of an early globalization in this period, finding no evidence of market integration in crucial commodities such as textile, foodstuffs and metals until the middle of the nineteenth century. In sum, the commodities imported to Europe were not vital to the development of a pre-industrial European economy. Manufacturing and consumption were local, and if goods moved they moved within a region and not across the sea. Rather than a socio-economic system, Emmer argues, the Atlantic was more a set of cultural values and institutions, in which free labour, private property, the economic role of women, the nuclear family and monogamy were practised, privileged and propagated from Europe across the seas.[77]

The two revolutions question demonstrates that we may not reduce the Atlantic system to a strictly materialist understanding of quantifiable socio-economic networks. Instead, we might interpret these networks in a deeper and broader ideological, intellectual or cultural context of economic relations.[78] These networks were inscribed in the expectation that trade would regenerate and fuse the interests of Atlantic republics and those of reformed monarchies. Political assumptions about Atlantic trade, in other words, guided policies and practices in the eighteenth century: Jefferson's advocacy of 'free bottoms, free goods' and the ideal of a most favoured nation status between republican peoples were not a mere sometime thing, not mere rhetoric to be trumped by raisons d'état. For the importance of Atlantic commerce in perception led to its highly politicized importance in practice. While the actual weight of Atlantic exchanges may have evolved over time, the political pressure of public opinion coupled with real market pressures created by consumer demand for 'populuxe goods' affected Atlantic political economy with profound impact on governments and peoples across the seas.[79]

The mutual expectations of a transparent republican diplomacy based on amity and commerce helped to create the crises that brought France and America to war by century's end. The disillusionment was not 'the fault' of Europeans mistaking America's 'struggle for neutrality' for belligerence and deceit as earlier diplomatic historians have held; nor did misunderstandings regarding the violence of the Terror and the revolutionary wars cause the falling out between the two revolutions.[80] Rather, the ideological arguments of republican commerce collided with such real crises as the American debt to France and the unfavourable balance of trade between the two nations. These conflicts endlessly called into question whether revolutionary republics and regenerated peoples should pursue 'business as usual' in diplomacy and commercial relations. 'Commercial republicanism' in the French Atlantic was a fragile practice indeed; and it haunted French–American relations up to the Haitian Revolution and the collapse of France's first empire in 1804.

## Notes

1. Support for this essay was given in France by the Groupe de recherche sur l'histoire intellectuelle, UPRES/EA 1569. Edward Larkin (2005) *Thomas Paine and the Literature of Revolution* (Cambridge: Cambridge University Press). Richard Price and Joseph Priestley, in celebrating the two revolutions, did not discuss the specific influences of America other than in general terms: see Price (1789) *A Discourse on the Love of Our Country* and Priestley (1791) *Letters to the Right Honourable Edmund Burke, occasioned by his Reflections*.
2. Tom Paine, *Rights of Man*, Part First, in Philip Foner (1993) *The Life and Major Writings of Thomas Paine* (New York: Citadel Press), pp. 299–301.
3. A controversial study argued that returning 'American' conscripts engaged in anti-feudal resistance during the 'Great Fear' of 1789: F. McDonald (1951) 'The Relationship of the French Peasant Veterans of the American Revolution to the Fall of Feudalism in France, 1789–1792', *Agricultural History*, XXV, 151–61.
4. Paine, *Rights of Man*, pp. 299–300.
5. The 'Furet school' and its political-ideological explanation of the maelstrom of 1789 predictably favoured Burke over Paine, for while Burke figures prominently in François Furet and Mona Ozouf (eds) (1988) *Dictionnaire critique de la Révolution française* (Paris: Flammarion), pp. 916–23, Paine does not receive an entry by himself. See further comments below.
6. Morris' collusion is disputed by Melanie Randolph Miller (2005) *Envoy to the Terror: Gouverneur Morris and the French Revolution* (Dulles, Va.: Potomac Books), pp. 117–19.
7. On historiographical genealogy, see Natalie Zemon Davis (1993) 'Censorship, Silence and Resistance: The *Annales* during the German Occupation of France', *Rivista di Storiografia Moderna*, XIV, 16–81.
8. Rebecca Spang (2003) 'Paradigms and Paranoia: How Modern is the French Revolution?', *American Historical Review*, CVIII, 1, 119–47.
9. Gordon Wood (1999) *The Radicalism of the American Revolution* (New York: Viking), p. 2. On radicalism and exceptionalism: *William & Mary Quarterly* Forum (1994) 'How Revolutionary was the Revolution? A Discussion of Gordon S. Wood's *The Radicalism of the American Revolution*', III, 51, IV, 677–716.
10. Keith Michael Baker (1990) 'Inventing the French Revolution', in *Inventing the French Revolution* (Cambridge: Cambridge University Press), pp. 203–23.
11. Annie Jourdain (2004) *La Révolution: Une exception française?* (Paris: Flammarion); Mlada Bukovansky (2002) *Legitimacy and Power Politics: The American and French Revolutions in International Political Culture* (Princeton: Princeton University Press); Jean-Louis Harouel (1999) *1798: La grande année des républiques sœurs. Mélanges en hommage à Jean Gaudemet* (Paris: Presses universitaires de France); Bailey Stone (2002) *The French Revolution in World-Historical Perspective* (Cambridge: Cambridge University Press).
12. Allan Potofsky (2002) 'French Lumières and American Enlightenment during the Atlantic Revolution', *Revue Française d'Études Américaines*, XCIII, 47–67.
13. 'Pour une histoire comparée des sociétés européennes' is reproduced in M. Bloch (1983) *Mélanges historiques*, I (Paris: Éditions de l'EHESS, Éditions Serge Fleury), pp. 16–40.

14. On taxation in the two revolutions, see Jeremy Popkin (2002) 'Not Over After All: The French Revolution's Third Century', *Journal of Modern History*, LXXIV, 801–21.
15. John Dunn (1972) *Modern Revolutions: An Introduction to the Analysis of a Political Phenomenon* (Cambridge: Cambridge University Press), p. 2.
16. David Hume (1963) 'Of National Characters', in *Essays: Moral, Political and Literary* (Oxford: Oxford University Press), p. 210. On nineteenth-century 'historicism', see Charles Rearick (1974) *Beyond the Enlightenment: Historians and Folklore in Nineteenth-Century France* (Bloomington: Indiana University Press).
17. Alexis de Tocqueville (1953) *Oeuvres complètes* (Paris: Gallimard), vol. 2, pp. 334–7.
18. Isabelle Olivero (1999) *L'invention de la collection: De la diffusion de la littérature et des savoirs à la formation du citoyen au XIXe siècle* (Paris: IMEC-MSH), pp. 148–9.
19. Françoise Mélonio (1993) *Tocqueville et les français* (Paris: Aubier), p. 255.
20. On American teaching and writing about the French Revolution: Lynn Hunt (1995) 'Forgetting and Remembering: The French Revolution Then and Now', *American Historical Review*, C, 1119–35. R.R. Palmer (1985) 'A Century of French History in America', *French Historical Studies*, XIV, 160–75.
21. André Burgière (1979) 'Histoire d'une histoire: La naissance des Annales', *Annales ESC*, XXXIV, 1344–59.
22. Denis Pasquet and Frederick Morrow Fling (1919) 'La Révolution française et la période napoléonienne aux États-Unis', *Revue de Synthèse Historique*, XXIX, 249, 260–9. Pasquet would later write his two-volume *Histoire politique et sociale du peuple américain: Des origines à 1825* (1924) (Paris: A. Picard).
23. John Harvey (2004) 'An American Annales? The AHA and the *Revue internationale d'histoire économique* of Lucien Febvre and Marc Bloch', *Journal of Modern History*, LXXVI, 578–621.
24. Volker Berghahn and Charles Maier (1998) 'Modern Europe in American Historical Writing', in Anthony Molho and Gordon S. Wood (eds) (1998) *Imagined Histories: American Historians Interpret the Past* (Princeton: Princeton University Press), pp. 393–414.
25. Alphonse Aulard (1921) 'La Révolution française et la Révolution américaine', in *Études et leçons sur la Révolution française* (Paris: Félix Alcan), pp. 59–134; Aulard (May 1925 and June 1925) 'La dette américaine envers la France', *La Revue de Paris*, III. Part 1, 319–38; part 2, 524–50. On the debt question, see Allan Potofsky (2006) 'The Political Economy of the Debt Debate: The Ideological Uses of Atlantic Commerce, from 1787 to 1800', *William & Mary Quarterly*, LXIII, 485–515; Philippe Sagnac (1924) 'Les origines de la Révolution française: L'influence américaine', *Revue des Études Napoléoniennes*, XXII, 27–45.
26. Philippe Sagnac, *Histoire général*, vol. 12: *La fin de l'ancien régime et la Révolution américaine (1763–1789)* (Paris: Presses universitaires de France), pp. 216, 243, 503; Olivier Bétourné and Aglaia Hartig (1989) *Penser l'histoire de la Révolution: Deux siècles de passion française* (Paris: La Découverte). Also, more recently: Elise Marienstras and Naomi Wulf (2001) 'Traduire, emprunter, adapter la

Déclaration d'indépendance des États-Unis: Transferts et malentendus dans les traductions françaises', *Dix-huitième Siècle*, XXXIII, 201–18.

27. See the pertinent comments of Cécile Vidal (2006) 'The Reluctance of French Historians to Address Atlantic History', *Southern Quarterly*, special issue: *Imagining the Atlantic World*, XLIII, 4, 153–89. One exception is Michel Vovelle (2000) *Les républiques soeurs sous le regard de la grande nation, 1795–1803: De l'Italie aux portes de l'Empire ottoman: L'impact du modèle républicain français* (Paris and Montréal: Harmattan).

28. Perhaps the finest of these many works is Gilbert Chinard (1931) *The Correspondence of Jefferson and DuPont de Nemours with an Introduction on Jefferson and the Physiocrats* (Baltimore: Johns Hopkins Press).

29. Bernard Faÿ (1923) *L'esprit révolutionnaire en France et aux États-Unis à la fin du XVIIIe siècle* (Paris: Edouard Champion). *Thèse complémentaire* (1923): *Bibliographie critique des ouvrages français relatifs aux États-Unis (1770–1800)* (Paris: Edouard Champion); *Bibliothèque nationale. Le fonctionnement et la réorganisation de la Réunion des Bibliothèques nationales de Paris: 15 juin 1940 à 31 décembre 1942, rapport présenté à M. le Maréchal de France, chef de l'État* (1943) (Paris: Bibliothèque nationale). The information on Faÿ partially derives from the BnF's official site, 'Les directeurs de la Bibliothèque nationale' (2004), 11: http://www.bnf.fr/pages/connaitr/pdf/administrateurs.pdf. A curious sideshow to Faÿ's career was his friendship with Gertrude Stein and Alice B. Toklas: Janet Malcolm (2007) *Two Lives: Gertrude and Alice* (New Haven: Yale University Press). On Faÿ's anti-masonic activities, see Jean-Paul de Lagrave (2003) *La vision cosmique de Benjamin Franklin* (Quebec: Septentrion), pp. 21–2; Luc Nefontaine (1994) *La Franc-Maçonnerie, une fraternité révélée* (Paris: Gallimard), pp. 82–4.

30. Bernard Faÿ (1927) *Revolutionary Spirit in France and America* (1927) (New York: Cooper Square).

31. In 1941, Faÿ's textbook *Civilisation américaine* was enthusiastically reviewed in the pages of *Modern Language Notes* as 'an example of the peculiarly French powers of broad synthesis and shrewd analysis'. See Herbert Brown (1941) *Modern Language Notes*, LVI, 4, 302–4.

32. Michel Cordillot (2002) *La sociale en Amérique: Dictionnaire biographique du mouvement social francophone aux États-Unis, 1848–1922* (Paris: Éditions de l'atelier), pp. 81–8, 167–70, 210–14.

33. Examples are J. Salwyn Schapiro (1934) *Condorcet and the Rise of Liberalism* (New York: Harcourt, Brace); James Michael Eagan (1938) *Maximilian Robespierre: Nationalist Dictator* (New York: Octagon Books); Geoffrey Bruun (1932) *Saint-Just: Apostle of the Terror* (Boston and New York: Houghton Mifflin); Eugen Newton Curtis (1935) *Saint-Just: Colleague of Robespierre* (New York: Columbia University Press).

34. Donald Greer (1935) *The Terror, a Statistical Interpretation* (Cambridge, Mass.: Harvard University Press). Greer (1951) *The Incidence of the Emigration during the French Revolution* (Cambridge, Mass.: Harvard University Press).

35. These caricatures derived from the popular image of Charles Dickens, *A Tale of Two Cities* (1859), adapted for Hollywood by Jack Conoway in 1935 and featuring Ronald Coleman and Basil Rathbone. See: Colin Jones, Josephine McDonagh and Jon Mee (2008) *Charles Dickens, a Tale of Two Cities and the French Revolution* (Basingstoke and New York: Palgrave Macmillan).

36. Molho and Wood (eds) *Imagined Histories*, p. 359.
37. Crane Brinton (1939) *The Anatomy of Revolution* (New York: W.W. Norton), p. 39.
38. Quoted by Linda K. Kerber (1997) 'The Revolutionary Generation: Ideology, Politics, and Culture in the Early Republic', in Eric Foner (ed.), *The New American History* (Philadelphia: Temple University Press), p. 32.
39. Clinton Rossiter (ed.) (1961) *The Federalist Papers* (New York: The New American Library), p. vii.
40. Ibid.
41. See the critique in this period of John Higham (1959) 'The Cult of the American Consensus: Homogenizing our History', *Commentary*, XXVII, 93–100; Higham (1994) 'Changing Paradigms: The Collapse of Consensus History', *Journal of American History*, LXXVI, 460–6.
42. Manuela Albertone (2007) 'Democratic Republicanism: Historical Reflections on the Idea of Republic in the 18th Century', *History of European Ideas*, XXXIII, 1, 108–30; Lucia Bergamasco (2005) 'Le républicanisme: Thème historique, paradigme historiographique', *Cahiers Charles V*, XXXIX, 15–43. See also Jonathan Scott (2004) *Commonwealth Principles: Republican Writing of the English Revolution* (Cambridge: Cambridge University Press), pp. 1–5.
43. See the account of Bernard Bailyn (2005) *Atlantic History: Concept and Contours* (Cambridge, Mass. and London: Harvard University Press), pp. 24–8.
44. Jacques Godechot (1983) *La grande nation, l'expansion révolutionnaire de la France dans le monde de 1789 à 1799*, 2 vols, first published 1956 (Paris: Aubier), p. 17. The 1965 American edition was tellingly entitled: *France and the Atlantic Revolution of the Eighteenth Century, 1770–1799* (New York: Free Press).
45. Godechot, *France and the Atlantic Revolution*, p. 17.
46. R.R. Palmer (1959 and 1964) *The Age of the Democratic Revolution: A Political History of Europe and America, 1760–1800* (Princeton: Princeton University Press) (vol. 1: *The Challenge*; vol. 2: *The Struggle*).
47. Jürgen Habermas (1997) *L'espace public: Archéologie de la publicité comme dimension constitutive de la société bourgeoise* (Paris: Payot) (first German edition: 1962). On the impact of Habermas, see Roger Chartier (1990) *Les origines culturelles de la Révolution française* (Paris: Seuil).
48. Keith Michael Baker and Joseph Zizek (1998) 'The American Historiography of the French Revolution', in Molho and Wood (eds) *Imagined Histories*, pp. 361–2.
49. Palmer, *The Age of the Democratic Revolution*, vol. 1, pp. 189, 234; vol. 2, pp. 115, 43–4.
50. Ibid., vol. 2, pp. 314, 513, 514.
51. Jacques Godechot (1974) *Un jury pour la Révolution* (Paris: Robert Laffont), p. 362.
52. Durand Echeverria and Everett C. Wilkie (1994) *The French Image of America: A Chronological and Subject Bibliography of French Books Printed Before 1816 Relating to the British North American Colonies and the United States* (London: Scarecrow Press) in 2 vols.
53. Durand Echeverria (1957) *A History of the French Image of American Society to 1815* (Princeton: Princeton University Press); Michèle Duchet (1971) *Anthropologie et histoire au siècle des Lumières* (Paris: Maspero).

44  Allan Potofsky

54. See Palmer's impassioned coda in Palmer, *The Age of the Democratic Revolution*, vol. 2, p. 575.
55. Lynn Hunt (1986) 'French History in the Last Twenty Years: The Rise and Fall of the Annales Paradigm', *Journal of Contemporary History*, XXI, 2, 209–24.
56. Hannah Arendt (1961) *On Revolution* (New York: Viking), pp. 110, 66–7.
57. On the distortions of excluding slavery in comparative revolutionary generalizations, see Isser Woloch (1990) 'On the Latent Illiberalism of the French Revolution', *American Historical Review*, XCV, 1452–70.
58. Brinton, *Anatomy*.
59. Theda Skocpol (1979) *States and Social Revolutions: A Comparative Analysis of France, Russia, and China* (Cambridge: Cambridge University Press), p. 7.
60. Stanley Eltkins and Erick McKitrick (1993) *The Age of Federalism: The Early American Republic, 1788–1800* (Oxford: Oxford University Press), p. 303.
61. David D. Bien (1990) 'François Furet, the Terror, and 1789', *French Historical Studies*, XVI, 4, 777–83.
62. François Furet and Mona Ozouf (eds) (1989) *A Critical Dictionary of the French Revolution* (Cambridge Mass.: Harvard University Press); Keith Michael Baker, 'Fixing the French Constitution', in *Inventing the French Revolution*, p. 305. For a trenchant critique of the *Dictionary* and its assumptions, see Woloch, 'On the Latent Illiberalism', p. 1460.
63. George V. Taylor (1967) 'Noncapitalist Wealth and the Origins of the French Revolution', *American Historical Review*, LXXII, 491–2.
64. Jacques Godechot (1958) 'Les relations économiques entre les États-Unis et la France de 1778 à 1789', *French Historical Studies*, I, 1, 26–39.
65. On the Atlantic consumer revolution, see Paul G.E. Clemens (2005) 'The Consumer Culture of the Middle Atlantic, 1760–1820', *William & Mary Quarterly*, LXII, 4 (October), 577–624. On French revolutionary artisanal revolts, see Allan Potofsky, *Constructing the Capital in the Age of Revolution: The Builders of Paris, from the Old Regime to the Empire* (Basingstoke and New York: Palgrave Macmillan), forthcoming; Daniel Roche (1997) *Histoire des choses banales naissance de la consommation (XVIe–XIXe siècle)* (Paris: Fayard); Michael Kwass (2003) 'Ordering the World of Goods: Consumer Revolution and the Classification of Objects in Eighteenth-Century France', *Representations*, LXXXII, 87–116.
66. Kenneth Morgan (1995) 'The Organization of the Colonial Rice Trade', *William & Mary Quarterly*, 3rd ser. LII, 433–52; Michelle Craig McDonald (2005) 'The Chance of the Moment: Coffee and the New West Indies Commodities Trade', *William & Mary Quarterly*, 3rd ser. LXII, 441–72. Brooke Hunter, 'Wheat, War, and the American Economy during the Age of Revolution', *William & Mary Quarterly*, 3rd ser. LXII, 505–26; David Hancock (1995) *Citizens of the World: London Merchants and the Integration of the British Atlantic Community, 1735–1785* (Cambridge: Cambridge University Press); Bertie Mandelblatt (2007) 'A Transatlantic Commodity: Irish Salt Beef in the French Atlantic World', *History Workshop Journal*, LXIII, 1, 18–47; J.H. Galloway (2004) *Tropical Babylons: Sugar and the Making of the Atlantic World, 1450–1650* (Chapel Hill: University of North Carolina Press).
67. Silvia Marzagalli (1999) *Les boulevards de la fraude: Le négoce maritime et le blocus continental 1806–1813. Bordeaux, Hambourg, Livourne* (Villeneuve d'Ascq: Presses universitaires du Septentrion).

68. Jean Tarrade (1972) *Le commerce colonial de la France à la fin de l'Ancien Régime: L'évolution du régime de "l'Exclusif" de 1763 à 1789* (Paris: Presses universitaires de France).
69. Jacob Munro Price (1973) *France and the Chesapeake: A History of the French Tobacco Monopoly, 1674–1791, and of its Relationship to the British and American Tobacco Trades* (Ann Arbor: University of Michigan Press) in 2 vols.
70. (2007) *American Historical Review*, CXII, 3.
71. Peter P. Hill (1988) *French Perceptions of the Early American Republic, 1783–1793* (Philadelphia: American Philosophical Association); Hill (1977) 'Prologue to the Quasi-War: Stresses in Franco-American Commercial Relations, 1793–1796', *Journal of Modern History*, XLIX; Hill (2005) *Napoleon's Troublesome Americans: Franco-American Relations, 1804–1815* (Washington, DC: Potomac Books).
72. See also Marc Belissa, Stéphane Bégaud and Joseph Visser (2005) *Aux origines d'une alliance improbable: Le réseau consulaire français aux États-Unis (1776–1815)* (Brussels: Peter Lang).
73. For example François Crouzet (1964) 'Wars, Blockades, and Economic Change in Europe, 1972–1815', *Journal of Economic History*, XXIV, 4, 573–4. The visible-hand interpretation is underscored by the disciples of Pierre Chaunu, such as Jean Meyer, Paul Butel and Patrick Villiers, who are interested above all in maritime issues, including navigation.
74. Hancock, *Citizens of the World*.
75. One recent effort in this direction is Kevin O'Rourke (2006) 'The Worldwide Economic Impact of the French Revolutionary and Napoleonic Wars, 1793–1815', *Journal of Global History*, I, 123–49.
76. Pieter Emmer (2002) 'In Search of a System: The Atlantic Economy, 1500–1800', in Horst Pietschmann (ed.) *Atlantic History: History of the Atlantic System, 1580–1830* (Göttingen: Vandenhoeck & Ruprecht), pp. 169–78. Also, Emmer (2003) 'The Myth of Early Globalisation: The Atlantic Economy, 1500–1800', *European Review*, XI, 1, 37–47.
77. Kevin H. O'Rourke and Jeffrey G. Williamson (2002) 'When Did Globalization Begin?', *European Review of Economic History*, VI, 23–50. See also a critique of their 'narrow definition of globalization' in Dennis O. Flynn and Arturo Giraldez (2004) 'Path Dependence, Time Lags and the Birth of Globalization: A Critique of O'Rourke and Williamson', *European Review of Economic History*, VIII, 109–17.
78. As exemplified by the rich argument of R. Darrell Meadows (2000) 'Engineering Exile/Social Networks and the French Atlantic Community, 1789–1809', *French Historical Studies*, XXIII, 1, 67–102.
79. Cissie Fairchilds (1993) 'The Production and Marketing of Populuxe Goods in Eighteenth-Century Paris', in Roy Porter and John Brewer (eds), *Consumption and the World of Goods* (New York and London: Routledge), pp. 228–48.
80. Albert Hall Bowman (1978) *The Struggle for Neutrality: Franco-American Diplomacy during the Federalist Era* (Knoxville: University of Tennessee Press).

# 2
# Democracy and Equality in the Radical Enlightenment: Revolutionary Ideology before 1789

*Jonathan Israel*

Keith Michael Baker has rightly stressed the 'complexity of the process of ideological elaboration that occurred' in France and neighbouring countries in the pre-revolutionary period (1770–89) and the 'great range of discourses upon which opposition to monarchical authority could draw' in the last decades before the Revolution.[1] He has also pointed out that many traditional notions, as well as a complex mix of new ideas, featured in the growing chorus of French protest and criticism. There is much to be said for this point of view; but it is arguable that it is open to criticism in one absolutely crucial respect.

In addition to these, there was a highly dynamic and perhaps decisively important ideological strain closely linked to the writings of Diderot, d'Holbach and Helvetius and such close allies and disciples as Condorcet, Volney, Brissot, Mirabeau, Paine and the Dutch democratic theorists of the 1780s. This stream of thought made no concessions at all to tradition, religion or existing institutions, and it was precisely this strain, I shall attempt to argue here, which arguably did most to establish and disseminate the ideology of equality, democracy and the supremacy of 'reason' in the transatlantic Western world during the 1770s and 1780s.

This thesis places particular emphasis on the 1770s and 1780s as a gestation period during which what I term the 'revolution of the mind' occurred and was spread widely, particularly in France, Britain and the Netherlands, by the disciples and publicists of the radical *encyclopédistes*. It was a 'revolution of the mind' which matured before the 'revolution of fact'. Furthermore, I shall argue, Radical Enlightenment principles played a key role – and in the case of France one might even say *the* key role – in shaping these revolutions insofar as both can be regarded as steps towards modern democracy and equality. However, the Radical

Enlightenment did this in ways which thus far scholars have paid scarce attention to. Essentially, what is being claimed here is that the most crucial intellectual factor in the creation of the core values of modern Western democratic republicanism was precisely the same chief factor that went into the creation of the ideology of 'reason' during the French Revolution (i.e. the anti-Rousseauist strain). What is more, this ideology also laid the foundation for what will be termed here 'the radical critique' of the American Revolution.

This state of affairs may immediately strike the reader as paradoxical, even strange. It suggests that the most formative intellectual factor in the making of the French Revolution, in its early stages, was a 'revolution of reason' already fully developed before 1789 and chiefly expounded by those whom Rousseau and the many religious *anti-philosophes* of the age termed (with strong overtones of disapproval) the *nouveaux philosophes*. Yet it is precisely this intellectual impulse towards democracy and equality that is the element in the equation most completely and insistently neglected by the historiography (including Baker) and by historians of political thought.

What is more, many readers are accustomed to thinking of the American Revolution, not the French, as the chief stepping-stone towards modern democracy and equality, and they tend to believe the American Revolution grew out of an 'Atlantic republican' intellectual and political tradition with strong roots in seventeenth-century English thought. Yet a number of scholars have noted that this way of viewing the rise of modernity leaves a number of gaps and transitions unexplained. In the first place, it fails to explain how Anglophone republicanism became democratic and egalitarian. In the second, it fails to explain how ideas contributed to the making of the two revolutions. As Manuela Albertone has expressed it, the 'link between republic and democracy was made explicit by the events of the American Revolution and the French Revolution'. However, historians' and philosophers' awareness of the revolutionary process leading towards democracy has not yet developed in such a way 'as to allow these historical periods to assume a central role in the current debate on republicanism'.[2]

This is largely unfamiliar terrain. There is a suggestion, however, that by far the most decisive phase in the process through which the values of democracy and egalitarianism became the core ideology and central value system of the Western world were the two decades immediately prior to the first major democratic movement in modern Europe (i.e. the Dutch *Patriottenbeweging* of 1780–87). Furthermore, the second major such movement, the 'French Revolution', amounts to more than just a challenging proposition or interesting thought-experiment. For the claim that what was frequently referred to in the closing decades of the *ancien régime* as *la philosophie nouvelle*, namely those radical ideas stemming from the work of the later Diderot and d'Holbach, was actually the chief factor in preparing the ground for this decisive transition does two things. It provides solid answers to questions which remain otherwise unanswered and gives us a richly suggestive vantage point from which to view both the American and French Revolutions in a much broader political and social, as well as intellectual, context than is provided by the discourse of 'Atlantic republicanism'.

The ideology dealt with in what follows – much neglected by modern scholars but nonetheless formidably powerful – was primarily French in origin. Yet its Spinozistic roots were decidedly not French, and its rapid spread in the 1770s and 1780s was arguably just as much Dutch, British and American, and to a lesser extent Italian and German, as it was French. Indeed, according to some representatives of the late eighteenth-century Radical Enlightenment, the French Revolution would better – and perhaps should actually – be called the 'General Revolution', as Tom Paine and his close friend, the American radical and participant in it, Joel Barlow, referred to that great upheaval. This is because there was arguably nothing inherently French about the principles and values that shaped it. Much of it took place outside France, and its significance for mankind was both universal and, as it seemed to Paine and Barlow, would prove lasting.

First, however, the reader needs to be convinced that there was a 'revolution of the mind' which preceded the 'revolution of fact'. The plausibility of such a thesis is significantly enhanced, it may be suggested, by the fact that there were various warnings and predictions on the eve of 1789 that a 'grande revolution', as one observer put it in 1788, was about to occur. These admonitions took it for granted that *la nouvelle philosophie* or *philosophisme*, as its enemies also often called it, was the likeliest or only causal agent behind the unprecedented general upheaval now widely envisaged and widely dreaded. One example is the lengthy *Analyse et examen de l'Antiquité devoilée, du despotisme oriental, et du christianisme devoilé* (Geneva and Paris, 1788), a work published anonymously but apparently written by the French *anti-philosophe* Charles-François Legros (1712–90). The *Analyse et examen* was a vehement counter-assault on the republicanism of Boulanger as expounded in the three books cited in its title, all prepared and published by d'Holbach in the 1760s. The work contended that it was precisely the *nouveaux philosophes* who were at odds with Rousseau, those friends of Boulanger – and particularly

Diderot and d'Holbach – who envisaged, desired and were providing the intellectual fabric for this 'grande revolution'.

On the pretext that men on earth are presently all wretched, miserable and wicked, this author warned, these thinkers accuse the governments of Europe day after day with 'disorder, misfortune and the corruption of humankind'. Is it not they who were constantly declaiming

> against the abuses they believe they see in the different political constitutions of Europe? Are they not trying to substitute these constitutions with other projects, other systems, real masterpieces, if we are to believe them, which alone can lead us along the road to happiness; isn't this an attempt to upturn public order?[3]

Here was the intellectual source of the 'revolution of the mind' prior to the Revolution. The thinkers he is referring to are those who contended that reason alone, and not sentiment, tradition or faith, is the sole guide in human life. This in opposition to the Lockean and sceptical views of Voltaire, Hume, Turgot and Condillac and, no less, in opposition to Rousseau's critique of 'reason', civilization and the arts and sciences. For if reason is *the* criterion, they held, then equality, democracy and individual liberty are the only justifiable social and political principles on which politics and the social order should be built.

It is clear, then, that there are a number of late eighteenth-century radical thinkers who rejected both Montesquieuan relativism, the entire Scottish Enlightenment, scepticism and Lockean empiricism on the one hand, and all theological criteria and Rousseauist sentimentalism on the other. These follow in the wake of the late Diderot, d'Holbach and Helvetius and include not only Condorcet, Mirabeau, Cerisier, Cloots, Maréchal, Naigeon, Volney, Brissot, Paine, Godwin and Barlow but also the more radical Dutch democrats, Gerrit Paape (1752–1803),[4] Schimmelpenninck, Irhoven van Dam, and British 'Unitarian', materialist radicals such as Joseph Priestley, John Jebb and, in large part, Richard Price. These are the intellectuals who declared their intention of following the light of reason alone and are the writers and publicists whom intellectual historians will perhaps eventually come to recognize as representatives of that revolutionary upsurge in Western thought which ushered modern equality and democracy into the world as a general principle and body of ideology.

Over several decades prior to 1789, both moderate Enlightenment observers and the French *anti-philosophes* had been taking note of the intrinsic tendency towards democracy and equality in a philosophical tradition which insists on upholding 'reason' as the sole and exclusive guide in human life. They had become accustomed to warning society that a great deal of danger lay in ideas which placed 'reason' on so high a pedestal. 'That kings are the servants of the people, to be obeyed, resisted, deposed or punished, as the public conveniency may require', objected Adam Smith, in 1759, 'is the doctrine of reason and philosophy; but it is not the doctrine of nature.'[5] In a similar vein, the German closet radical Georg Christoph Lichtenberg (1742–99), who was militantly anticlerical in his private views, remarked, soon after the advent of the French Revolution, that the 'political democrats' based themselves upon the 'monarchy of reason' and, consequently, energetically advocate equality and democracy. He seriously doubted, however, whether they were right to do so: 'Try to rule the world with a god whom Reason alone has enthroned', he objected, 'and you will soon see that it cannot be done.'[6]

The Radical Enlightenment thinkers met with some especially vigorous opposition from a rootedly anti-democratic, moderate mainstream Enlightenment which insisted, as Hume, Voltaire and Montesquieu all do in their different ways, that morality, law and society must be based as much, or more, on tradition, religion and the existing social hierarchy than on 'reason'. At the same time they were formidably assailed by Counter-Enlightenment, which was already surging in the 1770s and 1780s, and which rejected both the radicals' veneration of 'reason' and the idea of a balance between reason and tradition so dear to the moderate Enlightenment, insisting instead on the overriding, exclusive role of faith and authority in guiding human life. These writers viewed radical thought as the quintessence of all that is most to be feared and detested in society.

The radical thinkers expounded a *philosophisme* which not only rejected outright all existing European constitutions, but was also sharply critical of the new American constitution and political context. The newly born United States had failed to free the slaves, had not done enough to counter the religious intolerance of small-town America. It was also accepting with too much ease the slow but steady rise of an informal aristocracy, which Diderot especially warned against in his contributions to Raynal's *Histoire philosophique*. Mirabeau and Brissot were later to follow him in this. Equally, radical thought was contemptuous of those more cautious and traditional-minded friends of the American Revolution who opposed extending democracy and equality to Europe and hailing these ideals as universal values: 'That an avowed friend of the American revolution', protested Joseph Priestley, in his *Letters to the Right Honourable Edmund Burke* of 1791, 'should be an enemy to that of the French, which arose from the same general principles, and in a great measure sprung from it, is to me unaccountable.'[7] In fact, however, in the eyes of any theorist who insisted on the primacy of particular rights and particular constitutions, such as the special privileges of Englishmen, it was perfectly feasible and cogent, as Burke amply demonstrated, to champion the American Revolution while denying that other peoples necessarily had a right to have an 'American revolution' of their own.

What is more, a great many Americans who supported the revolution of 1776 made a point of opposing both full representative democracy and the idea of a universal rights-based equality. Most conservative and conventionally minded Americans – that is, most American political writers at the time – preferred to anchor their justifications for the American Revolution in British tradition, privileges and precedents, not in universal principles. Few had much use for philosophy, much less radical thought or any notion of universal rights or the basic unity of mankind. Indeed, Mirabeau, one of the prime exponents of this radical critique of the American Revolution before 1789, believed this continuing American addiction to everything British was detrimental to the fledgling republic. He, like Brissot, Paine, Barlow and others, saw it as the prime source and cause of emerging deficiencies and corruption, and not least the excessive deference to case law and to lawyers, evident in the new United States.[8]

There was a strong Hobbesian element in Burke's anti-democratic stance which Priestley picked up with unerring accuracy. It is highly important to establish correctly the intellectual lineage of the democratic and egalitarian ideology sweeping, not just France and the Dutch republic, but also British Unitarian and radical circles in the 1770s and 1780s. However, Priestley's observation is the clearest of indications that, whatever else it had, this ideology assuredly did not possess Hobbesian origins: 'you treat with ridicule', Priestley rebuked Burke, 'the ideas of the rights of men, and suppose that mankind, when once they have entered into a state of society, necessarily abandon all their proper natural rights, and thenceforth have only such as they derive from society'. This act of carrying over man's 'proper natural rights' from the state of nature into society begins not with Hobbes but specifically with Spinoza, and it was the very hallmark of the Radical Enlightenment.

Burke, of course, bitterly opposed the sweeping, universalist approach of the 'French theorists' and found in Hobbesian contract theory a useful resource for reinforcing his particularlist, anti-universalist stance. Priestley was absolutely right, though, to detect here a deep-rooted hostility on the part of Burke to a particular way of employing philosophy.

This was the growing tendency in the 1770s and 1780s, especially in Europe, to use philosophy to assert the universal liberty, equality and right to democratic participation of all men:

> It is one of the most curious paradoxes in this work of yours, which abounds with them, that the rights of men above-mentioned (called by you 'the pretended rights of the French theorists') 'are all extremes, and in proportion as they are metaphysically true, they are morally and politically false'. Now by metaphysically true can only be meant strictly and properly true, and how this can be in any sense false, is to me incomprehensible. If the above-mentioned rights be the true, that is the just, and reasonable rights of men, they ought to be provided for in all states, and all forms of government; and if they be not, the people have just cause to complain, and to look out for some mode of redress.[9]

There is no contractual element in the doctrine of universal rights during the 1770s and 1780s, or in the justifications for the people to take matters into their own hands to enforce them. We should look neither to Hobbes nor to Locke, and still less to the so-called 'Atlantic republican tradition' in our search for the real intellectual genealogy of the Radical Enlightenment's doctrine of equality, democracy and universal rights. In the wake of Pocock much emphasis has gone into stressing the centrality of the Atlantic republican tradition as a means of interpreting the age of revolutions. Despite this, however, it is arguable that the most crucial shaping and organizing factor – the Radical Enlightenment's ideology of democracy, equality and individual liberty – actually has no British origins or roots at all.

This new, specifically 'revolutionary' ideology stated that the moral and political transformation of man and his improvement or renewal on a better basis requires and can only be generated by a universal revolution driven by the active agent of *la philosophie*, and that this struggle, fought with the weapons of philosophy, is a fight forced on those capable of enlightenment by what d'Holbach deemed the truly brutal, destructive and savage ignorance of men 'and those who govern'.[10] It was, and remained, totally incompatible with the social, political, moral and educational conservatism and relativism of not just Hobbes and Burke, but also Montesquieu, Voltaire, Ferguson and Hume. For in the eyes of the late Diderot and d'Holbach, all existing societies were organized in the interest of the few at the expense of the many. 'A blind policy,' proclaimed d'Holbach, 'guided by interests entirely contrary to those of society does not permit men to become enlightened either about their own rights, or their true duties, or about the true ends of the association which it continually subverts.'[11]

The overriding problem in politics, as Diderot and d'Holbach understood it, was to prevent those being governed from becoming the prey of those who govern.[12] Eventually, Europe's monarchs, including such supposedly 'enlightened' despots as Frederick the Great and Catherine the Great, had somehow to be overcome or pushed aside. As for privilege and aristocratic fiscal exemptions, these, in the view of the radical *philosophes* Diderot, d'Holbach and Helvetius, negated every principle of equity, justice and morality and were the very contradiction of the 'general will' itself. In fact, declared d'Holbach, preceding Priestley (whose open call for the abolition of aristocracy came only some years later), all distinction of orders, privilege and forms of legal discrimination must be abolished.[13]

The central tenet in politics of the radical *philosophes* – those French, Dutch, German and British thinkers who adopted monistic, Spinozistic conceptions of the cosmos – was that a good government is one where legislation and the law-makers reject all theological criteria, separate government and legislation completely from religion, and seek to ensure by means of laws and institutional structures that education, individual interest and society's moral values 'concourir', as Helvetius expressed it, 'au bien général', understood in a purely secular sense.[14] Since inequality of wealth and status and the prevalence of monarchical, aristocracatic and ecclesiastical authority was then the overriding feature of European society, no one willing to apply the radical *philosophes*' criterion could possibly avoid Helvetius' and the other radical *philosophes*' conclusion that there were, therefore, scarcely any good governments and, furthermore, that only philosophy, or rather a turn towards 'la philosophie moderne' in formulating society's main social and political goals, could demonstrate what a good government and set of social values would look like.

Only the redoubled efforts of philosophy and enlightenment and nothing else, contended Helvetius, could combat the errors and dissipate the clouds which have hitherto prevented sovereigns and peoples alike from seriously attending 'to the things that are of most interest to them'.[15] No doubt a number of 'penseurs découragés', as d'Holbach referred to Voltaire, Hume, Rousseau and Turgot, try to convince us that it is useless to imagine philosophy can 'éclairer tout un peuple', claiming that neither philosophy nor the principles of true morality can be grasped by the common people:

> We will reply that to make a nation reasonable there is no need for all the citizens to be scholars or deep-thinking philosophers; it is enough that the nation be governed by respectable people.[16]

Doubtless the sciences, he granted, as well as most aspects of philosophy are beyond the capacity of the common run of men. But they are nevertheless very useful to them. Every day, the most ignorant, unlearned and fatuous of men use techniques based on principles which are altogether beyond them, the original discovery of which was due 'to the great efforts of human genius'.[17] Equally, the principles of true wisdom are hard to discover but, once found, can quite easily be put into effect by any well-meaning government. In short, philosophy may be something in which most people take no interest and which they cannot in the least understand; but it is also something relevant and useful to them to the highest degree.

The late eighteenth-century European world was one ruled over by monarchy. Its social hierarchy was dominated by the aristocracy, there were massive inequalities of wealth and legal privilege, its legal systems were extremely archaic, and it was intolerant of, and discriminated against, religious minorities, homosexuals and freethinkers, all of whom were systematically penalized. What remedy could there possibly be, asked d'Holbach in 1773, for 'the widespread degradation of society' which so many powerful factors seem likely to eternalize?[18] There is only one way to cure such ills – abolish the whole corrupt edifice and replace it with a more equitable society; and there is only one way to undertake such a task, namely by attacking 'error' and proclaiming 'the truth'. 'If error, as has been shown, is the source of all the evils of this world'; if men are only vicious, intolerant, oppressed and poor because they have totally wrong ideas about 'their happiness' and about everything else; then it can only be by fighting error with courage and resolution, by showing men their true interests and proclaiming 'des idées saines' that society's ills can be tackled. When the perceived defects of society are structural and deep and based chiefly on faith, a trust in authority and ignorance, then philosophy is not only the likeliest but also effectively the only agent powerful enough to organize and precipitate a rapid, all-encompassing revolution.

Unlike Voltaire, Montesquieu and Hume, the radical writers roundly rejected a British-style mixed monarchy, deeming it a recipe for dividing sovereignty, introducing unnecessary forms of corruption into politics, manipulating an electoral system which did not provide elected representatives in remotely equal ratios to electors, as well as preserving what was in effect a modified monarchy linked to the aristocracy. These writers included not only Boulanger, d'Holbach, Diderot, and all their disciples and acolytes, such as Condorcet, Cloots, Brissot, Mirabeau, Volney, Cerisier and their Anglophone allies – Tom Paine, Price, Priestley, Jebb, Godwin and Barlow – but also the radical Dutch democratic republicans – men like Gerrit Paape, Irhoven van Dam and Pieter Vreede. Gabriel Bonnot de Mably (1709–85), an austere republican fiercely hostile to Voltaire and an ally to *philosophisme*, had already condemned the British-style mixed monarchy as early as 1751, in his *Observations sur les Romains*.[19] Unlike Voltaire and the moderate mainstream Enlightenment, a movement which in the hands of Voltaire, Montesquieu, Hume and all the Scots was usually fervently anglophile, the Radical Enlightenment refused outright to recognize Britain, or any plea for particular traditions and privileges, as the ideal or the best available model.

However, Diderot and d'Holbach (unlike Rousseau) did not think the solution to society's urgent problems lay in Athenian-style direct democracy or in the Rousseauist cult of small republics either. The dismal story of the failure of the ancient direct democracies of classical Greece had been retold by Boulanger in his vividly written *Recherches sur l'origine du despotisme oriental* (1762) in a manner which convinced many that a true people's republic was one that was bound to revert to theocracy, the worst of conditions in Boulanger's eyes, owing to its invariably assigning popular cults and priests a central role in the affairs of the republic.[20] Since the common people cannot escape from the tyranny of priestcraft and demagogues on their own, Boulanger's message seemed to be that humanity must place its trust either in a form of constitutional monarchy which he calls *Nomarchy*, where the king has no other power than strictly to obey and help enforce laws based on reason, or else in the electorate's elected representatives.

Diderot, d'Holbach, Condorcet, Brissot, Mirabeau and Mably, like the Dutch democratic Patriots of the mid-1780s, wanted all men to be equally free in the sense that they should all enjoy equal protection under the law and equal liberty to pursue their own happiness, and hence their own ambitions and goals. Simultaneously, they refused to accept that this means direct participation of all men in the business of government, on the model of the ancient democracies. Horrified as they were by the ignorance and bigotry of the man in the street, such direct democratic government seemed to them, no less than to Immanuel

Kant, an impossible 'chimère', an invitation to tumult, licence and ruin, something incompatible with the general will and 'totally incompatible with our nature'.[21] How then could and can democracy and equality be based on enlightened ideas? That was the crucial democratic question for militant *philosophisme*.

Rejecting direct or 'simple democracy', as Tom Paine called it, which was based on the Athenian model and was of the sort recommended by Rousseau, the early architects of the philosophical democratic revolution searched for a different solution to the problem of how to organize a stable, effective democracy. The key political tool they came up with was the idea of political representation as a way of democratizing mixed monarchies and ultimately organizing stable, large-scale democracies. It was a concept sketched out clearly by Diderot, d'Holbach and their Parisian 'synagogue' in about 1763 for the article *Représentants* in the *Encyclopédie*. Henceforth, the idea figured prominently in the work of d'Holbach and Mably and also constitutes one of the principal differences between what we might call mainline European radical republican ideology in the 1760s and 1770s and the republican deviationism of Rousseau and Robespierre, with its very different conception of the 'general will', its rejection of reason as the chief criterion and insistence on virtue and sentiment as the true grounding of the general will.[22] It remained one of Rousseau's cardinal doctrines that popular sovereignty, being unlimited, is something that cannot be delegated and that representatives must therefore always be supervised and strictly mandated by their constituents.

Hence it turns out that the democratic egalitarianism of the 'revolution of the mind' that took place in France, Holland and in radical circles in Britain in the 1770s and 1780s, was not just unHobbesian, unLockean and unMontesquieuan, it was emphatically not Rousseauist either. On the contrary, Rousseau's political theses, and especially his insistence on small republics and the indivisibility of the 'general will', was the conclusion Boulanger, d'Holbach, Diderot, Helvetius and Mably explicitly and energetically strove to avoid while developing their new idea of democratic republicanism, as indeed did the Dutch democratic Patriot spokesmen of the 1780s. Moreover, d'Holbach and Diderot categorically denied that their model entails any diminution of individual liberty when compared with Rousseau's model. Sovereign in appearance, in reality the common people in a direct democracy are frequently the slaves of 'perverse demagogues' who know how to manipulate and flatter them. In a direct democracy, the people often have no real idea of what liberty is, and their rule can be harsher than that of the worst tyrant.

Liberty without reason, held d'Holbach, is, in itself, of little value: 'the history of most republics', he wrote, 'ceaselessly offers the revolting picture of nations bathed in their own blood by anarchy'.[23] The Radical Enlightenment was committed to representative democracy on principle precisely because it saw itself as a universal revolution of 'reason'.

The revolutionary character of the radical summons to transform government on an egalitarian and democratic basis, whether in its French, Dutch, British or American version, was thus clearly manifested in a call for a system of democratic elections, participated in by the citizens, with a view to choosing known, experienced and qualified representatives of the people who would be regularly changed, a system in which the hereditary and aristocratic principles would be totally eradicated. Supposedly, merit and rationality were to be the only criteria. Here was something approximating much more closely to what we would today call democracy than the originally medieval system of representation by 'estates' that still lingered in much of Europe in their day. The essential difference between representation according to the traditional model of the 'estates' and the new conception of an 'assemblée nationale', or 'senate', as propounded by radical *philosophes*, was the elimination of hereditary or privileged access (again something the American Founding Fathers could concur with). This went hand in hand with the inalienable right to convene regularly or whenever the representatives saw fit, along with effective control of the state revenues to ensure that these were spent 'to serve the true needs of the state' and not used by the prince, where there is one, to corrupt the 'representatives of the people', advance his own interest or sustain, as d'Holbach put it, 'la splendeur et la vanité d'une cour'.[24]

The *assemblée nationale*, which is d'Holbach's term for this new representative gathering, would also be empowered to establish regional assemblies and, last and most crucial of all, would control the armed forces. This assembly could never be dissolved by a monarch but could be by the people whenever it no longer faithfully performed its task of legislating and governing in the 'public interest'. Meanwhile, assuming this *assemblée nationale* did represent 'the general will' of society faithfully, it would always be justified in initiating armed action to oppose and suppress ambitious cliques, royal pretenders or would-be dictators intending to violate the 'general will'. If every individual of our species has 'the right' to defend himself against aggression, contended the late Diderot and d'Holbach, 'by what strange jurisprudence do apologists for monarchy and the churches deny to entire nations the right to resist their tyranny?'[25]

It was precisely their insistence that 'philosophical' reasoning – what we today would call mathematical-scientific reasoning – should be man's sole guide in ordering society and morality which pushed the Radical Enlightenment inexorably towards democratic republicanism. Equally, it was the contrary claim that the moral and social order cannot realistically be based on 'reason and philosophy' but must be anchored instead in sentiment and tradition which drove the moderate mainstream ever more strongly towards the defence of the social hierarchy and princely and ecclesiastical authority. The essential dichotomy of the Enlightenment, or what Voltaire, in 1770, called the 'civil war' among the 'incrédules', has a purely philosophical basis and was rooted in a fundamental split over moral theory, metaphysics and the status of reason. In short, it was a case of the Lockean Enlightenment (Voltaire and Hume) versus the Spinozist Enlightenment (Diderot and d'Holbach). However, its organizing power and revolutionary potential in the late eighteenth century derived no less, or perhaps even more, from social forces. If one wanted to be taken seriously by ruling elites and (or) princes and their courts as a reformer of law, the institutions and administration in the Europe and America of the 1770s and 1780s, then one had to endorse the existing social hierarchy based on a formal or (in America) informal aristocracy, the validity of existing institutions at least in broad outline and the validity of traditional religious values at least for the bulk of society. If, on the other hand, one criticized and rejected these to the point that no ruling elites or princes would promote one's career and prospects, then the only available support to be found was from those in society who harboured a deep sense of resentment against at least major aspects of the existing order.

If in his late philosophical texts Voltaire failed to counter democratic egalitarianism and d'Holbachian materialism effectively at court, among the *philosophes* or the public, he at least set out the characteristic positions of the secular moderate mainstream Enlightenment allied to kings, nobles and liberal prelates in a definitive fashion. Voltaire's philosophizing in the 1770s can be seen as his final attempt to block the progress of the Radical Enlightenment. Complimenting him on his *Lettres de Memmius*, in April 1772, the Prussian king called that work a masterpiece in which the most difficult issues were made accessible to busy men of the world. Frederick declared himself willing to sign up enthusiastically to 'ce symbole de foi philosophique'.[26] Needing to put as much distance as possible between the Enlightenment of the *nouveaux philosophes* and *Voltaireanisme*, it is striking also that Voltaire, after 1770, notably toned down the earlier ferocity of his attacks on Christianity and the churches even as he intensified his assaults on the *Système de la nature* (1770), *Le Bon-Sens* (1772) and the other major texts of *philosophisme*.[27] One of the most important contributions made by book history to our understanding of the Enlightenment in recent years is the clear and impressive evidence that it has provided of the widespread penetration of the Radical Enlightenment via a plurality of channels in France, the Netherlands and throughout Western Europe, especially after 1750. If the Radical Enlightenment began as a clandestine underground at the very fringes of society, there can be no suggestion that radical thought was marginal any longer after around 1750. It is true that historians, including Baker, appear to assume that it remained entirely marginal even in the 1770s and 1780s, and in fact barely discuss it at all, but that is precisely the crucial historical error that is being made. Here, the historians – the entire group from Cobban to Baker – have simply locked themselves into a gigantic error of historical interpretation. For the book evidence conclusively proves that traditional historiography has massively underestimated the impact of radical thought, especially – but by no means entirely – in France. Without doubt, this creates an urgent need to reassess our categories when trying to estimate the impact of particular kinds of ideology and ideas circulating in Europe immediately prior to 1789. In the search for the ideological basis of the late eighteenth-century Atlantic democratic revolutions, it is time to forget both Locke and 'Atlantic republicanism'; the important point is the Radical Enlightenment.

## Notes

1. Keith Michael Baker (1990) *Inventing the French Revolution: Essays on French Political Culture in the Eighteenth Century* (Cambridge: Cambridge University Press), p. 151.
2. Manuela Albertone (2007) 'Democratic Republicanism: Historical Reflections on the Idea of Republic in the 18th Century', *History of European Ideas*, XXXIII, 108–30, here p. 110.
3. Charles-François Legros (1788) *Analyse et examen de l'Antiquité devoilée, du despotisme oriental, et du christianisme devoilé, ouvrages posthumés de Boullanger* [*sic*] (Geneva and Paris), pp. 270–1.
4. On the development of Gerrit Paape's 'philosophical' democratic republicanism before 1789, see Jonathan Israel (2007) 'Gerrit Paape, "Wijsbegeerte", en de "Algemene Revolutie" van de mensheid', *Parmentier*, XVI, 13–22.
5. Adam Smith (1759) *The Theory of Moral Sentiments* (New York: Garland reprint 1971), p. 115.
6. J.P. Stern (1959) *Lichtenberg: A Doctrine of Scattered Occasions* (Bloomington: University of Indiana Press), pp. 238–40.

7. Joseph Priestley (1791) *Letters to the Right Honourable Edmund Burke occasioned by his* Reflections on the Revolution in France (Birmingham: Pearson), preface, p. iv.
8. Honoré-Gabriel Riqueti comte de Mirabeau (1784) *Considérations sur l'ordre de Cincinnatus* (London: Johnson), pp. 50–1, 91–2.
9. Priestley, *Letters*, p. 25.
10. Paul Henri Thiry, baron d'Holbach (1773) *Système social, ou principes naturels de la morale et de la politique* (Paris: Fayard reprint 1994), pp. 69–70.
11. Ibid., pp. 232–3.
12. Ibid., p. 276.
13. Paul Henri Thiry, baron d'Holbach (1773) *La politique naturelle ou discours sur les vrais principes du gouvernement* (Paris: Fayard reprint 1998), pp. 119–20.
14. Claude-Adrien Helvetius (1773) *De l'homme: De ses facultés intellectuelles et de son éducation*, 2 vols (Paris: Fayard reprint 1998), vol. 2, p. 917.
15. Ibid., p. 210.
16. Paul Henri Thiry, baron d'Holbach (1776) *La morale universelle ou les devoirs de l'homme fondés sur la nature*, 2 vols (Amsterdam: Marc-Michel Rey), vol. 2, p. 210.
17. Ibid., p. 211.
18. d'Holbach, *Système social*, pp. 551–2.
19. Gabriel Bonnot de Mably (1751) *Observations sur les Romains*, 2 vols (Geneva: Compagnie des Libraires), vol. 1, pp. 203–4; Jonathan Israel (2002) *Enlightenment Contested: Philosophy, Modernity and the Emancipation of Man, 1670–1752* (Oxford: Oxford University Press), p. 292.
20. Nicolas-Antoine Boulanger-d'Holbach (1762) *Recherches sur l'origine du despotisme oriental, ouvrage posthume de Mr B.I.D.P.E.C.* (Amsterdam: Marc-Michel Rey), vol. 1, pp. 248, 251–2, 255, 258; Legros, *Analyse et examen*, pp. 273, 384–5, 390.
21. d'Holbach, *Système social*, pp. 268–9, 276; d'Holbach, *La politique naturelle*; Immanuel Kant (1996) 'Toward Perpetual Peace', in M.J. Gregor (ed.), *Immanuel Kant: Practical Philosophy* (Cambridge: Cambridge University Press), pp. 322–5.
22. Albertone, 'Democratic Republicanism', pp. 116–17; with respect to Rousseau, see J. Miller (1984) *Rousseau* (New Haven: Yale University Press), pp. 64, 80, 116–18, 120; J.K. Wright (1997) *A Classical Republican in Eighteenth-Century France: The Political Thought of Mably* (Stanford, Calif.: Stanford University Press), p. 123.
23. d'Holbach, *La politique naturelle*, p. 275.
24. d'Holbach, *Système social*, pp. 276–80; d'Holbach, *La politique naturelle*, pp. 109–10, 166–7, 169.
25. d'Holbach, *La politique naturelle*, pp.112–14; d'Holbach, *Système social*, p. 285.
26. Frederick the Great to Voltaire, Sans-Souci, 22 April 1772, in Voltaire (1953–65) *Correspondance*, ed. Th. Besterman (Geneva: Voltaire Institute and Museum), vol. 38, p. 353.
27. John N. Pappas (1962) *Voltaire and d'Alembert* (Bloomington: Indiana University Press), pp. 127–8, 173.

# 3
# Between Republicanism and the Enlightenment: Turgot and Adams

*Maria Luisa Pesante*

For about thirty years republicanism has been claiming for itself increasingly broad swaths of the Age of Enlightenment. Thanks to numerous discoveries and reinterpretations of the period, a large number of versions of that period have emerged in which republican tenets have been opposed to, or superimposed on, Enlightenment points of view, or in which these two have been seen as simply moving in the same direction. Actually, it is not particularly easy to compare republicanism and the Enlightenment as historiographical paradigms. This is because the historical object known as republicanism has from the very beginning been proposed as a paradigm in and of itself, while the Enlightenment has rarely been considered one as such. In an attempt to shed some light on this issue, it is possible to contrast the work of two important historians who have both explored these phenomena, namely Franco Venturi and John Pocock.[1]

Venturi's work is emblematic of a general approach to the reconstruction of history which is completely uninterested in the discovery of paradigms as a means of organizing historical narratives. There is no way his view of the Enlightenment can be seen as a paradigm or a language, that is to say a way of looking at the world that structures political choices. Rather, it is to be viewed, within the context of a specific historical conjuncture, as a series of campaigns aimed at liberating the energies of historical individuals and societies from the powers, institutions, practices and customs that oppressed them. Venturi was always wary of Pocock's use of republicanism as a paradigm, both because of its very nature as a paradigm and because he saw it as an inherently conservative frame of reference. Venturi's version of republicanism, on the other hand, runs through his vision of the eighteenth century in four different forms. The first is the republicanism of the English Deists, including all the ways they influenced Europe and their model of a mixed constitution. The second is republicanism seen as a moral, not a political, choice in France in the 1740s and 1750s. The third is republicanism seen as a political solution – the kind that emerged after European princes had failed to reform their states in France and elsewhere. The last is republicanism as the moving spirit in the fight for national independence on the fringes of Europe, for example in Corsica or in Poland, and in the works of authors who took sides in those struggles, such as Rousseau. The relationship of these forms of republicanism to Enlightenment ideals and campaigns is defined by Venturi in different ways. However, the forms of republicanism are always seen by him as being purely instrumental in the way the Enlightenment intellectuals moved towards reforming action.[2]

John Pocock, on the other hand, has constructed his republican paradigm as just that – a paradigm, endowed with a specifically knowledge-based dimension which is seen as an inherent part of the citizens' choices. It needs to be noted that this paradigm encapsulates a number of highly important elements which are part and parcel of certain deeply held convictions of European agrarian societies. To be sure, these were elaborated within the paradigm into distinctive functions, using a specific vocabulary. However, they were shared well beyond the republican mode of interpreting events. It is enough to cite just one, which is of importance for the hypothesis being put forward here – namely the enjoyment of land-ownership as a way of deciding who is able to live as an independent being in the *polis* and who on the contrary falls within the sphere of action, and is subject to the interests of a superior.

Pocock's Enlightenments (in the plural), on the other hand, cannot be considered in any way paradigmatic. Certainly, they have very little to do with the language of rights, the obvious product of Protestant natural jurisprudence, which Pocock himself has described as the rival paradigm of civic humanism. Rather, the historian is dealing here with a situation in which a series of divergent political programmes and intellectual projects are present. Over the past thirty years, Pocock has increasingly attempted to create a vision of the Enlightenment which is many-faceted. It is not easy, however, to keep Pocock's narrative of the Enlightenments in line with his own republican paradigm, because his 'Utrecht Enlightenment' is characterized by disarmament of the citizens. This particular historical situation is seen in terms of the emergence of a system of states which had the aim of leaving behind themselves the wars of religion. In the past the churches and religious sects had been able to foment war by questioning the supremacy of civil authority.[3] The elimination of the power to do so in the future was by now possible because the monarchs had managed to deprive the citizens of the power of the sword and, as a result, the latter no longer had the means to wage civil war in the name of religion.

The target of this policy was enthusiasm, that is, the political and intellectual project aimed at liberating the creative and destructive energies of the spirit. As a result, the political debate taking place in Britain during the eighteenth century can be seen as inherently enlightened, because the conservatives are conceived of as capable of change, while the enthusiasts are incapable of reining in their desire for change. In Pocock's narrative the greatest fear of enlightened writers in post-Utrecht Europe was that the wars of religion would start up once more. This indeed was what seemed to happen when the French abandoned the good manners of the monarchy and the alliance with English freedom and began to move towards a revolution that would later lead to a counter-revolution.[4] In this context, it could be inferred, republicanism can only be monarchic, and a mixed constitution is not simply a compromise at a particular historical conjuncture. On the contrary, these are the only conditions in which the citizen's autonomy can somehow survive in the modern world, whereas any other type of republicanism is excluded. Thus, Pocock's Enlightenments, from Utrecht to Vienna, take the form of an intellectual option within the aporias of progress imposed on political thought by republicanism, and are an anti-republican reply to the citizen's right and duty to bear arms. It is more difficult to understand what is, in the context supplied by Pocock, the Enlightenment reply regarding that other precondition of virtue, land. To be sure, land-ownership was not put in doubt, but the value of it might be put at risk by trade and finance. And this leads to the question of the relationship between those followers of the Enlightenment who counted on agriculture to improve the world, and those who instead counted on commerce and manufacturing industry. As in the case of Venturi, the American republic may be seen as a crucial point here. If the American Revolution, which in Pocock's *Machiavellian moment* was the final episode in the history of the Renaissance, becomes the last war of religion of Old Europe, there is still something which needs to be understood about the relationship between republicanism, the Enlightenment, landed property and the right of citizens to bear arms.

The aim of this essay is to trace out some of the consequences of these two broad visions of eighteenth-century Europe by reading once more the most important passages of a well-known series of texts on the American Revolution which appeared in the period 1778–87, texts produced by a number of writers, including not only Price, Turgot and Adams, but also Mirabeau the Younger, Stevens, Dupont, Condorcet and Mazzei. At the centre of the debate that takes place in these texts is the famous letter from Turgot to Price, and Adams' reply to it in his *Defence*.[5] Venturi treated Turgot's letter as part of a continuum which went on to include the analyses that followed by Dupont, Condorcet and Mazzei, and considered it as essentially the way the Enlightenment interpreted the American Revolution. Since, according to Venturi's view, this was the first modern revolution betrayed by its Thermidorians, what Turgot had to say about the constitutions of the newly independent American states appears at one and the same time true – inasmuch as it foresees the compromise that will be reached at the end – and of secondary importance when compared to the criticisms that the Frenchman makes of certain specific policies, namely those relating to free trade and the freedom of religious practice. It is these criticisms, in fact, that Venturi concentrates on.[6] On the other hand, according to Pocock, Adams' answer to Turgot is an example of Harringtonian language; it should be read within that context, and there really is no need to compare it with Turgot's arguments against the balance of power and for a single-chamber system. But, according to Pocock, Adams is also a man of one of the Enlightenments, who defends the idea of a mixed constitution because he is aware that the human mind has to be kept within its limits.[7]

At the beginning of 1778 Turgot was both amazed at, and worried by, three facts. First, that the British government would now try to do everything in its power to bring the colonies to heel. Second, that the war would go on even longer than predicted, since the new American states were not prepared to agree on anything that fell short of independence. And third, that France had entered into some sort of armed conflict with Britain, even if outright war had not yet been declared. Back in 1776, Turgot had believed the first fact highly unlikely, as he thought the British government could not possibly make such a serious mistake concerning their real interests. The third he had firmly recommended avoiding. Regarding the second, Turgot's belief in the inevitable final victory of the colonies had never faltered.[8] In 1778, however, it seemed that this victory would now have to be seen as the outcome of a worst-case scenario – a prolonged conflict which might lead to the formation of a military caste and a spirit of conquest among the Americans. This in turn would prevent this new actor on the stage of history from realizing its potential as a force for universal emancipation. As far as England was concerned, Turgot was now bitterly disappointed that the senseless policy of its government had continued to receive public support throughout the previous two years, and also that so few writers had rallied to the cause of the independence of the colonies. He concluded that the errors that were being made were not due simply to the government, but rather to an attitude deeply rooted in British society, and that it was in fact its political culture that was responsible.[9] This was the context in which he directly attacked one of the cornerstones of British republicanism, the idea that the mixed constitution was sufficient enough to guarantee the liberty of the citizens. He aggressively asked Price:

> How comes it that you are almost the first of the writers of your country, who has given a just idea of liberty, and shewn the falsity of the notion so frequently repeated by almost all republican writers, that liberty consists in being subject only to the laws, as if a man could be free while oppressed by an unjust law.[10]

This was a crucial point, because it was directly related not only to the omnipotence of the composite sovereign in the mixed British constitution but also to the omnipotence of the legislature in a republican constitution as defined at that time. Not by chance did Adams attempt to deny that any republican author would ever have supported an opinion such as this.[11] Turgot was referring here to a fundamental breaking point between the position taken up by Price and English republicanism, which he was perfectly familiar with. He had used this language in his *Réflexions* of 1776 when he had explained the – albeit remote – hypothesis of the British government going bankrupt. This would have placed limits on the power of the court and placed the strength of the nation back in the hands of the landowners, who loved liberty as much as any other Englishman, yet were less apt to succumb to the illusions produced by vanity and greed than were the populace. This shift of influence from court to country would have rendered 'the British constitution more solidly republican than it is today'.[12] In 1776, then, Turgot had no qualms about talking of a republican constitution in the form of a mixed constitution with different possible balances of power. However, this was something he was no longer willing to do in 1778.

Turgot's *Lettre* also marks his distance from Price, who continued to think in terms of a mixed constitution, and focused his criticisms of the British parliament's omnipotence on the question of representation in the House of Commons. Price argued, in fact, that this representation was both incomplete and inadequate, and that the representatives in the Commons were not answerable to those they represented, but he did not question the relationship of king, lords and commons in parliament.[13] As is well known, when Turgot outlined his plans for representation in his 1775 *Mémoire sur les municipalités*, the logic behind it was very different. He thought that the only class that should be represented was that of the landowners. This idea derived from his own economic theories and those of the Physiocrats, which in this case ran along very much the same lines.[14] The idea that a single-chamber system was the necessary consequence of the abolition of every type of order within society; the idea that representation be restricted to landowners; the idea of national interests coming together for the good of the body politic as a whole: these seem to be, in the impassioned and anxious line of reasoning of 1778, the natural outcome of the same vision that had given life to his paper on the municipalities. In 1778, Turgot presents the single-chamber system as the only possible solution for a republic. In effect, this is exactly the approach to institutional questions adopted later on by the republicans in the National Assembly, while the liberals and monarchists supported the idea of a two-chamber system with an executive branch independent of the legislature and a balance of power.[15] Does this mean that the *Mémoire* is already an implicitly republican text, or that Turgot had become a republican between 1775 and 1778?

One possibility is that he already *was* a republican while serving under the French monarchy, a monarchy which could certainly not be described as 'well-tempered'. In this case, he would have remained sincerely loyal to that monarchy despite his republicanism as long as his position in government required it of him. However, if we do not wish to accept this hypothesis and instead ask *how* he might actually have become a republican, the answer seems to lie in the rationale of his plans for municipal reform. He expected his project for representation at municipal level to set off a difficult and risky political process. Turgot, and Mirabeau before him, had elaborated for a monarch the idea of the landowners' representation in the context of a monarchical system. The king was the legislative power within the latter, and the task of the representatives of the landowning class was an administrative one, accounting for most of the executive function within the country.[16] It is difficult to find a vision anywhere else that compares with this – with a legislative power which is so unitary that it is monocratic and an executive power which, on the other hand, is widely distributed.

In his *Mémoire*, the executive is clearly subordinate to the legislative power. However, Turgot believed that when his plan had been pushed through and put into action, and his National Assembly of Municipalities set up, the relationship of power between the authority of the crown and 'the general will of the nation' which the Assembly would express would inevitably change.[17] 'Turgot told me', wrote the abbé de Véri, that at that point the political power of the nation would have acquired 'such strength that it would inevitably transform the present monarchic constitution', and that the thirty provincial Assemblies, united as one, would be backed by the force of the nation as a whole, as had happened in the American Congress.[18] In this case, as the diarist noted, Turgot believed that France could have become a republic, even if this might mean a civil war. But in this case how would a situation in which the legislative power resided solely with the crown and the executive function was in the hands of the representatives – the basic structure foreseen by Turgot's *Mémoire* – have to change? Bearing in mind the idea of a single chamber made up solely of representatives of the landowners – the model Turgot proposed for the American states – which institutional organ would fill the role played by the legislative power of the absolute monarch in the *Mémoire* and which was to be the executive? When this question is asked, the apologia for a single-chamber system contained in the two sentences of Turgot's *Lettre* seems rather less clear in meaning.[19]

Let us attempt to follow the line of argument Turgot himself might have followed, if we want to credit him with the conclusion not only that a true republic could not be governed by anyone else than the representatives of the landowning class – a republican point of view and one that was entirely shared by English republicans – but also that those representatives would only be able to carry out that role successfully in a republic, and never in a monarchy. In order to understand Turgot's position, it is necessary to leave to one side both the debates which would arise later on in the Constituent Assembly and the assumption that in a monarchy it is obviously the crown that is the seat of executive power, a power which is at one and the same time strong and independent. It is also necessary to leave behind the idea that, if the monarchy is to be excluded, it necessarily follows that an executive power must be set up which is not autonomous but which derives its power from the legislative assembly, the only assembly necessary in a republican constitution. The point of view of the Physiocrats, too, must be abandoned.[20] How far Turgot was from the latter may be measured by his approach to the question of how the net product should be divided between the crown and the representatives of the landowning class. For the Physiocrats, this point was crucial in explaining why there was no risk the overweening power of the crown would abuse that power:

> Hereditary sovereignty makes the sovereign the co-owner of the *net product* of all the lands under his dominion: as such, his interest is identical to that of all landowners who, owning these lands as if they were undivided shares, exploit them or allow them to be exploited, taking a share of *this net product* which constitutes their due as co-owners. Hence it is as important to him as it is to them that this *net product*, thanks to abundant production and just prices, reaches the highest possible level.[21]

'Comme par indivis' Lemercier wrote. In a society which is necessarily unequal, founded as it is on the private ownership of land, the nation cannot be considered as a single body, and hence cannot be a legislator. However, the landowning class cannot be a legislator either, without the co-ownership of a hereditary monarch. Only this will guarantee that the interests of all landowners will come together. Otherwise, the landowners as individuals, subject as they are to different and conflicting passions and interests, would never be able to constitute a single body. If we can attribute to Turgot exactly the words written for him by Dupont in his *Mémoire*, Turgot proposed the creation of precisely those 'liens sociaux' which were missing and which would have transformed the nation into a single unified whole.[22] He would do this both by using the administrative functions of the representatives, starting at the level of the village, and thanks to his plans for civil education. What is more, in his *Lettre* he wrote that the land belongs to individuals, not to the nation, nor, by implication, to a monarch. This train of thought implies a means of establishing a cohesion of interests that is different from the co-ownership of the net product. If, on the contrary, Turgot's position is reduced to the central position of the Physiocrats,[23] there is a risk of seeing the emergence of republicanism in his circle as inevitably evolving out of Physiocratic theories rather than as a complicated process involving the way the *turgotistes* reshaped their own ideas.[24]

One of the aims of Turgot's plan was to create a *citoyen fractionnaire*, a figure who would have the right to take part in municipal administration by dividing a vote up into fractions, depending on how much land was owned by each *citoyen fractionnaire*, such as to arrive at the minimum quota of revenue from land-ownership necessary for the right to vote (which was the minimum necessary to support a family). There was also a multiple vote for those who, on the other hand, earned a revenue which was a multiple of the minimum quota. This would have allowed the complex institution of municipal representation to be at one and the same time broadly inclusive and yet able to differentiate between the smaller and the larger landowner, while remaining impervious to the effects of the greater number and the incompetence of the former. Equal representation (i.e. representation which is indifferent to the legal standing of individuals) of land which is unequally distributed was an institution capable of reflecting most naturally the features of the productive and social structure of a nation. We can assume that Turgot was not ignorant of the fact that, if it were applied to the situation in the new American states, it would have led to a legislature with a social make-up noticeably different from that of the French one. Political power would be distributed more fluidly and in a less hierarchical fashion.

A logic of the cohesion of interests would still have applied perfectly, which, however, was rather different from the logic of the cohesion of interests foreseen by the Physiocrats; and it was the logic which Condorcet attributed to Turgot in 1786, while his own consideration of the choices made by the Americans was in full flow:

> If the deputies are divided into different orders, a new sanction is given to the inequality between them; and the deputies of the more popular orders, already held in lower consideration, are so also because of the place attributed to them. You should keep the citizens united among themselves, but instead they are divided, and this marks the divide that separates them even more clearly ... If the different orders have shared interests, why not leave this in the hands of an assembly in which these orders are joined together? If they have opposing interests, is it perhaps from an assembly in which they are kept separate that you can expect decisions which are reasonable and procedures carried out with impartiality?[25]

Condorcet was arguing about the separation into orders of the representatives because he wanted to point out that any simple recognition of the superior numbers of deputies voted in by the lower classes would have reduced the importance of the upper orders too much, and any attempt to make the numbers even would have made the actions of deserters from the lower orders decisive. This last worry was similar to the one expressed by Adams.

Hence Turgot, while envisaging a legislature made up of the representatives of landowners and characterized by the degree of equality that American society would naturally have bestowed upon it, was able to see it as capable of creating cohesion between the different interest groups by allowing them to compare their viewpoints with one another, rather than by separating them. The limits to this point of view were determined by Turgot's belief that the United States was bound to remain an agricultural society until such a time as the whole of the continent had been conquered. This conquest was necessary because it was impossible to have a frontier with a territory that was not part of a state.[26] The Americans had no other choice than to produce agricultural goods and exchange them with Europeans under a regime of free trade until all the land available had been converted into agricultural land and the increase in the population had reduced to a subsistence level the high wages in American manufacturing industry, which at that time rendered American manufactured goods uncompetitive in the international marketplace.[27]

Turgot applied to the situation in America the same structure of legislative and executive power that he had elaborated for the plan laid out in his *Mémoire*. A single legislative assembly is the organ which substitutes the absolute legislative power of the crown, and this power cannot be shared in any way. If the system of representation is such that the legislature speaks with the voice of the nation, then the legislative power of the crown would be cancelled. However, the monarch, or the figure that fulfils the same role as the monarch, would not be invested with executive power, in a reversal of roles. What would the executive be then? Turgot describes exactly the same scheme for the new American states as he does in his *Mémoire*, with the idea of a pluralist, stratified administration:

> I do not think they are sufficiently careful to reduce the kind of business with which the government of each state is charged within the narrowest limits possible; nor to separate the objects of legislation from those of the general administration, or from those of a local and particular administration; nor to institute local permanent assemblies, which by discharging almost all the functions in the detail of government, make it unnecessary for the general assemblies to attend to these things, and thereby deprive the members of the general assemblies of every means, and perhaps of every desire, of abusing a power which can only be applied to general objects, and which, consequently, must be free from the influence of the little passions by which men usually are agitated.[28]

As can be seen, Turgot is not thinking at all here in terms of a weak executive dependent on the legislature, of the kind that was to emerge in the French republican point of view a few years later. Rather, he is thinking about the guarantees given by a clear separation of two centres of public authority, each with its own structures and tasks. This idea of a complete separation of the sovereign power's functions was exactly what was missing from the theory and practice of the mixed constitution.[29] In a constitution such as this, the balance of powers is only possible because separate branches of the sovereign power share some functions, and can compete over them. According to Turgot this competition was to be a cause of unavoidable conflict, while the imperfect separation would not guarantee liberty.

It is not possible to say whether or not at this point Turgot had become a republican, in the sense that he believed either that a republican constitution was the best one possible, or else that it was both possible and to be hoped for in France. The passage from Condorcet regarding this point is by no means conclusive.[30] However it seems fairly clear that Turgot's idea of a monarchy could be neither that of a monarchy with a king as absolute legislator nor one that was part of a mixed constitution without a separation of powers. Both of these were incompatible with the political situation which would have emerged as a result of his most important plan for political reform. A kind of republicanism by default might be the most appropriate definition. It certainly has its roots in a specific, innovative economic theory, but it also overlaps a great deal with one of the basic principles of English republicanism, namely the belief that only land-ownership can form the basis of a relationship between an individual and public power, and hence the ability of the individual to act in the political sphere. One well-known concept of all the debates regarding citizenship in England (and before these in the sixteenth-century Italian republics) appears in the *Mémoire*. The exclusion of those who are not landowners is justified by the fact that they are foreigners who are here today and gone tomorrow, in the search for work or profit, and hence they have no fixed interest in the country as such. This point is useful because it allows us to establish with greater precision the distance between the intermittent republican impulses that emerged in Turgot's circle before the Revolution and the republicanism of the English-speaking countries. The two express ideas about the relationship between property and liberty which are as similar as the terms used to express them are different. This can be seen as proof either of how powerful the language used in both cases was or else of the use to which the presumed misunderstandings between the two could be put.

There is a considerable amount of irony in the fact that Adams reprehended Turgot because he knew nothing of Harrington's incomparable invention, namely the 'balance of property', when the heart of Turgot's political vision is the idea that there is a perfect correspondence between land-ownership and the right to govern.[31] When Adams wrote the first volume of his *Defence* he had not read the *Mémoire*, which was only made public by Dupont in 1787, in his posthumous collection of Turgot's works. However, in 1786 Condorcet had given a great deal of space to illustrating this idea in his *Vie de Turgot*. For the rest of his long life, and in following editions, Adams would have been more than able to acknowledge this, if he had wanted.

There is also a certain irony in the fact that, in the letter, itself subtly ironic, in which he gave Mably his advice on how to go about writing his history of the American Revolution, Adams explained that it was in the true sense of the term the universal history of that period, and that, however, the key to the understanding of that history was local history. This latter could be reconstructed in terms of the four crucial administrative institutions of the district, the schools, the churches and the militia, where the functions of the first two were described in exactly the same way that Turgot had described them.[32]

John Pocock has placed the *Defence* firmly within the language and the canons of Harringtonian republicanism, explaining that the misunderstandings which the work became the victim of were essentially due to fact that its critics, more or less honestly, believed that Adams was talking of a hereditary aristocracy whereas he was in fact talking about a natural aristocracy.[33] Actually, to a true Harringtonian, the idea of a 'balance of property' in Turgot's plan for municipal representation would have seemed capable of controlling the balance of power perhaps even too rigidly. According to Pocock, the correspondence between the distribution of land-ownership and that of power in *Oceana* was aimed at excluding any kind of compatibility between a feudal aristocracy and any form whatsoever of political liberty. Once this aristocracy disappeared, though, Harrington believed that the distribution of power among landowners would not be directly proportional to the distribution of land.

The unequal distribution of property, in fact, would have created an authority rather than a power. Only authority would have allowed between the few and the many, who are all independent because they are all landowners, a relationship of deference as free recognition of the superiority of the former by the latter on the one hand, and, on the other, acceptance of the role of debating and advising, with no power of deliberation, by the former. Of course, it must be borne in mind that property is a term which excludes those who are not landowners.

Landowners exercise power over non-landowners, but not authority over them. It is this power alone which, in its turn, reciprocally enables the few and the many to exercise authority and to express deference in freedom.[34] There are a number of hints at this kind of power in Harrington, even if it clearly did not constitute a problem for him, as it was to at the end of the following century.

The problem is that Adams does not interpret Harrington in the same way that Pocock does. In his *Defence*, the 'balance of property' is seen precisely in terms of power. What is more, the lack of this power in the American states is the starting point of his process of reasoning:

> In America, the balance is nine-tenths on the side of the people: indeed there is but one order; and our senators have influence chiefly by the principles of authority, and very little by those of power.[35]

In Adams' Harringtonian terms, this set-up guarantees that America is a republic. However, in America there is a lack of that power over non-landowners which makes relative equality between landowners possible. Furthermore, the influence which, as it is not power, is not limited by the material dimension of ownership, risks spreading out pathologically if the few and the many are not segregated into two separate chambers.[36] Adams' thought, then, is to be seen as an answer to a situation in which land-ownership no longer works as a means of discrimination, and the authority of the few, which the many spontaneously recognize, but which is not sufficiently rooted in differences of ownership, cannot be made stable by these differences. The few are obviously that natural aristocracy which, explicitly or implicitly, becomes an unavoidable term of reference in every form of republicanism which emerges within the context of a mixed constitution. A republicanism of this type, in fact, is obliged to define a hereditary aristocracy in very narrow terms, as a legal and hereditary distinction for public office, and to define natural aristocracy, on the other hand, in very broad terms, made up not only of personal characteristics summed up by virtue, but also a number of ascriptive characteristics, namely, in classical terms, goods bestowed on the individual by fortune, such as wealth and family position, but also knowledge.

The presence of wealth and position alongside virtue has always posed an insoluble problem for every republican theory applied to landowning or merchant oligarchies. It was well known to the fifteenth-century Italian civic humanists, from Bracciolini's *De nobilitate* (1440) onwards. It was also openly debated among them in the kind of dialogue which allowed the writer to lay out a problem without necessarily providing an answer for it. In English republicanism it is less of a theme, but it is nonetheless always present, and is resolved by considering the goods bestowed on the individual by fortune as a condition or sign of virtue, a condition which allows one to develop virtue, or a sign that allows the many to recognize virtue and elect it to office in a free state. This of course does not resolve the problem entirely, and as a result a sense of tension between language and politics remains in republican discourses. Adams reasons it out by using an all-inclusive definition of qualities or goods bestowed on the individual by fortune. He tends to blur the distinction between these and the qualities of the mind, 'merit, or talents, virtues, services, and, what is of more moment, very often ... reputation'.[37] When the qualities of the mind are reduced to fame, as he writes a few lines later, the reader should be warned that what appear to be signs of virtue are at least doubtful, may be false, and are no guarantee of virtuous behaviour in the future. Indeed, they are not even necessary for the many to recognize that a famous man is in some way superior and must hence be deferred to. At this point natural aristocracy is the fruit of the tendency of the many to defer to he who is already more powerful than they, rather than the ability to rationally discern greater ability to discuss problems and to point to alternative solutions.[38]

In this context, where fortune itself has become the child of imagination, we, however, may well ask what meaning might persist in the historical distinction English republicanism made between hereditary aristocracy – that is, a stable form of attributing the goods of fortune and the public functions connected to it – and a natural aristocracy – that is, a recognition of personal abilities which have developed thanks also to the goods bestowed on the individual by fortune, both material and immaterial. If we look at the way Adams reduced merit to fame, namely by looking at the former as an object of the imagination – the faculty which, in English republicanism of the eighteenth century, was competing with corruption in putting liberty at risk – it is easier for us to find a place for his answer to Turgot:

> There is then a certain degree of weight, in the public opinion and deliberations, which property, family and merit will have: if Mr Turgot had discovered a mode of ascertaining the quantity which they ought to have, and had revealed it to mankind, so that it might be known to every citizen, he would have deserved more of their gratitude than all the inventions of philosophers. But as long as human nature shall have passions and imagination, there is too much reason to fear that

these advantages, in many instances, will have more influence than reason and equity can justify.³⁹

Since Turgot was interested in destroying the privileges of a hereditary aristocracy, he wanted to define as accurately as possible his natural aristocracy of landowners in purely economic terms. His definition, like that of English republicans, included leisure, which made landowners eminently capable of holding public office, and he certainly thought, as indeed Harrington had, that he had found the way to measure, with a criterion that was both sure and visible to every citizen, the weight that the material good on which society was founded, in all possible ways of distributing it, should have in public deliberations. So the more selective nature of his definition seems to be the real difference between him and Adams.

Adams' reasoning, then, seems to undermine the same conceptual tools he was working with himself, namely the idea of a balance of power and the notion of a natural aristocracy. This is because he was applying them to a situation which did not meet the conditions necessary for them to have any real meaning. In the United States it was impossible to make any kind of distinction between landowners and non-landowners that could somehow be used as the basis for establishing constitutional orders. Turgot reworked this distinction and gave it a legitimate basis once more by marrying it to an economic theory, after which he took it to the point at which it demanded the establishment of a republic for it to become reality as a political fact. At this point, however, he had before him a republic which was ignoring it, and it is this that he found both disturbing and worrying. Turgot and Adams come into contact with one another at the point at which the American Revolution was making it impossible to take as read that crucial distinction English republicanism and some French Enlightenment thinkers had interpreted in terms of two different paradigms.

Both paradigms, over and above the difficulty of translating their languages, are interpretations of a basic feature in European agrarian societies, namely the relationship between land proprietorship and political freedom. Since in the civic humanist paradigm virtue was construed as excellence, that is, a zero-sum game, in America there was too much land and not enough people for it to be able to sustain the necessarily ambiguous relationship between land and virtue. For Adams, this meant that only for a very short while in the present could the government avoid showing its stern face, the face to be seen, not in the legislative process, but in the executive's application of the law – precisely the kind of approach that demonstrates the executive as necessarily unpopular, and thus in need of strong guarantees, namely independence from the legislature, and a power of veto.[40] For Turgot, on the other hand, it meant that at the moment land-ownership could exercise its function as a means of social differentiation and agricultural development, but could not yet cause the specialization of the economic functions necessary for progress. Hence it is America that forces Condorcet to confront the problem of political citizenship, meaning that the new state is the model, yet Europe cannot follow this model, at least not for the moment, and not for a long time ahead.[41]

I would now like to put forward some tentative conclusions with regard to the two asymmetrical historiographical frames of reference whose movements have been traced here. Venturi interprets Turgot's idea of perfectibility in the same way that Pocock interprets Adams' idea of corruptibility – namely, in isolation. Both Turgot and Adams are closeted by their historian within their own paradigm, and neither Venturi nor Pocock compares the position of the author he analyses with the paradigm of the other author. In this way, it becomes more difficult to identify the point at which the relationship between the paradigms changes, and contrasting paradigms reveal what they have in common. As Venturi was clearly uninterested in the constitutional problems so prominent in the republican tradition, he firstly fails to acknowledge the importance of Turgot's point of view regarding these problems when compared to single policies, however important. Second, he dismisses as a residual Physiocratic prejudice that distinction between landowners and non-landowners which is the very heart of Turgot's political stance. This is so because Venturi wanted to keep any enterprise of the Enlightenment at a safe distance from old natural jurisprudence, as he used to call it. Thus he was not prepared to explore the aporias of equality within the language of natural rights.

Pocock, on the other hand, translates back into the republican language of natural aristocracy Adams' belief in the intrinsically hierarchical turn of man's mind. This enables him to tell us that it was 'an English-derived brand of republicanism' Adams was defending against Turgot's thesis that a republic could not be constructed by reshaping a mixed constitution.[42] Recognizing this invincible inclination to submit to a leader seems to be a far cry from English republicans' restricted yet strong sense of a desire for independence in men. The fact is that Adams was arguing in a situation where too much available land had dissolved the discriminating function of landed property, and virtue with it. So the question seems rather to be why Adams would not recognize that Turgot, on the contrary, was arguing precisely on the assumption of the landed proprietors' capacity to be only legislators. An answer to this question might explain why Adams chose that strange way of naturalizing the problem instead of historicizing it.

Comparing and contrasting republicanism-oriented interpretations of the eighteenth century to the Enlightenment versions of that history seems to me, for research purposes and for the present moment, more fruitful than any blunting of their differences. As far as I am concerned, tunnel history is fine, and need not prevent us from discovering the points at which tunnels criss-cross. This also implies that construing the Enlightenment more as a historical paradigm might be useful.

## Notes

1. On the distinction between paradigm as political ideal and interpretative matrix see J.G.A. Pocock (1983) 'Cambridge Paradigms and Scotch Philosophers: A Study of the Relations between the Civic Humanist and the Civil Jurisprudential Interpretation of Eighteenth Century Social Thought', in I. Hont and M. Ignatieff (eds) *Wealth and Virtue: The Shaping of Political Economy in the Scottish Enlightenment* (Cambridge: Cambridge University Press), pp. 235–52.
2. F. Venturi (1971) *Utopia and Reform in the Enlightenment* (Cambridge: Cambridge University Press); F. Venturi (1984) *Settecento riformatore*, IV/2 (Turin: Einaudi), pp. 927 ff. on Poland; F. Venturi (1987) *Settecento riformatore*, V/1 (Turin: Einaudi), pp. 3 ff. on Corsica. On Venturi's explorations of republican ideas see M. Albertone (ed.) (2006) *Il repubblicanesimo moderno: L'idea di repubblica nella riflessione storica di Franco Venturi* (Naples: Bibliopolis).
3. J.G.A. Pocock (1999) *Barbarism and Religion*, I, *The Enlightenments of Edward Gibbon, 1737–1764* (Cambridge: Cambridge University Press), pp. 7–9, 292–302.
4. J.G.A. Pocock (1999) 'Enlightenment and Counter-Enlightenment, Revolution and Counter-revolution: A Eurosceptical Enquiry', *History of Political Thought*, XX, 127–8.
5. A.R.J. Turgot, 'À Monsieur Price, Londres', Paris, 22 March 1778, in R. Price (1785) *Observations on the Importance of the American Revolution* ... (Dublin: White), pp. 88 ff. (hereafter *Lettre*); J. Adams (1797) *A Defence of the Constitutions of Government of the United States of America, against the Attack of M. Turgot* ... , 3rd edn, 3 vols (Philadelphia: Cobbett).
6. Venturi, *Settecento riformatore*, IV/1, pp. 96–9, 129–30.
7. J.G.A. Pocock (1989) ' "The Book most Misunderstood since the Bible": John Adams and the Confusion about Aristocracy', in A.M. Martellone and E. Vezzosi (eds), *Fra Toscana e Stati Uniti: Il discorso politico Americano nell'età della costituzione Americana* (Florence: Olschki), pp. 181–201.
8. A.R.J. Turgot (1776) 'Réflexions rédigées à l'occasion d'un mémoire remis par Mr de Vergenne au Roi sur la manière dont la France et l'Espagne doivent

envisager les suites de la querelle entre la Grande-Bretagne et ses colonies', in G. Schelle (1923) *Œuvres de Turgot et documents le concernant*, vol. 5 (Paris: Alcan), pp. 384 ff.
9. Turgot, *Lettre*, pp. 89–91.
10. Ibid., pp. 111, 91.
11. Adams, 'Defence', vol. 1, p. 124.
12. Turgot, 'Réflexions rédigées', p. 386.
13. R. Price (1777) *Additional Observations on the Nature and Value of Civil Liberty, and the War with America*, here quoted from (1991) *Political Writings* (Cambridge: Cambridge University Press), pp. 78–82, 91–2, 95–6.
14. A.R.J. Turgot (1775) 'Mémoire sur les municipalités', in G. Schelle (1923) *Œuvres de Turgot et documents le concernant* (Paris: Alcan), vol. 4, pp. 575 ff. See M. Albertone (2004) 'Il proprietario terriero nel discorso fisiocratico della rappresentanza', *Studi Settecenteschi*, XXIV, 181–214; A. Alimento (2004) 'Tra coerenza dottrinale e progettualità riformista: Il ruolo dei proprietari nelle proposte del movimento fisiocratico', *Studi Settecenteschi*, XXIV, 153–80; A. Alimento (1988) 'Tra fronda e fisiocrazia: Il pensiero di Mirabeau sulla municipalità (1750–1767)', *Annali della Fondazione Luigi Einaudi*, XXII, 97–140.
15. K. Baker (1990) *Inventing the French Revolution* (Cambridge: Cambridge University Press), pp. 281 ff.; M. Hulliung (2002) *Citizens and Citoyens: Republicans and Liberals in America and France* (Cambridge, Mass.: Harvard University Press), pp. 58 ff.
16. 'Your majesty can therefore see himself as an absolute legislator and rely on his good nation to execute his orders', Turgot, 'Mémoire', vol. 4, p. 575.
17. J.-A.-N. Condorcet (1786) *Vie de monsieur Turgot* (London), p. 49.
18. G. Schelle (1923) *Œuvres de Turgot et documents le concernant* (Paris: Alcan), vol. 4, pp. 627–8.
19. When interpreting Turgot's text, Troper's distinctions must be borne in mind: M. Troper (1980) *La séparation des pouvoirs et l'histoire constitutionelle française* (Paris: Pichon & Durand-Auzias).
20. M. Albertone (2008) ' "Que l'autorité souveraine soit unique": La séparation des pouvoirs dans la pensée des Physiocrates et son legs: Du despotisme légal à la démocratie représentative des Condorcet', in S. Baume and B. Fontana (eds) *Les usages de la séparation des pouvoirs* (*The Uses of the Separation of Powers*) (Paris: Houdiard), pp. 38–68.
21. P.-P.-F.-J.-H. Le Mercier de la Rivière (1767) *L'ordre naturel et essentiel des sociétés politiques* (London: J. Nourse), here quoted from Le Mercier de la Rivière (2001) *L'ordre naturel* (Paris: Fayard), p. 157; see also pp. 128 ff., 460 ff.
22. 'The cause of the ill, Sire, depends on the fact that your nation does not have a constitution. It is a society composed of different orders, which are ill joined, and a people who are linked one with the other by very few social ties', Turgot, 'Mémoire', vol. 4, p. 576.
23. L. Charles and Ph. Steiner (1999) 'Entre Montesquieu et Rousseau: La Physiocratie parmi les origines intellectuelles de la Révolution française', *Études Jean-Jacques Rousseau*, XI, 124.
24. On Condorcet's rather slow turn to republicanism see G. Magrin (2001) *Condorcet: Un costituzionalismo democratico* (Milan: Angeli), pp. 19–55.
25. Condorcet, *Vie de monsieur Turgot*, pp. 141–2.

26. Turgot, *Lettre*, pp. 100–1.
27. Turgot, 'Réflexions rédigées', p. 392.
28. Turgot, *Lettre*, pp. 115, 94–5. Turgot's vocabulary in this passage might lead one to think of a remnant of that separation of powers according to legislative aims that Troper (*La séparation*, pp. 114–15) discovered in some natural lawyers.
29. D. Wootton (2006) 'Liberty, Metaphor, and Mechanism: "Checks and Balances" and the Origins of Modern Constitutionalism', in D. Womersley (ed.), *Liberty and American Experience in the Eighteenth Century* (Indianapolis: Liberty Fund), pp. 209–74.
30. Condorcet, *Vie de monsieur Turgot*, p. 262.
31. Adams, *Defence*, vol. 1, pp. 159–60.
32. Ibid., pp. 388–92.
33. Pocock, 'The Book most Misunderstood since the Bible', p. 188.
34. J.G.A. Pocock (1976) 'The Classical Theory of Deference', *American Historical Review*, LXXXI, 516–20.
35. Adams, *Defence*, vol. 1, pp. 168–9.
36. Ibid., pp. 139–41.
37. Ibid., pp. 109–12, 116–17, 158.
38. Pocock, 'The Book most Misunderstood since the Bible', pp. 191–2.
39. Adams, *Defence*, vol. 1, p. 118.
40. Ibid., pp. 120–1, 362–3, 381–2.
41. Condorcet, *Vie de monsieur Turgot*, pp. 263–4; J.-A.-N. Condorcet (1788) 'De l'influence de la Révolution de l'Amérique sur l'Europe', in F. Mazzei, *Recherches historiques et politiques sur les États-Unis de l'Amérique septentrionale* ..., IV (Colle: Froullé), pp. 241–2. As far as I know this was the first publication of Condorcet's 'short work' (p. 213); Mazzei's fourth volume was published between the first and second of Adams' *Defence*.
42. Pocock, 'The Book most Misunderstood since the Bible', p. 185.

# 4
# Nicolas Bergasse and Alexander Hamilton: The Role of the Judiciary in the Separation of Powers and Two Conceptions of Constitutional Order

*Pasquale Pasquino*

Since the end of the eighteenth century the separation of powers has been an essential element and, in a sense, a synonym of modern constitutionalism.[1] It may be important to spell out from the outset two underlying dimensions of the question that will be discussed here:

A. The separation of powers was conceived of generally as a technique, a mechanism or an instrument of constitutional engineering, and more specifically as an anti-despotic, anti-absolutist organizational principle of government, and not as a goal in itself – the goal being instead and famously individual freedom.[2] Now, in order to understand the alternative French and American interpretations of this instrumental constitutional principle it is worth stepping back and focusing briefly on the difference between two major possible understandings of this idea of individual freedom.

On the one hand, and notably according to Montesquieu,[3] it seems to be the same as *Rechtssicherheit*, that is, the idea that the commandments of political power in a given society ought to be both stable and general, since stability and generality are the essential characteristics of good (moderate) government.[4] This implies that commandments need to have the abstract form of laws,[5] meaning here stable rules, made by the sovereign legislator under a 'veil of ignorance' as to the concrete application of the rule. The relevant consequence, intrinsically linking law and liberty, is that under such a 'rule of law' the members of the society are able to foresee the consequences of their actions. That is to say, they are free from the fear that a new rule will be enacted in the course of their actions, rendering them illegal or even irrelevant because they are the necessary steps in order to achieve a given aim. It also means they are free from the fear that a rule will be used against a specific individual whom the sovereign/legislator wants to disqualify, assault or oppress. On the other hand, the guarantee of individual freedom may require more than the stability and generality of the commandments. It may also mean carving out a sphere of action that will be outside the reach of political power, a sort of sacred space that simply should/ought not be invaded by any commandment or legislation whatsoever.[6]

B. No less relevant, and connected with these different intuitions concerning the constitutional aim of protecting individual freedom, we will see that the doctrine of the separation of powers, incorporated respectively into the American and French constitutional matrices, as has already been hinted at, is not at all the same. Indeed these embody, more interestingly, two different versions of the same principle – and specifically two different conceptions of the stability of a constitutional, anti-despotic legal and political order.

This essay will focus essentially on point B. above, and more precisely on the question of the constitutional role of the judiciary within the two versions of the separation of powers. To do this, it is useful to compare two important thinkers and political actors of the end of the eighteenth century: the Frenchman Nicolas Bergasse and the American Alexander Hamilton. Both good lawyers, they were involved in the constitution-making process on the two sides of the ocean. The Lyonnais Bergasse was a member of the first Constitutional Committee of the National Assembly in 1789; the New Yorker Hamilton was one of the active participants in the Philadelphia convention in 1787 and was also one of the authors of the *Federalist Papers*, still the most respected commentary on the US constitution even today.

Nicolas Bergasse (Lyon 1750–Paris 1832) was born into a bourgeois family, studied law, as did a large number of the members of the first French Constituent Assembly, and became a member of the Parisian bar. Well known to the public because of the famous Kornmann *affaire*, which opposed him to Beaumarchais, he was elected to the Estates General as representative of the Third Estate and became one of the members of the first *Comité de constitution* during the summer of 1789. On 12 September, when the Assembly rejected the constitutional project presented by the *monarchiens* Mounier and Lally, based on bicameralism and the king's power of absolute veto, he resigned. Bergasse was one of the few survivors of the Terror among the moderate members of the *Constituante*; after the Revolution he became an ultra-conservative.[7]

Alexander Hamilton (West Indies 1755 or 1757–New York 1804) was 'an Army officer, lawyer, Founding Father, American politician, leading statesman, financier and political theorist'.[8] He is important here as the author of no. 78 of the *Federalist Papers*, in which he presented a very remarkable doctrine relating the constitutional role of the Courts of Justice in protecting individual freedom. We shall return below to considering Bergasse's contribution to French constitutional theory.

Nicolas Bergasse represented, with Mounier, Lally-Tollendal and Clermont-Tonnerre, the most moderate and Montesquieuan trend within the political spectrum of the French Constituent Assembly.[9] Famous for his report on the organization of judicial power, which laid the foundations for the laws of 1790, he is also the author of an important text, published when he resigned from the Constitutional Committee, which gives a clear idea of his view on the constitutional separation of powers: the *Discours sur la manière dont il convient de limiter le pouvoir législatif et le pouvoir exécutif*.[10] In this booklet Bergasse aims at exposing 'moderate opinions' (*Discours*, p. 4)[11] concerning the way a constitution can guarantee individual freedom. To achieve this goal, the essential function of the constitution is to contain legislative and executive power (*Discours*, p. 8). Here there is a first important element to highlight. According to our author the three powers of the Montesquieuan classification boil down actually to two, since the judiciary is part of the executive.[12] Bergasse's anti-despotic constitution has the twin task of limiting these two powers (in his conception the king and the elected bicameral parliament plus the royal veto, which implies a partial overlapping of them) and avoiding the attribution *in toto* of distinct functions to the same agency or branch of the government. Different configurations have to be excluded from the constitutional order, not only the exercise by the same agency of the three functions (L+E+J would indeed represent absolute despotism), but also (1) J+L, (2) E+L and (3) E+J.[13]

(1) If the judge were also the legislator, there would be a danger that he could exercise his function arbitrarily, here in the sense of not independently from the identity of the litigants. Driven by his passions and prejudices, the judge-legislator would be a constant threat to the equal and 'blind' neutrality and impartiality of justice. He would legislate in the absence of the 'veil of ignorance' that has to protect the plaintiff and the defendant or the parties in a trial from the partiality of the judge,[14] and put all of them under the protective mantle of abstract legislation.

(2) If L and E were unified, the king (or an elected president), exercising legislative and executive power alone, would concentrate within himself too much power, which is for the moderates a constant and overwhelming threat to individual freedom.
(3) If E and J were in the same hands, there would be a single judge, at least in the last instance – again a danger of irresistible power for the subjects, notably those used to the arbitrary exercise of *justice retenue* under the French *ancien régime*.[15]

The positive recipe Bergasse offers is, as we know, the separation of powers/functions. The judge has to be distinct and subordinated to legislation. According to Bergasse, the reason is fairly simple: 'ce n'est que par la loi que se maintient la liberté'[16] (*Discours*, p. 13). It is worthwhile pausing to examine this claim, as it seems intuitive, but in fact requires some consideration.

The argument here is not to oppose the legislators to the judges, where the first would be impartial, virtuous and motivated by reason and the latter arbitrary and moved only by harmful passions. Such an idea would be simply preposterous, and contradicted by any even superficial perusal of the real world. The point, as already hinted at, has to do with the supposed distance between the legislator and the citizens/subjects, and with the general abstract form of statute law. The judge and his decision are considered too close to the parties, with the consequence of making neutrality more difficult to achieve. Bergasse, like the men of the Revolution, has no intuition that the contrary might be true – that justice as *epieikeia*[17] implies exactly the proximity he fears above everything else. But this is not the point here. Equally, the executive has to be distinct and subordinated to the legislative power. So containment seems to consist in attributing to the two branches and a half specific functions. Legislators lay down (general) statutes and the executive with the judiciary apply and enforce them. But here a new question arises, which is prima facie difficult to make sense of:

> We have to put limits on legislative power through executive power to avoid arbitrariness in the constitution, so that once we establish a constitution able to promote freedom, it keeps its equilibrium and it is no longer possible for the legislature, the most dangerous of all powers when it is not limited, to undermine its structure and create confusion in its organization. (*Discours*, p. 14)

The claims of this passage need some clarification. First, it is clear that stability – literally the immobility of the constitution – is a paramount preoccupation, and understandably so. If the constitution is the organization of political power that guarantees individual liberty, independent of the meaning of this expression, it is evident that the constitution has to be stable. In other words, it has to be the organization of a polyarchy that makes it impossible for the organized powers to subvert the organizing machinery. It has to be a rule creating or redefining institutional forces that the rule has to govern/dominate. This is at one and the same time the challenge and the puzzle of each constitution-making enterprise, the point that can be at the same time the weakness or the superiority of the idea of a modern written and rigid constitution, such as those of America and France, vis-à-vis the British tradition of a constitution based on convention. Now this enterprise, if it wishes to be sensible and perhaps successful, needs to identify the weak spots in the machine, the points of tension and friction where the machine might go overboard and cease to function, in order to fix it and prevent the breakdown of the system. Bergasse, like James Madison in a different political context – and that is the second comment – identifies a special weak point, an extreme danger for constitutional stability, in the very existence of the legislative power. He does not tell us why here, but the argument of the 'despotism of the many' is at hand.[18]

The answer, in any event, is once again the same as that spelled out by Montesquieu in the Book of the *Spirit of Laws* devoted to the constitution of England.[19] Along with the specialization of powers, Bergasse suggests splitting legislative power among three actors – two houses and the king. It is not necessary to enter here into the details of his proposal, which encountered strong, stubborn opposition inside the Constituent Assembly. But two arguments are worth remembering (*Discours*, pp. 35 ff.). On the one hand, the bicameral system, by increasing the amount of deliberation, would by the same token increase the probability that the law will be an expression of reason and general interest rather than of particular interests and passions. Here we find the classical eighteenth-century trilogy of reason, passions and interests and the idea that law is not any form of authorized commandment but only that which expresses the general will and collective reason as a result of a decisional process which goes here under the name of deliberation. This term does not refer to a specific way of discussing nor a well-defined mechanism of decision-making. Notably, the role of majority and minority in the decision-making process is not discussed and it seems to play no role in the political theory of the French Revolution. Deliberation is a synonym of disinterested and impassionate decision-making that would follow on from rendering this process somehow slow and complex. On the other hand, the king's veto would protect him as the head of the executive from incursions by the legislature,[20] since 'the legislative power inevitably has the tendency to invade the other powers, when nobody is able to place a check on its action' (*Discours*, p. 68).

From all that we have seen so far, it is clear that the judiciary does not play any active role in maintaining the stability of the constitutional order. This is the result of a balance inside the legislature and of a quite rigorous separation of the functions,[21] such that the special executive function called judiciary – the settlement of litigation – has to be attributed to specialized magistrates. Their task it is to adjudicate conflicts through the strict application of general norms (*lois*) that are the result of deliberation and the expression of the general will.

Nicolas Bergasse was more famously the author of the remarkable report on the *organisation du pouvoir judiciaire* presented to the Assembly on 17 August 1789.[22] This text is relatively well known and it was the basis of the very important laws enacted by the Constituents in August and November 1790, but it is worth considering in the perspective of these pages.

In this text the specialized branch of the executive called the judiciary is presented as particularly dangerous since 'There are no limits to the impact of judicial power.'[23] This is contradictory only prima facie with the thesis we have just considered. In the *Discours* Bergasse was indeed presenting the judiciary as it would look *after* his constitution had been enacted; here, in the *Report*, he starts historically from the status quo ante – the *ancien régime* – and logically from the consideration that, in general, judicial decisions are those which may directly infringe upon citizens' civil freedom. Montesquieu's line was still in the minds of the men of the Revolution: 'judicial power, so terrible among humans'.[24] This is why it is so important to organize very accurately this *puissance* (power), which here means 'function'.[25] The two main points that it is important to single out[26] in this project for the organization of judicial power are, first, the strict subordination of judges to the letter of the law, and, second, the mechanism through which they are appointed.

As to the first point, the crucial element – as we have already seen – is the illusion of 'purifying'/emptying judicial decisions of any discretionary power. In Bergasse's language that means completely separating legislation and adjudication:

> Judicial power shall be badly organized if those who exercise it take part in the legislation, or *can have any kind of influence whatsoever* on the production of laws. (*Discours*, p. 5, my italics)

The immediate consequence is the even more extraordinary illusion that the judge can apply the statute laws without interpreting them:

> Judicial power will be ill conceived when the judge has the dangerous privilege of interpreting a statute or of supplementing it through interpretation. Since it can clearly be seen that if the statutes can be interpreted, developed in their meaning, or, what amounts to the same thing, enforced on the basis of the will of a single individual [the judge], citizens are no longer under the protection of the law, but under the power of those who interpret or modify the statute through their interpretation of it; now, the power of a man over another man is essentially what we want to abolish through the institution of a legal government, so it is clear that this power would become overwhelming, if the faculty of interpreting the statutes were to be abandoned to the person who has to apply it. (*Discours*, pp. 9–10)[27]

The twin concepts of general will/law versus particular will/arbitrary power here return as a mantra that has the power to disseminate the extravagant fiction of a judge without discernment and will.

As far as the mechanism for appointing judges is concerned, Bergasse proposed a system[28] which was somewhat different from the one chosen by the constitution of 1791.[29] The rule he suggests is that 'the prince alone appoints the judges; but he will be allowed to select only from among the candidates designated by the citizens' (*Discours*, p. 17), by which he meant the representatives of the people. It was a system able in principle to guarantee the dependence[30] of the judges on the new sovereign: the nation.

The mechanism for appointing federal judges was one of many issues which became the object of serious discussion during the ratification of the constitution prepared by the Philadelphia convention in 1787. Alexander Hamilton took on the task not only of defending in the *Federalist Papers* the exception to the rule, namely that the members of the judiciary represented vis-à-vis the republican principle of political accountability, but more generally of rebutting the criticism spelled out by one of the most articulate and acute challengers of the constitution, the anti-federalist Brutus – probably Melancton Smith. Already in no. 39, James Madison had hinted at a situation whereby the judiciary was organized on the basis of the elective principle at the foundation of the republican government the Americans were about to establish in the thirteen former British colonies.[31] Here I will focus on paper no. 78, in which Hamilton presented his original doctrine of the judiciary and its role in the constitutional order. This was a doctrine different not only from the one we have just examined in the texts by Bergasse, but also, and more surprisingly, from the one his co-author J. Madison presented in sections 47–51, which many of the readers of the *Federalist* believe contains the authoritative, definitive description of the American version of the separation of powers.

As we are going to see, unlike in the schemes of Bergasse and Madison, judicial power plays for Hamilton a capital and active/positive role in maintaining constitutional equilibrium, guaranteeing the hierarchical structure of the legal system and the superiority of constitutional norms vis-à-vis the statute laws passed by the Congress.

Brutus claimed[32] that the US Supreme Court, created by Article 3 of the constitution, gave exorbitant powers to this agency, and the anti-federalist added that if the federal judges 'are to be rendered totally independent, both of the people and the legislature, both with respect to their offices and salaries... they will operate to a total subversion of the [member-]state judiciaries, if not, to the legislative authority of the states'.[33]

It is evident from the context that Brutus, with his second argument, was trying to preserve the judicial and legislative competences of the member-states vis-à-vis those of the central/national government. However, the main point for my argument here has nothing to do with the federal structure of the American constitution but with the criticisms levelled at an 'independent' judiciary – independent from popular control through repeated elections. Moreover, the anti-federalist claimed that 'This article vests the courts with authority to give the constitution a legal construction, or to explain it according to the rules laid down for construing a law.'[34]

If Brutus is right – as was probably the case, even though he exaggerated his arguments for reasons of political rhetoric – it is wrong, to begin with, to attribute to the Chief Justice Marshall the invention of judicial review in America. This is because the critic of the Philadelphia constitution saw correctly that this was implied by that constitution.[35] In any event, Publius, here the lawyer behind the pseudonym, Hamilton, felt compelled to answer the criticism and to make explicit the content of Article 3 of the constitution. As we will see, in his answer he will not contest the role that Brutus attributes to the Supreme Court, but will insert it into a highly imaginative concept of the balance of powers and into a unique form of constitutional self-enforcing equilibrium, where the judiciary plays a major role in stabilizing that equilibrium and the goal that it has to guarantee – individual freedom.

To clarify what is being said here we need to step back a moment. Madison, in paper no. 39, wrote that the principle of republicanism consists essentially of the popular authorization (through periodical elections) of the major governmental organs. Now in a post-aristocratic,[36] post-monarchical society like the US at the end of the eighteenth century, only an election attributing a mandate *pro tempore* can justify the exercise of governmental power by men over men (the government of women for almost one century after the establishment of the American constitution was assigned to fathers and husbands, since women had no citizenship in representative government at its origins – on both sides of the Atlantic). Madison introduced an exception to that principle: not only were the federal judges not elected by citizens but they had a mandate for life, restricted only by the rule of customary English public law: good behaviour. As Madison wrote:

> If we resort for a criterion to the different principles on which different forms of government are established, we may define a republic to be, or at least may bestow that name on, a government which derives all its powers directly or indirectly from the great body of the people, and is administered by persons holding their offices during pleasure, for a limited period, *or* during good behavior. (Which means for life, provided they do not transgress the laws of the country and, hence, independently of their decisions).[37]

In a different section, no. 51, the best-known text in the *Federalist* concerning the separation of powers, Madison comes back to the 'exception' represented by the federal judiciary in relation to the republican principle of popular authorization *pro tempore*. The Philadelphia constitution takes away from the citizens the choice of judges and the possibility of popular sanction, derogating to the principle according to which:

> it would require that all the appointments for the supreme executive, legislative, and judiciary magistracies, should be drawn from the same fountain of authority, the people, through channels, having no communications whatever with one another.

The arguments that Madison offers in order to justify this deviation from the constitutional norm as to the appointment of judges are neither entirely clear nor persuasive. Actually, we are here confronted with a double exception/derogation. Indeed, the federal judges are not only unaccountable to the voters, but they are also not 'independent', since their appointment (and career, we might add) depends on the joint will and decision of two other branches of government: the President and the Senate. Notice that by 'independence' is meant here that the three powers have distinct/independent sources of popular authorization and are accountable only to the citizens/voters.[38] There is, to be sure, a third anomaly in the Madisonian model concerning the structure of the judiciary, since the judges play no constitutional role as a counter-power (and not even one of self-defence, as in the case of the executive, thanks to the presidential veto). The reasons put forward for these anomalies in the organization of the third power by Madison in the same section were:

> first, because peculiar qualifications being essential in the members, the primary consideration ought to be to select that mode of choice which best secures these qualifications; secondly, because the permanent tenure by which the appointments are held in that department, must soon destroy all sense of dependence on the authority conferring them.[39]

As has already been pointed out above, these arguments are not entirely persuasive, since elections were considered by the Founding Fathers – as they were by the Athenians – as a good mechanism for selecting the best citizens, the elite. Hence it is not entirely clear (and there is no equivalent for this in Montesquieu's chapter on the English constitution) why it would be necessary for judges to have a system of selection different from the one adopted for the other high magistracies, notably presidential appointment with consent of the Senate.[40] The second argument is persuasive, but only up to a point,[41] since tenure makes the judges independent of those who have appointed them. The consequence is that the independence absent in the mechanism for appointing judges is restored, so to speak, by the absence of accountability.[42] It is a fact that Madison wanted to give to the judiciary a structure at the same time quite unique and derogatory as to the rule valid for the other organs of constitutional rank, but/and no role in the celebrated American doctrine of the balance of powers.

If we turn now to section 78 of the *Federalist*, the fabric of the government and the specific role of the judiciary inside it look very different. Hamilton comes back to the criticisms levelled at the constitution concerning the organization of judicial power: first, the mechanism for appointing judges and, second, and even more important, the magnitude of its powers. On the first point, he adds some remarks at the end of his text which supplement those spelled out by Madison. However, he devotes the bulk of his argument to the second point. For Hamilton, the life tenure of judges limited only by the principle of good behaviour is a crucial constitutional value. An independent judiciary – independent here in the sense that it has no need to fear the other powers, since its members cannot be dismissed because of decisions the elected branches (or the citizens) do not like – is, in a republican regime, the equivalent of an independent judiciary in a monarchical system. If under a monarchy it represents an 'excellent barrier to the despotism of the prince', in the republican system that the Americans were going to establish 'it is a no less excellent barrier to the encroachments and oppressions of the representative body'.[43]

It is immediately evident that we are here looking at the problem from the perfectly clear point of view of a liberal doctrine of government. In the optic of absolute representation or of pure representative democracy (the one supported by the Jacobin tradition) it is just not conceivable to speak of encroachments of representative organs, elected and accountable to the voters. In French public law from the Revolution through to part of the Fifth Republic, the elected representatives express the general will, exactly as the constituent power does. Hence the paradox of two equal powers of which one (the constituent power) is – fictionally – superior to the other (the legislative one). This also gives rise to the thesis according to which the legislative majority is infallible, just like the pope of the Catholic Church.

The difference between the American and the French constitutional tradition (to which Elisabeth Zoller has once again drawn attention[44]) has to do with a different way of conceiving of the very idea of a constitution. Briefly, it is possible to summarize this in the following way. On the European continent, constitutional rigidity has been for a long time – mainly up to the Second World War in fact – quite fictional. In the best of cases, when the rigid constitution was stable, it had the rationalizing function of avoiding discussing the rules for decision-making and the tasks of governmental organs each time they had to make decisions and enforce them.[45] It is enough to think of the *Déclaration* of 1789, in which there is only a 'réserve de la loi' concerning fundamental rights, which means that they are at the disposal of the legislative power. In fact, rights have to yield before the law (*loi*), and may even disappear completely. In the United States, the principle of constitutional rigidity has the function of creating a barrier for the 'legislative vortex' (Madison) and demands an institutional guardian. Hamilton, in fact, wrote:

> The complete independence of the courts of justice is peculiarly essential in a *limited* constitution. By a limited constitution I understand

one which contains certain *specific exceptions to the legislative authority*. [My italics][46]

Hamilton is extremely clear on one point: the guardian of the limited/rigid constitution has to be the Courts of Justice, since it is their task and duty to refuse to apply statutes contrary to the constitution. Now, our author has to face the objection which claims that this function makes of the judiciary a sort of unchecked sovereign, and in any event a power superior to that of the legislature. At this point he presents a doctrine of popular sovereignty that allows him to dismantle the classical doctrine which from Bodin onwards established the supremacy of the legislative power. If the latter (unlikely in Bodin) is a constituted power, hence a delegated one and as such subordinate to the constitution, it will not be possible to conceive of 'the deputy ... greater than his principal; that the servant is above his master; that the representatives of the people are superior to the people themselves'.[47] From the point of view of American constitutionalism, since the will of the representatives cannot replace or absorb the will of the voters it follows that

> It is far more rational to suppose that the courts were designed to be an intermediary body between the people and the legislature, in order, among other things, to keep the latter within the limits assigned to their authority.[48]

Hamilton added here a number of arguments we find again in the opinion expressed in 1803 by Chief Justice Marshall in *Marbury* v *Madison*.[49] What matters to us are specifically the answers paper no. 78 opposes to Brutus' thesis, according to which the federal judiciary, because of its function as guardian of the legislative power, would become the new sovereign.

The main arguments are two. On the one hand, 'the purse and the sword', over which the judiciary has no control. On the other, the dichotomy between will and judgment.

The first argument cannot easily be disproved. The Supreme Court (USSC) not only is not in command of the budget of the nation,[50] but it is also unable to impose its decisions alone. Without the support of the executive power, the opinions of the USSC based on *Brown* v *Board of Education* would have remained unenforced, similar to the results of the German *Bundesverfassungsgericht*'s decision to take down the crucifixes from classrooms in Bavaria. Without the cooperation at least of the executive branch, the constitutional power of the judiciary can frequently end up as just a *flatus vocis* rather than the *sic voleo sic jubeo* of the baroque sovereign.[51]

The second argument is based on the opposition between *will* and *judgment*. I do not know of any persuasive commentary on the dichotomy used by Hamilton. Hence, here is one interpretation of it.[52] By 'will' it seems evident that he meant the political will of the citizens or of the elected representatives: the number, the majority stays here 'pro ratione'. Hamilton wrote:

> The courts must declare the sense of the law; and if they should be disposed to exercise WILL instead of JUDGMENT, the consequence would equally be the substitution of their pleasure to that of the legislative body.[53]

It is clear what he had in mind with 'will'. He meant the discretionary will of a political majority. But how should we interpret 'judgment'? The *Oxford English Dictionary* states, at point 8.a., that 'judgment' means the 'faculty of judging; ability to form an opinion; that function of the mind whereby it arrives at a notion of anything; the critical faculty; discernment'. At point 3.a. it says, 'The sentence of a court of justice; a judicial decision or order in court'. Now, the opinion of a court of justice is a *judgment* and not just an example of *will*, since it has to be justified through a *ratio decidendi* which ought to have the form of a 'public reason'[54] and not an expression of the will of a segment of the society that derives its legitimacy from the principle of majority will. There is no point in objecting that the court sometimes may decide by majority, since this minimalist and technical conception of majority rule as a decision-making mechanism is not the same thing as the principle used to legitimize the democratic dimension of the will expressed by elected representatives. Were they the same, not only would the specific character of the judicial decision disappear, but so would the specific character of democracy which the critics oppose to the courts' power, since democracy simply equated to majority rule would be indistinguishable from the decision-making mechanism of any kind of oligarchy whatever, as Aristotle and Pufendorf already noticed in the past. What I am saying is that it does not make sense to claim that there is no difference between courts and parliaments, given that both may decide using majority rule, since the same principle is utilized in any and every oligarchic sovereign body. In terms of a logic such as this, all the differences would disappear where it is much more interesting to look at them.[55]

Courts of Justice need the cooperation of the other organs of government in order to enforce their decisions and are under an obligation to give written and public reasons for their opinions. Moreover, they have for Hamilton, who in this point deviated significantly from the younger Madison, a paramount role to play in the stabilization of the constitutional order; courts are a coordinated and essential power in the American constitutionalism.

According to *Federalist* 78:

> it is not with a view to infractions of the Constitution only, that the independence of the judges may be an essential safeguard against the effects of occasional ill humors in the society. These sometimes extend no farther than to the injury of the private rights of particular classes of citizens, by unjust and partial laws. Here also the firmness of the judicial magistracy is of vast importance in mitigating the severity and confining the operation of such laws.[56]

A guarantee of constitutional rigidity and the protection of the citizens' fundamental rights, these are the functions that the American constitution assigns to the Courts of Justice, according to Alexander Hamilton.

At the end of his text he comes back to one of the exceptions Madison considered concerning the appointment of federal judges derogating to the electoral principle. We find here an argument that the judge Coke used in his polemic against King James I: exercising judicial power cannot be a prerogative of the political power – not even the power of the sovereign of England. It is function of a specific expertise, the knowledge of positive law:[57]

> It has been frequently remarked, with great propriety, that a voluminous code of laws is one of the inconveniences necessarily connected with the advantages of a free government. To avoid an arbitrary discretion in the courts, it is indispensable that they should be bound down by strict rules and precedents, which serve to define and point out their duty in every particular case that comes before them; and it will readily be conceived from the variety of controversies which grow out of the folly and wickedness of mankind, that the records of those precedents must unavoidably swell to a very considerable bulk, and must demand long and laborious study to acquire a competent knowledge of them. Hence it is that there can be but few men in the

society who will have sufficient skill in the laws to qualify them for the stations of judges.[58]

It may be worthwhile to discuss here a question which became the subject of a strange discussion during the debates of the French Constituent Assembly in 1795 (Year III): what is the nature of judicial control? In the words of Thibaudeau: is that control internal or external? But this would be the subject of a different essay. So perhaps it is best to end this discussion by citing the title of a recent book by Alec Stone Sweet. The constitutional *Rechtstaat*, the state that knows nothing of absolute sovereigns and the only one compatible with the institutional pluralism established by the separation of powers is inevitably, and since 1787 from the point of view of constitutional doctrine, *Governing with Judges*.[59]

For Bergasse, and this is the conclusion I would like to suggest, a good constitution is a governmental machine able to produce *lois* – resulting from the deliberation of the two houses and the executive veto – that judges have to apply without interfering with the legislative sovereign power. Here there is no hierarchy of norms but only a hierarchy of functions. All the *lois* are constitutional. And freedom is obedience to the *lois*.

For Hamilton, however, a good constitution is one under which judges refuse to apply statutes contrary to the constitution, those enacted *ultra vires*, beyond the competence of constituted powers. The legislature is *not* a sovereign power and moreover there is no mechanism and no quality of deliberation able to guarantee good legislation with certainty. The passions and interests of legislators – an agent and not the principal of political business – can always produce the oppression of individual freedom (the freedom of specific and isolated individuals). In this sense, a true hierarchy of norms also functions as a guardian of the courts of justice. Freedom consists in the expectation that political power will refrain from intervening in a sphere that the constitution puts outside the reach of the legislators.

It is not too difficult to see which model was the exception in the eighteenth century, only to become the rule in the twentieth.

## Notes

1. The general systematic discussion of this topic is still to be found in Carl Schmitt (1928) *Verfassungslehre* (Munich and Leipzig: Verlag von Duncker und Humblot). See especially the second section: 'The liberal element of the modern constitution' (*Der rechtstaatliche Bestandteil der modernen Verfassung*) pp. 123–220. For the history of the doctrine see: M.J.C. Vile (1998) *Constitutionalism and the Separation of Powers*, 2nd edn (Indianapolis: Liberty Fund);

G. Silvestri (1979–84) *La separazione dei poteri*, 2 vols (Milan: Giuffrè); for the introductory remarks on the judiciary and the separation of powers see A. Marongiu (1972) 'Il posto del potere giudiziario nella dottrina della separazione dei poteri', in *Studi in memoria di Carlo Esposito* (Padua: Cedam), vol. 1, pp. 679–93.
2. Bergasse wrote, for instance, that the aim of a constitution based on the separation of the powers is 'la garantie de la liberté individuelle'; see N. Bergasse (1789) *Discours sur la manière dont il convient de limiter le pouvoir législatif et le pouvoir exécutif dans une monarchie* (Paris), p. 10 – hereafter *Discours*. James Madison on the other side of the Ocean wrote the same in the *Federalist Papers* no. 51: 'In order to lay a due foundation for that separate and distinct exercise of the different powers of government, which to a certain extent, is admitted to all hands to be essential to the preservation of liberty...'.
3. In Book XI of his *Spirit of Laws*.
4. Schmitt, *Verfassungslehre*, p. 279 (French tr., Paris: Presses universitaires de France, 1993), writes: 'la séparation entre législatif et exécutif doit empêcher cette combinaison de normes générales et de prescriptions particulières individuelles; est despotique tout gouvernement qui peut prendre des décisions particulières sans être lié par des lois générales, fermes et durables'.
5. This point was made already very clearly by Locke, see his *Second Treatise* No. 131: 'whoever has the legislative or supreme power of any common-wealth, is bound to govern by established standing laws, promulgated and known to the people, and not by extemporary decrees'.
6. A contemporary example of the different way of perceiving individual freedom can be seen concretely considering the difficult transatlantic debate concerning the French law about the ban on wearing a headscarf in French public high schools (not, by the way, in the universities, which are also public institutions). From the French point of view, the rule is general and non-discriminatory since it bans any religious symbol (not just the Muslim ones). From this perspective, both a rule allowing any religious symbols and the one forbidding all of them are 'laws' and so a legitimate exercise of legislative power. From the point of view of the American idea of freedom, the simple fact that a law regulates this type of behaviour seems an egregious infringement upon individual liberty. In other words, rights are, in the French legal tradition, under the protection of the (general) law, whereas in the United States they are under the protection of the constitution, since there is a real hierarchy between laws and the constitution!
7. About his life there is only one quite mediocre biography: Louis Bergasse (1910) *Un défenseur des principes traditionnels sous la révolution: Nicolas Bergasse, avocat au parlement de Paris, député du tiers état de la sénéchaussée Lyon 1750–1832* (Paris: Librairie Académique Perrin).
8. Hence the slightly pompous Wikipedia, *s.v.*
9. On the constitution drafted by this group and the reasons for its defeat see my (1998) *Sieyes et l'invention de la constitution en France* (Paris: Odile Jacob), Ch. 1, 'La balance du législatif', pp. 15–30.
10. See n. 2 above.
11. 'Moderate' has here the meaning it has in Montesquieu.
12. The same position in a text by Duport (29 March 1790) 'Principes et plan pour l'établissement de l'ordre judiciaire', in *Archives Parlementaires* 1st ser.,

vol. 12, p. 410: 'ce que l'on appelle improprement le pouvoir judiciaire. Je dis improprement parce qu'il n'y a réellement de pouvoir dans l'ordre judiciaire que le pouvoir exécutif'.

13. The apparent conundrum – why bother with the judiciary since it is not a third power? – can probably be clarified in the following way. Notwithstanding the fact that the judiciary is not a *power*, the combined exercise of that *function* conjunctly with one of the two powers represents a threat to liberty, for reasons I try to clarify in the text.

14. I cannot discuss here the largely utopian approach which lies behind this conception of the separation of legislative and judicial power. It is evident that between the arbitrary justice of the *cadi* (by the way a quite perfunctory and discriminatory representation of the Muslim-Turkish judge) and the perfect impartiality of a blind judge bound only by the letter of statute law there are a lot of different realistic possibilities more interesting than these *images d'Epinal*. The reader of Italian can look up the serious remarks on this question by Gustavo Zagrebelsky (2007) *La virtù del dubbio* (Rome and Bari: Laterza), pp. 153–6.

15. 'Justice retenue' was the part of the judicial power, originally the first mark of sovereignty, that the French king never agreed to delegate to his Courts of Justice (which exercised only 'justice déléguée'. On this distinction, see J.-P. Royer (1996) *Histoire de la justice en France* (Paris: Presses universitaires de France), notably pp. 90 ff. Bergasse's argument, which is easy to understand from a historical point of view, seems logically unpersuasive in terms of his own theory. If the judges are, as he claims, part of the executive power, and since this last is bound by the strict application of the law, E+J would seem both inevitable and not dangerous. We can speculate that he believed that the strict application of the law would have been possible only if the judges were independent from the king, since otherwise the great power of the latter would have destroyed any subordination to the law when he had to apply the statutes as the final judge. This might be the reason why the executive power assigned to the judges, that is, the judicial function, had to be independent from the monarch (or the elected chief of the executive), who should not exercise more than the executive function, *stricto sensu*. I will come back to this question when analysing Bergasse's report on the organization of the judiciary.

16. This can be translated as: 'Law is the only guarantee of freedom.'

17. The Greek ἐπιείκεια; 'Aristotle says that it is the function of the *dikastes* (juror/judge) to judge according to *dike* ("justice"), but that the *diaitetes* (arbitrator) should make his decision according to *epieikeia*. It is conventional therefore to translate *epieikeia* as "equity", since this is a standard and convenient way to describe "fairness" or "natural justice" as opposed to the strict application of legal rules. There are however certain problems here. "Equity" in English law can mean simply "fairness", but it is also the name given to the system of law developed originally by the Court of Chancery (the Lord Chancellor's court) to provide relief in cases where to apply the rules of the common law would have seemed manifestly unfair. "Equity" in this sense is itself a body of rules; it is found only in countries which base their legal system on the common law, and it is clearly not what Aristotle is talking about. It should indeed be noted that Aristotle's statement of theory receives

little acknowledgement in Athenian practice. When a litigant in an extant speech pleads for the application of natural justice in his favour, he characteristically describes this as *dike* and not as *epieikeia*.' See S.C. Todd (2003) *A Glossary of Athenian Legal Terms* (Austin: University of Texas Press), selections by Michael de Brauw. For a contemporary and original version of this Aristotelian concept of justice see G. Zagrebelsky (2000) *Le droit en douceur* (Paris: Économica).
18. Later on in his *Discours* he writes: 'le pouvoir législatif, dès qu'il est illimité, devient despotique' (p. 68).
19. It is important to notice that Bergasse's Upper House did not have the aristocratic character of the English House of Lords, a point, however, on which he was not able to persuade the Constituent Assembly!
20. Here again the argument is similar to that presented by Madison in the *Federalist Papers*.
21. The exceptions are the king's veto, making him co-legislator, and the judicial function of the Senate acting as a court as to the political responsibility of the ministers ('*les agens du prince*', *Discours*, p. 20). On pp. 27–8 Bergasse defends his thesis from the criticism of violation of the separation of functions.
22. It was also published in the *Moniteur Universel*, I, 340 ff.
23. I am quoting here from the English translation; the French original says: 'L'influence du pouvoir judiciaire n'a point de bornes' (p. 3, copy of Bibliothèque nationale FB-20910; p. 2 of the same text on the web, easier to access and the one I will quote from hereafter. See http://www.justice.gc.ca/fr/ps/inter/rev_002_ber/index.html).
24. *Spirit of Laws*, B. XI, ch. 6. Bergasse writes: 'The influence of judicial power is something that has an impact, so to speak, on our daily life, and on each single moment of it; and since what has such continual impact will inevitably influence greatly all our habits, it is understandable that of all the public powers the one that changes us most, for good or bad, is without any doubt judicial power', p. 2.
25. 'We cannot dispute the huge impact judicial power has; now, if its influence is without limits, if the judiciary is stronger than all the other public powers, it follows that there is no other public power that we need to limit and place checks on more precision than with this; there is none that we have to organize with more restless carefulness and meticulous precautions', p. 3.
26. Notably in comparison with Hamilton!
27. If the judge has a doubt concerning the interpretation of statute law, he has to ask the legislative body to clarify the meaning of the law: 'Judges will be allowed in no way to interpret statutes; and in the case of ambiguity of the statute, they have to turn to the legislative body for the provision, if necessary, of a more precise statute' (*Discours*, p. 19). We see here the origin of another unique invention of the French Revolution: the so called *référé legislatif*, introduced in 1790 and never actually used! See J.L. Halpérin (1987) *Le Tribunal de cassation et les pouvoirs sous la Révolution (1790–1799)* (Paris: LGDJ).
28. For details, see *Titre V et dernier: De l'élection et de la nomination des juges*, in *Discours*, pp. 25–6.
29. Article 2 of Ch. V on judicial power disposes: 'Justice will be delivered by judges elected by the citizens for a limited mandate, and appointed by "lettres-patentes" of the king, who cannot reject the popular choice.' The

98  *Pasquale Pasquino*

elective character of the judiciary has been typical of the French legal tradition for more than a century, but only in theory, since in practice it has never been really applied.
30. Simply in terms of the appointment of judges!
31. I will come back to this question later in the text.
32. Brutus XI, 31 January 1788.
33. Pp. 293–4. I am quoting from R. Ketcham (ed.) (1986) *The Anti-Federalist Papers* (New York: Mentor Books).
34. P. 295.
35. Evidence in M. Farrand (1911) *Records of the Federal Convention of 1787* (New Haven: Yale University Press), vol. 2, pp. 144, 299; see also J. Elliot (1859) *Debates in Several State Conventions on the Adoption of the Federal Constitution* (Philadelphia: J.B. Lippincott), 2nd edn, in 5 vols. See vol. 1, p. 380; vol. 2, pp. 290, 488; vol. 3, p. 553.
36. 'Could any further proof be required of the republican complexion of this system, the most decisive one might be found in its absolute prohibition of titles of nobility, both under the federal and the State governments; and in its express guaranty of the republican form to each of the latter' (*Federalist*, no. 39).
37. That the author is referring by the last expression to the judicial power becomes evident if we read what is written a little later in no. 39: 'According to the provisions of most of the constitutions, again, as well as according to the most respectable and received opinions on the subject, the members of the judiciary department are to retain their offices by the firm tenure of good behavior.'
38. Not to each other, as in the parliamentary regime for the executive vis-à-vis the legislative branch.
39. Much later on, Robert Badinter, the president of the French Constitutional Council will speak of 'devoir d'ingratitude' of the members of the Council towards their electors, notwithstanding the fact that these are appointed only for a nine-year term and not for life.
40. To be sure, it would be possible to object that exercising judicial power implies specialized knowledge, and specifically familiarity with the positive laws of the country. It is not clear though why the judges could not have been chosen by the voters from a list of candidates qualified for the job from specialists in law; and need they be appointed by the other branches?
41. Up to a point, since the remark is appropriate *only* for the Justices of the Supreme Court, who cannot be promoted by the political/elected organs to a higher position! Not for the other judges.
42. Here again, we find the two meanings of independence to which I referred earlier in the text.
43. J. Rakove (ed.) (2003) *The Federalist: The Essential Essays* (Boston and New York: Bedford/St Martin), p. 197.
44. See her (2006) *Introduction au droit public* (Paris: Dalloz).
45. On this aspect of constitutional rigidity see Steven Holmes (1995) 'Precommitment and the Paradox of Democracy', in *Passions and Constraints* (Chicago: University of Chicago Press), pp. 134–77.
46. Rakove, *The Federalist*, p. 198.
47. Ibid., p. 199.

48. Ibid.
49. The parallel between Hamilton no. 78 and *Marbury* v *Madison* has already been dealt with in E.-M. Erlick (1926) *La séparation des pouvoirs et la Convention fédérale de 1787* (Paris: Sirey), p. 166.
50. Decisions of Supreme/Constitutional courts may of course have an impact on redistributive justice (in France, for instance, the *Conseil constitutionnel* has to approve the budget); but when interference was too important, courts had to step back and leave these types of decisions to the legislative bodies.
51. Rakove, *The Federalist*, p. 198: 'It [the judiciary] may truly be said to have neither Force nor Will, but merely judgment; and must ultimately depend upon the aid of the executive arm even for the efficacy of its judgments'.
52. Which I owe largely to Valerio Onida.
53. Rakove, *The Federalist*, p. 200.
54. The expression is used in a more general sense, as is well known, by John Rawls.
55. We should notice that courts interpreting the constitution exercise – like any agency of decision-making – some discretionary power (a point made at the beginning of the twentieth century both by C. Schmitt and H. Kelsen; see especially C. Schmitt (1912) *Gesetzt und Urteil* (Munich: Beck; 2nd edn 1969) in the absence of which it is difficult to speak of 'decision'. What matters in this context is to draw attention to the fact that both courts and legislative assemblies exercise their discretionary power under constraints which are not the same for the two types of institution.
56. Rakove, *The Federalist*, pp. 201–2.
57. See P. Pasquino (2003) 'Prolegomena to a Theory of Judicial Power', *Law and Practice of International Courts and Tribunals*, II, 1, 11–26.
58. Rakove, *The Federalist*, pp. 202–3.
59. Alec Stone Sweet (2000) *Governing with Judges* (Oxford: Oxford University Press).

# 5
# Neutrality and Trade in the Dutch Republic (1775–1783): Preludes to a Piecemeal Revolution

*Koen Stapelbroek*

## American state-building, neutrality and the Dutch commercial republican legacy

Comparing the geographical characteristics and the political, economic and social history of America and the European continent, eighteenth-century political thinkers emphasized their great differences. Mostly, eighteenth-century writers stressed that history since the fall of the Roman Empire had created conditions that placed a heavy burden on European states and blocked any chance to further develop economic growth and generate legal and social change. In the words of Ferdinando Galiani, writing in 1776, 'the time has come for the total downfall of Europe and for the transmigration to America. Here everything falls into decay: religion, laws, the arts, sciences; and everything will be newly built in America.'[1] Still, since European power struggles and interstate economic rivalry were played out on a global scale (of which the modern history of America itself was a product), American state-building and the general redesign of modernity that writers like Galiani alluded to would have to directly engage with these constraints.

The combination of America's distinctive characteristics and the inescapable immersion of the new state into European-led global power politics in the aftermath of the acquisition of independence translated into a crucial challenge for federalists and republicans alike. Hamiltonians and Jeffersonians devised rival nation-building strategies that simultaneously exploited the natural and historical-institutional advantages over the Old World and secured American sovereignty against military and political threats posed by European states. In this regard, the 1793 declaration of neutrality was of great significance. Bypassing any claims related to the 1778 Franco-American Treaty of Amity, the declaration formally defined the stance taken by the newly independent state towards the Old World. Moreover, and more importantly, it represented a vision of the future of international economic development, foreign trade and the interstate system, with as many internal, national (including constitutional) as external policy ramifications. Through the declaration of neutrality in 1793 (and in the course of the episodes involving Genet[2]) as well as in Jefferson's Barbary War and the American protection of its neutrality in the Mediterranean in the next decade, different perspectives on the relations between trade, war, economic development, finance and policy emulation were played out in an international context.[3]

This external manifestation of the internal crystallizing of American statehood, in the engagement with the topic of political neutrality and foreign trade, I want to suggest, resembled the way in which Dutch politicians and political thinkers during the War of American Independence discussed rival scenarios and understandings of Dutch neutrality. The challenge for the Dutch (which they failed to live up to) was how, in the context of European commercial competition and its frequent spilling over into warfare, neutrality could be made integral to the promotion of Dutch trade and be made congruent with the security of the Dutch republic.

A great deal has been written about whether the country that was responsible for setting up New Amsterdam,[4] that traded intensively with the thirteen states between 1775 and 1783 and whose merchants held great sympathies, as well as commercial and political hopes, for American independence, left any marks on the American national identity, such as through the transmission of republican ideas of freedom, or even in the American Declaration of Independence.[5] In this chapter I will not engage with the Dutch legacy in the history of American independence, or even take up a position with regard to the (intertwined) Atlantic and republican traditions.[6] Instead, I will deal with these issues much more indirectly, by giving a rough outline of how we might begin to understand in a different way, and in connection to each other, the significant number of relatively understudied sources – notably pamphlets – that were published in the United Provinces between 1775 and 1783. Here, different views of the future role of America, once independent, in the international scene were discussed, along with competing outlooks on what alliances with other states were the most natural, based on Dutch commercial and political interests. I will suggest, contrary to the commonly held views among Dutch historians, that despite the presumed particularism of Dutch politics, the different visions of the future of the commerce of the republic were much more coherent with those that existed in other European countries than hitherto has been recognized. By grasping the wider logic of rival positions in the debate on the role the Dutch republic should take in the course of the War of American Independence, the contours of the processes that culminated in the Patriot Revolt of 1787 and the later Batavian Revolution may be understood in a new light. Eventually – but this falls outside the scope of this essay – the neutrality debate in the United Provinces may prove to be a useful context for comparison with early American points of view on how to turn neutrality into a key principle of commercial politics.

## The Dutch republic during the War of American Independence reconsidered

At the time of the War of American Independence, the United Provinces were in disarray. A country no longer among Europe's dominant nations, with an economy allegedly in decline, the future of the state was at stake in a number of disputes that were not simply party political conflicts of interest played out at different administrative levels within the republic. Not that the supposedly age-old party divide between supporters of the House of Orange and the States could ever be simply reduced to domestic politics. In the 'Golden Age', struggles within the Dutch republic had always been connected – in the long war of independence with Spain, followed by three Anglo-Dutch wars – to its precarious existence in the international arena. Yet, typically, in 1672, when the Dutch provinces were invaded by France, England and the Bishop of Munster, much of the enormous pamphlet debate that raged across the country concerned faction politics, contested interpretations of the nature of the Dutch republic as defined in the Union of Utrecht of 1579 and alternative social-political orders grounded in different understandings of proper republican citizenship. Within this debate, De Witt's regime of 'True Liberty' (1650–72), was portrayed as a perfidy of Dutch virtue, constitutional balance and integrity and, along the same lines, was criticized for its failure to secure the state in foreign politics.

By the second half of the eighteenth century the dominant discourses of Dutch politics themselves had not changed a great deal. Indeed, political battles were still fought over the dead bodies of De Witt, Barnevelt, de Ruyter and Tromp. But it was their underlying nature that had assumed a new form. However much Dutch political culture outwardly retained the fixed categories of later seventeenth-century oppositions, underneath its apparent continuous focus on republican virtue its dividing lines were determined by rival visions of the future of international commerce and the reforms needed to regenerate the republic's economy. During the eighteenth century, Dutch political debate, famously, became ever more strenuously linked to the issue of commercial decline and restoration.[7] Yet it has been largely overlooked by historians how discussions about counteracting the waning of Dutch economic supremacy from the middle of the seventeenth century (when it reached its peak) to the 1740s onwards developed. Consequently, historical accounts construe the political thought of the era as linking the 'Golden Age' to the inauguration of the Liberal Constitutional Monarchy in 1848, while neglecting an important dimension.

At the moment, the second half of the eighteenth century is still understood by Dutch historians first and foremost as the beginning of a notoriously drawn out revolutionary trajectory that lasted from 1780 to 1848. From 1776, the aggressive campaigns by the French and English ambassadors Vauguyon and Yorke created the immense pressure on Dutch neutrality that caused the outbreak of the Fourth Anglo-Dutch War in 1780. During this period, the Patriotic movement gathered the strength that led to the abortive Patriot uprising of 1787 and the 1795 French invasion and Batavian Revolution, which gave way to what for a long time was seen as the 'restoration' of true Dutchness in 1813.[8] From the nineteenth-century orthodoxy confirmed by the work of H.T. Colenbrander onwards,[9] the historiography of this period has been subject to many ideologically driven revisions[10] and a great many details in the careers and the political contacts and actions of the main figures in Dutch political life between 1775 and 1783 are now well known. Still, the main relevance of the period even at this stage can only be described in terms of what follows, instead of on its own terms.[11]

Before the outbreak of the War of American Independence, Dutch political life was already a strangely complex patchwork of diplomatic, administrative, financial and commercial powers and influences. This was due on the one hand to Dutch institutional structures, with their different levels of formal administrative and military power, in which the Stadtholder fulfilled a curious ever-disputed role.[12] On the other hand, this situation was a natural consequence given the United Provinces' nature as a trading republic. The international significance of Dutch trade made European states recognize the importance of maintaining sway in Dutch politics. Moreover, it was crucial for European states to ensure they had the opportunity to get loans from Amsterdam financiers in wartime. Possibly for these reasons, diplomatic circles in The Hague had evolved into hotspots for sensing changes in international relations, and European states sent their most able foreign envoys to the United Provinces – not primarily to negotiate with the government about military alliances and treaties, but to act almost as consuls in the politically crucial spheres of trade and state debt finance.

The international role of the republic in its turn reflected on domestic political processes. In times of war and for as long as the republic stayed neutral, its commercial and financial services became an attractive source of wealth for Dutch (mainly Amsterdam) merchants and bankers. Yet this situation exposed the state to political pressures by belligerent states, which demanded the strictest neutrality based on their diverging interpretations of, for example, definitions of contraband in treaties with the Dutch. The different interests of Amsterdam capitalists and traders and the Hague politicians, along with the immersion in their affairs by foreign ministers, consuls and secret agents, created huge latent tensions. At the outbreak of the War of American Independence these tensions flared up and intensified when foreign agents started to milk their Dutch contacts. As international pressure increased, European states sent more diplomats to the United Provinces. Meanwhile, the main question was: would the republic manage to stay neutral?

During the Seven Years War – the major previous global military and economic conflict – the United Provinces had just managed to stay neutral, but the War of American Independence was a different kind of conflict, precisely because the trade of neutral powers became a more important, more organized and in the end more threatening aspect for the British. From the start of the conflict, Great Britain made it clear that they expected the Dutch to be favourable to their cause by requesting, in 1775, the use of the Scotch brigade,[13] itself a symbol of the Protestant succession and the dynastic alliance between the Hanoverians and the House of Orange. After initially agreeing, the Dutch set impossible conditions and implicitly refused. A series of further incidents followed, when the expectations of the British were not met by the behaviour of the Dutch: the first salute to a ship flying the American flag by the governor of the Dutch island of St Eustatius and the alleged contraband trade in the Caribbean,[14] the welcoming of the American privateer John Paul Jones with his captured English ships on the island of Texel,[15] and the seizure off the coast of Newfoundland of a ship carrying Henry Laurens and his papers, including a draft treaty of amity and commerce between the United States and the United Provinces.[16] These incidents were more symbolic (even if they became a *casus belli*) than of real importance, but they polarized Dutch public opinion as much as they gave the British and

French envoys motives to make demands to the States General and in these ways influence the political debate over the true Dutch commercial and political interests in the War of American Independence.

Between 1778 and 1780 a series of memoranda were drawn up by the British ambassador Yorke and his French counterpart Vauguyon that were published and translated immediately. Other foreign ministers immediately sent them home and extracts of these memoranda were invariably published in foreign journals like the *Notizie del Mondo*. In these memoranda, Vauguyon stressed the Dutch right to free trade, upheld the terms of the 1674 treaty with England – which comprised the 'free ships, free goods' principle[17] – and urged the Dutch to demand that the English respect their legal rights. Aware of the crucial importance of Amsterdam, the French offered separate trade privileges to this city and to Haarlem. The city of Amsterdam, rather than the country as a whole, was addressed by the French; the language of the address was economic interest. Yorke, on the other hand, busied himself mainly with threatening the Dutch, whose anti-English sympathies for American independence had inspired what he claimed seemed a more than merely commercially interested trade with the American rebels and France.

This, indeed, was what the entire debate was about: not simply short-term economic interests, but long-term prospects for Dutch trade that involved ideas of future alliances, trade privileges and shifts in the balance of power. More important than any of the high-profile accusations and justifications involving St Eustatius, John Paul Jones and Laurens was the interaction of competing perceptions of how to preserve the small trade republic in decline in writings of the time. The return of Stadtholder William IV in 1747 – while the republic was at war with France – the short-lived *Doelistenmovement*, the discussion about tax and land-lease reform and the sale of offices in 1748 and the debate about a limited free-port system in 1751 formed a series of events that set off the development of what turned into the movement of the Dutch Patriots. What has not been recognized sufficiently, despite the fact that key figures in later times (like Elie Luzac and Isaac de Pinto) were already active at the time, is that in the course of time, for example in the struggle over De Witt's legacy in 1757 – in the middle of the Seven Years War – Dutch political thinkers, influenced by a larger European debate on these matters, developed rival perceptions of the best viable long-term political economic strategy for the United Provinces. Between 1770 and the Patriot Revolt of 1787 the future of the Dutch economy and foreign politics were discussed through a famous prize essay competition and a series of wide-ranging pamphlet debates. These writings form the context in which the major Dutch political and economic treatises of the time (by Luzac, Kluit, etc.) are to be placed and compared with the works by foreign commentators that deal with the crisis in the United Provinces. They also form the clearest political expression of how different visions of the future of international commerce and how to restore the neutrality of trade in the interstate system clashed with each other in the Dutch republic.[18]

## Orangists and Patriots on neutrality: a basic outline

When Stadtholder William V decided in November 1775 that lending the Scotch brigade to Britain was a mere matter of politeness and most of the provinces had already consented, the Overijssel delegate to the States General, Baron Joan Derk van der Capellen tot den Pol, objected and published in the form of a pamphlet a truly remarkable speech opposing the decision.[19] Van der Capellen, who was to become the most prominent, but also the most visionary Patriot thinker, argued that to help Great Britain by sending troops was not to stay neutral, but to participate in the conflict, which could be of great consequence. Since the Dutch interest resided in trade, commercial interests had to be pursued consistently, not be neglected or brought into danger. The best protection was by maintaining strict neutrality – which van der Capellen understood as impartiality.[20] To lend Britain the Scotch brigade was the opposite of what had to be done in order to restore Dutch trade to its old glory and was a sign of the influence of 'some' (i.e. supporters of the House of Orange), which had been so detrimental to the republic that its decline was best understood as unnecessary self-destruction.[21]

But the influence of these same figures reached beyond this: 'The fire that is burning in America is more than able to set light to the whole of Europe, which is full of fuel.' By sacrificing its wealth to the greatness of England, the Dutch republic was to blame for this situation. It had upset the balance of power and put into power a monarchy at sea more powerful than had ever been seen. A monarchy that was 'indifferent' (*onverschillig*) to the House of Bourbon, which desired freedom and the freedom of trade[22] for the whole of Europe. Lending the Scotch brigade to Britain seemed, in the light of earlier policies, a minor matter, but was in reality the beginning of a chain of events that would result in 'another war with one of the most powerful neighbouring countries [i.e. France] which, in reality, because of shared interests, is our natural ally and one that cannot wish otherwise than that there should always be a neutral and, by means of trade, a flourishing republic like this one present, one that is endowed with a great number of ships and a capable navy to protect it in times of war, in order to continue its Commerce and Navigation, which would otherwise be hindered, to mutual advantage of both'.[23]

Van der Capellen had more reasons for objecting to the decision to send troops. 'What', he asked, 'did we get for our participation by England's side in the War of Succession, so deadly for us, when the English managed to obtain America, Minorca and Gibraltar, the keys to the entire Mediterranean? We got nothing, apart from an empty treasury, the worthy fruit of our hot-headedness.'[24] He continued that 'the advantages of commercial treaties, which on our side are so carefully observed and where we demand no more than what the law of nature and nations already entitles us to, *free ships free goods*, we are denied. Our ships on the open seas, the seas that belong to the Creator alone, are searched and confiscated ... goods are declared contraband that are not at all and we are treated as if we are not a free people.'[25] Finally, van der Capellen compared the American rebellion to the Dutch revolt and justified it: 'if even the barbarians [i.e. native Indians] ... do not become embroiled in this hateful unnatural fight of brother against brother ... how much more hateful would it be then to see a people do so that itself was enslaved and held that name, but ultimately liberated itself'.[26] While the Americans simply claimed their natural human rights to political freedom, not from the executive powers of the British, but from God, the contrast with the abuses of the House of Orange and its sustained support for the creation of a supranational Anglo-Dutch (but really British) empire could hardly be greater.[27]

This short text contained all the ingredients of later debates and of van der Capellen's more famous *Aan het Volk van Nederland* ('An Address to the People of the Netherlands') (1781), with its emphasis on the balance of power, the idea of the restoration of Dutch commerce, the 'natural' alliance with France because of a shared interest in free trade and his critique of the House of Orange that was squandering Dutch liberty, wealth and power by facilitating the rise of a British universal monarchy and its regime of global commercial oppression. An immediate response appeared in the same year. Not so much van der Capellen's *Advis* against lending troops to Britain, but more so its underlying principles[28] were refuted in three pamphlets published by Isaac de Pinto, who was often referred to as 'the Jew pensioner of England' because he had been rewarded with a £500 annual payment for advising the English government at the 1763 peace negotiations. Yet the suggestion that Pinto was a hired pen does injustice to the sophistication of his arguments and his long-standing advocacy, from the late 1740s on (when he wrote a *Tribut*

*Patriotique* containing financial policy proposals for William IV[29]), of the Anglo-Dutch alliance in the balance of power. In 1776, Pinto published three pieces in which the political and constitutional principles underlying van der Capellen's vision of international trade and politics were refuted.[30]

More direct opposition to the vision of the Dutch republic and international trade presented in van der Capellen's *Advis*, which nonetheless did not polemicize openly with the Overijssel nobleman, was contained in a pamphlet published in 1778 by an anonymous *Bon hollandais à ses compatriotes*.[31] Understandably, from its contents, it was repeatedly attributed to Isaac de Pinto.[32] The pamphlet was followed by a sequel in 1779[33] and both received many highly critical responses.[34] The *Bon hollandais* agreed with van der Capellen that the natural interest of the republic resided in commerce, but insisted that the Dutch and the British had a shared interest in maintaining the balance of power. The position of the British was threatened by the loss of their colonies, that of the Dutch by the loss of a global equilibrium of great powers if France became the main superpower. The *Bon hollandais* argued that 'trade is not a property, but an accidental possession'.[35] Preserving the conditions of international equilibrium was absolutely crucial for the Dutch if they wanted to retain their trade.

This perspective of shared interest inspired the alliance that came into being in the Anglo-Dutch treaties, not only of 1674 and 1678, but also in the 1667 Treaty of Breda.[36] Taken as a whole, these treaties, so the *Bon hollandais* argued, stipulated that both states had an interest in not hindering each other's trade, provided this did not affect the essential requirements of statehood. Thus the 1667 treaty dictated that in case of 'necessity', any further agreements, such as the 1674 articles on the principle of 'free ship, free goods' – which had been ambiguously defined anyway – became subordinate to the direct political needs of the state that found itself in a dire situation. Invoking Grotius time and again, and arguing that the 'right' of a state to act in a particular fashion was determined by calculations of 'justice' and 'utility' together, the *Bon hollandais* pointed out that the British only objected to the trade by the Dutch in naval stores with the French, while allowing all other forms of trade. Dutch insistence on their interpretation of the 1674 treaty as a neutral commercial nation was all the more remarkable, the *Bon hollandais* added, since really commerce should be defined not only as carrying goods from place to place for other states, but also selling these goods. If there were no speculating over price, carrying goods turned into 'commission' and was no longer properly trade or in tune with the essential nature of the trading republic, and stopped being politically neutral.[37] The best option under the present conditions was to give in to the British claims, which were reasonable enough, both to avoid the short-term risks of being involved in warfare and losing the commercial advantages of neutrality and to secure a long-term alliance with Britain in order to preserve the viability of the republic as a commercial entity in the modern world.

The *Bon hollandais* firmly rejected all suggestions that the American colonies were in the same position that the republic had found itself in when it declared itself independent from Spain. These were part of an ideological offensive that should have no place in politics. Politicians had neither the luxury nor the right to be tempted by rhetorical strategies that confounded national interest with the interest of humanity. Whatever ideas of free trade might be expressed and commercial promises for the Dutch be attached to them, in reality there would prove to be no foundation supporting these ideas. The truth was that the American states did not have any credit, did not have anything to offer the Dutch and if they were ever to become independent they would immediately turn into a dangerous competitor for the Dutch and a direct threat to international stability. As an independent entity, the United States would soon develop into a commercial state with land and all other kinds of natural resources, and would be interested not only in conquering Dutch trade, but also its colonial possessions, whereas the British in the present situation could not but allow the Dutch to retain whatever colonies and trade they had acquired. There were no complementary interests connecting the republic to America, whether in politics or in commerce. Appeals to historical precedent were misguided. In fact, 'our ancestors understood that England could guarantee our possessions in Europe and in the Indies and help us keep our trade'.[38]

To seek to replace that security by adhering to the promises of free trade by French and American propaganda was to flirt with disaster. Dutch merchants had a naïve perception of commercial gain. The decisive factors they did not recognize sufficiently were that the Americans were striving to establish themselves as a territorial commercial power, and rather than having anything to offer, posed a threat to the Dutch, while the French, unreliable debtors that had always abused Dutch territorial integrity, were led by a political aspiration not to maintain the balance of power, but to attain universal hegemony through the defeat of Britain.

The *Bon hollandais* first of all recommended the Dutch keep on investing capital in the British state debt.[39] This, I believe, may well have been a criticism of the efforts by van der Capellen and others in the later 1770s (before John Adams came on the scene) to raise a loan for the United States in the Dutch republic.[40] Moreover, the *Bon hollandais* made a strong plea for changing the administration of the Dutch colonies so as to transform them into an integrated part of a global, sectorially balanced, Dutch economic system. The aim here was to one day arrive at the stage that the 'cultivating commercial nations', that is, territorial commercial societies, had reached.[41] The model here was England, which had managed to reinvent its own vulnerable trade-based existence and turn itself into a great power. This, rather than hanging on to nostalgic feelings about the past of Dutch trade and mythical competitive advantages deriving from heroic frugality and virtue, was the only way to secure the Dutch state in the modern world.[42]

## Neutrality lost and the downfall of the republic

The debate between the Dutch Patriots led by van der Capellen and Orangists holding the views of Pinto and the anonymous *Bon hollandais* resembled in many ways the challenge that European states faced in the second half of the eighteenth century to reconceptualize their sovereignty and identity as a choice between competitive emulation among open cosmopolitan societies or peaceful coexistence among closed commercial societies. On the one hand, French publicists like Antoine-Marie Cerisier and Honoré Gabriel Riqueti Mirabeau, and the American agents C.W.F. Dumas and later John Adams, attempted to persuade the Dutch of the commercial benefits of free trade and support for the American cause by exploiting anti-English feelings. On the other hand, Orangist pamphleteers defended the long-term advantages of the old alliance with England and urged the republic to develop its colonial agriculture in much the same way as the English had done. But the main divide was not initially between these parties. In 1778, when van der Capellen and the Amsterdam mayors, led by van Berckel, took part in attempts to replace the privileged relationship with the English with new ties with the American colonies they embarked on a visionary project to simultaneously restore Dutch commercial greatness and the neutrality of trade that had been corrupted by political jealousy between Europe's dominant states.

Van der Capellen and the Amsterdam mayors ultimately aimed at separating trade from the balance of power by controlling the behaviour of dominant territorial states in maritime affairs. The course of action they followed was based first of all on using finance and the events of the American rebellion to withdraw Dutch funds from the English national debt and invest them in loans to the Americans. The problem they encountered was that American credit was deemed low by Amsterdam financiers and the interest rates that were paid by other nations were higher than the American Congress could afford. One solution they came up with was to replace interest payments with transferable land certificates in the former colonies. Van der Capellen also launched a campaign to convince moneylenders that the sincerely republican form of government of America made that state much more creditworthy than tyrannical England. He then advised Franklin to reciprocate by offering the Dutch advantages, commercial privileges and legal guarantees on payment of interest. At the same time, Dumas published an essay by Arthur Lee, who argued that American independence would be the vehicle for restoring international trade to its previous, ancient, free character. The main state standing to profit from this wholesale global changeover in the nature of foreign trade was the United Provinces. Hence America with its investment opportunities and the republic with its financial sector and interest in trade were natural allies.[43]

Exerting financial control over the balance of power was a key component in the long-term strategy that was being developed, a strategy which was not only extremely risky, but which was also created with a certain amount of self-awareness. It was an eighteenth-century commonplace that historically small free states like Venice and the Dutch republic, that were miserably situated in infertile marshes and lagoons, could create 'wealth without abundance' by transporting and exchanging goods produced by more fortunate territorial monarchies. Thus interstate systems of commercial functions arose. While it was also widely understood that trade had become heavily politicized and an object of power politics for territorial states, the plan devised in 1778 aimed at reclaiming the old commercial republican tradition, not by returning to a pre-modern interstate order, but by exploiting the greater jealousy of territorial states of each other's trade, as opposed to the comptoir trade carried on by politically insignificant republics. Along with a financial shift, the plan required that the position of the Dutch be shored up by treaty-based trading privileges. In 1778, William Lee, brother of Arthur Lee, negotiated a draft treaty with the Amsterdam mayors should American independence be recognized by the United Provinces. The main motive for the negotiations was that among Amsterdam merchants there was a fear that the commercial promises that the new Atlantic world held in store would turn into direct threats if the English were to accept American independence in exchange for exclusive trading privileges. The Americans would exploit this fear consistently until 1782. Significantly, the draft treaty, as it emerged from London after the capture of Laurens and his papers, included an article that provided for the return of New York to the United Provinces (and a number of similar rewards for other allies and formal neutrals), along with the guarantee of unlimited free trade.[44] But where the Amsterdam mayors would have hoped for a smooth transition from Anglo-Dutch to American–Dutch privileged ties their vision would soon look like a curiously opportunistic utopian scheme inspired by nostalgia for the old times of Dutch trade supremacy.

From 1779 on, the British envoy Yorke threatened ever more emphatically that his country would stop seeing the Dutch as a 'privileged' nation and that enduring abuses of neutral trade for alleged contraband would be a just reason for abandoning the 1674 treaty or even for declaring war.[45] At the same time, it became clearer that the Americans were not going to play the part the Dutch wanted them to play in the scheme invented by the Amsterdam mayors. In 1779, Cerisier might have cited the winner of the 1771 prize essay competition on the restoration of Dutch commerce, van den Heuvel, that 'one should never let an opportunity for obtaining any privilege escape',[46] but free trade with America was not a privilege at all.[47] Whereas, unlike other neutral states, the Dutch profited from the 1674 Anglo-Dutch Treaty, the Americans promised rights for free trade to all nations, thinking – as European contemporaries like the *Bon hollandais* feared and Americans anticipated – that they would emerge as the superior commercial state precisely through reciprocal free trade while claiming to be the friends of mankind.[48]

When the Dutch were invited by Catherine the Great to join the League of Armed Neutrality they encountered a similar problem. To join the League meant not just claiming for themselves in the face of England the right to free ships and free goods, but also extending that right to all other neutral states in the League, thereby losing an exclusive and very profitable, even if contested, advantage over, for example, Sweden and Denmark. The Amsterdam mayors in particular, attracted as they were to an anti-English alliance, still tried to extend the aims of the neutral alliance from protecting neutral trade at sea to a full-blown territorial defensive alliance before agreeing to join the League. When this was refused by the Russian empress and the Laurens papers with the Amsterdam scheme were found at the same time, Britain declared war and the Dutch were no longer neutral.

If at this point Adams expected to be able to raise a big loan, conclude a treaty of commerce and amity and have the Dutch recognize American independence, he was wrong. The Dutch did what Rijklof Michaël van

Goens recommended, following the example of De Witt's policy in the Second Anglo-Dutch War: not unnecessarily offend England even in time of war and hope that the previous alliance could be restored on its original conditions.[49] The pamphlet in which van Goens made his case itself was a response to a memorial by Adams in which he revealed himself as appointed by the American Congress to 'negotiate natural Alliances in Europe'. In this text Adams hijacked the former Governor Thomas Pownall's argument that America would offer infinite markets to Europe and offered unlimited free trade to the republic.[50] Yet, the suspicions of the value of this offer were too great for the Dutch to be persuaded. Adams himself blamed the Stadtholder William V and the new mayor of Amsterdam Rendorp, who sought to reconcile England and the republic – while Catherine the Great offered to mediate to save her League of Armed Neutrality. However, van der Capellen's judgement that the Dutch regents were too cowardly to commit themselves to America,[51] along with the fact that the greedy enthusiasm of Amsterdam merchants and financiers for the American cause was wearing off, was a more important factor in explaining the hesitations of the Dutch to side with France and America.

Adams wrote his *Memorial* to the Dutch after a conflict with Vergennes about an American default payment on a loan to the French, which affected American credit. Increasingly frustrated and desperate to make his mission succeed, and justly uncomfortable about the support lent to him by the French, Adams addressed the Dutch directly and in the process also gave away an insight into his strategy: 'It is hoped', he declared, that 'the example' of the Dutch 'be followed by all the Maritime Powers, especially those which are Parties to the late Marine Treaty'.[52] By offering free trade to all European states interested in competing with British commercial power, and the Dutch first of all, the Americans hoped to be recognized as an independent state, raise their credit and get cheaper loans, and by exploiting the polarization in the Old World on the issue of neutral trade create dramatic ruptures between Britain and other states. The Dutch were a major target, as were the states that had acceded to the League of Armed Neutrality.[53]

To stir up the Dutch against the English, people like Cerisier had argued that Dutch ownership of global trade had been 'stolen' by the English. The latter even ingeniously manipulated the investment of Dutch money into English funds to rob the Dutch.[54] So far, however, these arguments had lost in public opinion to the arguments of writers like the *Bon hollandais*, who rehearsed William Temple's classical warning that the 'abaissement' of England does not mean that their lost commerce will fall to the Dutch.[55] Privately, even Adams himself did not share the vision he was supposed to sell to the Dutch that they might be able to reconquer their trade through free trade with America. Instead, he envisaged America as a natural superpower, capable of overwhelming Europe. This was based on the idea that 'ours is the richest and most independent Country under Heaven'.[56]

Nevertheless, Adams' gamble paid off, not directly, but by preparing the ground for the famous full-blown resentful attack in the same year by van der Capellen on Stadtholder William V and the political culture that brought down van Berckel, blocked any alliance with France and America and refused to claim the rights and privileges of the Dutch in foreign trade. The publication of the *Address to the People of the Netherlands* engendered what one writer has described as 'a perfect revolution'.[57] The work itself contained no arguments that had not already emerged in debates since 1775, but its presentation and timing made it a bombshell. Suddenly, public opinion switched around and Adams found that negotiations on loans restarted, and after the provinces – Friesland, Holland and Westfriesland to begin with – proposed to the States General to recognize the American territories as a sovereign state, Adams was received by the Prince of Orange on 19 April, soon after which negotiations on a treaty commenced, a treaty which was signed by both parties in October.[58]

Thus, when the peace negotiations in Paris started soon after the treaty with the United States was ratified, the republic ended up in the worst possible position. The free ships–free goods principle, which Catherine the Great hoped would be an integral part of a general peace treaty, was denied by the British to all parties. The Dutch position was so hopeless and negotiations moved so slowly that their case could not even be included in the general peace of 1783. Once peace was restored in 1784 the Amsterdam capital market was plunged into a crisis that was not only in some part caused but also reinforced by the political tensions and stand-offs in the republic.

When in 1781 Cerisier chose to use in the logo of his journal *Le Politique Hollandais* the 1674 treaty as the symbol of the Dutch role in the heroic struggle for independence of the American states, he could not have made a more relevant choice.[59] The Dutch cherished the privilege they acquired in 1674 and saw themselves as the champions of free trade. Both were exploited as much as the Dutch themselves allowed by American agents and French publicists and served direct and more strategic commercial as well as political ends. The history of the Dutch republic in the War of American Independence provides a window as much on the struggle of the last commercial republic to reinvent itself and adapt itself to the modern world, as it does on the challenge that the American republic that would emerge would face in aligning itself with the commercial political rivalries of the Old World. With regard to Dutch history, I want to question the judgement by Schulte Nordholt that the British declared war on the Dutch because 'in the long run the Dutch became too unimportant to be treated with respect'.[60] Rather it is the case that in 1780 the neutrality of trade in war became too crucial an issue for the British to allow the Dutch to join the League of Armed Neutrality and thus aid in making the free ships–free goods principle become universal in international trade. We can only guess how necessary or how consequential the Fourth Anglo-Dutch War really was, but what deserves more serious attention is how late eighteenth-century thinkers envisaged the way that the reform of the law of neutrality might inaugurate a new global commercial-political order. Through exploring the Dutch case in the second half of the eighteenth century, we can develop a better understanding of why, for example, the highly influential Dutch international lawyer Cornelis van Vollenhoven, who was also the author of *De eendracht van het land*[61] and defender of Dutch colonialism and Grotian principles of international law, launched a massive attack on the law of neutrality in *The Three Stages in the Evolution of the Law of Nations*[62] at the end of the First World War.

## Notes

1. To Mme d'Épinay, 18 May 1776; see Ferdinando Galiani (1881) *Correspondance avec Mme d'Epinay, Mme Necker, Mme Geoffrin, &c. Diderot, Grimm, d'Alembert, De Sartine, d'Holbach, &c.*, 2 vols (Paris: Lucien Perey & Gaston Maugras), vol. 2, p. 462.
2. See Chapter 10 in this volume by James R. Sharp.
3. See Mark Somos, 'Armed Neutrality and Early American State Building: Alexander Hamilton's Political Economy', in Koen Stapelbroek (ed.), *Trade and War: The Neutrality of Commerce in the Inter-State System* (forthcoming). For the conditions under which Franco-American amity disintegrated see Allan Potofsky (2006) 'The Political Economy of the Debt Debate: The Ideological Uses of Atlantic Commerce, from 1787 to 1800', *William & Mary Quarterly*, LXIII, 3, 489–516 and Paul Cheney (2006) 'A False Dawn for Enlightenment Cosmopolitanism? Franco-American Trade during the American War of Independence', *William & Mary Quarterly*, LXIII, 3, 463–88. For a more diplomatic, historical approach to Jeffersonian neutrality that concentrates less on economic strategy, see James Sofka (2000) 'American Neutral Rights Reappraised: Identity or Interest in the Foreign Policy of the Early Republic?', *Review of International Studies*, XXVI, 4, 599–622; James Sofka (1997) 'The Jeffersonian Idea of Security: Commerce, the Atlantic Balance of Power, and the Barbary War 1786–1805', *Diplomatic History*, XXI, 4, 519–44.

4. See for example (out of many) the high-profile book by Russell Shorto (2004) *The Island at the Center of the World: The Epic Story of Dutch Manhattan and the Forgotten Colony that Shaped America* (New York: Thorndike Press).
5. See Wijnand W. Mijnhardt (2005) 'The Limits of Present-day Historiography of Republicanism', *De Achttiende Eeuw*, XXXVII, 1, 81–7.
6. Thus my approach in its focus on alternative visions of neutrality and trade politics differs from S.R.E. Klein (1995) *Patriots Republikanisme: Politieke Cultuur in Nederland (1766–1787)* (Amsterdam: Amsterdam University Press), J.W. Schulte Nordholt (1982 (original Dutch, 1979)) *The Dutch Republic and American Independence* (Chapel Hill: University of North Carolina Press), F.W. van Wijk (1921) *De Republiek en Amerika: 1776 tot 1782* (Leiden: E.J. Brill), Francis P. Renaut (1924) *La neutralité hollandaise durant la guerre d'Amérique (1775–1780)* (Paris: Graouli) and Friedrich Edler (1911) *The Dutch Republic and the American Revolution* (Baltimore: Johns Hopkins University Press).
7. For a short analysis and overview of this major theme in Dutch eighteenth-century historical writing, see my introductory essay in the forthcoming volume *Dutch Decline in Eighteenth-Century Europe*.
8. A.N.J. Fabius et al. (1913) *'t Herstelde Nederland: Zijn opleven en bloei na 1813* (Amsterdam: van Kampen).
9. H.T. Colenbrander (1897) *De Patriottentijd: Hoofdzakelijk naar Buitenlandsche Bescheiden* (The Hague: Martinus Nijhoff). The most recent major contribution to the historiography of this period is N.C.F. van Sas (2005) *De Metamorfose van Nederland* (Amsterdam: Amsterdam University Press). For more perspective see the earlier response to van Sas' leading ideas by E.H. Kossmann (1988) 'Nabeschouwing', in H. Bots and W.W. Mijnhardt (eds), *De Droom van de Revolutie* (Amsterdam: De Bataafsche Leeuw), pp. 141–2.
10. For just one of many historiographical overviews of earlier interpretations by Colenbrander, Geyl, Vijlbrief and De Wit see E.O.G. Haitsma Mulier (1983) 'De Geschiedschrijving over de Patriottentijd en de Bataafsche Tijd', in *Kantelend Geschiedbeeld* (Utrecht: Het Spectrum), pp. 206–27. See also E.H. Kossmann (1988) 'Nabeschouwing', in H. Bots and W.W. Mijnhardt (eds), *De Droom van de Revolutie* (Amsterdam: De Bataafsche Leeuw), pp. 135–43, and in the same volume A.E.M. Janssen 'Over Nederlandse patriotten en hun historie: Enige historiografische kanttekeningen', pp. 7–17. In English see Margaret C. Jacob and Wijnand W. Mijnhardt (1992) 'Introduction', in *The Dutch Republic in the Eighteenth Century: Decline, Enlightenment, and Revolution* (Ithaca, NY: Cornell University Press), pp. 1–15.
11. I. Leonard Leeb (1973) *The Ideological Origins of the Batavian Revolution* (The Hague: Martinus Nijhoff) for example tried to understand the period before 1785 in terms of the later patriotism. See Jonathan Israel (2007) *'Failed Enlightenment': Spinoza's Legacy and the Netherlands (1670–1800)* (Wassenaar: NIAS) for an attempt to break with this orthodoxy.
12. Writers like William Temple (1673), *Observations upon the United Provinces of the Netherlands* (London), pp. 75–120 spent many pages explaining the curious institutional and informal power structures of the republic to their audience.
13. A part of the Dutch army that had existed since the War of Dutch Independence for which soldiers used to be recruited with Stuart permission

in Scotland. The brigade was called to England to deal with the Jacobite uprisings of 1715 and 1745 (Edler, *Dutch Republic and American Revolution*, pp. 28–32).
14. Ibid., pp. 38–62.
15. Ibid., pp. 62–9.
16. Ibid., pp. 151–2.
17. Which Yorke called the 'infernal' treaty, 'one of the plagues of my life' (Schulte Nordholt, *Dutch Republic and American Independence*, p. 15).
18. The absence of these themes and the obsession with Colenbrander's legacy is what makes Chapters V–VII of J.S. Bartstra (1952) *Vlootherstel en Legeraugmentatie (1770–1780)* (Assen), otherwise a fine study of Dutch naval defence, such unsatisfactory reading.
19. Joan Derk van der Capellen tot den Pol, *Advis door Jonkheer Johan Derk van der Capellen tot den Pol over het verzoek van zyne Majesteit den Koning van Groot Brittannie raakende het leenen der Shotsche [sic] Brigade*, the transcription of his speech given at the meeting of the States of Overijssel 14–16 December 1775 (Knuttel 19069). Translated into French (1775, Knuttel 19070) and triggering responses *Brief van een vyand der kwaadspreekenheid aan zyn vriend te Rotterdam; aangaande het ... Advis, door jonkheer Johan Derk van der Capellen tot den Pol ... raakende het leenen der Schotsche brigade* (1775, Knuttel 19071), *Onpartydige en vrymoedige aanmerkingen, over het bekend advis van jr. J.D. van der Capellen tot den Pol* (1776, Knuttel 19127), *Hollandsche vrymoedige bedenkingen, over het ... Advis van jonkheer J.D. van der Capellen tot den Pol, briefsgewyze voorgesteld door een j.....r* (1776, Knuttel 19128) and *Vrye gedachten van een jong welmeenend patriot, over het berugte Advys van jonkheer Johan Derk van der Capellen tot den Pol* (1776, Knuttel 19128a). Knuttel refers to the pamphlet collection of the Royal Dutch Library in The Hague, which was catalogued by W.P.C. Knuttel. It needs to be added here that I have not had time to explore other Dutch archives, which is important since the Royal Dutch Library's collection is not as complete as is often supposed.
20. 'If his Majesty the King of Great Britain is offered the use of our troops? Then, the American shall not be lacking the same,' van der Capellen, *Advis*, p. 3. In a similar way, van der Capellen would be furious about the free transit that German soldiers ('slaves', because they were not defending their fatherland) were granted in 1777 through the Dutch Provinces, J.D. van der Capellen (1782, Knuttel 20137), *Address to the People of the Netherlands* (London), p. 113. Also van Wijk, *De Republiek en Amerika*, pp. 11, 32–3, 102, 139 on this issue, which formed the first platform for the younger Mirabeau to mingle in Dutch affairs (Schulte Nordholt, *Dutch Republic and American Independence*, p. 32).
21. Van der Capellen, *Advis*, p. 2.
22. Ibid., p. 3.
23. Ibid., p. 4.
24. Ibid., pp. 4–5.
25. Ibid., p. 5.
26. Ibid., p. 6.
27. Ibid., pp. 6–7.
28. Van der Capellen translated and published works by Price (1776 and 1777), Priestley (1783) and Fletcher (1774). For the influence of British civic

118  Koen Stapelbroek

humanists and dissenters in the Dutch republic, see Chapters 2 and 5 of Klein, *Patriots Republikanisme.*

29. See Ida Nijenhuis (1992) *Een Joodse Philosophe: Isaac de Pinto (1717–1787)* (Amsterdam: NEHA), pp. 13–14, 36–7 and Ida Nijenhuis (1987) 'Een vroeg manuscript over geldcirculatie van Isaac de Pinto', in Fred van Dam (ed.), *Benedictus homini homo: Liber amicorum voor Dr. J.Z. Baruch* (Amsterdam: n.p.). The wider context and principles of Pinto's manuscript merit more in-depth study.
30. Isaac de Pinto, *Lettre de mr. ***** a mr. S.B. ... au sujet des troubles qui agitent actuellement toute l'Amérique Septentrionale* (1776, Knuttel 19122), *Seconde lettre de M. de Pinto, à l'occasion des troubles des colonies, contenant des réflexions politiques sur ... l'etat actuel de l'Angleterre* (1776, Knuttel 19124) and a *Réponse de mr. J. de Pinto, aux observations d'un homme impartial, sur sa lettre à mr. S.B. ... au sujet des troubles qui agitent actuellement toute l'Amérique Septentrionale* (1776, Knuttel 19126). Pinto was criticized in *Observations d'un homme impartial sur la lettre de Mr. ***** à Mr. S. B. docteur en médécine* (1776, Knuttel 19123) and *Nouvelles observations, sur la seconde lettre de Mr. de Pinto, à l'occasion des troubles de l'Amérique Septentrionalle. Pour servir de suite aux Observations d'un homme impartial sur la premiére lettre de Mr.\*****  (1776, Knuttel 19125).
31. *Discours d'un bon Hollandois à ses compatriotes, sur différents objets intéressants* (1778, Knuttel 19189, Dutch translation 19190 and with criticisms added republished in 1779, Knuttel 19242). I will refer to the 1779 Dutch translation, i.e. Knuttel 19242, as *Welmeenend hollander.*
32. The pamphlet was attributed to Pinto in 1779 in three pamphlets criticizing the *Bon hollandais* (Knuttel 19243, 19245 and 19248). See also Nijenhuis, *Een Joodse Philosophe*, pp. 30, 43, who encountered – but doubts the truth of – the same attributions to Pinto, which she traced back to Dérival de Gomicourt (1779) *Lettres Hollandaises*, vol. 1, pp. 141, 267–8. See also (1779), vol. 3, p. 178.
33. *Second discours d'un Bon Hollandais à ses compatriotes* (1779, Knuttel 19246).
34. See from 1778, Knuttel 19191-2, in French and in Dutch, by Antoine Marie Cerisier. I will refer to *Onpartydige bedenkingen van een welmeenend Hollander* (19192). In 1779 more replies followed (Knuttel 19242-55), among which Cerisier's, *Suite des observations impartiales d'un vrai hollandais* (Knuttel 19247).
35. *Second discours*, p. 15.
36. *Welmeenend hollander*, p. 36.
37. *Second discours*, p. 18.
38. *Welmeenend hollander*, p. 55.
39. Ibid., pp. 69–71.
40. Edler, *Dutch Republic and American Revolution*, pp. 74–84.
41. *Second discours*, p. 9.
42. *Welmeenend hollander*, pp. 66–7.
43. See Edler, *Dutch Republic and American Revolution*, pp. 74–7.
44. See the *Notizie del Mondo* (1780) 23 October, p. 718. The Florentine journal gives very good insights on the course of events in the autumn of 1780.
45. Yorke to the States General on 21 March 1780, quoted by Edler, *Dutch Republic and American Revolution*, p. 134. Yorke's memorials in 1779 were of the same tone and revolved around the same issue.

46. Cerisier, *Suite des observations impartiales d'un vrai hollandais*, p. 10.
47. However, John Adams used the argument that was very effective in Amsterdam in particular that if the Dutch were not quick enough to recognize American independence they would be denied the right to free trade.
48. See the remark by John Adams below, made from the perspective that would rule the American debate about neutrality of the 1790s between federalists and Jeffersonians.
49. R.M. van Goens, *Consideratien op de memorie aan H.H. MM. Geadresseerd door John Adams* (1781, Knuttel 19508). Other pamphlets by van Goens arguing the same position are *L'Ésprit du Sistème politique de la Régence d'Amsterdam* (1781, Knuttel 19757), a response to a pamphlet by Hendrik Calkoen, and the allegorical satire *Zeeven Dorpen in Brand* (1781, Knuttel 19768–80). Van Goens contributed, between 1781 and 1783, to the Orangist journal *De Ouderwetse Nederlandsche Patriot* and wrote together with Isaac de Pinto an unpublished (and unstudied) work in 1783 on the same issues, the title of which, *Examen impartial des intérêts actuels de la République par rapport à une alliance*, is itself a direct response to the subtitle of the most important work in this entire debate, the *Address to the People of the Netherlands* (1782) (*Aan het Volk van Nederland* (1781)) by Baron van der Capellen tot den Pol, which called for an immediate alliance with France.
50. John Adams, *A Memorial to their High Mightinesses, the States General of the United Provinces of the Low-Countries* (1781, Knuttel 10506), p. 6.
51. See Schulte Nordholt, *Dutch Republic and American Independence*, p. 197.
52. Adams, *Memorial*, p. 11.
53. Curiously, America itself – a belligerent, not a neutral state – made an attempt to join the League of Armed Neutrality, perhaps indicating that the League was seen by the Americans primarily as a support instrument for the reform of maritime law, Edler, *Dutch Republic and American Revolution*, p. 167.
54. Cerisier, *Onpartydige bedenkingen*, pp. 6, 28, 39–41, 57–60.
55. *Second discours*, pp. 55–6. Cf. the implicit response by Cerisier, *Suite des observations*, p. 43.
56. Schulte Nordholt, *Dutch Republic and American Independence*, p. 142.
57. Edler, *Dutch Republic and American Revolution*, p. 229.
58. See ibid., pp. 214–32.
59. See van Wijk, *De Republiek en Amerika*, p. xxviii.
60. Schulte Nordholt, *Dutch Republic and American Independence*, p. 16.
61. C. van Vollenhoven (1913) *De eendracht van het land* (The Hague: Martinus Nijhoff).
62. C. van Vollenhoven (1919 (Dutch original, 1918)) *The Three Stages in the Evolution of the Law of Nations* (The Hague: Martinus Nijhoff).

# Part II
# Free Trade and Democratic Revolutions in Eighteenth-Century Europe and America

# 6
# Thomas Jefferson and French Economic Thought: A Mutual Exchange of Ideas

Manuela Albertone

## Democracy and agrarian ideology

Alexander Hamilton's *Report on Manufactures*, presented to the American Congress on 5 December 1791, is a clear witness to the dangers that supporters of the development of manufacturing industry in the United States at the time saw in the theories of the Physiocrats.[1] It is both an expression of the economic plans of the Federalists, opposed to Thomas Jefferson and the republican party's idea of an agrarian democracy, and a forceful attack on both the principles and the language used by the Physiocrats – their idea 'that agriculture is not only the most productive, but the only productive, species of industry', their notion of a 'net surplus' and their belief that the work of the 'classes of artificers' – the Physiocrats' *classes stériles* – did not actually produce wealth at all. If, in terms of economic theory, the secretary of the Treasury aimed at negating the principles of the French *économistes*, in political terms his attack was aimed directly at Thomas Jefferson, who had returned from France in 1789 after spending five years there, and whom George Washington had recently nominated secretary of state.

For the most part, Hamilton and Jefferson were at loggerheads with one another over issues of foreign policy and the economy. However, over and above the differences in their characters, their opposition to one another was, more generally, the opposition of two radically different kinds of political culture. During the time he had spent in France, Jefferson's republican principles had become firmer and firmer, as had his rejection of monarchy in all its forms, and he now used his experience as an observer of the situation in Europe to support attacks on the Federalists' own monarchical aims.[2] For Jefferson, there was a close connection between all the targets of his attacks on Hamilton and the

Federalists – their dislike of France, their adherence to the British model, their commercial and financial power, linked to Great Britain, their support for the banking system, and their belief in the central importance of paper currency and a strong executive.[3]

There are clear echoes here of the ideology of the *country party*, and indeed there can be little doubt that the *country* ideology, with its criticisms of the English financial system, helped inflame debate in the revolutionary period in America.[4] Jefferson's own dislike of *banking mania*, for example, is a constant of his thought,[5] undermining as he felt it did republican virtues. It is only too true that this mistrust was also fed by his ideas about economics which, however, were always used as an answer to immediate problems and never became a systematic philosophy as such.

It is, in fact, rather difficult to gain a clear picture of Jeffersonian thought, partly because of its complexity and partly because of the contradictions that coexisted within it between Jefferson's philanthropist outlook on the one hand and his support for slavery on the other, or between his political realism and the radical nature of his ideas, which, however, his political realism never suffocated. Jefferson was a quintessentially American figure, and oddly enough his experiences in Europe helped to make him even more so. While living in France in the period immediately preceding the Revolution, in fact, he assimilated European culture, observed the differences between the political situations in its countries and took in the ideas that were then circulating, including the way that America was coming to be seen as a radical ideal in Europe.

Scholars are thus still attempting to identify a central hub around which Jeffersonian thought revolves and a coherent link between his thought and his political actions. As of yet, however, there is no widespread consensus about how to interpret them or about the presence of a central philosophy in his intellectual and political development. Different historiographical approaches have given rise to a variety of ways of viewing Jefferson. He has been seen as a liberal influenced by the writings of Locke;[6] as a politician with an organic, community-based vision of society borrowed from the Scottish philosophers;[7] as a thinker in the tradition of civic humanism, in all its most recent interpretations or adaptations; or even as a representative of an individualism that was to manifest itself in the market economy of capitalism, which was emerging in this very period.[8] These various interpretations have highlighted different sides of Jefferson's personality, a personality whose contradictions can be traced back to the radicalism of the intellectual and the pragmatic efficiency of the administrator,[9] both present in a single figure. With his idealism on the one hand and his realism on the other, Jefferson has come to represent the way that the identity of America and the Americans defined itself in terms of its relationship to different traditions within European culture. From this has emerged an original, shared system of thought which was more than just a network of relations between Europe and America. Rather, it was a synthesis of the matching of concepts and notions, the result of like-minded thinkers sharing, analysing, rebutting and modifying their theories and beliefs in a complex interchange of ideas.

Jefferson, the author of the Declaration of Independence, a document in which he expressed no pretensions to original thought,[10] and the man who first coined the term 'Americanism',[11] was in many ways the product of the ideas that had been circulating freely in the cosmopolitan culture of the long, eventful eighteenth century; he was also a leading figure in the American Revolution and an eyewitness to the beginnings of French revolutionary activity; and throughout his life he remained a believer in the central importance of France and France's political and economic culture.

Jefferson's approach to economics, in fact, was the fruit of a current of thought ready to respond to the needs of the political and economic situation as they really were. This is as true of agrarianism as it is of a belief in free trade, the principle of commercial reciprocity, protectionism and the encouragement of local manufactures, as well as a wariness of banks and accumulated wealth and a dislike of the idea of public credit. At the same time, however, this current of thought was coherent in the way it had developed. It is at its most characteristic in the way it picks up on French economic thought and in particular the connection between economics and politics that is a part of it, from Physiocracy right through to the work of Jean-Baptiste Say.

The first and only real overview of Jeffersonian thought written by Jefferson himself is his *Notes on the State of Virginia*. This is the only work he published that was not written as a response to a particular political or social question. It is also, incidentally, the work that earned him his reputation as a writer. At its centre is the idea that economics and politics are connected with one another – an idea that runs throughout his life and writings. The *Notes* were written in 1780–81 as a reply to a number of questions posed by François de Marbois, secretary of the French delegation in Philadelphia, and became for Jefferson an opportunity to give his own interpretation of the state in which he lived. He did this in the form of a commentary on political economy, and in the work his preference for agriculture becomes clear, developing all the economic and political connotations of that belief.

The *Notes* are a detailed description of the largest agricultural and economically most important state in America – a true natural history of the region, as it was described at the time.[12] It places nature at the centre of its discussion of both economics and politics. Here nature becomes one with the very idea of America and the American spirit. It is nature as opposed to history, expressed stylistically in two distinct ways: first, it is the object of detailed scientific investigation; second, through the Romantic sensitivity of the description of the *Natural Bridge*, it gives voice to a sense of a national identity, in much the same way as St John de Crèvecoeur does in his *Letters from an American Farmer*.[13] Just as in the *Letters* penned by the Norman nobleman, in fact, centre stage is given to an ideology and sociology that are felt to be distinctly American:

> Those who labour in the earth are the chosen people of God, if ever he had a chosen people, whose breasts he has made his peculiar deposit for substantial and genuine virtue... While we have land to labour then, let us never wish to see our citizens occupied at a workbench, or twirling a distaff. Carpenters, masons, smiths, are wanting in husbandry: but, for the general operations of manufactures, let our work-shop remain in Europe.[14]

Over and above the Puritan Millenarian tone, Jefferson sees the nation essentially in terms of one particular social class – that of the farmers who till the soil, 'a people which preserve a republic in vigour'. In his plan for the growth of the American economy, the prime importance of agriculture was, as far as Jefferson was concerned, correlated to certain political principles that are in line with his modern republicanism. These principles are clearly laid out in the *Notes*: a refusal of coercive government, the untouchable principle of majority rule, the right to revise the constitution, the abolition of primogeniture, respect for the freedom of the press, the emancipation of slaves and the need for a system of public education.

'In so complicated a science as political economy, no one axiom can be laid down as wise and expedient for all times and circumstances, and for their contraries,'[15] Jefferson wrote to Benjamin Austin in 1816, when justifying his acceptance of the need to develop American manufacturing industry further, on the heels of the difficult economic situation that followed the 1812 war. Despite this, however, in the same letter Jefferson expressed his firm opinion that agriculture was still the most important branch of the economy.[16]

It has been made clear that the economic thought of Jefferson, whose pragmatism always expressed itself as the realistic approach of an intellectual called upon to fulfil a number of important political roles, changed direction a number of times. After his return from France, as has been seen, he believed in a policy of free trade, combined, however, with the notion of reciprocity. Once he became president, on the other hand, he accepted the idea that it was important to strike a balance between various areas of economic activity and aim at conciliation at a national level. Thus in 1805 Jefferson turned towards protectionism, a move influenced by the course of the Napoleonic wars.[17] Yet it is in any case true that, for Jefferson, agriculture remained a personal passion, and was always to be at the centre of his economic thought, a cornerstone of his politics, the foundation of his radicalism and an expression of his identity as an American.

Like George Logan and John Taylor, the other theorists of American agrarian democracy, Jefferson was an agronomist, as well as a landowner.[18] He scrupulously recorded all his experiments in his *Farm Book*; he was curious about new species of plants, annotating them as he discovered them in his *Garden Book*; and, like other Southern plantation owners, he was aware of how intensive farming could impoverish the soil, so he followed a plan of land improvement, used artificial fertilizers and the rotation system, encouraged the introduction of new types of crops and helped promote American agricultural societies.

This ideal of an agriculture which transformed and regenerated the land[19] set America up in opposition to a Europe full of cities.[20] During the time he spent in France and England, Jefferson was struck by the widespread poverty he saw there, which he felt was the result of both political and economic factors, such as the monarchy and the world of privileged wealth and the fact that commercial and manufacturing interests were considered to be more important than those of the agricultural community. America with its farmers, on the other hand, represented an alternative model of a dynamic economy and political stability, and for Jefferson this was always an essential part of his opposition to England.[21]

Jefferson's political battle in Virginia was based on the central importance, in both political and social terms, of land-ownership, of ways of avoiding the land falling into the hands of the few and ways of ensuring that all had access to it. Hence he secured the abolition of the laws of entail and primogeniture. He also ensured that the state award fifty acres of land to every voting adult who was not already a landowner. This move in itself was a reflection of his republican, anti-aristocratic beliefs. Influenced by the writings of Locke,[22] Jefferson believed that land-ownership was legitimized by a notion of ownership not perceived as a natural right,[23] a position which induced him, when confronted with the poverty he found in France, to make some extremely radical statements: 'I am conscious that an equal division of property is impracticable. But the consequences of this enormous inequality produce so much misery to the bulk of mankind, legislators cannot invent too many devices for subdividing property'.[24] Once he had returned to the United States, Jefferson would no longer take up such a clear position, partly because he no longer felt such a need to, given the ease with which the white man could gain access to land.[25] Despite this, however, his belief that land-ownership was 'the gift of social law' remained firm.[26]

Jefferson saw land as being of fundamental political importance not just because it encouraged social cohesion; he also felt it was of central importance from an economic point of view. If his agrarianism was most marked up to 1790, and if he moved from an economic policy based on self-sufficiency[27] to a programme of agricultural specialization[28] with the *First Message* he presented to Congress in 1801, this has nothing to do with the flexibility and pragmatism of a policy which was continually aimed at guaranteeing that the interests of agriculture came first. True, under the influence of the economic thought of Jean-Baptiste Say and the post-Physiocrats (rather than his reading of Adam Smith, whose work, even though he recognized its importance,[29] he felt rather distant from), Jefferson came round to the idea that it was necessary to strike a balance between the different areas of economic activity. Despite this, however, his plan to stimulate the growth of manufacturing industry, his adoption of certain protectionist measures and the principle of commercial reciprocity itself were always subordinate to, and a function of, the primacy of agricultural production: 'An equilibrium of agriculture, manufactures, and commerce', he wrote in 1809,

> is certainly become essential to our independence. Manufactures, sufficient for our own consumption, of what we raise the raw material (and no more). Commerce sufficient to carry the surplus produce of agriculture, beyond our own consumption, to a market for exchanging it for articles we cannot raise (and no more). These are the true limits of manufactures and commerce.[30]

### Jefferson and the way Physiocratic thought was received in America: an economic and political heritage

Jefferson did not see agriculture as being simply a political and economic factor. It was also at the heart of his theoretical thought, and led to

Jefferson's lifelong interest in the French economists. As we have seen, the author of the *Notes on the State of Virginia* repeatedly affirmed his belief in the prime importance of agriculture. When he arrived in Europe, then, Jefferson already had a firm belief in the value of agriculture. What is more, his political ideas had already matured.

Over the years, and after his experiences in France, his theoretical convictions became firmer and firmer. In 1792, in a circular to American consuls, he expressed his agrarianism thus: 'A prosperity built on the basis of agriculture is that which is most desirable to us, because to the efforts of labor it adds the efforts of a greater proportion of soil.'[31] In 1805, in a letter recounting his preparations for a new edition of his *Notes*, which never actually saw the light of day, he described the situation he found himself in when he declared his opposition to the development of American manufacturing industry in 1781: 'I had under my eye, when writing, the manufacturers of the great cities in the old countries.' This is further confirmation of Jefferson's belief in the supremacy of agriculture, a belief based on the principle that agricultural production was increased 'by the creative energies of the earth'.[32] In 1813 he came back to this idea once more, speaking of labour 'employed in agriculture, and aided by the spontaneous energies of the earth'.[33] In 1816, he wrote the now famous letter to Benjamin Austin, in which he explained the reasons that had led him to accept the inevitable growth of manufacturing industry. He described the principles that had guided him in his actions, recognizing the validity of their theoretical premises, even if the situation had now changed radically:

> to the labor of the husbandman a vast addition is made by the spontaneous energies of the earth on which it is employed: for one grain of wheat committed to the earth, she renders twenty, thirty, and even fifty fold, whereas to the labor of the manufacturer nothing is added.[34]

Jefferson's continual references to the notion of the land as a creator of wealth inevitably lead to the question of how important Physiocracy actually was for Jefferson's economic thought.[35] As we have seen, in his *Report on Manufactures*, Hamilton attacked the economic theory founded on the concept that it was agriculture, and agriculture alone, that was truly productive in economic terms. Jefferson and his followers responded through the writings of George Logan, an authentic American Physiocrat; and the stand taken by Logan in his writings was uncompromising.[36]

Jefferson himself did not feel he could take part in the debate openly, partly because of his characteristic prudence and partly because his position in the government did not allow him to do so. However, he supported Logan in his campaign against the secretary of the Treasury. Yet it is difficult not to admit that, over and above Jefferson's essential pragmatism, his standpoint on a number of fundamental theoretical issues was different from that of the French *économistes*. He differed from them on the foundation of land-ownership and the central importance, in both political and economic terms, of the small landowner. He also had different ideas about which landowners should be taxed, and how.[37]

Despite these differences, French economic thought was an ongoing point of reference. After his return to the United States, in fact, Jefferson's contacts with the *Idéologues* and the post-Physiocratic writers became even more intense. Nevertheless, for him Physiocracy remained the starting point for the science of political economy, and through his reading of the French economists he became aware not only that it was part of an ongoing French intellectual tradition, but also that it was a specifically French mode of thought.[38]

In 1816 Jefferson penned a brief excursus on the history of political economy which was heavily influenced by his contacts with Du Pont de Nemours. In this piece, written as a foreword to the *Treatise on Political Economy* – the American translation of Destutt de Tracy's *Traité de la volonté* – Jefferson placed the science of political economy within a theoretical framework defined by the concepts of Phyisocracy. Notwithstanding the critical debates that took place in this period, which essentially led to the Quesnay school of thought[39] becoming less and less important, and which Jefferson followed with great attention, his principal aim was always that of favouring the spread of the ideas of the French school of political economy as opposed to that of the English writers:

> Political Economy, in modern times, assumed the form of a regular science, first in the hands of the political sect in France, called the Economists. They made it a branch only of a comprehensive system, on the natural order of Societies. Quesnia [*sic*] first, Gournay, Le Trosne, Turgot, and Dupont de Nemours, the enlightened, philanthropic, and venerable citizen now of the United States, led the way in these developments, and gave to our enquiries the direction they have since observed.[40]

When Jefferson arrived in France in August 1784, he quickly became a part of revolutionary circles, taking part in the debate that would eventually lead to revolution itself. This was thanks in part to his contacts with the *Américanistes*, who looked to America as a model for their own plans for reform, a group where the political rationalism of the Physiocratic tradition survived in Condorcet, Du Pont de Nemours and La Rochefoucauld. It was also thanks to his friendship with Franklin, who preceded him as the American ambassador to France and who played an important role in keeping alive an interest in Physiocracy in the group that was later to become the *Idéologues*.[41]

Jefferson's time in Paris was an intensely stimulating period for him, a period in which he acquired ideas. As political events accelerated, he elaborated his theories, and this led not only to a confirmation of his rejection of the English political model, but also increased his detachment from British culture, through his original reading of French political rationalism and its revolutionary implications. The positions he takes up and the judgements he makes begin to change and become more concrete from the Paris years on. What emerges is a more mature awareness of what it means to be American and the contribution made to the concept of an American identity by French thought.[42]

The thinkers Jefferson came into contact with most frequently in Paris were Lafayette, La Rochefoucauld and Condorcet.[43] He was particularly close to Condorcet – they were linked by common beliefs in democracy and the perfectibility of man.[44] Throughout his life, Jefferson had a deep admiration for his *philosophe* friend, and while in Paris he also became instrumental in making Condorcet's writings known, sending them to his American correspondents.[45] Condorcet's ideas about ownership led him to develop the idea of representative democracy, in the same way that Jefferson's reflections on ownership had led him to do the same, and this was reinforced by the belief that good government would speed up the spread of land-ownership.[46]

A follower of the rationalist tradition, one of whose essential points of reference was Physiocracy and the connection between economics and politics that was a part of it, Condorcet was one of the best-informed and most assiduous collectors of information regarding the situation on the ground in America,[47] and it was precisely in the period 1786–88, the years in which Jefferson was in France, that Condorcet expounded his constitutional theory in the form of a discussion about the nature of the new state. With his *De l'influence de la Révolution d'Amérique sur l'Europe*, Condorcet launched one of his most severe critiques of the English model, 'that Machiavellian system', as he called it, to which he opposed the originality and potential of the United States,[48] laying down the foundations of his ideas: Physiocratic economic theory, republicanism, his critique of the balance of powers, the principles of the freedom of the press and of religion, the principle of equality and the universal importance of the rights of man. With his *Lettres d'un bourgeois de New-Heaven à un citoyen de Virginie*, on the other hand, he produced the first formulation from a French thinker of the idea of representative democracy.[49]

In his *Essai sur la constitution et les fonctions des Assemblées provinciales*, penned in 1788, Condorcet came out against summoning the Estates General and opposed the idea of forming a National Assembly, according to the line laid down in the *Mémoire sur les municipalités*, which Du Pont de Nemours had written in 1775 for Turgot.[50] Thus, on the eve of the French Revolution, Jefferson was in a position to witness at first hand the development of a writer as he moved towards the democratic ideal, a writer who had understood the political implications of the Physiocrats' economic theory. Condorcet, then, had firm Physiocratic convictions, such as the idea that wealth produced by the land was the foundation of national unity. These beliefs were made manifest in a detailed system of decentralized representative assemblies, and were directly linked to discussions about the creation of Provincial Assemblies which only landowners would be allowed to attend. These were one of the most representative expressions of the Physiocratic plans for reform,[51] whose evolution led Condorcet to the elaboration of a detailed plan for participatory democracy.[52]

Jefferson was a supporter of the rights of the individual American states, and hence appreciated French projects for decentralized political participation, sharing their attacks on the *parlements* and the corporative interests of the society of orders: 'This nation is risen from the dust,' he wrote in August 1788, 'They have obtained, as you know, provincial assemblies in which there will be a more perfect representation than in our states assemblies.'[53] The beginnings of revolution in France thus made clear to Jefferson a constitutional model which was directly opposed to the British one, based on the balance of power and checks and balances.[54]

In Condorcet's rationalist political approach, as among the groups where the approach of the Physiocrats to the relationship between politics and economic science was particularly strong, the unity of national interest was seen as being an expression of natural laws, which governed politics. This was in clear opposition to the English model based on history and tradition lauded by Montesquieu. This was the context in which an important change came about in Jefferson's thought.

Montesquieu appears as early as 1774 in Jefferson's writings. In his *Commonplace Book*, where he made notes on the authors and the works he was reading, Montesquieu is the writer Jefferson writes about most. He had already approached Montesquieu's work in the preceding decade, coming to him through Blackstone, Voltaire and Beccaria.[55] His first real criticism of the *Esprit des lois* appears in 1790,[56] and from that point on Jefferson's criticisms of Montesquieu recur repeatedly. He became, in fact, the main – almost the only – critic of an author whose work had become a classic of American political thought.[57] Jefferson's rejection of Montesquieu's anglophilia was due in part to his critical attitude towards the balance of power as envisaged by the English model and the political relativism theorized by Montesquieu, which the Physiocrats developed strong theoretical arguments against, sustaining the idea of the unity of the law.[58] In 1809, three months after Jefferson's second presidential term had come to an end, he set about attempting to publish Destutt de Tracy's *Commentaire sur Montesquieu*. Like de Tracy, he rejected Montesquieu's relativism and the stress Montesquieu laid on history and tradition, and he does so in the same terms as Condorcet. This can be seen by comparing Condorcet's refutation of these ideas in the first published edition of the *Observations sur le vingt-neuvième livre de l'Esprit des lois*.[59]

Hence Jefferson distanced himself from Montesquieu when he came into contact with Parisian thinkers – and this at a time when, in the United States, the author of the *Esprit des lois* had already become a reference point for those political groups that were inspired by the English political model. From this point on, Jefferson would see Montesquieu as emblematic of the exaltation of Great Britain, in opposition to the American model.[60]

### 'The earth belongs to the living'

Jefferson derived from this radical idea of a break with the past and the refusal of tradition and history as political reference points one of the cornerstones of his thought, which he gave clearest shape to during the years he spent in Paris – namely, the theoretical legitimization of the principle of constitutional revision. He used as his starting point the idea that 'the earth belongs in usufruct to the living', as he says in the letter he sent to James Madison on 6 September 1789.[61]

During the first revolutionary debates concerning the public debt inherited from the *ancien régime*, Jefferson took up the position that the debt should be redeemed, on the basis of his belief that one generation was not authorized to pass on its debts to the succeeding one. In line with this idea, he also believed that a constitution could not be legitimized for more than one generation – which he calculated as lasting nineteen years, in line with Buffon's calculations:

> The question Whether one generation of men has a right to bind another, seems never to have started either on this or our side of the water. Yet it is a question of such consequences as not only to merit decision, but place also, among the fundamental principles of every government. The course of reflection in which we are immersed here on the elementary principles of society has presented this question to my mind.[62]

There are a number of hypotheses about the birth of this, a principle which is at the basis of modern political thought, and which emerged in the course of the democratic revolutions of the eighteenth century.[63] Jefferson's realization of how innovative this concept was, and his awareness of the way the revolutionary period in France was stimulating intellectual debate about the principles upon which society is founded, clearly indicate that Jefferson developed this idea within the context of revolutionary Paris. It was an idea which was to become a vital point of reference for all Jefferson's thought.

The idea of detachment from tradition in the name of future generations was already at the heart of Jefferson's proposals for the abolition of the laws of primogeniture and entail, an act through which Jefferson intended to change the social structure of the state of Virginia, originally modelled on that of England. Yet his revolutionary standpoint on this question was clearly formulated in theoretical terms for the first time only when Jefferson came into direct contact with the thinkers he met while in Paris, and in particular with two thinkers who were close to the Physiocrats: Condorcet and Richard Gem.

Jefferson elaborated his idea in the first week of September 1789, during which he was laid up due to a slight illness. He was probably encouraged in this by his personal physician, Richard Gem, 'a very sensible man, a pure theorist, of the sect called the economists, of which Turgot was considered as the head', as Jefferson described him.[64] Gem gave him a written description of a scheme he had devised to deal with the problem of the public debt. It contained, couched in more or less the same terms, the idea Jefferson himself had outlined to Madison in his letter.[65] Gem himself drew up a declaration of rights, inspired by Physiocratic ideas, which reserved the right to vote for *propriétaires du territoire*, sanctioned 'the absolute freedom of industry and commerce' and fixed *l'impôt territorial unique*.[66]

Jefferson's letter followed the same lines as Gem's ideas: 'I set out on this ground, which I suppose to be self-evident', he wrote, much in the language of Locke:

> that the earth belongs in usufruct to the living: that the dead have neither powers nor rights over it. The portion occupied by any individual ceases to be his when himself ceases to be, and reverts to society.[67]

In line with the idea that property is not a natural right, Jefferson believed that the public debt the state contracts should not last for more than one generation.[68] More than one of his arguments led him to a position close to that of the Physiocrats: the central importance of land, a distaste for public debt, the idea that this implied an aggressive foreign policy and a rejection of the English political model. What is more, Jefferson here clearly picks up once more on the distinction between natural law and civil law, an idea dealt with by Condorcet in 1786 in his *Vie de Turgot*, in order to delegitimize any action that might attribute to land-ownership an eternal, inalienable right.[69]

In accordance with the idea that the earth belongs to the living, Jefferson, in the same letter to Madison, claimed that the constitution of a state could not, on principle, be held to be legitimate for a period longer than that of a single generation:

> On similar ground it may be proved that no society can make a perpetual constitution, or even a perpetual law. The earth belongs always to the living generation... Every constitution then, and every law, naturally expires at the end of 19 years. If it be enforced longer, it is an act of force, and not of right.[70]

So it was that, during his stay in Paris, Jefferson gave shape to the principles of the rights of each generation and the right of a people to revise the constitution by which it was governed.[71] In the same period, and more precisely on 30 August 1789, Condorcet, too, had stressed the need for regular conventions for the revision of the constitution.[72] In his *Lettre à M. le comte de Montmorency*, in fact, Condorcet picks up on this idea once more, an idea he had already outlined in his essay on the provincial assemblies, in which he recognized the intellectual debt he had towards American constitutional models.[73]

Thus, in the course of this to and fro of intellectual theories and opinions – and it was a process which went far beyond individual thinkers simply being influenced by one another – an original idea began

136 *Manuela Albertone*

to take shape, and it was the fruit of the coming together of political rationalism on the one hand and the democratic ideology on the other.[74] The principle that 'the earth belongs to the living' remained at the very heart of Jefferson's political thought[75] and, along with Thomas Paine's *Rights of Man*, became a fundamental building block of the ideologies of the democratic revolutions.[76] When he returned to the United States, Jefferson turned this idea into an instrument in the fight for republican agrarianism. In the ten-year battle between Federalists and Republicans that was to follow, the theoretical foundations Jefferson had acquired for his standpoint, which had taken shape in the period he spent in France, while that country was crossing over from the *ancien régime* into the Revolution, became a determining factor. He realized that political economy was the instrument he could use to reinforce the republican idea that politics, economics and society were all connected with one another; and he also realized that the Physiocratic approach provided this viewpoint with a model for growth founded on agriculture and on the conception of economics as a science, a science whose foundations, as Jefferson himself always recognized, had been laid down by the French economists. In Paris, Jefferson frequented circles where the Physiocratic tradition and the economic foundations of the right to representation that went with that tradition, as made clear from Du Pont de Nemours to Condorcet, survived within the context of a political rationalism which, through contact with the experiences of the American Revolution, had identified the principles of representative democracy. Only after his return did Jefferson entrust George Logan with the task of attacking the Federalists' economic plans, and Logan did so by basing himself on the principles of the Physiocrats.

Jefferson himself placed the central importance of the land, and its connection with the rights of the individual, at the very heart of a radical ideology which even went so far as to recognize the right of each generation to rewrite the constitution that governed it. Thus Jefferson comes to symbolize a synthesis of political pragmatism and political rationalism, a synthesis which had come about and matured in the period he had spent in France.

## Jefferson and Du Pont de Nemours: a mutual exchange of ideas

Du Pont de Nemours constantly played the role of intermediary between Jefferson and French intellectual circles after the latter's return to the

United States. Right up to Du Pont's death in 1817, he represented for Jefferson a living link with Physiocracy. This was especially the case after Du Pont de Nemours decided to move to America after the coup d'état of 18 Fructidor V.[77] During his first stay, Du Pont and Jefferson continually exchanged letters, and their correspondence demonstrates just how close their thinking was to each other's. Du Pont expresses all his distrust of Alexander Hamilton and of Hamilton's economic policies, while Jefferson shares Du Pont's distrust of Bonaparte.[78]

These are the years in which Jefferson's relations with the *Idéologues* became even more intense, years in which he followed post-Physiocratic French economic thought closely. Jean-Baptiste Say sent him a copy of his *Traité d'économie politique* at the beginning of 1804,[79] just as Jefferson was in the process of reading the second edition of Malthus' *Essay on the Principle of Population*, and Malthus' work became for him a new opportunity to ponder over Physiocracy. It was in the 1803 edition, in fact, that Malthus mentioned Du Pont de Nemours and his arguments in favour of keeping the price of grain high.[80] It would be perfectly acceptable to suppose that Jefferson was confirmed in his reading of Malthus by Du Pont himself; it needs to be remembered that Du Pont published his *Examen du livre de M. Malthus* after his return to the United States. Jefferson also shared Du Pont's opinion that Malthus was superior to Smith in terms of the level of his theoretical thought.[81]

Du Pont's final stay in France lasted from 1802 to 1815, during which time Jefferson informed him of the American government's decision to encourage the growth of manufacturing industry as a result of the Continental Blockade. Jefferson also encouraged Du Pont to write a treatise on finance, which Du Pont sent him on 14 September 1810.[82] Du Pont's aim in this treatise was to convince the Americans to abandon the customs system, avoid using indirect taxation and base their fiscal system on a land tax, the Physiocratic *impôt térritorial*. Thus the treatise was faithful to the Physiocratic point of view. A land tax, Du Pont felt, was the only way of ensuring a flow of capital for the newly born American manufacturing industry and protecting 'the middle class, that virtuous, honest, hard-working, liberal class'.[83] These pages were clearly written by a Du Pont who had read his Say, a Du Pont who knows about the situation in America but who remains essentially a Physiocrat. What is more, Du Pont clearly perceived the special way in which French economic thought had been received in America and was aware of an opportunity to gather information about American ideas on economics, including the ideas that were emerging from the unique nature of the situation in the United States.[84]

Jefferson was impressed by Du Pont's work and the logic of the Physiocratic thought that lay behind it,[85] and immediately set about arranging for it to be translated.[86] However, with the realism that was typical of him, Jefferson defended the American government's economic policy and did not share Du Pont's belief that the country's finances needed to be reorganized in relation to the growth of manufacturing industry there.

The debate between Jefferson and Du Pont lasted for the whole of 1812, and became more intense when Du Pont set about reading Destutt de Tracy's *Review of Montesquieu*, which he believed had been written by Jefferson.[87] This work had in fact been published anonymously, and some even believed that it had been penned by one of Du Pont's circle; but Du Pont himself had no doubts about the matter:

> you have inserted a brief dedication, as if the book were being offered to the United States by a Frenchman... But there is no Frenchman in America, nor in France, who could have sustained an argument so difficult with such severe logic and in such surprising depth.[88]

The version of economic science which Du Pont expounds in his letters is that of the Physiocrats: 'it is in this that the whole *Théorie de l'Impôt* consists'.[89] Yet it has been enriched by a reading of contemporary writers. Du Pont does not as yet have any clear notion of the concept of capital, but he does speak of *travail utile*, of *salaire des ouvriers*, of *profit*, and of *services* offered to the *entrepreneurs de culture*. He links Malthus to the Physiocrats using the same arguments he will later adopt in his *Examen*,[90] in order to support his idea of the superiority of agriculture. He also talks in detail in particular about Book XI of the *Review*, concerning liberty and the constitution – which Jefferson himself had translated – outlining his own political position and the distance between his own liberalism and Jefferson's democracy.[91] In any case, Du Pont was so impressed by the work that he decided to translate it.[92]

The correspondence between Jefferson and Du Pont and Du Pont's mistaken belief that it had been Jefferson himself who had written the work give us a precious insight into the long-lasting presence of Physiocracy and the way it related to economic science at the beginning of the nineteenth century. At the same time, it also allows us to define clearly, through the close relationship between Jefferson and the *Idéologues*' circles, the way in which French economic thought was received in America.

In the same period, and especially after his return to America, Du Pont acted as intermediary between Jefferson and Tracy, who wanted to see his *Commentaire* published.[93] Du Pont, Say and Tracy together embody a welter of economic theories that were in opposition to the ideas of Hamilton and which could be employed at a time in which the United States was suffering from the depreciation of its paper currency and the nation itself was divided by fierce debate over the banks and public credit.

In 1813 Jefferson encouraged the editor Duane to publish translations of both Say's work and Tracy's.[94] Jefferson had by now become convinced of the inevitable need to stimulate American manufacturing industry, even if he still believed in the primacy of agriculture.[95] He had become convinced of the need to create a balance between different sectors of the economy and of the need to encourage the growth of manufacturing, not only because the situation abroad required it, but also because of his reading and his contacts with the French economists. He communicated his beliefs to Du Pont.[96]

In May 1815 Du Pont returned to the United States and immediately made contact with Jefferson once more. In January 1816 he sent President James Madison his *Sur l'agriculture et les manufactures aux États-Unis*, in which he put forward his thoughts on the American economy, explaining why he felt it was necessary for the United States to foster the growth of its native manufacturing industry. The text is the fruit of the rich intellectual debates of the time, and in it can be seen the political science of the period filtered through the thought of Jefferson and the surviving influence of the Physiocrats at the beginning of the nineteenth century. Du Pont's arguments have lost the dogmatic tones of the language of the Physiocrats, and his point of view is essentially the one he shared with Jefferson. Du Pont, too, states his belief that there is a need to balance the various sectors of the economy and increase the output of manufacturing industry in function with agriculture. 'Agriculture is a manufacturing industry like all the others; however, it is even more important as it supplies all other branches of manufacturing industry with their means to survive and their raw materials,'[97] he writes. To bolster his argument that the United States should create a system of manufacturing industry that will reinforce agriculture, Du Pont states a number of principles that demonstrate how his view of economic science has been brought up to date: he speaks of *débouchés*, of *services*, and makes the distinction between producer and consumer, between the salary of the worker and the capital of the entrepreneur, even if he is at this point dealing with 'agriculture, which is the starting point for everything and towards which everything returns'.[98] This text also contains, repeated almost word for word, the criticisms to be found in the *Examen du livre de M. Malthus* concerning the excessive importance that England was giving to manufacturing industry.[99] In the same fashion,

Du Pont's work reflects the way Jefferson had expressed his admiration for certain aspects of Malthus' work. Jefferson, in fact, shared Du Pont's opinion that the situation in America was exceptional, and gave the lie to Malthus' theory, an idea that Du Pont was to develop in his *Examen*, published a year later.

The link between different sectors of the economy and the need to foster the growth of manufacturing industry had been confirmed, as far as Du Pont was concerned, by the special nature of the situation in America. In his *Observations sommaires sur l'utilité des encouragemens à donner aux manufactures américaines*, which he sent to Jefferson on 31 March 1816, Du Pont developed an analysis of the value of manufactured products which, among other things, had the aim of showing how every type of expenditure ultimately profited agriculture, and this, in his opinion, made dangerous a policy which encouraged industry to the detriment of other types of economic activity, and especially agriculture.[100] So after his return to the United States, Du Pont changed his position slightly, and in this he was influenced partly by his discussions with Jefferson.

During these same months, however, both Jefferson and Du Pont made it clear that their political points of view were different from one another, and this illustrates a certain distance between the democratic spirit of the ex-President and the liberal outlook of the old Physiocrat. This difference of opinion came out into the open when the fledgling South American republics asked Du Pont for his opinion of their plans for a new constitution. For Du Pont, to restrict the participation in the political process to landowners derived directly from the Physiocratic 'principle of evidence'.[101] Jefferson's position, on the other hand, was different. His definition of a republic was essentially one and the same as the concept of representative democracy, and this showed how he was at variance with the ideas of Du Pont:

> We both of us act and think from the same motive. We both consider the people as our children, and love them with parental affection. But you love them as infants whom you are afraid to trust without nurses, and I as adults, whom I freely leave to self government.[102]

Jefferson shared the non-dogmatic spirit of post-Physiocratic French economic thought and its clarity when compared to Smith, even if for him Physiocracy remained a point of reference, partly because of his friendship with Du Pont de Nemours. The exchange of ideas between France and the United States, then, was mutual. Through his ideas on economic science Jefferson helped to re-establish the unity of the French tradition; and the ideas of the ageing Du Pont, the critic of Say who was, however, sensitive to the way his American friend spurred his thought, are a clear witness to this.

## Notes

1. A. Hamilton (1885–86) 'Report on Manufactures', in H. Cabot Lodge (ed.), *The Works* (New York and London: G.P. Putnam), vol. 3, pp. 294–300.
2. Th. Jefferson to G. Washington, Paris, 2 May 1788, in Th. Jefferson (1950–) *The Papers*, ed. J.P. Boyd (Princeton: Princeton University Press), vol. 12, p. 128.
3. Jefferson to Washington, Monticello, 9 September 1792, in Jefferson, *The Papers*, vol. 24, p. 355. Cf. D.R. McCoy (1980) *The Elusive Republic: Political Economy in Jeffersonian America* (Chapel Hill: University of North Carolina Press); C.D. Matson and P.S. Onouf (1990) *A Union of Interests: Political and Economic Thought in Revolutionary America* (Lawrence: University Press of Kansas).
4. Cf. J.G.A. Pocock (1975) *The Machiavellian Moment: Florentine Political Thought and the Atlantic Republican Tradition* (Princeton: Princeton University Press); McCoy, *The Elusive Republic*.
5. Jefferson to A. Stuart, Paris, 25 January 1786, in Jefferson, *The Papers*, vol. 9, p. 218.
6. Cf. J. Dunn (1985) *Rethinking Modern Political Theory: Essays, 1979–83* (Cambridge: Cambridge University Press).
7. M. White (1978) *The Philosophy of the American Revolution* (Oxford: Oxford University Press); G. Wills (1978) *Inventing America: Jefferson's Declaration of Independence* (Garden City and New York: Doubleday).
8. J. Appleby (1984) *Capitalism and a New Social Order: The Republican Vision of the 1790s* (New York: New York University Press); I. Kramnick (1982) 'Republican Revisionism Revisited', *William & Mary Quarterly*, LXXXVII, 629–54.
9. Cf. B. Bailyn (2003) *To Begin the World Anew: The Genius and Ambiguities of the American Founders* (New York: Alfred A. Knopff), pp. 37–59.
10. Jefferson to H. Lee, Monticello, 8 May 1825, in Thomas Jefferson (1984) *The Writings*, ed. M.D. Peterson (New York: Library of America), p. 1501.
11. In opposition to 'Anglomany'; the expression is to be found in the letter to C.F. De Volney, Washington, 8 February 1805, in Thomas Jefferson (1903) *The Writings*, ed. A. Lipscomb and A. Bergh (Washington: Thomas Jefferson Memorial Association), vol. 11, p. 68.
12. Cf. Thomson to Jefferson, 6 March 1785, in Jefferson *The Papers*, vol. 8, p. 16.
13. Cf. M. Albertone (2006) 'The French Moment of the American National Identity: St John de Crèvecoeur's Agrarian Myth', *History of European Ideas*, XXXII, 28–57.
14. Th. Jefferson (1954) *Notes on the State of Virginia*, ed. E. Peden (New York: Norton), pp. 164–5.
15. Jefferson to B. Austin, 9 January 1816, in Jefferson, *The Writings*, ed. D. Peterson, p. 1372.

16. Ibid., p. 1370.
17. Cf. W. Grampp (1946) 'A Re-examination of Jeffersonian Economics', *Southern Economic Journal*, XII, 263–82; R. Ellis (1973) 'The Political Economy of Thomas Jefferson', in L. Weymouth (ed.), *Thomas Jefferson: The Man, His World, His Influence* (London: Weidenfeld and Nicolson), pp. 81–95.
18. A.C. Miller (1942) 'Jefferson as an Agriculturist', *Agricultural History*, XVI, 65–78; *Thomas Jefferson's Farm Book* (1953), ed. E. Morris Betts (Philadelphia: American Philosophical Society).
19. Cf. also L. Marx (1964) *The Machine in the Garden: Technology and the Pastoral Ideal in America* (New York: Oxford University Press).
20. Jefferson to James Madison, Paris, 20 December 1787, in Jefferson, *The Papers*, vol. 12, p. 442. The same strong image was to remain with him until his final years. Cf. Jefferson to William Johnson, Monticello, 12 June 1823, in *The Writings*, ed. Lipscomb and Bergh, vol. 15, p. 442.
21. Jefferson to Horatio G. Spafford, 17 March 1814, in *The Writings*, ed. Lipscomb and Bergh, vol. 14, p. 120.
22. 'The earth is given as a common stock for man to labour and live on' (ibid.). Cf. J. Locke (1960) *Two Treatises of Government*, ed. P. Laslett (Cambridge: Cambridge University Press), Book II, Ch. 5, § 27, 31, 48–9, 186, 188, 201.
23. Cf. F. McDonald (1985) *Novus ordo seclorum: The Intellectual Origins of the Constitution* (Lawrence: University Press of Kansas).
24. Jefferson to James Madison, Fontainebleau, 28 October 1785, in Jefferson, *The Papers*, vol. 8, p. 682.
25. Cf. S.N. Katz (1976) 'Thomas Jefferson and the Right to Property in Revolutionary America', *Journal of Law and Economics*, XIX, 481.
26. Jefferson to Isaac McPherson, Monticello, 13 August 1813, in Jefferson, *Writings*, ed. Peterson, p. 1291.
27. Cf. Grampp, *A Re-Examination of Jeffersonian Economics*.
28. Jefferson's first clear declaration in favour of commercialized agriculture appears in a letter dated 4 May 1787, one month after the publication of *De la France et des États-Unis*, written by Brissot and Clavière to encourage trade between the two countries. Jefferson expressed his appreciation of this work (Jefferson to Brissot, Paris, 16 August 1786, in Jefferson, *The Papers*, vol. 10, p. 262).
29. Cf. M. Albertone (2008) 'Un cas de circulation des idées économiques: Th. Jefferson, P.-S. Du Pont de Nemours, J.B. Say, A.L.Cl. Destutt de Tracy. Continuité et discontinuité de la pensée économique française et de sa réception aux États-Unis', in A. Tiran (ed.), *Jean-Baptiste Say: Postérité et Influences* (Paris: Economica Classiques Garnier).
30. Jefferson to James Jay, Monticello, 7 April 1809, Jefferson, *The Writings*, ed. Lipscomb and Bergh, vol. 12, p. 271.
31. Jefferson, 'Circular to Consuls and Vice-Consuls', 3 May 1792, in Jefferson, *The Papers*, vol. 23, p. 618.
32. Jefferson to Mr Lithson, Washington, 4 January 1805, in Jefferson, *The Writings*, ed. Lipscomb and Bergh, vol. 11, p. 56.
33. Jefferson to John Melish, Monticello, 13 January 1813, in Jefferson, *The Writings*, ed. Peterson, p. 1268.
34. Jefferson to Benjamin Austin, 9 January 1816, in ibid., p. 1370.
35. Cf. V. Parrington (1927) *Main Currents in American Thought* (New York: Harcourt, Brace).

36. Cf. M. Albertone (1995) 'George Logan: Un physiocrate américain', in B. Delmas, Th. Demals and Ph. Steiner (eds), *La diffusion internationale de la physiocratie (XVIIIe–XIXe)* (Grenoble: Presses universitaires de Grenoble), pp. 421–39.
37. Tax exemption for small landowners was part of Jefferson's broader plan for the redistribution of wealth (Jefferson to James Madison, Fontainebleau, 28 October 1785, in Jefferson, *The Papers*, vol. 8, p. 682). He also affirmed his opposition to a direct tax on land, preferring instead the application of a levy to the agricultural surplus on the sale of products. (Jefferson to James Madison, Paris, 8 December 1784, in ibid., vol. 7, p. 558).
38. Jefferson had many of the works of the Physiocrats in his library, including the first edition of *Physiocratie* (cf. *Catalogue of the Library of Thomas Jefferson* (1952), ed. E. Millicent Sowerby (Washington: Library of Congress), vol. 1, nos. 216, 1195, 1264; vol. 3, nos. 2370, 2371, 2372, 2373, 2374, 2375, 2377, 2432, 2433, 2436, 3551, 3617).
39. Cf. Ph. Steiner 'Quels principes pour l'économie politique? Charles Ganihl, Germain Garnier, Jean-Baptiste Say et la critique de la physiocratie', in Delmas et al., *La diffusion internationale de la physiocratie*, pp. 209–30.
40. A.-L.-Cl. Destutt de Tracy (1817) *A Treatise on Political Economy* (Georgetown, Washington, DC: J. Milligan), *Prospectus*, p. III. Jefferson also encouraged the American editions of Say's and Destutt de Tracy's works in an attempt to oppose Ricardo. Cf. M. Albertone (2003) 'Les rapports de Jean-Baptiste Say avec Thomas Jefferson et la réalité américaine', in J.-P. Potier and A. Tiran (eds), *Jean-Baptiste Say: Nouveaux regards sur son oeuvre* (Paris: Economica), pp. 631–52.
41. Cf. A.O. Aldridge (1963) *Benjamin Franklin et ses contemporains français* (Paris: Didier).
42. Cf. O. Vossler (1980) *Jefferson and the American Revolutionary Ideal* (Washington, DC: University Press of America); J. Appleby (1982) 'What is Still American in the Political Philosophy of Thomas Jefferson?', *William & Mary Quarterly*, XXXIX, 287–309.
43. Cf. D. Malone (1948–74) *Jefferson and His Time* (Boston: Little, Brown).
44. Jefferson to W. Green Munford, Monticello, 18 June 1799, in Jefferson, *Writings*, ed. Peterson, p. 1064. Cf. M. Albertone (1997) 'Condorcet, Jefferson et l'Amérique', in A.-M. Chouillet and P. Crépel (eds), *Condorcet: Homme des Lumières et de la Révolution* (Fontenay and Saint-Cloud: ENS Éditions), pp. 187–99.
45. Jefferson to William F. Dumas, 26 September 1786, Jefferson, *The Papers*, vol. 10, p. 354; Jefferson to James Madison, 31 July 1788, in ibid., vol. 13, p. 441; Jefferson to James Madison, 12 January 1789, in ibid., vol. 14, p. 437.
46. Cf. M-J.-A.-N. Caritat de Condorcet (1847–49) 'Essai sur la constitution et les fonctions des assemblées provinciales', in A. Condorcet O'Connor and M.-F. Arago (eds), *Oeuvres* (Paris: F. Didot frères), vol. 8, p. 133 (hereafter *Oeuvres*).
47. Cf. K.M. Baker (1975) *Condorcet: From Natural Philosophy to Social Mathematics* (Chicago and London: University of Chicago Press).
48. M.-J.-A.-N. Caritat de Condorcet, 'De l'influence de la révolution d'Amérique sur l'Europe' (1786), in *Œuvres*, vol. 8, p. 18. Cf. D. Echeverria (1968) 'Condorcet's "The Influence of the American Revolution on Europe"', *William & Mary Quarterly*, 3rd ser., XXV, 85–7.

49. M.-J.-A.-N. Caritat de Condorcet, 'Lettres d'un bourgeois de New-Heaven à un citoyen de Virginie', in F. Mazzei (1788) *Recherches historiques et politiques sur les États-Unis de l'Amérique septentrionale* (Colle and Paris: Froullé), vol. 1, p. 361. Cf. N. Urbinati (2004) 'Condorcet's Democratic Theory of Representative Government', *European Journal of Political Theory*, III, 53–75.
50. Condorcet, 'Essai sur la constitution et les fonctions des assemblées provinciales', p. 496.
51. Cf. M. Albertone (2004) 'Il proprietario terriero nel discorso fisiocratico sulla rappresentanza', in *Fisiocrazia e proprietà terriera*, special issue of *Studi settecenteschi*, XXIV, 181–214.
52. The scheme for decentralized representation is to be found in *Lettres d'un bourgeois de New-Heaven* and in the plan for a constitution drawn up by him in 1793.
53. Jefferson to William St Smith, Paris, 2 August 1788, in Jefferson, *The Papers*, vol. 13, p. 458. In his autobiography, he discusses Calonne's project for provincial assemblies, expressing his appreciation of the scheme (Jefferson, 'Autobiography', in A. Koch and W. Peden (eds) (1993) *The Life and Selected Writings of Thomas Jefferson* (New York: Random House), p. 69.
54. Jefferson to Diodati, Paris, 3 August 1789, in Jefferson, *The Papers*, vol. 15, p. 327.
55. Cf. G. Chinard (1926) *The Commonplace Book of Thomas Jefferson: A Repertory of His Ideas on Government* (Baltimore: Johns Hopkins University Press).
56. Jefferson to Thomas Mann Randolph Jr, New York, 30 May 1790, in Jefferson, *The Papers*, vol. 16, p. 449.
57. Jefferson to Nathaniel Niles, 22 March 1801, in Jefferson, *The Writings* (1893–99), ed. P.L. Ford (New York: G.P. Putnam and Sons), vol. 8, p. 24; to William Duane, 12 August 1810, in Jefferson, *The Writings*, ed. Lipscomb and Bergh, vol. 12, pp. 407–8; to Destutt de Tracy, 26 January 1811, in Jefferson, *The Writings*, ed. Ford, vol. 9, p. 305; to Thomas Cooper, 10 July 1812, in Jefferson, *The Writings*, ed. Lipscomb and Bergh, vol. 13, p. 178.
58. Cf. M. Albertone (2008) 'Que l'autorité souveraine soit unique: La séparation des pouvoirs dans la pensée des Physiocrates et son legs: Du despotisme légal à la démocratie représentative de Condorcet', in S. Baume and B. Fontana (eds), *Les usages de la séparation des pouvoirs* (Paris: M. Houdiard).
59. On the reasons why Condorcet is believed to be the author of the *Observations*, despite the fact that none of his papers have survived, cf. Baker, *Condorcet*, p. 446.
60. Cf. Appleby's essay, 'What is Still American'.
61. Jefferson to James Madison, Paris, 6 September 1789, in Jefferson, *The Papers*, vol. 15, pp. 392–7.
62. Ibid., p. 392.
63. H.E. Sloan (1995) *Principle and Interest: Thomas Jefferson and the Problem of Debt* (New York and Oxford: Oxford University Press).
64. Jefferson to James Madison, Paris, 12 January 1789, in Jefferson, *The Papers*, vol. 14, p. 437. Together with Quesnay, Gem treated one of Smith's students in Paris (cf. *The Monthly Magazine; or British Register* (1821), LI, no. 351, 139).
65. *Proposition Submitted by Richard Gem* (c. 1–6 September 1789), in Jefferson, *The Papers*, vol. 15, pp. 391–2.
66. Ibid., vol. 14, p. 439.

67. Jefferson to James Madison, Paris, 6 September 1789, in ibid., p. 392.
68. Ibid., p. 395. Jefferson repeats Gem almost word for word (p. 392).
69. *Oeuvres*, vol. 5, p. 142.
70. Ibid., pp. 395–6. Jefferson's opinions concerning the rights of each generation demonstrate that he did not share the evolutionist approach of the Scottish philosophers.
71. The principle of constitutional revision is also to be found in his discussion of the Declaration of Rights in the summer of 1789, as witnessed by the exchange of letters between Jefferson, Lafayette and Gem.
72. M-J.-A.-N. Caritat de Condorcet, *Lettre à M. le comte de Montmorency*, in *Oeuvres*, vol. 9, pp. 372–3.
73. Condorcet, 'Essai sur la constitution et les fonctions des assemblées provinciales', p. 223.
74. The same idea can also be found in the same period in Le Mercier de La Rivière, with reference to the nationalization of the properties of the crown (P.-P.-F. Le Mercier de La Rivière (1789) *Canevas d'un code constitutionnel, pour servir de suite à l'ouvrage intitulé: 'Les voeux d'un François'* (Paris and Versailles: Vallat-La-Chapelle, Veillard), p. 33.
75. Cf. Jefferson to John W. Eppes, Monticello, 24 June 1813, in Jefferson, *Writings*, ed. Peterson, pp. 1280–1; to Joseph C. Cabell, Monticello, 17 January 1814, in Jefferson, *Writings*, ed. Lipscomb and Bergh, vol. 14, pp. 67–8; to John Taylor, Monticello, 28 May 1816, in ibid., vol. 15, p. 18; to Thomas Earle, Monticello, 24 September 1823, in ibid., p. 470; to John Cartwright, Monticello, 5 June 1824, in ibid., vol. 16, pp. 44, 48.
76. Cf. Th. Paine (1971) *Rights of Man*, ed. H. Collins (Harmondsworth: Penguin Books), pp. 63–4. On the question of who is to be viewed as the originator of this idea – Jefferson or Paine – cf. Sloan, *Principle and Interest*.
77. Du Pont de Nemours to Jefferson, 27 August 1798, in *The Correspondence of Jefferson and Du Pont de Nemours* (1931), ed. G. Chinard (Baltimore: Johns Hopkins University Press), p. 7. In 1800 Du Pont drew up a plan for national education for the University of Virginia for Jefferson and played an important role in the negotiations for the Louisiana Purchase in 1803. (Cf. M. Albertone (2004) 'Du Pont de Nemours et l'instruction publique pendant la Révolution: De la science économique à la formation du citoyen', *Revue Française d'Histoire des Idées Politiques*, XX, 353–71.)
78. Du Pont de Nemours to Jefferson, New York, 7 January 1801, in *Correspondence*, ed. Chinard, p. 33; Jefferson to Du Pont, Washington, 18 January 1802, in ibid., p. 37.
79. Jefferson to J.B. Say, 1 February 1804, in Jefferson, *Writings*, ed. Peterson, p. 1144.
80. T.R. Malthus (1803) *An Essay on the Principle of Population*, 2nd edn (London: J. Johnson by T. Bensley), p. 458.
81. P.-S. Du Pont de Nemours (1817) *Examen du livre de M. Malthus sur le Principe de Population* (Philadelphie: P.M. Lafourcade), p. 30.
82. Du Pont de Nemours to Jefferson, Paris, 14 September 1810, in *Correspondence*, ed. Chinard, p. 158. The manuscript is kept at the Eleutherian Mills Historical Library, *Papers of Pierre Samuel Du Pont de Nemours*, The Winterthur Manuscripts, series B, no. 44; this consists of eighty-seven pages written by a copyist and carrying Du Pont's handwritten corrections.

83. Ibid., no. 16.
84. Ibid.
85. Jefferson to Du Pont, Monticello, 15 April 1811, in Jefferson, *The Writings*, ed. Lipscomb and Bergh, vol. 13, pp. 37–8.
86. Jefferson to Du Pont, Monticello, 28 February 1815, in ibid., vol. 14, p. 257.
87. A.L.-Cl. Destutt de Tracy (1811) *A Commentary and Review of Montesquieu's Spirit of Laws* (Philadelphia: W. Duane).
88. Du Pont to Jefferson, 25 January 1812, in *Correspondence*, ed. Chinard, pp. 179–80.
89. Ibid., p. 189.
90. Ibid., p. 184. Cf. Du Pont, *Examen*, p. 2.
91. Du Pont to Jefferson, 14 April 1812, in *Correspondence*, ed. Chinard, p. 194.
92. Ibid., p. 195. Cf. also Jefferson to Duane, 4 April 1813, in Jefferson, *The Writings*, ed. Lipscomb and Bergh, vol. 13, p. 230; Du Pont to Tracy, Paris, 14 August 1816, Eleutherian Mills Historical Library, series A, Correspondence.
93. Cf. G. Chinard (1925) *Jefferson et les Idéologues d'après sa correspondance inédite* (Baltimore and Paris: Johns Hopkins University Press and Presses universitaires de France).
94. Jefferson to Duane, Monticello, 4 April 1813, in Jefferson, *The Writings*, ed. Lipscomb and Bergh, vol. 13, p. 229. Cf. Albertone, 'Les rapports de Jean-Baptiste Say'.
95. Jefferson to J. Melish, Monticello, 13 January 1813, in Jefferson, *The Writings*, ed. Lipscomb and Bergh, vol. 13, pp. 207–8.
96. Jefferson to B. Austin, Monticello, 9 January 1816, in Jefferson, *Writings*, ed. Peterson, pp. 1370–1.
97. P.-S. Du Pont de Nemours, 'Sur l'agriculture et les manufactures aux États-Unis', in *Correspondence*, ed. Chinard, p. 240. Hints of Du Pont's new standpoint had appeared in the *Décade philosophique*, IV (December 1794–February 1795), 'Lettre aux auteurs de la décade sur les économistes'.
98. Du Pont de Nemours, 'Sur l'agriculture et les manufactures aux États-Unis', p. 241.
99. Ibid. Cf. Du Pont, *Examen*, p. 19.
100. 'Observations sommaires sur l'utilité des encouragemens à donner aux manufactures américaines', in *Correspondence*, ed. Chinard, pp. 254–5.
101. Jefferson to Du Pont de Nemours, Poplar Forest, 24 April 1816, in ibid., p. 258.
102. Ibid.

# 7
# The Question of Slavery in the Physiocratic Texts: A Rereading of an Old Debate

*Marcel Dorigny*

Research into the theoretical foundations of anti-slavery and abolitionism have concentrated upon the philosophical, theological and more generally ethical origins of the condemnation of colonial slavery, focusing above all on the foundation of abolitionist societies at the end of the century in England, the United States and France. The actors most systematically cited in this domain – often in a contradictory manner – are the great names of the Enlightenment: Montesquieu, Voltaire, Rousseau, Diderot and, of course, Raynal.[1] This recourse to the 'great ancestors' of the anti-slavery movement is certainly legitimate, and the reinterpretation of their work is always interesting. However, there is a whole area of the dominant culture of the Enlightenment of the eighteenth century that has been studied too rarely and only partially from the angle of slavery, and particularly colonial slavery, which was the mode of general development for the tropical islands possessed by the great European powers. It views the Physiocratic intellectual tradition and doctrine, not in the context of the existence of the colonies and the particular mode of their relations with the *métropole* – an approach generally condemned by the Physiocrats as forms of monopoly and protectionism – but rather with reference to slavery as a type of human relation and the imposition of a particular labour relation upon a part of the population. However, this dimension of the political economy of the epoch was not ignored by the refined Physiocratic authors; it is even legitimate to say that their reflections in this area constituted in a certain fashion the true realization of their overall vision of the world, the nature of social relations and, even more so, the formation and the distribution of the wealth of nations.

Clearly, it is impossible in this brief text to take into account all the authors belonging to the vast Physiocratic movement of the last part of the eighteenth century. The approach proposed here will be to analyse not only the texts of some of the major authors of the school, such as Mirabeau, Baudeau and Dupont de Nemours, but also some of the later, more marginal contributors, such as Turgot and Herrenschwand. The case of Condorcet, widely studied by others, will be left aside, but not without reminding the reader that his work on this subject summarized, practically all by itself, the quintessential doctrine of the school from its origins, even if he may have later distanced himself from this heritage.

Three points of view will be examined. First, the condemnation of slavery as a violation of human rights and a danger for the colonies; second, the condemnation of slavery as an archaic form of labour; and third, how to end the system of slavery, which, despite the fact that it was continually condemned, was still a vigorous institution.

## A violation of human rights and a danger for the colonies

If the Physiocrats were first and foremost economists, in the quasi-modern sense of the term, they were not detached from the overall analysis of human societies, which they conceived of as profoundly coherent and as subject to the independent laws of political regimes and the habits of the past, including its errors. Thus, before it was criticized from the perspective of economic usefulness, slavery was described in terms of the violence which fundamentally underlined it. Even before the birth of the Physiocratie, as formulated by Quesnay in 1758, Mirabeau had clearly condemned slavery on moral grounds, not only as it had been practised since the beginning of time, but especially the way it was practised by the Europeans in their colonies. A passage from the first edition of *L'ami des hommes* is explicit on this point:

> At first we had imagined bringing the slaves to our southern colonies to subject them to the cultivation of the land, that is to say, giving the art and labour of working the land secondary importance, that which must truly be of the utmost importance to man ...
> 
> But slavery, in its original state, as barbaric and unnatural as it was, even as it corrupted the masses, degraded and intermingled nations, eliminating all harmony, all pity, all delicacy, all humanity; slavery, in its earliest forms, while it remained more despotic in law than that which exists today, was in fact more endurable and less dangerous. Our slaves in America are a distinct race of people, distinct and separate by the most indelible trait from our own, by this I mean to say

their colour, a colour which consequently inherits this sort of misfortune from nature. The original slaves were people who resembled their masters; ... On the other hand, these slaves have been found in the most barbaric of states. They come to us as brutes, endowed with an instinct which we cannot comprehend, all the same in our eyes. We throw them into the cowsheds with their brethren, we overburden them with work for the benefit of the masters; and through these habits and practices is born at the heart of fraternal law and during a century enlightened by excellence, the most odious and, if I can say, the most impious of servitude.

Thus, in every conceivable way, this method has equally inevitable and ruinous consequences.[2]

This text makes two observations that, from Mirabeau's point of view, lead unequivocally to his condemnation of the colonial practice of slavery:

- the fact that agricultural work is somehow degraded, and those who carry it out are reduced exclusively to the condition of servitude, when, in fact, working the land ought to be the most noble of human activities.[3]
- the racial character of colonial slavery, something that was not present in ancient societies but had become the sole criterion for modern slavery. By putting into place this degenerative practice, based on the exploitation of one race peculiar to the human species, the Europeans had created in their colonies the conditions of their own undoing.

Another nefarious consequence of exclusively African slavery – for Mirabeau – was the inevitable submergence of whites by blacks and métis in colonial societies, due to a dependency on the large numbers of 'imported' Africans. This conquest of power by the blacks would be the inexorable result, first, of the demographic imbalance between the two populations and, second, of the fact that the work was done exclusively by blacks and métis, while whites increasingly lived in indolence. Whatever solution was adopted by the masters to conserve their power, it could only lead to one outcome:

> If we place these unfortunate creatures under the yoke, as we generally do as a necessary precaution for the well being of our colonies, the cultivation of the land, which remains their exclusive domain, languishes as a result, their population is stunted by their inherent misery

and all of the disorders which follow; women have abortions to rid themselves of a burden; within the culture of the small field which is left to them for their subsistence, they become dishonest and even criminal and as a result of the constant loss of labour that this odious system inflicts upon these people we are forced to continually replace them at an even greater cost to Africa ...

The most industrious Negros are able to teach themselves arts and to learn various crafts, which wrests from the White population this secondary but rewarding source of income. Little by little, the slave population grows as that of the masters diminishes; all of the work and activity is shared amongst the slaves while the masters become indolent and filled with pride: it is for us to judge where this evolution leads.[4]

Thus, the result of the policy of importation created ever greater reliance on the slave trade – since the atrocious living conditions reduced the birth rate – and the increasing dependency on slaves in all areas of social and economic life accelerated the process of racial mixing, thus rendering inevitable greater inequality between the two populations. The result would be the seizure of the control of the islands by the slaves at the expense of the Europeans:

> The seduction of profits, and of greater remuneration gained through the work of their slaves, forces them to use their slaves for such tasks as navigation and even military functions. Even the simplest of men have enough sense to understand the advantage of freedom. There is even a preconceived notion amongst many of them that God first created the land for the Redskins, then the Whites and finally for the Blacks and one can find counties on the Islands where they are already subjected to obedience.[5]

The reliance upon slavery thus proved itself to be, at once, contrary to natural law and to the interests of the European colonies themselves, whose lazy and corrupt white population would inevitably fall under the domination of the more numerous and active black population. Such was the portrait sketched by one of the most widely read Physiocrats. Mirabeau's reflections – far from expressing his desires, was rather a cry of alarm – underlining an often misunderstood characteristic of anti-slavery thought of the eighteenth century. The inevitable independence of the colonies in the New World was not systematically seen as being primarily a case of 'white independence', in the hands of the Creole colonizers; rather, it threatened to be a case of 'black independence', at the hands of Africans who had become the great majority. Fervent supporters of the rebels during the American Revolution, the Physiocrats were not, however, well disposed to the idea of the blacks acquiring independence – in fact, quite to the contrary.

The abbé Baudeau, the most active propagator of the Physiocratic doctrine, in its most elaborate form, explicitly confirmed this: slavery was a violation of the founding principles of the social contract; that is to say, the very liberty of individuals that constitute society:

> *Personal liberty* is thus the first condition presupposed in the practice of *natural law*, in this state of multitude; the first *attack* possible by a man against his brethren would thus be to violate the *ownership* of his person in order to routinely prevent him from making liberal use of his bodily functions to satisfy his own needs and his own desires. It is clear that nature has created all other animals who live in this state of seeking as free: the strong do not enslave the weak. Has nature refused the same advantage only to man? The question is not difficult to answer.[6]

Baudeau then defined human labour as presupposing the ownership of one's own person. Thus, free labour and ownership of one's own person formed the framework of natural law. The consequence of freedom and of personal property guaranteed by natural law is the absolute refusal of all form of servitude and slavery, under any pretext whatsoever:

> It [natural law] is thus to be considered as *prohibitive* of attacks on, and usurpation, of ownership [labour and personal liberty]. There are to be no exceptions to this rule, whose institution does not depend on the volition of man but rather descends directly from the Supreme Being and the Author of Nature: therefore, there is no reason, no existing authority who can make exceptions. The perpetrators, the accomplices, the agitators of this barbaric and criminal custom who turn men, both *white and black*, into slaves of warring pirates or merchants will find their inevitable condemnation in this *natural law*. Violators of the first law of justice or injustice, there is no horror or price which would not be considered legitimate for or against them to be judged according to the principle of their domination over the unfortunate that they have reduced to servitude. If man is permitted to infringe not only upon land-ownership and personal property but also upon *personal liberty* which is the basis of the other two, then

theft, assassination and the ravaging of human flesh are just and innocent.[7]

If another major figure of the Physiocrat movement, Le Trosne, did not find it useful to develop his arguments in detail, it was because, in his eyes, the debate was decided by the very terms in which it was elaborated. Le Trosne worked out as a clever rejoinder another point of view on the slave trade and slavery, which he viewed as the very negation of rights:

> I will not consider the natural law of this trade here. Is it permissible to purchase men with the intent of subjugating them in slavery? Is it permissible through this trade to promote and to foster all of the crimes which these barbaric nations are engaged in, and the wars which they continually wage in order to maintain it? Would the Europeans want to be treated as such? Is justice applicable to the relations between the Europeans and the Africans? Or does the difference between white and black require other principles and a different morality? All of this is not my domain.[8]

The condemnation of all forms of slavery could not be more explicitly expressed in a time where the possession of the sugar islands of the French monarchy had just been consolidated by the clauses of the Paris treaty, thus resolutely promoting slavery as an option to ensure the prosperity of the French colonies after the abandonment of Canada.

## An archaic form of work

Not only was slavery condemned as a permanent violation of natural law, it was also criticized in even stronger terms by the Physiocrats because it was economically inefficient. As early supporters of the absolute liberty of social relations, which rested exclusively upon free agreements between free economic agents, they could not, without violating the principles of their established dogma, permit the bond which made the slave's work for his master an absolute constraint, a bond that escaped the rules of supply and demand. Outside the labour market, once purchased by man, making him property of the same order as an animal or a plough, the work of the slave was taken from him by force and not by the consent of contract (not even a tacit one). Under these conditions, the work furnished could never attain the level of perfection, attachment and application necessary for a rewarding productivity for the master. This failing was essentially the same as for all forms of constrained work: the chores imposed upon peasants in the French countryside, as well as slavery, were both targeted by the anathema launched by the Quesnay school against all forms of labour that was not free.[9]

The verdict was formulated in these terms by Turgot in a text dedicated to the formation of wealth in a chapter that is not often cited, despite its very explicit title: 'How the Farming of Slaves is Little Profitable and Very Expensive for the Master and for Humanity', dated November 1766:

> The slaves have no motive to carry out the work which is forced upon them with the intelligence and care which could ensure their success; as a result this work is hardly productive at all.
>
> The rapacious masters know no better than to force their slaves to accomplish ever harsher tasks, tasks that are ever more relentless and violent, in order to compensate for this lack of production. These excessive tasks take their toll and result in the loss of many slaves, so in order to maintain the necessary number of slaves for the cultivation of the land, the masters are thus required to acquire even more. As such, they do not provide their slaves with a salary, but they do spend exorbitant sums to procure these poor workers and as it is always war which creates the initial capital for this trade, it is clear that it can only exist through an enormous destruction of men.[10]

Thus, according to this schema, forced work is not profitable for anyone: the slave is mistreated to such an extent that he has no affection for his work, the master derives little net product from his land, the population of workers is always insufficient due to the low birth rate and, as a result, the master is obliged to constantly purchase new slaves, while Africa is depopulated by the slave trade. The image that emerges from this is increasingly pessimistic, far from the idyllic descriptions of rural society happily practising the precepts of the economists – seen from the point of view of a Mirabeau or a Badeau – and allows for few future prospects for the colonies that have been developed in such a fashion, no more than it does for Africa.

At the end of the century, an analysis made by one late adherent of the Physiocratic school would not differ at heart: the development of the tropical colonies by slavery is the reason why they are so backward, while free labour had created the prosperity of the American continental colonies, at least in the north:

> If the colonies that the European nations created in the New World had had the misfortune of being established and maintained through

a system of slavery as are those on the islands of this vast continent, this industry would never have taken root in the colonies; the absolute dependence of their *métropole* would have been their share and America would not have so quickly produced thriving nations.[11]

The link between underdevelopment and the generalized practice of slavery could not be more explicitly established. Where slavery did not exist, or at least where it did not constitute the exclusive motor of agricultural production, colonial societies prospered. Where slavery was omnipresent, poverty inevitably established itself and, as a corollary, the close dependency of the colonies on the metropoles that furnished all they were incapable of producing.

In 1766, Mirabeau again condemned the lack of productivity under slavery in even more incisive terms. According to him, this underproductivity was due exclusively to the fact that slavery was fundamentally contrary to the laws of nature, according to which only mutual respect inspired the zeal of the worker, for he finds in it his own personal interest. In a paragraph explicitly entitled 'Slavery is the perversion of the natural order,' we read this:

> Ancient barbarity had imagined slaves for this [to assume all of the work on the land by non-landowners]; an unnatural expedient, experience has shown its lack of validity in the success of large agricultural plantations. The losses in products over a large territory cultivated by hard labour, the multitude of atrocious precautions that ancient laws established for the protection and maintenance of the masters, their subjugation and the omission [*intercadence*] of their wellbeing in areas where this custom persists, even for the commodities of choice, and which provides nevertheless almost no solid wealth for three generations; all of these things, I would say, demonstrate how futile human efforts can be when nature resists. It is indeed unnatural to assert that two similar beings are enemies, and place them in the position where they are obliged to become so; especially those whose mutual and reciprocal assistance is necessary. It is a perverse and forced form of agriculture which can only subsist in a large kingdom to the great detriment of the nation and the eventual ruin of the state.[12]

The author of *L'ami des hommes* again took up one of the most decisive arguments against slavery, one that his brother had presented to him several times in the past, when he was serving as Intendant to Martinique, to underscore the reasons for the low productivity of innumerable slaves put to work under harsh military discipline on the plantations:

> Thirty-five thousand arms destined to work the land will not accomplish what two thousand could do elsewhere. As such, slavery appears to me to be an evil, even if it is considered purely from the point of view of the cupidity in which its origins lie.[13]

With such arguments, reportedly formulated by an observer who was attentive to, and prudent, about the colonies he administered, it is easy to understand that the followers of Physiocratic theories could not, in any way, see the system of plantation slavery as a model compatible with their aspirations for increased agricultural production, notably through a rapid generalization of the division of labour and the introduction of new techniques designed to replace – as far as possible – raw 'manpower'. The social ideal and the economic model described in Mirabeau's famous 'Agricultural Kingdom' – a liberal utopia based upon the Physiocratic thesis – rested upon large farms cultivated by salaried workers, not slaves. The colonial plantation was antithetical to this model.

Even Le Mercier de la Rivière, the only Physiocrat to accept slavery as a mode of work in the sugar colonies, insisted equally upon the underproductivity of forced work, and especially its elevated costs when compared to those of the free European labourer; but he did not draw the same conclusions. To remedy the excessive cost, due principally to the fact that it was becoming increasingly expensive to import negroes from Africa, it was necessary, according to this line of reasoning, to promote a rise in the birth rate by improving living standards and working conditions for the slaves, while also introducing a significant proportion of free workers from Europe or other continents that were not colonized, who would work side by side with slaves on the plantations. In order to lower the price of negroes, Le Mercier also elaborated the idea of authorizing importations from slave traders from other countries – and especially England – as well as the French negotiators that had benefited thus far from French monopoly, the so-called 'exclusif'. Thus, from Le Mercier's perspective, it was the introduction of the free market that, first, had allowed slavery to develop in peripheral regions of the empire, and had then made slavery a constituent element that counterbalanced the disadvantages of the absence of this same market in terms of a pure logic of slavery. This was a curious paradox that was not adopted by the other followers of Quesnay's doctrine. We will come back to the atypical analysis of Le Mercier in the conclusion.

## How to end the condemned but still vigorous institution of slavery

After having roundly condemned slavery as both barbarous and underproductive, and thus as a form of work that did not even satisfy the main reason for using slaves, namely the search for ever-increasing wealth – one might expect forceful proposals for the abolition of the practice the Physiocrats had so completely stigmatized. In reality, there was nothing of the sort: the Physiocrats did not transform themselves into militant abolitionists. For them, anti-slavery was an essential point in their doctrine, indispensable and intellectually coherent with a general theory of society developed over the course of several thousand pages. But this position of principle was not destined to be implemented immediately in the way colonial societies were run, however perverse their values and the way they functioned were. If Dupont de Nemours had reproached Turgot for his lack of ardour on the slavery question in his discussion on the offences of servitude, Turgot might have replied that this system, fundamentally bad for the kingdom and the colonies, still had good days ahead. For its deficiencies were not apparent to the slaveholders. On the contrary, they felt they earned a considerable income through the practice of slavery:

> Franklin also demonstrated that the work done by blacks is even more costly than it appears at first glance, because of the constant need for replacements, and while I could not agree more concerning our islands, there is an advantage to having slaves, not for the colony but for the owner who wants to produce costly commodities in order to make a quick fortune through this business. I believe that I have provided, in this text, the reasons which render the work of slaves useful in a country where wealth and business take precedence over the population. You may not know that in the islands, a good worker is paid 6 pounds a day; this comes out to about 1,500 pounds per year.[14]

Turgot was thus perfectly aware that the idea of replacing slaves with free workers – or even transforming slaves themselves into salaried workers – would run up against two obstacles. On the one hand, it would be very difficult to find a sufficient number of workers, given the climatic conditions and the difficult nature of the work. On the other hand, their salaries would be at least double that paid in Europe for agricultural work, due simply to the imbalance between supply and demand. For Turgot, one point was certainly clear: slavery served the immediate interest of masters and, as a consequence, it was not possible to convince them of its perversity, even from a financial point of view:

> If I had the time, I would also write a large tome to prove to you that it is unnecessary to correct me. I would simply tell you summarily: it is impossible to infer from what I have said that slavery was not beneficial to any society, even in its infancy. As for individuals who own slaves, that is a totally different question. I would very much like for you to be right in asserting that slavery is good for no one, for it is an abominable and barbaric injustice, but I fear that you would be wrong, for this injustice can sometimes be beneficial to those who practise it. The human race is not fortunate enough for injustice to always be immediately punished.[15]

In such conditions, any idea of abolition was impossible, bearing in mind that the *économistes* did not see themselves at all as recommending a break with the established order. On the contrary, they saw themselves in terms purely of a dynamic of reform, faithful to the principles of 'Enlightened Despotism'. This is what Mirabeau formulated in perfectly clear terms:

> One would ask, what is the solution? I am not ignorant of the fact that the worst of abuses is to try to attack head on and to destroy all at once abuses which are engrained in the nature of things. As a result, I will not try to banish the custom of Negroes; but do you want to limit it and soon render it useless? Promote the cultivation of land in the colonies.[16]

The lack of political proposals for guiding colonial societies towards a definitive end of slavery should not, however, lead us to underestimate the impact of the anti-slavery positions taken up by the Physiocrats, described in part above. In the middle of the eighteenth century, such theoretical considerations – stripped of all philanthropic or moralistic connotations – belonged to a body of writings still being created, and which would not become the 'vulgate' of the abolitionist movement until late into the nineteenth century. In order to measure the radical nature of the Physiocratic condemnation of colonial slavery, it is necessary to cite, by way of contrast, a passage from the pen of Jean-François Melon, one of their predecessors and an economist, but one opposed to what he described as the 'sect' of Quesnay. In fact, Melon constructed a long apology for slavery in his text on commerce, seeing in this system an efficient and protective system for slaves themselves, thanks to the *Code noir*, a practice which did not contradict principles of rights in any way: 'The use of slavery authorized in our colonies teaches us that slavery does not contradict religion or morality.'[17] With Mirabeau, Turgot, Dupont or Le Trosne, the hierarchy of values changed fundamentally, and we cannot seriously challenge their full defence of anti-slavery positions, but none of these illustrious figures became full-fledged abolitionists. The Physiocrats condemned slavery in unequivocal terms, but did not propose any credible means of breaking with the system. This represented an apparent paradox for a group of men so closely aligned with the social and political elites of the monarchy; they were prudent reformers, but never revolutionaries before their time.

This extreme prudence would also be echoed among French abolitionists (and among the British) at the end of the 1780s. By founding the Société des amis des noirs, these liberals, largely intellectual inheritors of debates surrounding Physiocracy during the 1770s, did not propose immediate abolition, but a progressive way out, by slow extinction, prudently set up by legislation that would protect both property and persons.[18]

Thus the path traced by the Physiocrats would become a permanent part of the abolitionism of the eighteenth and nineteenth centuries – long after the direct influence of the doctrine, as articulated in the 1760s and 1770s, had passed, and would be reflected in the most liberal of arguments of writers such as Adam Smith, among others. Denouncing the inefficiency of forced labour, in fact, was one of the common points of abolitionist arguments, on the same level as those that emphasized the inhumanity of slavery, and even more so, of the slave trade itself. Of the Physiocratic anti-slavery heritage, the abolitionists of the 1780s retained, above all, the need not to provoke a brutal rupture with the colonial order that was already in place. The movement preferred to emphasize the need for laws that would progressively lead to a future where slave labour would disappear by stages, to be replaced finally by free wage labour. The initiative for such a project could only come from an enlightened government, and never from the slaves themselves. The fixed Physiocratic horizons for the colonies on the issue of slavery presupposed the end of slavery, but the way of doing away with it was not established at all, not even in the vaguest of forms. Several decades later, the emergence of political abolitionism reappropriated the heritage that tried to eliminate slavery from the colonial societies, all the while preparing the various stages and the political solutions to be put into practice.

The analysis proposed here has left aside one of the major authors of the Physiocratic school – Le Mercier de la Rivière – mentioned in passing above, and to whom we must return in a moment, in order to underline his originality, which put him on the margins of the Physiocratic tradition with regard to the analysis of colonial slavery.[19] This deliberate choice is explained by the particular character and, to be truthful, atypical position defended by this essay. Le Mercier was, in effect, the only member of what his adversaries called the 'Sect of the Economists' to justify the principle of slavery as an ordinary mode of production for the tropical colonies, and this in the name of the very principles of Physiocracy – that is to say, the search for the highest possible agricultural output capable of creating a maximum net product. For Le Mercier, the slavery regime that ruled in the Caribbean islands was a sort of foreshadowing of the social and economic order advocated by the Economic school: work on the plantation was framed by strict discipline, each person being assigned a specific task, and under the strict surveillance of an overseer. The transformation of products – notably sugar – demanded the respect of a rational order of tasks; each stage of the process of transformation was observable; therefore – and this is probably the heart of the argument – this form of colonial agriculture was fully integrated into the financial and commercial networks. The initial investment of capital is important (the famous 'advances' of the Physiocrats) and could only be guaranteed by large landowners. The concentration of financial capital is thus more advanced than in France, where micro-exploitation of land was more important. Moreover, colonial production was exclusively destined for large-scale commercial ventures perfectly integrated into the general circulation of wealth on a global level, challenging artificial borders and their disastrous tariffs. For Le Mercier, the fact that production was exclusively assured by slaves did not pose a problem to his resolutely optimistic vision of the sugar colonies as a sort of prefiguring of perfect agricultural societies. The disappearance of the notion – however central – of free labour and the freedom to enter into labour contracts between owners, farmers and salaried workers, did not call into question the integration of the slave economy in the ideal schema of Physiocratie, according to his interpretation.

The decisive role of human labour for the agricultural development of the colonies was taken into account by Le Mercier. Along with the two factors of production identified by Quesnay and Mirabeau – the fixed capital 'advances' and the land – the slave plantation added a third factor that was also indispensable: that of human labour, assured exclusively by slaves. From the special nature of colonial plantations, Le Mercier derived a 'heretical' theoretical conclusion with regard to Physiocratic doctrine: the 'Net Negro Product', a radical notion completely foreign to pure Physiocracy. In this way, while labour by itself only created new wealth in the eyes of the economists of the school, the work specific to the slave is the only kind to share with the earth and the fixed capital *avances* an eminent role in the mechanism through which wealth is produced in societies.

Le Mercier's theoretical innovation thus situated slavery at the heart of the colonial system and explained the importance that he attached to the establishment of protectionist legislation for slaves, the active agents of production.

There is, therefore, room to question the coherence of Le Mercier's arguments and especially their compatibility with the theses of other members of the school, all of which led to a radical condemnation of slavery, opening the path to the future programmes of anti-slavery societies – all of which were, more or less, intimately related to the vast liberal movement born of the decline of Physiocracy, which began in the period 1775–80, revolving around Jefferson and Franklin in the United States and Condorcet, Clavière and Say in France.

The case of Le Mercier should not, however, obscure the central analysis of the nature and inadequacies of slavery by the Physiocrats. With this analysis, they contributed a great deal to discrediting this practice. They did not, however, delude themselves (and the example of Turgot is eloquent in this respect) with regard to the ability of slave owners to resist arguments that relied upon a strict macro-economic logic, even if these arguments demonstrated the low level of actual production derived from slave labour in comparison with that derived from free labour, and even without taking into account the barbaric nature and inhumanity of slavery, contrary to all human rights. The Physiocrats should also be reinstated as part of the long chain of those who were engaged – often swimming against the tide of their social milieux – in the denunciation of slavery, both in the name of the principle of natural rights and in the name of the 'new science' founded upon the immutable principles of individual liberty, the market and competition between the actors of human activity.

The Physiocratic view of slavery was largely grounded in a situation which had two aspects – one political and the other theoretical – that largely explains its various positions. On the one hand, it unites with other ideas emerging at the end of the 1750s regarding the theory of the *produit net*, the nature of work and the exclusive role of the land in the production of wealth. On the other hand, this school of thought is grounded in the economic crisis of colonial slavery, characterized by the rapid increase in the price of slaves, due to an increase in demand and growing moral opposition to slave traffic. The Physiocratic response to this situation was perfectly in line with their fundamental vision of society: a rejection of slavery, both as a way for human beings to appropriate other human beings and as an archaic and underproductive form of labour.

The cessation of the slave trade would have been an appropriate response, opening the way to a slow conversion of colonial societies to free wage labour. But this abolitionist line was never formulated by the Physiocrats themselves. They were indeed favourable to the widespread opinion held by the most enlightened metropolitan colonists, who realized the extent to which, in such a short time, the future of a system that rested on such inequalities and on such a feeble amount of production by agricultural labour had been compromised; and agricultural production was the founding stone of all human societies, according to the doctrine of the *produit net*. At the same time, however, the Physiocrats would never become actively engaged in the struggle for abolitionism.

## Notes

1. See, for instance, the summary recently proposed by Nelly Schmidt (2005) *L'abolition de l'esclavage: Cinq siècles de combats XVIe–XXe siècles* (Paris: Éditions Fayard).
2. Victor Riquetti de Mirabeau (1756) *L'Ami des hommes ou Traité de la population* (Avignon), vol. 3, pp. 390–2.
3. The whites' refusal to work the land as a result of the spread of slavery as a way of handling all the agricultural work, had been underlined by the Bailli de Mirabeau, writing to his brother *l'ami des hommes*, during his time as administrator in Martinique: 'Self-esteem, which often serves as a call to work elsewhere, prevents it here; no white man would allow himself to be seen as similar to a negro who, as a result of his colour, is condemned to such tasks; no one would want to expose himself to such mockery', 'Letter written by the Bailli de Mirabeau to his brother, 12 January 1755', cited by Lucien Brocard (ed.) (1902) *Doctrines économiques et sociales du marquis de Mirabeau* (Paris: Giard), p. 221, n. 2.
4. Mirabeau, *L'Ami des hommes*, p. 394.
5. Ibid., p. 395.
6. Nicolas Baudeau (1767) *Exposition de la loi naturelle* (Paris: Lacombe), p. 7.
7. Ibid., pp. 55–6.
8. Guillaume François Le Trosne (1707) *De l'ordre social* (Paris: Debure), pp. 711–12.
9. For an analysis of the different forms of forced labour, see Yann Moulier-Boutang (1998) *De l'esclavage au salariat, économie historique du salariat*

*bridé* (Paris: Presses universitaires de France); see in particular Ch. 9, pp. 213–41, devoted to a study of the comparative costs of slaves and free labourers in the French and English Antilles and colonial North America.
10. Gustave Schelle (ed.) (1914) 'Combien la culture exécutée par les esclaves est peu profitable et chère pour le maître et pour l'humanité'. *De la formation et de la distribution des richesses*, in *Œuvres de Turgot et documents le concernant* (Paris: Alcan), vol. 2, p. 545.
11. J.F. de Herrenschwand (1786) *De l'économie politique moderne: Discours fondamental sur la population* (London: Hookham), p. 54.
12. Mirabeau (1766) *Philosophie rurale, ou économie générale et politique de l'agriculture pour servir de suite à l'ami des hommes* (Amsterdam: Marc Michel Rey), vol. 1, p. 137.
13. Letter from the Bailli de Mirabeau to his brother, 14 September 1754, cited by Brocard, *Doctrines*, p. 221.
14. Letter to Dupont, Limoges, 6 February 1770, in Schelle (ed.), *Œuvres de Turgot*, vol. 3, p. 375.
15. Letter to Dupont, Limoges, 20 February 1770, in ibid., p. 378.
16. Mirabeau, *L'Ami des hommes*, vol. 1, p. 393.
17. Jean-François Melon (1723) *Essai politique sur le commerce*, cited by Brocard, *Doctrines*, p. 202, n. 1.
18. See Marcel Dorigny and Bernard Gainot (1998) *La Société des amis des noirs. 1788–1799: Contribution à l'histoire de l'abolition de l'esclavage* (Paris: Éditions Unesco).
19. On Le Mercier de la Rivière, see most notably, L. Ph. May (1975) *Le Mercier de la Rivière, aux origines de la science économique* (Paris: Éditions du CNRS), as well as an old article, by the same author (1932) 'Le Mercier de la Rivière intendant de la Martinique (1759–1764)', *Revue d'Histoire Économique et Sociale*, pp. 44–74. More generally the study of the 'colonial doctrine' of the Physiocrats has not been the subject of any recent studies; the work by André Labrouquère (1927) *Les idées coloniales des Physiocrates* (Paris: Presses universitaires de France), which is a little dated, remains the only overview available. Pernille Røge's thesis, in course of publication at Cambridge University Press, will provide important new ideas.

# 8
# 'A New Kind of Federalism': Benjamin Constant and Modern Europe
*Biancamaria Fontana*

In a conference paper published in 1993, Beatrice Fink set forth persuasively the ambiguities in Benjamin Constant's famous anti-Napoleonic pamphlet *De l'esprit de conquête*. On the one hand she credited the author with a modern, cosmopolitan vision of the new Europe that emerged from France's revolutionary conquests; on the other she exposed the doubts and incongruities expressed in the text, reaching the conclusion that what Constant described there was 'not just one, but several Europes'.[1]

It would be pointless to try to impose theoretical coherence upon a work like *De l'esprit de conquête*, where the understanding of the new European political reality is inextricably bound up with the immediate problems opened by the collapse of Napoleon's regime. It is instructive, however, to look more closely at the tensions and difficulties that surfaced at the time in Constant's broader analysis of an integrated European system. In the climate of eager expectation of Napoleon's defeat it is not surprising that the emperor's ambition to create a French superpower, built upon autocratic rule and military conquest, should be dismissed, by one of his political opponents, as anachronistic and contrary to the natural development of modern European societies. And yet the experience of forced political and administrative unity put to the test some of Constant's own most cherished assumptions: the superiority of a cosmopolitan Europe of rights over separate identities and national egoisms; the irresistible advantages of representative government in ruling large states; the benefits of free market relations among nations; the peaceful and unifying effects of commerce.

In *De l'esprit de conquête* – a work that on its publication in 1814 proved as successful as its author had hoped – Constant was determined to celebrate the triumph of the modern republic over its historical enemies: the ancient republican regime of the Jacobins and Bonaparte's military empire. But, as later events showed, the victory had been a narrow one, and in the process the 'bourgeois liberal republic' – considered as a model for modern European society – had very nearly come apart at the seams.[2]

In 1814 Constant built his attack against Bonaparte's regime upon the same well-rehearsed argument he had used, in the late 1790s, to denounce the Jacobin dictatorship: the irresistible development of commercial society had created in the citizens of modern European nations a powerful need for independence and individual satisfaction that was incompatible with any form of authoritarian governance. Thus the attempt to limit arbitrarily this new liberty, either in the name of republican virtue or in that of imperial grandeur, was doomed to fail. In this perspective, deeply rooted in the tradition of classical political economy, it was the development of the market, and its consequences upon civil society, that decided the viability of political institutions.

The strength of representative government – as Constant had theorized it – was precisely that it appeared best suited to this new type of civic identity, since it guaranteed both a high degree of personal independence and an adequate measure of participation in political decisions. Moreover, representative government, being committed to the maximization of individual freedom and prosperity, seemed naturally opposed to any dangerously aggressive line in foreign policy, favouring the development of peaceful commercial relations over aggressive competition and military conflict.[3]

Looking back, this over-optimistic belief not just in the natural affinity between representative government and commercial progress, but in their harmonious and synchronic development, was giving too many hostages to fortune. In 1799 the coup of Brumaire, though alarming to liberal observers, had still seemed preferable to the dangers of a return of the Jacobins, or to the dismal prospect of a monarchical restoration. But the rapid evolution of the Consulate into domestic despotism, and its growing commitment to foreign conquest, had soon led Constant to view Bonaparte as the arch-enemy of modern liberty – a conviction that had gained strength during his brief experience of political opposition at the *Tribunat* and the long years of exile that followed.[4] And yet, for all the brilliant rhetoric deployed in the 1814 pamphlet, his judgement on the anti-modern vocation of the empire was far from being as clear cut and consistent as it appeared at first.

If the empire was so opposed to the interests of modern commercial society, why had it lasted for so long and commanded such large consensus? Why had the French economy flourished during this period, in spite of the destruction caused by the war, instead of falling into the kind of crisis that, only a few years back, had rapidly sunk the revolutionary regime? No doubt the unification of a large part of Europe under French rule had been mainly – if not exclusively – achieved by means of military conquest. Yet at least, through this experience, the vague cosmopolitan ideals of the Enlightenment – Europe as a cultural community or as a single large republic – had been transformed into political reality. Was a comparable result imaginable by any other means? Constant himself did not reject the political and civil conquests of the Revolution, even though the experience of the Terror had been part of their genesis. Questions like these, if not explicitly formulated, could not be altogether avoided in pronouncing a final verdict on the empire. Constant's subsequent political fluctuations, and his controversial decision to support Napoleon during the Hundred Days, though largely motivated by reasons of immediate opportunity, reflect to some extent the uncertainty of this judgement.[5]

## Unity and uniformity

One of the features of the new imperial Europe most eloquently denounced by Constant was uniformity, the imposition from above of the same system of governance to territories and populations originally distinguished by different customs and traditions. The notion of uniformity was borrowed from the *Esprit des lois*, from the short chapter 'Des idées d'uniformité' (XXIX, 18). There, Montesquieu described how rulers of empires (the examples given were those of Charlemagne and China) were sometimes tempted to impose the same practices on different subject populations, with the ambition of achieving 'a kind of perfection' in governance. This imposed uniformity may touch on simple practical things, such as weights and measures, but also more substantial ones, like religion. Montesquieu expressed a balanced judgement on this inclination. In his view, the genius of a ruler consisted precisely in knowing when it was best to have uniformity, and when differences were preferable.[6] However, the chapter was often read by commentators as a critique of uniformity.[7] The same theme served a more explicitly polemical purpose in the *Reflections on the Revolution in France* (1790), where Edmund Burke used it, to great rhetorical effect, to describe the new territorial division of France introduced by the revolutionary government. The partition of the country into *départements* designed by 'square measurement' served to illustrate a political logic that preferred artificial symmetries to natural diversities. The straight lines traced by the 'state surveyors' of the Convention to create new regions, ignoring the sinuous natural contours of the landscape, became the symbol of an ideology that valued abstraction more than reality, and opposed empty bureaucratic schemes to the real needs of the people.[8]

In his writings – beginning with the unpublished draft 'Principes de politique' of 1806[9] – Constant echoed Burke's hostility to the 'love of symmetry' of the revolutionary government; he then went on to show how the same 'spirit of system' characterized Bonaparte's despotic rule. Thus, in pages that carry an unmistakable Rousseauian flavour, he conjured up a vivid picture of the new Europe as a vast desert, a vacant space where isolated individuals, deprived of their original attachments and identities, were confronted with a distant, anonymous, despotic power. In this perspective the 'living variety' of local identities, traditions and aspirations was opposed to the deadly 'mechanisms' of uniform governance, which reshaped, flattened and even 'mutilated' every dimension of people's lives, down to the most intimate ones. In the polished version of 1814 he wrote:

> We are always hearing about the great empire, of the whole nation, abstract notions that have no reality. The great empire is nothing independently of its provinces. The whole nation is nothing separated from the parts that compose it ... If they are successively stripped of what they hold dearest, if each of them, isolated so as to be made a victim, reverts, by a strange metamorphosis, to being a portion of the great whole, to serve as the pretext for the sacrifice of another portion, real beings are sacrificed to abstract ones. The people as individuals are sacrificed for the sake of the people *en masse*.[10]

Thus the new Europe created by Bonaparte paid a double price for its unity: on the one hand the loss of the richness of local diversities and autonomies, on the other the isolation of citizens and the relentless surveillance and interference of a remote despotic authority.

For all its rhetorical appeal, this critique of artificial uniformity was not, however, free from ambiguity. In other passages of the same work, Constant presented the same notion of uniformity in rather different terms. In modern times, he explained, the citizens of European nations had acquired similar tastes, lifestyles and aspirations; rather than being divided by old differences and rivalries, they had come to form a single, indistinct 'mass of people':

> While in the past each nation formed an isolated family, the born enemy of other families, a great mass of human beings now exists that,

despite the different names under which they live and their different forms of social organization, are essentially homogeneous in their nature.[11]

This similarity of tastes and interests was given by Constant as the main reason why modern European nations – unlike their pre-modern counterparts – had nothing to gain from being at war with one another, and could not identify with Bonaparte's ambitions of conquest. This image of European nations forming a single, homogeneous population recalled the cosmopolitan vision of some Enlightenment writers. But for Constant the main unifying agent – before any other political or cultural factor – was unquestionably the development of the market:

> The infinite and complex ramifications of commerce have placed the interest of societies above the frontiers of their own territory; the spirit of the age triumphs over the narrow and hostile spirit that men seek to dignify with the name of patriotism.[12]

Detachment from one's original community or nation meant that people were free to decide where and how they wished to live; if their own country no longer suited them, they could choose another. Exile no longer represented the kind of moral death sentence that the ancients had regarded as the most severe of punishments to be inflicted upon a citizen. This mobility of individuals mirrored the freedom commerce created through the circulation of property. In the modern world, wealth, in the form of credit, could not be kept by law or by force within the frontiers of single states, but flowed wherever it was most convenient for it to be, towards those countries that favoured its growth.[13]

Clearly, in Constant's own terms, the 'bad' uniformity imposed by bureaucratic despotism and the 'good' one created by commerce were very intimately related, or at least produced very similar effects. They deprived people of their traditional attachments, 'denationalized' them, turned populations into masses of isolated, anonymous, mobile individuals. In practice it was impossible to tell apart the respective influences of commerce and uniform rule, as these overlapped and reinforced each other. Thus the claim that the uniformity of the new system was an alien mould forced upon reluctant European societies coexisted uneasily with the view that uniformity was to a large extent the natural, inevitable consequence of commercial development.

## War and commerce

Another problematic issue in Constant's attack on the empire was the opposition he established between war and commerce. As he claimed in a famous passage:

> We have finally reached the age of commerce, an age which must necessarily replace that of war, as the age of war was bound to precede it. War and commerce are only two different means to achieve the same end, that of possessing what is desired.[14]

This classical argument about the historical sequence that brought civilization to reject war as a means of the acquisition of material resources was used to stress the anachronistic character of a regime that found in territorial conquest its main raison d'être. The endless military campaigns necessary to sustain Bonaparte's ambitions were not compatible with the habits and aspirations of ordinary European citizens, whose only wish was to enjoy freely and safely the fruits of their labour. By wasting human lives, destroying resources, obstructing trade and restricting liberties, the conquering empire went against the natural evolution of modern societies and was therefore doomed to a rapid decline.

While Constant's passionate denunciation of the intolerable disruption caused by the war was bound to gain credibility with the prolongation of the conflict, the same could not be said of his claim that the politics of conquest must necessarily lead to economic stagnation and impoverishment. In the same pages where he set forth the opposition of war and commerce, Constant described in vivid terms the contemporary phenomenon of a 'military race acting on self-interest alone', showing that war could in fact be turned into a formidable machine in the interest of material gain.[15]

For ancient conquerors the sheer impulse of fighting and the love of glory were far more important than the occasional bounty of war. Their barbarous violence was somewhat ritualized, exercised according to tradition, and not just motivated by gain. The new breed of modern conquerors, on the other hand, subordinated their aggressive practices to 'commercial calculation' alone. They pursued their aim with rational efficiency and were prepared to do anything to satisfy their material interests.

In presenting this portrait of the new conquerors as 'reborn Vandals', Constant added the caution that this type of regime would need to last longer than a generation before it completed the transformation from ancient to modern conquest; and yet his analysis led to the inevitable (if unexpressed) conclusion that there were in fact possible synergies at work between war and commercial interest. Even his recurrent descriptions of the person of Bonaparte as cold, calculating, guided by self-interest alone, and surrounded by a court of meretricious opportunists, seemed to point to the new phenomenon of a purely utilitarian power, unfettered by any ideological or moral constraints. Rather than the enemy of modern liberty, the emperor appeared as the incarnation of its ugly hidden features – greed, indifference, selfishness – and of the unsuspected dangers it carried with it.[16]

As the war came to an end, some foreign observers – who could not be suspected of Bonapartist sympathies – were prepared to recognize the multiple advantages that France had derived from its war-oriented economy and from its conquests. The question was raised in the pages of the influential Whig journal *Edinburgh Review* by Sir James Mackintosh, an old friend of Constant and a prominent liberal writer.[17] In a review of *De l'esprit de conquête*, Mackintosh expressed his appreciation for Constant's book, but set forth some reservations about his friend's views on the state of the French economy.

Constant, he claimed, had been too rigid in his negative assessment of Bonaparte's policies. The confusing circumstances of the war should not obscure the durable social and economic advantages that France had gained since the Revolution. It was in fact impossible to separate the experience of the empire from the deep transformation of French society set in motion by the revolutionary process, a transformation that Bonaparte's regime had pursued and consolidated. Mackintosh stressed in particular the considerable improvement of French agriculture – the transfer of land and capital from the old aristocracy to an active and capable middle class that had been integrated with the landed classes through the acquisition of nationalized properties. He also indicated among the benefits of the regime the creation in the occupied territories of local elites of competent bureaucrats and administrators.[18]

In his writings Constant had always associated the progress of commercial society with free trade. His fidelity to the Smithian tradition had naturally led him to condemn the aggressive French protectionism that culminated in the experience of the Continental Blockade, and to celebrate England as the champion of economic freedom. Things appeared in a different light to English observers, who knew the extent to which their nation's economic success had been sustained all along by 'illiberal' policies, such as the suspension of the convertibility of the pound sterling, the introduction of the income tax or the continuing control exercised over corn prices.[19] In 1815 the Tory government had little difficulty in obtaining wide parliamentary support for a further extension of the Corn Laws to sustain domestic agricultural interest, against the vocal opposition of free traders.[20] The heated debate that followed saw a prominent political economist like Thomas Malthus taking up a position in favour of protectionist policies, indicating France as an example to be followed.[21]

There is no evidence of how Constant responded to Mackintosh's review, though his journal records various meetings with the author in 1815–16.[22] In any case, it is reasonable to assume that his retrospective verdict on the empire would not be substantially altered by a more open-minded recognition of its economic achievements. As Germaine de Staël argued in her *Considérations sur la Révolution française*, Napoleon had used the attack against English trade as 'a sort of crusade', rallying around him domestic commercial and industrial interests. But the short-term advantages that French manufacturers derived from those protectionist policies had to be set against the damage caused by the prolonged disruption and instability of European markets and the consequent decline of confidence that affected the entire system.[23]

What the fluctuations and contradictions in *De l'esprit de conquête* did show, however, was that the economic interests of large social groups could be effectively served, for reasonably long periods of time, by a regime that violated both the freedom of trade and political freedom, a prospect that had not really been taken into consideration in Constant's previous works.

## Federalism: decentralizing representation

The ambiguities associated with uniformity – so suggestively evoked in *De l'esprit de conquête* – were formulated by Constant in more pragmatic and coherent terms in his discussion of the possible role of federalism in representative government. He first addressed the subject at the turn of the century in his unpublished work *Fragments ... d'une constitution républicaine dans un grand pays*,[24] then returned to it in the unpublished *Principes de politique* of 1806,[25] and finally dedicated a chapter to it in the *Principes de politique* of 1815,[26] at the time of his short-lived collaboration with Napoleon. As is always the case with Constant, some passages and formulations reappear in almost identical form in the different texts, but the focus of the arguments shifts significantly through time.

In the *Fragments*, written when the Napoleonic adventure had only just begun, Constant presented a general discussion of 'federalism' as a possible response to the difficulties in the governance of large states.

The aim of the exercise was to prove that – contrary to Montesquieu's influential view – large and densely populated nations could in fact be successfully run by representative institutions of a republican kind. In a chapter dedicated to what he called *pouvoir administratif* he set forth the respective advantages of small and large states, adjusting to some extent to his purpose the received wisdom of eighteenth-century writers on the subject.[27]

Small states, he argued, were superior to large ones as regards morality and justice, and offered greater tranquillity and happiness to their citizens. Large states, on the other hand, were more effective in protecting their citizens from foreign aggression and in preserving their independence. As small states were generally very attached to their customs and traditions, they were less open to improvement and less conducive to 'enlightened' policies. The real problem with large states was that the strength of their governments, which was necessary in order to rule over a vast territory and a large population, could easily degenerate into despotism.

How was it possible to combine the efficacy of strong, centralized regimes with the happy freedom of small local ones? Federalism seemed the obvious solution; but the term – Constant explained – was generally used incoherently to designate very different institutions. If by federalism was meant the external association of independent states – like Holland or Switzerland – then the institution was 'especially vicious'. Even the American model, though far and away the best of these 'gouvernements fédératifs' (confederations), was unsatisfactory, since the authority of its central government had thus far proved insufficient and in need of reinforcement.[28] In spite of his critique of the American constitution, the 'good' form of federalism Constant was proposing resembled in fact very closely the federalist ideal of a balanced combination of local and central power:

> Each partial society must be dependent – to a greater or lesser degree, even for its internal arrangements, on the general association, and federalism properly so called is a defective institution, unless it presupposes such mutual dependence. But at the same time the internal arrangements of the particular factions, insofar as they have no influence upon the engagements these factions have with the general association, must remain in a state of perfect independence.[29]

Here Constant could draw upon the extensive analysis developed on the subject by Jacques Necker, since his failed attempt in the 1770s to decentralize French administration by creating locally elected provincial assemblies. In his writings, Necker had identified the main obstacle to the reform of French government in the unwillingness – first of the monarchy, and later of the revolutionary regime – to surrender any portion of the power concentrated in national institutions and in the capital to local authorities.[30] Constant subscribed to this view, arguing that the constitutions of 1791 and 1795 failed to articulate successfully the competences of central and local powers, while the most recent constitution of 1799 simply turned local powers into the 'blind instrument' of the executive. In order to avoid these errors, the constitution of a large nation must make a clear distinction between executive and administrative power. Naturally administrative institutions were part of the executive, but unless they were decentralized and enjoyed a high degree of autonomy, the machinery of the executive could not function adequately:

> This leads us to establish a truth that we regard as fundamental. Until now administrative power has been considered as a dependent branch of executive power. On the contrary, if administrative power must never obstruct the executive, it should not be dependent on it.[31]

As Necker had convincingly argued, what was at stake was not just the efficiency of government, but its legitimacy in the eyes of the people. Decentralization was efficient because local problems could be better understood and dealt with at a local level. But, more importantly, people would be far readier to accept any legislative measures that emanated from authorities they could recognize and identify with. When the measures were new and disruptive – as in the case of structural reforms – this recognition became even more vital. The same logic worked for the political class. If the representatives of the people spent all their time in the capital city, busy with the preoccupations and intrigues of national politics, they would lose touch with the preoccupations of their electors and neglect their interests.

These views on the need to give a decentralized form to administrative power reappeared, virtually unchanged, in the text of the *Principes de politique* of 1815, written to illustrate the new constitution that Constant had drafted, on Napoleon's demand, during the Hundred Days, the never-to-be-applied *Acte additionnel aux constitutions de l'empire* of 22 April 1815.[32]

The constitution did not in fact make any provisions for the autonomy of 'municipal powers', the question being postponed to further legislative interventions once peace would be restored. Yet in his commentary Constant took the opportunity to reassert his belief in the need to introduce into internal administration 'a great deal of federalism', but a federalism 'of a new kind', that is to say the same combination of local autonomy and central authority he had originally outlined in the *Fragments*. This was, he concluded, the only possible means to achieve 'peaceful and lasting patriotism'.[33]

## Federalism: consensus and legitimacy

In the *Fragments*, the question of federalism and of the relation between central and local authorities focused upon the nature of executive power and upon the problems connected with the administration of large states. Empires appeared fleetingly in the text merely as historical examples of large political units. In the 1806 *Principes de politique* the issue was the same – the relations between centre and periphery – but the context and the perspective of the discussion had shifted. The 'large state' had now acquired the contours of a modern empire, where the problems of governance went beyond the original question of the efficient execution of the law.

In particular, Constant examined what he described as 'three dangerous ideas' in the practice of government: these ideas were uniformity, stability and the 'inconsiderate desire for premature improvements'.[34] The notion of 'uniformity' – borrowed from Montesquieu and destined to play a central role in *De l'esprit de conquête* – was introduced here for the first time. The other two dangerous ideas – stability and premature improvements – were both errors of judgement about the timing of reforms. The former was the attitude that consisted in clinging to the past, resisting necessary changes. The latter was the ambition to introduce novelties when popular sentiment was still unprepared for them and hostile to them.

In discussing the issue of uniformity, Constant repeated a number of arguments about the disadvantages of large political units and the need for federalism that he had already presented in the *Fragments*. Here, however, the original example of 'a nation of twenty million people' featured alongside references to an empire ruling over different populations and facing a far more significant degree of political and cultural diversity. The hostility of local administrators towards measures emanating from a centralized bureaucracy was replaced by the active resistance of peoples defending their own identities and way of life against alien rule.

In some respects, the structure of the problem was the same – how to make the best of the advantages of large political units while minimizing their disadvantages. In dealing with ordinary administration, Constant's solution was that representation must be decentralized. Decisions over matters of local concern should be taken by locally elected (and locally resident) authorities. National decisions having an impact upon local interests should be subjected to a degree of local control. The precise form this transfer of power to localities was to take remained unspecified, but the general principle was clear enough: a people's right to exercise control over political and administrative decisions increased whenever these initiatives concerned them more directly and immediately. Unless this principle was respected, the representatives of the people could not perform their role adequately:

> Placed in the capital, far away from the portion of the people which has elected them, representatives lose sight of the uses, needs and way of life of those they represent. They indulge in general ideas of equalization, symmetry, uniformity, mass changes and universal reforms that cause widespread upheaval, disorder and uncertainty. This tendency must be opposed ... The larger a state is, the more a single electoral body is inadmissible; the stronger a central authority is, the more choices need to come from below, not from above.[35]

However, the relations between the central authority and the citizens became more problematic when what were at stake were not just measures of ordinary administration, but important, wide-reaching reforms. This is where the question of timing, of stability and premature improvements became crucial. Constant had argued all along that large states were more favourable than small ones to progress and enlightened reforms. Large nations were generally more advanced and open to new ideas, while a strong central government could more easily overcome factional resistance to change. Whatever their form of government, large states introducing far-reaching reforms seemed to require a certain degree of authoritarian initiative, to break down existing practices. History had proved this to be true in the case of absolute monarchies, like eighteenth-century Prussia and Russia, just as it had in the case of republican regimes like America or revolutionary France.

The difficulty was that, on the one hand, without this 'authoritarian' impulse from above the reforms would never be realized; on the other, the very fact that the initiative came from above aroused hostility and resistance in the population. The experience of the French Convention showed how public opinion could reject the same measures it had previously demanded just because the initiative came from the government. Napoleon's empire was the most recent example of this kind of dilemma. Possibly some of the improvements introduced by the French administration were not worth the disruption they had cost. But what about those 'acts of justice' in the field of human rights that French conquest had made possible? Should they be rejected in order to respect the prejudices of the most backward sections of the European population? And what about those enemies of progress who wished to bring back serfdom, religious intolerance or torture on the strength of popular sentiment?

In response to this kind of question, Constant maintained that the only way to establish durable improvements was to introduce them gradually, respecting as far as possible public opinion, and refraining in any case from acts of force or injustice towards particular individuals. Interestingly, he believed that the ordinary mechanisms of political representation were inadequate in these cases to show what people really wanted. They were inadequate partly because it was not possible 'to count suffrages' on particular issues (apparently he did not contemplate the possibility of referendums) and partly because, when sensitive issues were at stake, people might react negatively to the decisions of their representatives, even if they had originally voted for them and regarded their mandate as legitimate. The example he offered was that of the suppression of convents during the Revolution. Things would have been very different if, instead of driving people out of them regardless of their feelings and their personal circumstances, the doors had been opened to those who wished to leave. There were domains of public action where popular consensus had to be tested and eventually won over outside the ordinary procedure of election – through open discussion, controversy, the circulation of information and such like. Important reforms must be introduced gradually precisely to give people the time to react, to criticize and eventually adjust to novelty.[36]

In 1815 Constant was still reasonably optimistic about the state of public opinion, claiming that the natural evolution of modern European societies would necessarily lead them towards justice and progress, and that rulers must simply 'obey time' in order to do the right thing.[37] In later years this militant optimism would be replaced by a more mitigated judgement about the tendency of public opinion towards progress. In 1829, the year prior to his death, he wrote:

> It is in vain that we talk of enlightenment, liberty, philosophy. The abyss may open under our steps; savages may overpower us; impostors may rise among us; and, far more likely, our governments may become tyrannical.[38]

Yet if anything this sombre perspective would strengthen the writer's belief in the need to give more scope to popular aspirations and sentiments through consultation and debate.

To conclude, Constant's vision of European nations as part of an integrated political and economic system emerged from the context of the meteoric rise and fall of the French Empire. Inevitably, much of what he wrote on the subject was embedded in those ephemeral circumstances, and in the climate of conflict and instability they generated. In particular, the severe crisis that accompanied the collapse of Napoleon's regime made it very difficult for him – as for most of his contemporaries – to look at the future of European society with reasonable clarity and detachment. The fitful and dispirited entries in his journal for the years 1815–16 convey very vividly this sense of confusion and helplessness, of political disarray and existential turmoil.[39]

However, two centuries later, some of Constant's intuitions about the predicament of modern European states and about their governance have not lost their power, and can still speak to our own preoccupations and difficulties. Constant understood that the needs, expectations and way of life of the citizens of modern Europe were bound to become increasingly similar and interdependent. Beyond any contingent events, strong historical forces, of which commerce and credit were the most powerful, were in fact leading irresistibly in that direction. This was not a novel idea, as it had been anticipated, from different perspectives and with varying appreciations, by some Enlightenment writers. But what Constant brought to it was an especially realistic and pragmatic understanding of the implications of this process of unification. On the one hand he did not subscribe to Rousseau's belief that European states, having lost their original national identities, were 'rushing towards their ruin'[40]; on the other, he did not see the advent of an enlightened, cosmopolitan society as an effortless transition that European governments and their citizens could simply take in their stride. On the contrary, he argued that a great deal of political effort and ingenuity – as well as of luck – would be necessary to make the somewhat inhospitable habitat of modern Europe at all viable for its population.

Being the anonymous subjects of vast, interdependent states would not necessarily make people lose their souls, as Rousseau had anticipated; but it would generate much unease and create a powerful need for alternative forms of identity and recognition. Without some correctives – such as 'a great deal of federalism' and recurrent appeals to public opinion – political authorities were bound to become far too alien and distant to command any real loyalty. A decentralized administration could reduce the distance between the people and the state; but it was not within the power of representation to give full expression to public opinion, address broad questions of collective interest or shape popular consensus. Indeed representative government – the political system Constant had so militantly advocated all his life – could only offer a partial and somewhat inadequate solution to the problem of the relations between modern citizens and their rulers.[41]

## Notes

1. Beatrice Fink (1994) 'L'Europe de Constant vue à travers *De l'esprit de conquête'*, *Le Groupe de Coppet et l'Europe, 1789–1830*, Actes du Ve Colloque de Coppet (Tübingen, Lausanne, Institut Benjamin Constant and Paris: Jean Touzot), pp. 97–105 (p. 105).
2. See John Dunn (1994) 'The Identity of the Bourgeois Liberal Republic', in Biancamaria Fontana (ed.), *The Invention of the Modern Republic* (Cambridge: Cambridge University Press), pp. 206–25.
3. On Constant's relation to the political economy tradition, see Biancamaria Fontana (1991) *Benjamin Constant and the Post-Revolutionary Mind* (New Haven and London: Yale University Press).
4. On the evolution of Constant's political career, see Paul Bastid (1966) *Benjamin Constant et sa doctrine* (Paris: Librairie Armand Colin), vol. 1; Kurt Kloocke (1984) *Benjamin Constant: Une biographie intellectuelle* (Geneva: Droz); Dennis Wood (1993) *Benjamin Constant: A Biography* (London: Routledge).
5. See Constant's own account of this experience in the *Mémoires sur les Cent-Jours*, to be found in Kurt Kloocke, Jean-Charles Biaudet and André Cabanis (eds) (1993) *Oeuvres complètes* (Tübingen: M. Niemeyer), vol. 14.
6. Montesquieu, *De l'esprit des lois*, in Roger Caillois (ed.) (1951) *Oeuvres complètes* (Paris: Gallimard), vol. 2, p. 882.
7. See for example the commentary by Condorcet (1780) 'Observations sur le vingt-neuvième livre de *L'esprit des lois*', in Antoine-Louis-Claude Destutt de Tracy (1970) *Commentaire sur L'esprit de lois de Montesquieu suivi d'Observations inédites ... de Condorcet* (Geneva: Slatkine). I am grateful to Bernard Manin for drawing my attention to this text, a reproduction of the Paris edition of 1819.
8. Conor Cruise O'Brien (ed.) (1973) *Edmund Burke's Reflections on the Revolution in France* (Harmondsworth: Penguin Books) p. 287.
9. On the status of this manuscript in relation to Constant's published works see Etienne Hofmann (1980) *Les 'Principes de politique' de Benjamin Constant: La genèse d'une oeuvre et l'évolution de la pensée de leur auteur (1789–1806)*, 2 vols (Geneva: Droz), in particular vol. 1.
10. Benjamin Constant (1814) 'De l'esprit de conquête et de l'usurpation', in Marcel Gauchet (ed.) (1997) *Écrits politiques* (Paris: Gallimard); I am quoting from my English translation in B. Constant (1988) *Political Writings* (Cambridge: Cambridge University Press), p. 77.
11. Ibid., pp. 52–3.
12. Ibid., p. 54.

13. See also the development of this concept in Part II, Ch. 14 of *De l'esprit de conquête*, in ibid., pp. 140–2.
14. Ibid., p. 53.
15. See Ch. 4 of the same work, ibid., pp. 56–9. With this idea of a modern 'military race' Constant put a new spin on the eighteenth-century fear that a militarized nation might gain supremacy in Europe by emancipating itself from the constraints of the national debt. For a contemporary example of this view see Robert Walsh (1810) *A Letter on the Genius and Disposition of the French Government, including a View of the Taxation of the French Empire* (Philadelphia: Hopkins and Early); for an ambitious historical reconstruction of the debates on public debt see Michael Sonenscher (2007) *Before the Deluge: Public Debt, Inequality and the Intellectual Origins of the French Revolution* (Princeton: Princeton University Press).
16. On the image of Napoleon as a utilitarian, calculating agent cf. Germaine de Staël in Jacques Godechot (ed.) (1983) *Considérations sur la Révolution française* (Paris: Tallandier), Part IV, pp. 353 ff.
17. Mackintosh's best-known work remains his reply to Burke's *Reflections* (2008): *Vindiciae Gallicae: A Defence of the French Revolution 1791* (London: Palgrave Macmillan). On Mackintosh's life and career see Robert Mackintosh (ed.) (1836) *Memoirs on the Life of the Right Honourable Sir James Mackintosh*, 2 vols (London: Moxton); Patrick O'Leary (1989) *Sir James Mackintosh: The Whig Cicero* (Aberdeen: Aberdeen University Press).
18. James Mackintosh, 'France', *Edinburgh Review*, XXIV (November 1814) and XXV (February 1815).
19. For an overview on eighteenth-century debates on free trade see Istvan Hont (2005) *Jealousy of Trade, International Competition and the Nation State in Historical Perspective* (Cambridge Mass. and London: Belknap Press of Harvard University Press), Introduction; on the English debate during the Napoleonic wars see Biancamaria Fontana (1985) *Rethinking the Politics of Commercial Society: The Edinburgh Review, 1802–1832* (Cambridge: Cambridge University Press).
20. William Smart (1910) *Economic Annals of the Nineteenth Century*, 2 vols (London: Macmillan), vol. 1, pp. 445–60. See also François Crouzet (1958) *L'économie britannique et le blocus continental: 1806–1813*, 2 vols (Paris: Presses universitaires de France).
21. Thomas Robert Malthus (1815) *The Grounds of an Opinion on the Policy of Restricting the Importation of Foreign Corn* (London: John Murray).
22. After Waterloo Mackintosh helped Constant to find an English publisher for his *Mémoires sur les Cent-Jours*, see Norman King (1978) 'Après les Cent-Jours: Trois lettres de Benjamin Constant écrites en 1815', *Cahiers Staëliens*, XXV, 25–44.
23. Germaine de Staël in Jacques Godechot (ed.) (1983) *Considérations sur la Révolution française* (Paris: Tallandier), p. 404.
24. Benjamin Constant in Henri Grange (ed.) (1991) *Fragments d'un ouvrage abandonné sur la possibilité d'une constitution républicaine dans un grand pays* (Paris: Aubier).
25. See n. 9 above. For an English translation of the 1806 *Principes* see Benjamin Constant, in E. Hofmann (ed.) (2003) *Principles of Politics Applicable to all Governments* (Indianapolis: Liberty Fund), tr. Dennis O'Keeffe.

26. Benjamin Constant, 'Principes de politique', in Marcel Gauchet (ed.) (1997) Écrits politiques (Paris: Gallimard), pp. 303–506; B. Constant (1988) Political Writings (Cambridge: Cambridge University Press), pp. 169–305.
27. Constant in Grange (ed.) Fragments, Book VIII, Ch. 9.
28. In particular Constant claimed that the weakness of the American federal government had prevented the abolition of slavery (Constant in Grange (ed.) Fragments, p. 406). I found no evidence that Constant read the Federalist Papers; the only American authors he cites are Franklin, Jefferson and Paine.
29. Constant in Grange (ed.) Fragments, p. 408 (all translations from Constant's French texts are my own).
30. This theme was first set forth in his Mémoire de M. Necker au Roi sur l'établissement des administrations provinciales (1781) and continued to appear in all his major works, including Du pouvoir exécutif dans les grands états (1792), De la Révolution française (1796) and finally Dernières vues de politique et de finances (1802). See Henri Grange (1974) Les idées de Necker (Paris: Klincksieck), pp. 390–6.
31. Constant in Grange (ed.) Fragments, p. 410.
32. On the Acte additionnel see Jacques Godechot (ed.) (1979) Les constitutions de la France depuis 1789 (Paris: Flammarion), pp. 225–39.
33. See Ch. 12 of the Principes de politique: 'Du pouvoir municipal, des autorités locales et d'un nouveau genre de fédéralisme', in Gauchet (ed.), Écrits politiques, pp. 423–30; B. Constant (1988) Political Writings (Cambridge: Cambridge University Press), pp. 251–5.
34. Hofmann, La genèse, vol. 2, p. 385.
35. Ibid., p. 392.
36. Ibid., pp. 410–11.
37. See yet another reformulation of this perspective in the chapter added to the 4th edition of De l'esprit de conquête, 'Des innovations, des réformes, de l'uniformité et de la stabilité des institutions', in Gauchet (ed.), Écrits politiques, pp. 279–90; Constant, Political Writings, pp. 149–57.
38. Benjamin Constant (1829) Mélanges de littérature et politique (Paris: Pichon et Didier), p. 388.
39. Benjamin Constant (1957) 'Journaux intimes', in Alfred Roulin (ed.), Oeuvres (Paris: Gallimard), pp. 730–89.
40. Jean-Jacques Rousseau (1772) 'Considérations sur le gouvernement de Pologne', ed. Jean Fabre, in B. Gagnebin and M. Raymond (eds) (1969) Oeuvres complètes, 4 vols (Paris: Gallimard), vol. 3, pp. 951–1041 (p. 954).
41. On the limitations of representative government in this respect see Benjamin Constant (1819) Discours de la liberté des anciens comparée à celle des modernes, in Gauchet (ed.) Écrits politiques, pp. 589–619; Constant, Political Writings, pp. 307–28.

# 9
# Industry, Government and Europe: From the Mercantilists to Saint-Simon

Gino Longhitano

## 1

In October 1814, six months after Napoleon had left Fontainebleau for the island of Elba, a 112-page pamphlet appeared in Paris entitled *De la réorganisation de la société européenne*. The work, printed by Adrien Egron, was written by Henri de Saint-Simon and Augustin Thierry, 'son élève', and carried the subtitle *De la nécessité et des moyens de rassembler les peuples de l'Europe en un seul corps politique en conservant à chacun son indépendance nationale*. Saint-Simon contributed the ideas,[1] while Augustin Thierry, still only nineteen years old, organized them and put them into a shape fit for publication as a book.

At that time France was just coming out of a period of revolution and war, and liberals hoped that this chapter in France's history, characterized by internal conflict and complicated still further by international conflict, was now definitively closed. Louis XVIII made his own the Charter of 1814, whose basic tenets had been laid down by the Napoleonic Senate, adding a Preamble which attempted to change the sense of the Charter but which in fact accepted its contents. It seemed that this was the best way to put an end to the period of crisis which the country had been going through for years and to bring back together the scattered threads of the 'liberal' revolution. More than a few people, then, considered the 1814 Charter the best constitution that France had ever had. It accepted the social consequences of the revolutionary process, but left out of play the masses, who liberals, from Madame de Staël down, considered responsible for the disasters of the period dominated by Robespierre and Napoleon. It also seemed capable of putting an end to internal conflict through a civilizing process which viewed the Revolution part of the evolution of French liberty – a process which had given France a constitution which brought it closer to England. True, it still needed to be seen if this constitution would transform the French political system into one which was little more than representative or if it would furnish the country with the tools necessary to create a parliamentary government. Even in England, though, this area still seemed to be a rather grey one.

The problem of the international conflict remained, of course. That conflict had shattered any certainty of pacific progress in which the eighteenth-century idea of the *douceur* of commerce had come to reign over political relations between nations. Had not the sad days of commercial wars returned with the way England had declared war on French industry and with the Continental Blockade that was France's response? What had happened to the anti-mercantilist movement of the eighteenth century and the ideas of Jean-François Melon, which had pointed to the ability of the market and commerce to pacify international relations and resolve internal and international conflicts that may have arisen due to the economic situation? Now that the French Revolution had come to a close, would it be possible to find a way to peace and European unity? Would the Congress of Vienna, which was just about to begin, be capable of handling the problem of peace through its treaties? And where had that sudden outburst of warlike spirit that had set fire to Europe come from? Was it just a product of the Revolution itself, or had other factors contributed to it?

A few months before – the preface was dated 22 April – another pamphlet had come off the presses at Le Normant in Paris. It was the third edition[2] of a work by Benjamin Constant that was to influence the political debate greatly and which, in future years, was to become a fundamental reference point for French liberal thought: *De l'esprit de conquête et de l'usurpation dans leurs rapports avec la civilisation européenne*. This work held the spirit of conquest, represented by Napoleon,[3] as responsible for the war in Europe. This spirit of conquest was an anachronistic one,[4] despite the fact that, in certain circumstances, war, which was the way in which it showed its face, was, according to Constant, 'dans la nature de l'homme' (p. 197).[5] Was it possible to say, however, given the 'current situation of the European peoples', where that love of war lay? Was it part of their national characters, or was it due instead to the force of circumstance? Since it was not possible to give a positive answer to this question, the only conclusion that was possible was that 'in order to lead nations to war and conquest, it is necessary to upset the situation in which they find themselves. This is something that never happens without inflicting many ills upon them and going against their character, and this never happens without indulging their vices in many ways.'[6]

In ancient times, when the population was divided into small independent neighbourhood groups, men had to use arms to conquer land, a sense of security, independence and an existence for themselves, even at the expense of war. 'In this sense, the world today is the exact opposite of the ancient world.'[7] In circumstance such as these, then, war was natural. But over the centuries things changed. The populations of Europe – Constant goes on – were now organized into a variety of social forms and no longer lived in small isolated groups, and they all tended towards peace. 'We are now in the Age of Commerce, an age which necessarily substitutes the Age of War, just as the Age of War necessarily preceded it.'[8] And again:

> The ultimate aim of modern nations is repose, and, with repose, prosperity, and, as the source of prosperity, industry. War is an increasingly inefficacious way of reaching this aim. What it brings does not offer, either to individuals or nations, benefits which equal the results of peaceful labour and the regular exchange of goods, labour and services.[9]

Constant's argument was inspired by the themes of classical economics as re-elaborated by Jean-Baptiste Say, and was anti-Bonapartist with respect both to international relations and to national institutions. It would not be long before it conquered liberal politics in Restoration France. Charles Comte's and Charles Dunoyer's *Censeur européen* and Saint-Simon's *L'industrie* would soon appear as the logical continuation of this line of thought. Later still, Augustin Thierry would make Constant's theory the central reference point of his historical work, from his *Vues sur les révolutions d'Angleterre* through to the *Histoire de la conquête de l'Angleterre par les Normands*, and from *Considérations sur l'histoire de France* to the *Essai sur l'histoire de la formation et des progrès du Tiers État*. Classical economics, which took economics out of politics, became the foundation of the liberal 'political' model that used these ideas as a basis upon which to construct itself and its own history. The French Revolution gave rise to a concept of democracy, reintroduced politics to the social arena, gave the masses a role to play in regulating the balance of power within society, brought with it the idea of egalitarianism and ended by creating Robespierre and Napoleon, who, to the liberals, seemed nothing more than a 'Robespierre à cheval'; but it also placed in jeopardy the process through which that model could be realized and interrupted its development. Napoleon, Robespierre and Louis XIV were seen as being a part of this process. Later, Tocqueville would underline this idea very clearly, and would transform Louis XIV, the representative of a 'strong' state, an idea also proposed by the supporters of egalitarianism, into the 'father of modern socialism'. Napoleon was the symbol of the spirit of conquest and usurpation, and his defeat seemed to have remedied the situation. But would peace now return?

## 2

If Constant's writings revolved around general principles, those of Saint-Simon and Thierry dealt in a more concrete fashion with the details of European history as seen from a political perspective. Their arguments differed from those of Constant on a number of points, but the spirit was essentially the same. Europe knew no peace because the institutions of the countries that go to make it up were different from one another. How then would it be possible to create institutions that are the same? On what principles should these institutions be founded? What did the history of Europe teach us about this?

The *Réorganization de la société européenne* was aimed at the parliaments of France and England. It showed the members of both those parliaments how, before the sixteenth century, all the nations of Europe formed 'a single body politic, peaceful within and armed against the enemies of its constitution and its independence'.[10] It was a body politic united passively by the Roman Catholic religion and actively by the clergy of the Church of Rome. Of course, this was not the model which Saint-Simon and Thierry had in mind, nor did they believe that it would be possible to return to it. The authors considered the government of the clergy – like the governments of all the peoples of Europe at that time – an aristocratic hierarchy. General opinion had it that the power of the clergy was superior even to that of kings, and as such it acted as a brake on the ambitions of the sovereigns of the individual nations and created a balance of power in Europe. The court of Rome ruled over all the other courts, just as the latter ruled over their respective peoples. Europe was one great aristocracy subdivided into a number of smaller local aristocracies, all of whom were dependent on the Church of Rome, all of whom were subject to its influence, its judgements and its decrees.

For all its limitations, that government managed in some way to ensure the maintenance of peace. However, it also had a weakness – it was an institution founded on a general opinion, and thus could not last any longer than the general opinion upon which it was founded. Luther destroyed that sense of respect that was the foundation of the clergy's power, and threw that particular model of European unity into disarray.

At that point, half of Europe threw off the chains of papism and destroyed the only link that kept it tied to the rest of the continent. The long war of religion that followed created a Europe made up of independent sovereign states, but it was the Europe of sovereigns, not of the people.

A new European order arose from the Treaty of Westphalia, called at the time the 'balance of powers', but it did not bring peace in its train. 'Europe was divided into two confederations, each of which attempted to stay on a par with the other: it was like creating a war and then maintaining it through constitutional means.'[11]

In order to preserve that balance of power, all that the individual nations had done was to expand their military might. Since the Treaty of Westphalia, war had been the condition in which Europe habitually lived. England, guided by governments which believed that the idea of liberty was a domestic issue, had profited from this struggle for a balance of power and constructed its own might upon it, to the detriment of the other European nations. Separated from the rest of the continent by the sea, it no longer had anything in common with the other nations of Europe. It had its own national religion and a government that was different from the other governments of Europe. However, it had also provided itself with a constitution founded on what should be at the basis of every constitution: the liberty and happiness of the people – but of its *own* people. From that point on, its political aim was supreme domination. It had nurtured the arts of navigation, commerce and industry, and had discouraged other nations from doing the same wherever possible. It had given its support to arbitrary governments, keeping for itself the liberty and goods that these offered:

> Its gold, its arms, its politics – it used everything in an attempt to maintain this so-called balance of power which, by setting the nations of Europe against one another and thus destroying them, left it free to do whatever it wished with impunity.[12]

As a result:

> this colossal English power threatens to subdue the whole world. This is how England, free and contented within and hard and despotic without, has managed for a century to play the whole of Europe for a fool, toying with it as it wishes. This situation is too monstrous to continue. It is in Europe's interest to free itself of this tyranny, which is so noisome to it, and it is in England's interest not to tarry too long, lest Europe, armed, come and free itself of its own will.[13]

But even England was aware that this situation could not last, despite the opposition of the Tory party to the idea. The damage produced by widespread, drawn-out war had made it clear that it was time to change that policy, and the lessons of economic science pointed in the same direction. The France of the age of the Charter seemed to offer Europe the chance to move forward as one towards a confederation of states bound together by shared institutions, as was medieval Europe, but whose foundations were radically different. It was to be a Europe ruled over by a general government which was to the peoples what the national governments were to individuals. Of course, this common foundation needed to be discovered. The nineteenth century was too distant from the thirteenth. It would be better for Europe if it now adopted a constitution based on principles drawn from the nature of things as they were, rather than on a set of transitory beliefs or opinions. England had shown the way to go by being the first nation to do away with the feudal system within its borders. Even if it wished to, though, England could not change the state of things in Europe on its own. In southern Europe the power of the Catholic Church was sill used as an instrument to keep people in a state of servitude and uphold the despotic rule of princes. The peoples of two nations, however, had freed themselves of despotism, and the positive outcome of the French Revolution had laid the basis for a union between France and England. Now that France had experienced the damage caused by war and was flushed with the strength given it by its new institutions, it could – according to our authors – unite with England to become the centre of liberal principles in Europe. Little could be expected from the Congress which was about to take place in Vienna. The interests represented by the states that were gathering there were the interests of monarchs and governments, not the common interests of the peoples of Europe. Political power in most of the states taking part was in the hands of despotic governments. How would it be possible then to identify the common interest of the peoples of Europe?

## 3

'Everybody says that Europe is in a violent situation at the moment. But what is the nature of this situation? How has it arisen? Has it always been like this? Can it come to an end? These are questions that remain without an answer'[14] was the reply of the two authors. Political ties were like social ties; the power of one and the other could be assured by similar motives. However, it was not a question of sentiment. What really counted were *interests*. When people united, as when men united, what was needed was some form of organization. Europe would not have peace simply by virtue of treaties and Congresses. Despite the vices and the ambitions of the popes and their priests, Europe had not gone to war often during the Middle Ages, and the wars that had taken place were of little importance. Religious unity, which was at the basis of all, held up, but its existence was a precarious one, because the Christian idea of *brotherhood* could only appeal to sentiment, not to the common *interests* of peoples. The crisis precipitated by Luther had thus paved the way for different attempts at universal domination. Charles V, Philip II, Louis XIV, Napoleon and the English had aimed at it one after the other. Two plans had emerged to put an end to the wars which the system of the 'balance of powers' in Europe was powerless to prevent. The first had been formulated by Henry IV, who, however, had not had enough time to put it into action. The second, formulated by the abbot of Saint-Pierre, was based on a general confederation of all the sovereigns of Europe, and foresaw the establishment of a permanent congress of plenipotentiaries, with a diet in which the sovereigns would have the right to vote. The ongoing power of the monarchs would be guaranteed in the face of any hostile action by a foreign power or any act of rebellion on the part of the people. The diet would act as arbiter, and would be able to banish any sovereign who broke the treaty. The object of the scheme was to ensure perpetual peace for all. It was, though, utopian, because it had as its starting point the interests of the sovereigns themselves. If it had been put into action, Saint-Pierre's plan would not have guaranteed peace and would have preserved what remained of the feudal system, rendering it indestructible. It was a plan that would preserve peace among the crowned heads. The situation as it was in Europe during the fifteenth century, according to the authors, was 'far superior to the Abbot of Saint-Pierre's plan'.[15] Of course, the application of its principles made it corrupt. What is more, the general opinions that were at the foundation of government power in Europe were run through with anachronistic superstitions which the clergy upheld in order to preserve their own power and hinder any spread of enlightened ideas. Now, however, the development of scientific ideas was progressively eating away at popular superstition.

The constitution that could ensure peace in Europe had to come from the application of the sciences. These had to be put to use in creating the best possible constitution for Europe. Saint-Simon and Thierry went into detail on this point, explaining how the European constitution ought to work, how a European parliament could be made up, how the liberal constitutions already in place in France and England could give rise to a constitution for all European peoples, and how the local interests of the individual states and the interests of Europe as a whole could be made to move forward as one.

By common accord, France and England would come together to establish a European parliament. Representatives of the other European nations would then adhere to this one by one as they progressively came to share in the common interest. There was a need to create a Europe made up of its peoples.

The common interests of the European peoples would be made manifest in this parliament. However, the representatives chosen by the people would have to be the right ones:

> Only merchants, scientists, magistrates and administrators should be called upon to constitute the Chamber of Deputies of this great parliament. Everything that has to do with the common interests of European society, in fact, can be related to the sciences, the arts, the law, commerce, administration and industry.[16]

## 4

*L'industrie*: The word was out. Three years later, with *L'Industrie*, the two authors went into this idea in greater depth. Industry was the basis of a new constitution suited to the times. It represented the common interest of the people. Global society rested on industry. Industry was the only thing that guaranteed its existence, the source of all its riches and all its prosperity.

The starting point was the idea of the nation, of what nations were in terms of the relationships that link them to one another and of the relationships between them over the course of the centuries. A nation was a group of people bound together by interest. The Greeks were a nation because they fought together against the Persians. The Italian city states that fought together against Barbarossa were a nation. Devout Europeans who threw themselves against the nations of Islam at the time of the Crusades were a nation. But none of these nations lasted very long because the interests that bound them together were of a transitory nature. 'A nation means a *league*, and a league means a unity of effort. Wherever there is something which men are striving for together, there, and only there, is there a nation.'[17] According to these writers, whenever men think in the same way and wish for the same things, they become a nation, irrespective of the lands they come from, the languages they speak, or the governments, habits, or customs they have.

Their belief was, then, that nations come together, destroy themselves and maintain their existence on their own. Men from different lands who speak different languages are part of the same nation if they have the same interests in common. Only the *populace* believes that a foreigner is worthy of derision. The enlightened man believes a foreigner is a member of the same society as himself, a man whose efforts go in the same direction as his own, a man who has the same aim as himself: the wellbeing and liberty of all mankind. The common herd believes that a foreigner is an evil man who is only concerned with harming those around him by selling his goods without buying any in return, by taking money off others. He is a man whose industry needs to be undermined, to the point that he has nothing left to sell and must buy everything, so that his money can be taken off him. The common herd, however, is living in the past. The governments of Robespierre and Napoleon were upheld by 'the most ignorant part of the French population'. It is the *élites* who truly represent civilization; and yet, if we were to observe the political situation as it is, there were still many states in which it was the voice of the *populace* that decides what is to be done.

The reason they gave was that civilization only advances very slowly. In ancient times, they related, the peoples were essentially military in character. Any pacific form of work was carried out by slaves. At that time, the major industry was war. Only when the European city states started to free themselves did peaceful endeavour become a part of the natural life of the state, transforming itself from the passive activity that it had been in the past to become the active part of the life of the state. Freedom from feudal serfdom and the establishment of an age of peace, now the aim of the state, are linked to this event. These two changes were the trigger for all the revolutions of the past, and from them will emerge all the revolutions of the future.

Over the course of time, nations had changed both in form and content:

> At the beginning the nations were soldiers who fought together loyally. They were barbarous, yet noble. Then they turned into small merchants intent on fighting for a place to set up their workshops and stealing customers so that they could sell more. Today they are rich merchants with huge commercial concerns, numerous factories and large amounts of accumulated capital. This new situation is very different from the preceding one, but the behaviour it gives rise to is different, too. Will the nations hold their spirit at a lower level than their fortunes?[18]

The line the two authors took is clear. In the years that follow, Augustin Thierry would develop this basic theory in a quite extraordinary fashion to produce a broad historical model of events. Industry, he felt, guaranteed the internal and external equilibrium of nations and was the condition through which peace within nations and between nations was established. Economics, re-elaborated on the basis of the principles found in J.-B. Say's *loi des débouchés*, was now the key to national and international peace. It had been taken out of the hands of the politicians and given back to civil society at large, and it was economics which eliminated social conflict. Seen as the basis of a nation's riches and power, on the other hand, economics became the raison d'être for the spirit of conquest.

## 5

This, according to Thierry, was the reason why it was necessary to divorce the idea of industry from those models which linked it to a view of economic activity as the basis of the riches and power of a state. It needed to be divorced from that spirit of conquest through which the states had managed trade. It is also why it was necessary to destroy the influence of Colbertism, which continued to influence British policies and those of Napoleon. In any case, Thierry asked, hadn't Napoleon said that he wanted to defend French industry from the English? Hadn't industry been an affair of state from Colbert's time on? And hadn't England also declared war on French industry? And wasn't this the idea of industry that united the ill-understood interests of the populace, drunk with its egalitarian pretensions, and the illiberal forces and governments of Europe?

In reality, of course, industry was an activity that employed labour which could not support itself; as such, it had become a favourite subject for reflection, and had given rise to that concept of the *social face* of mercantilism which John Maynard Keynes appreciated so much in the 1930s and which the liberal tradition has opposed so strongly ever since the eighteenth century. In an agrarian society, in which there is a monopoly of the landowning classes who produce the means of subsistence, it became important to increase that section of the population which was not involved in agriculture, because it produced, with the fruits of its labours, a surplus of riches and power for the state that was the discriminating factor in any comparison between two nations of the same size. But in order to increase the number of people involved in trade and manufacture, it was necessary to protect them and ensure that the resources were available to reduce unemployment. This could be done by intervening in the economy with tools designed to get the poor into employment and produce goods that could be sold both at home and abroad by guaranteeing access to these markets, keeping an eye on costs and ensuring that industry was competitive. To do this, it was also important to ensure that the cost of living at home was not so high as to cause an internal crisis for labour and industry alike. Alternatively, it was also possible – as England had done with its Poor Law – to balance out the effects by providing welfare. Agriculture could not live according to an absolute logic of its own. Colbert had pegged French grain exports in order to keep prices lower in France than abroad, and he did this so as to ensure French industry continued to enjoy one of the few advantages it had over England – lower labour costs. For the mercantilists, industry was in conflict with the landowners, the class that had a monopoly over the means of subsistence, and the mercantilist state intervened in this conflict by favouring industrial growth, which was a tool to ensure population growth and increase national power. This was the idea of industry which was seen as the offspring of the spirit of conquest, but also something that disturbed the equilibrium of the landowning classes, and it was this idea of industry which liberals needed to destroy. But how could they do that? Was there some kind of tradition which French liberals could appeal to for help?

In France, the Physiocrats had clearly identified the way in which mercantilist politics worked, and had opposed it strongly. They also attempted to demonstrate how ineffective it was. And they had attacked those policies forcefully, defending landowners and agrarian capitalism. For the Physiocrats, popular policies based on industrial development were both ineffective and counterproductive. Work could not produce wealth. It was *sterile* whenever it was not linked to the land, extracting from the earth the riches which God had placed there to ensure the survival of men. If it was seen as a variable independent of the production of wealth from the land – wealth which, according to the Physiocrats, was linked to the logic of capital investment in agriculture – industrial labour became simply a cost. Favoured by the interventionist policies of the state in industry, it could not help but increase the burden on the economy and the size and social breadth of the sterile classes. And these classes, politically speaking, were dangerous. Ultimately, it was the landowning classes and agriculture that paid the price for the full employment of resources. For the Physiocrats, these were policies which reproduced once again the damaging effects of the annonarian laws of the Roman Empire. They believed that the artificial growth of the sterile classes jeopardized the economic and social balance of a *royaume agricole*, and ended up by jeopardizing also the 'material constitution' of the state. The most suitable constitution for a *royaume agricole* was, of course, based on a monarchy. But these policies risked pushing a nation towards the sad destiny of the 'républiques commerçantes', deprived of land and financially dependent on agricultural nations. Just as trading nations were dependent on agricultural nations, so the sterile classes within a *royaume agricole* were 'paid for' by agriculture. Now, their 'salaries' would be pushed to subsistence level by the market and by competition between workers. The amount of money available for salaries, from whichever sector of the economy it came, ultimately derived from agriculture; hence the level of those salaries would be commensurate with that part of agricultural wealth that could be used to this purpose. It was useless to expect the salaried, non-landowning class to grow at the expense of agricultural production. This would only end by jeopardizing the natural order of a *royaume agricole*. This was even more true if the classes involved were the salaried sterile classes of industry. The economic system had to be entrusted to the free functioning of the mechanisms of the *marché général et commun des nations commerçantes*. In this way it would regulate itself. The mercantilist policies of France had altered the basis upon which agricultural products and the cost of industrial labour were exchanged. Over a twenty-year period, the price of grain had fallen when compared to the price of shoes. Boisguilbert had said the same when criticizing Colbertist interventionist and fiscalist policies. Quesnay had repeated it when he accused the French state of using Colbertist economic policies in the middle of the eighteenth century. The *bon prix* of agricultural products – and of grain in particular, the most representative of all – is the reference point of the system of prices and the equilibrium between the social classes. The process by which wealth is created had no need for intervention. It just had to be left alone. All that was needed was to make sure the market was allowed to work according to the natural laws that governed it, and the processes by which wealth was created and social subsistence was supplied would work for the best, as the graphs and figures of the *Tableau économique* demonstrated. Only by coming into line with the natural order of things could conflict be avoided both within the nation and with other nations, and the only authority that could guarantee this was a representative of legal despotism whose job it was simply to ensure that the natural laws of the market were maintained. If industry were left subject to the mechanisms that made the market work and made compatible with the mechanisms that governed the system of production, it would not conflict with the general interests of society in the shape of the production of wealth. But rather than increasing industrial output, the Physiocrats argued, it should be reduced to bring it into line with agricultural production, on which it depends and which pays for it! What would happen – Mirabeau asked – if the sterile classes, who earned their living through trade and industry, were to grow to such an extent that they would politically threaten the social equilibrium of a *royaume agricole*? Who would be able to control them from within a political system which had granted them suffrage?

Of course, the Physiocrats were supporters of a form of economic liberalism which did not take as its starting point the interests of the individual; only interest 'bien entendu' was acceptable. Society, they believed, was hierarchical. And the role of the landowners, disciplined by the fact that they had to spend all that they earned as land rent, was so prominent in the Physiocratic model that it ended up by destroying any form of political alliance with the emerging bourgeoisie. The aim of the social model they proposed was to identify within the economy the skeleton of civil society and 'despotically' solve any conflict of interest in accordance with the 'natural functioning' of the free market. However, this confluence of interests around the *bon prix* of grain left too much space available for the landowners. Only they were allowed to deal with matters of agriculture, trade, industry and taxes in the new state institutions proposed by the Physiocrats, namely the provincial assemblies. It seemed to their critics that for the Physiocrats the landowners were the only real members of the nation. But, as their critics of the mid-nineteenth century said, were they really the only members of a nation? And was there any real basis for free trade in grain, something the landowners asked for as a way of 'naturally' controlling the economic and social equilibriums within the country? Was grain just a product like all other products, considering how important it was for the survival of the people? And was the market, freed of interventionist politics aimed at maintaining the equilibrium within it, really fair in the way it resolved conflict, when society was itself based on inequality? For Graslin, Forbonnais and Necker, the answer was no. They were, however, 'mercantilists' – not particularly kind to landowners and perhaps a little 'socialist', too.

The Physiocratic model was also embarrassing for many others. It was for Voltaire, Diderot and Turgot after the publication of Mercier de la Rivière's *Ordre naturel et essentiel des sociétés politiques*. How was it possible to accuse trade and manufacture of attempting to create a monopoly, they asked, when the social model being proposed revolved around the 'natural monopoly' of the landowning classes? Condillac (in *Le commerce et le gouvernement, considérés relativement l'un à l'autre*, 1776) tried to turn the basis of this on its head by making traders into the main means of production. The central importance of the landowner, then, was becoming an embarrassment, and it was to become even more embarrassing after the Revolution. As a result, the Physiocrats, those great discoverers of the role of the market, were discredited. Only with the explosive effects of Ricardo's theory of land rent did French liberals re-evaluate the Physiocratic approach to the problem in the 1840s, opposing it to Ricardian 'socialism'.[19]

At this point Adam Smith became a better option.[20] There was nothing about the constitution of a *royaume agricole* coming into conflict with the industrial sterile classes in the *Wealth of Nations*. On the contrary. There, everything started from an abstract notion of labour whose aim was to eliminate conflict between the forms it takes and the connotations it has. It is this abstract notion which becomes the general basis of the wealth of nations. The division of labour is a 'natural' consequence of the tendency of men to barter the surplus of the fruits of their labour in order to better satisfy their needs. Smith defines productive and unproductive labour in a way which is very different from the Physiocrats' definition of the productive and sterile classes. One extensive chapter of Smith's work attacks the 'commercial or mercantile system', but he uses a different kind of argument to do so.[21] Mercantile policies equate national wealth with power and believe that wealth can be increased by 'politically' attracting wealth away from the international flow of riches. Smith condemns these ideas because they are policies which were based on monopolistic systems and are the fruit of intervention in civil society from the outside. They are also opposed to the liberty of the individual and limit that liberty. These policies are leftovers from the economics of the Middle Ages, based on the creation of monopolies and the tools of corporations. They favour the privileged few and work against the interest of the consumers who go to make up society as a whole. Smith's anti-mercantilist approach, then, is the basis of liberal economic theory in the early part of the nineteenth century, the first proofs of which are Saint-Simon's and Thierry's works, which already start to appear between 1814 and 1817. Their anti-mercantilist approach does not make explicit reference to ownership, as the Physiocrats do; it hides behind the approach.[22] And it is an anti-mercantilist approach – conveyed through the work of Jean-Baptiste Say – which lends itself well to throwing into the same boiling pot ancient empires bent on conquest, feudalism, the Navigation Acts, absolute monarchies, the Poor Law, Colbertist policies, the English Corn Laws, Robespierrian price-fixing and Napoleon's Continental Blockade.

And all of this is presented as the old arsenal inherited from the social and political *ancien régime*. Modern society is seen as an independent development coming straight out of medieval cities populated by serfs who have escaped from the feudal system of the surrounding countryside and have organized forms of production and governments free from any kind of political control. These are the roots of the history of the Third Estate according to the model later to be created by Augustin Thierry on the basis of developments within the medieval tradition of the communes. Modern society, then, was born when economic activity was liberated from the control of feudal political power. This is not to say that inequality and conflict are altogether absent, but the economy that developed in these communes 'résout en elle-même au moins pour l'essentiel, la question du politique et de la régulation du social'.[23] Smith is anti-Machiavelli and anti-Colbert. What is more, for him capital derives from savings and from the fruits of individual labour. It, too, is labour – accumulated labour. The division of wealth at a national level operates according to the 'natural' working of the *law of value*. Any other means of distributing wealth is therefore unnatural.

According to this line of thought, this is why state intervention in the economic life of the country is made one with feudalism and war. It is a heritage from ancient times in which war was the greatest of industries. It is the offspring of the spirit of conquest. This kind of intervention is dangerous not because it damages the landowning classes or the tenant farmers, as Quesnay had it, but because it attacks the economic liberty of all. It is the result of the theory and practice of the abusive interference of politics in economic life, which is part of civil society. Society ought to be governed by the market. The state should limit itself to ensuring that the markets are working well and guaranteeing the liberty of the people and their property, which represents the fruit of the labour of individuals. It should intervene as little as possible and cost as little as possible. The state must simply act as a 'gendarme'. As a state of law.

# 6

These are the lines along which the thought of Saint-Simon and Thierry ran, benefiting of course from the way Jean-Baptiste Say had reworked the thought of Smith. And these are the lines along which their political and historiographical contribution to the 'légende bourgeoise'[24] of the history of capitalism also ran. Theirs was a form of capitalism based on the free market and born out of the 'internal' story of the bourgeoisie, free from any type of state intervention. It was based on the reformulation of the concept of industry. The concept of industry was reformulated to accommodate this model, and it was this new concept of industry, they believed, which was the basis for that common interest that binds together modern states and can act as a source of inspiration for their constitutions. If economic life at both a domestic level and an international level was governed by the market, they argued, conflict would be avoided and domestic and international peace would be assured. State intervention in the economy was not in the interests of the people. It was the heritage of the militaristic spirit of times past, based on the desire for conquest, something that still drove many European governments. What is more, this kind of intervention satisfied and fed, in many cases, the unjustified egalitarian demands of the *populace*. In addition, these governments maintained huge standing armies which were unproductive, costly and were a way for those in power to despotically control the people. They, too, were a vestige of the ancient feudal system, and both France and England[25] had freed themselves of them. England, France and the United Provinces, they wrote, had all acquired the social values typical of the modern world. They had done away with feudalism, that feudalism which, according to our two authors, Napoleon had tried to recreate. This was why these countries were able to lead the peoples of Italy, Germany and Spain towards a new united Europe based on the interest of its peoples. From this process the new European nation would emerge, based on the values of industry. European Russia would also be able to become a part of it, once it had freed itself from the Tartar barbarism of 'Muscovy'. Europe at that time was still a chaotic mix of principalities, kingdoms, empires and petty dukedoms. It was impossible to see the nations themselves because most of them were oppressed by their governments, but they were there, behind the scenes, waiting to come out into the open. Now nations, the argument went, were like large industrial concerns. The aim of social organization was to satisfy the needs of everyone. The riches that satisfy the needs of the individuals were produced by capital investment and the industry of the citizens working together, as in a private company. National income was divided among the citizens and the part each one receives was his private income. Everyone received an income on the basis of his or her contribution in terms of capital and of labour. The European Nation would be born on the basis of these principles:

> All of the people who work in a country, taken as a whole, form a great industrial company that embraces all the industrial companies to be found within the frontiers of that country. All of the people

who work in the world, taken as a whole, also form a great industrial company, which embraces all of the companies of the nations. The aim is always the same – to produce. On the basis of the nature of things, as happens in every industrial company, wealth is produced through a combination of the industry and capital of all the peoples. On the basis of the nature of things, this wealth is distributed in a perfectly natural way and ends up with different peoples in proportion to how much capital and industry each people has contributed. Capital and industry – these are the natural organs through which wealth is created. A people that has them will necessarily increase its wealth. A people that does not have them will necessarily remain poor. But these are delicate organs, and will not allow themselves to be touched. They develop and work on their own. If you apply any kind of instrument to them, they will be harmed. Any external force that is used in an attempt to help them, rather than strengthening them, will paralyze them; rather than helping them to work, it will disturb and destabilize them.[26]

Hence theirs was a model of 'Utopian Capitalism' in which politics was eliminated from the economy and the market was able to resolve conflict at both a domestic and an international level. This model was a fundamental part of early nineteenth-century French liberalism. The reasons that lay behind it and the way it was delineated differ of course, and, from the 1820s onwards, it would create two models that move in the same direction, but along two different lines. The first led to the *industrialism* of Say, Dunoyer and Charles Comte, who Thierry would abandon Saint-Simon for, moving over to the *Censeur européen*. This school of thought radicalized 'the economic approach to society, introducing the terminology of utility and rational behaviour'. On the other hand, Saint-Simon and his followers, such as Bazard, Saint-Amand, Enfantin and Auguste Comte, would move towards 'New Christianity' and try to bring back 'a moral dimension that the economic approach either left out or restricted to the domestic sphere'.[27]

It was a model whose influence would spread as far as the thought of Karl Marx, who appreciated the notion of class struggle invented by liberal historians for the occasion – but only the struggle between the nobility and the Third Estate. Marx would, however, criticize the 'bourgeois science' which derived from Smith because the theory of value which inspired it was not capable of explaining capitalist society as it really was. This in turn was because Smith lacked the tools that would allow him to discover the mechanisms by which the labour force was 'exploited', identifying in savings the source of the formation of capital, and not in the privatization of the means of production. This in turn would give rise to another Utopia – the one which would find the political solution for the conflicts created by 'real capitalism' and the way the law of value effectively worked in the socialization of the means of production and the end of the state.

## 7

That state, however, was one of the lightest, the least costly, the least interventionist of all, and both Saint-Simon and Thierry appreciated the way that it had established an alliance with the 'industrious' classes over the course of the centuries. Hadn't the Third Estate been aided, they asked, by its anti-feudal alliance with the French monarchy? Hadn't it found in this alliance the strength to resist the nobility and clergy over the centuries, and in the end win out against them? But what Saint-Simon and Thierry really appreciated about this alliance was the way that it led from the charters of the medieval communes straight to the Charter of 1814. It was an alliance with a monarchy, they felt, which had accepted the need to reduce the influence of the old and new forms of feudalism that surrounded it and had thrown its lot in with the history and formation of the Third Estate and the whole of the French 'industrial' class, the foundation of that national party which Saint-Simon would invite Louis XVIII to bind even more firmly to his throne in 1820.[28]

When Charles X resolved the ambiguities inherent in the Charter with his July Ordinances, Thierry – like all liberals – would find in the monarchy of Louis Philippe the full and complete incarnation of their social and political[29] desires. But that illusion was only to last eighteen years. Social conflict, which the market ought to have eradicated forever, suddenly re-exploded once more in an altogether new and unexpected fashion in the shape of the workers' revolution in Paris in February 1848. It was a revolution 'full of the same spirit and the same threats that the worst period of the first had manifested'. In fact, it reintroduced the masses to the political arena, and it would astound and disturb Thierry 'first as a citizen, and then as a historian'.[30] The model had exploded!

## Notes

1. The idea of building international order on the foundations of 'the common interest of the peoples that go to make up European society', by reorganizing Europe, which would have brought with it the reorganization of the member-states, had already been launched by Saint-Simon in his *Mémoire sur la science*

*de l'homme* and the *Travail sur la gravitation*. Cf. H. Gouhier (1936) *La jeunesse d'Auguste Comte et la formation du positivisme* (Paris: J. Vrin), vol. 2, p. 302.
2. The first edition was published by the Hahn press at Hanover in January 1814.
3. 'This work was written in Germany in November 1813 ... If I had written this work in France, or at the present time, I would have expressed myself differently on a number of points. To the horror that Bonaparte's government aroused in me was added, I admit, a certain sense of impatience with the nation that laboured beneath his yoke. I know better than anyone else how odious this yoke was to that nation, and I suffered when I saw how its courage was betrayed and how its blood was spilt in order to keep it in a state of servitude.' B. Constant (1814) *De l'esprit de conquête et de l'usurpation* (Paris), pp. v–vi.
4. 'How long each power lasts depends on the proportion that exists between its spirit and its times. Every century awaits a man who, in some way, will become its representative. When this representative appears, or seems to appear, all the forces of the moment group about him. If he represents the general spirit faithfully, his success is guaranteed. If he deviates from it, his success is in doubt. If he continues to pursue a path which is not the right one, the assent that upheld him will abandon him, and his power will fail.' Ibid., p. 2.
5. 'It is not true that war is always an ill. At certain ages in the history of mankind, it was part of the nature of man. It favoured the development of his greatest, most attractive faculties. It gave him a wealth of riches to enjoy. It taught him greatness of soul, adroitness, self-control, courage, and a fearlessness in the face of death, without which man can never say to himself that he will not commit any crime or act of mean-mindedness. War teaches him heroic devotion and bestows on him sublime friendships.' Ibid., pp. 3–4.
6. Ibid., p. 5.
7. Ibid., p. 6.
8. Ibid., p. 7.
9. Ibid., p. 8.
10. Cl.-H. de Saint-Simon and A. Thierry (1814) *La réorganisation de la société européenne* (Paris), p. xi.
11. Ibid., p. xiii.
12. Ibid., p. xiv.
13. Ibid.
14. Ibid., p. 23.
15. Ibid., p. 30.
16. Ibid., p. 53.
17. Saint-Simon (1868) 'L'industrie, seconde partie, Politique', in *Œuvres de Saint-Simon* (Paris), vol. 1, p. 26.
18. Ibid., p. 42.
19. The introduction to the second volume of Eugène Daire (1846) *Collection des principaux économistes* (Paris), pp. vii–lxxxviii, dedicated to the Physiocrats, is indicative in this respect.
20. 'Smith's book was the strongest, most direct and most complete critique that has ever been made of the feudal system. Every one of its pages is a demonstration that the communes and industry were eaten up by this system, which was not useful to them in any way, and that governments, in the way they

were formed, tended to ruin their peoples, as they did nothing else except consume, while the only way to accumulate wealth was to produce. His book could be seen as a collection of detailed rebuttals of all the ways governments operate, and consequently as a demonstration of the need for people to change both the principles and the nature of their governments if they want to stop living in misery and enjoy peace and the fruits of their labours. At the same time, this work contained the proof that, if a nation wishes to live well, it has to follow the example of manufacturers, merchants, indeed of any industrious person. As a consequence, the budget of any nation that wishes to become rich and free had to be run on the same basis as the budget of any industrial enterprise. The only reasonable aim that any nation could have was that of producing as much as possible with the lowest possible administrative costs.' Saint-Simon, 'L'industrie', in *Œuvres de Saint-Simon*, vol. 3, pp. 154–5.
21. See L. Herlitz (1964) 'The Concept of Mercantilism', *Scandinavian Economic History Review*, XII, 2.
22. For Saint-Simon, in fact, 'owners rule over non-owners, not because they are owners as such; they are owners and they rule because, taken as a whole, they are more enlightened than non-owners' (*Lettres d'un habitant de Genève*, cited in Gouhier, *La jeunesse d'Auguste Comte*, vol. 2, p. 301, note.
23. P. Rosanvallon (1979) *Le capitalisme utopique: Critique de l'idéologie économique* (Paris: Seuil), pp. 60–1.
24. On the 'légende bourgeoise' of capitalism in Thierry, cf. F. Fourquet (2002) *La richesse et la puissance: Une généalogie de la valeur (XVIe–XVIIIe siècles)* (Paris: La Découverte), pp. 49 ff.
25. When the battles of the English Radicals and their realization that it was impossible to change the electoral system a few years later made it clear that things were not as simple as they seemed in England, Thierry and the men of the *Censeur européen* would come to the conclusion that the heritage of an *esprit de conquête* is still strong there, and would turn their attention instead to the American model, free from the taint of feudalism. An impertinent character of one of Flaubert's novels would remind them that the United States is tainted by an even more heinous sin: slavery.
26. Saint-Simon, 'L'industrie', in *Œuvres de Saint-Simon*, vol. 1, pp. 69–70.
27. G. Faccarello and Ph. Steiner (2008) 'Interest, Sensationism and the Science of the Legislator: French "philosophie économique", 1695–1830', *European Journal of Economic Thought*, XV, 1, 1–23.
28. 'The political existence of the Bourbon dynasty in France, like that of the industrialists, began at the same time. The ancestors of the Bourbons first placed the crown on their heads in the eleventh century, and it was in the eleventh century, too, that the freedom of the industrialists became a matter of general policy in our country. There is an important point to note here, and it is the object of this first observation – namely, that from that time right up to the beginning of the present revolution, the Bourbons and the industrialists have always supported one another ... The Bourbons should admit that their claims have always been supported by the industrialists and that they owe their position of great power to the support they have always had from the industrialists. The Bourbon dynasty, then, owes a great deal to the industrialists. For their part, the industrialists should be aware of the civil

and political position of their ancestors at the beginning of the third race and will be forced to admit that their forefathers were no more than slaves. Let them think about what has happened over the centuries since then, see how their social condition has continually improved, and note the reasons which have principally caused this increase in their civil and political importance. They will become firmly convinced that the success they have achieved is due to the continual protection afforded to them by the Bourbon dynasty against the feudal barons who lorded over them', in *Considérations sur les mesures à prendre pour terminer la Révolution*, IIIe lettre, in *Œuvres de Saint-Simon*, vol. 3, pp. 52–4.
29. On the opposite side of the fence in the same period, Louis Blanc will develop the idea of a positive continuum leading from Colbert, to Law, Robespierre, Napoleon I and socialism.
30. A. Thierry (1853) *Essai sur l'histoire de la formation et des progrès du Tiers État* (Paris), p. x.

# Part III
# The American and the French Revolutions: From Two Continents a New Political World

# 10
# France and the United States at the End of the Eighteenth Century

*James Roger Sharp*

The French Revolution transformed not only the way that Americans of the early republic perceived France, but also greatly influenced how they saw their own nation. They viewed France as a mirror and used that reflection to analyse the historical progress of their own society. In other words, events in France after 1789 seemed to many Americans as a kind of yardstick for measuring and evaluating the future course of their own country against the failures and successes of the Revolution and Republicanism in France. But they were also disheartened by any French failures or challenges, as ominous forebodings of potential problems in the United States as well.[1]

In the years from the French Revolution down to the end of the eighteenth century, American politics was critically polarized between two proto-parties – the Federalists, led by George Washington, John Adams and Alexander Hamilton, who controlled the government, and their Republican opponents led by Thomas Jefferson and James Madison. The major catalyst in this bitter and union-threatening division was the French Revolution. The Federalists were suspicious and eventually bitterly hostile to the French revolutionaries, whereas the Republicans enthusiastically embraced the efforts to establish republican government in France.

Earlier, colonial Americans had had a negative image of France. Americans shared the bias and prejudice of their English Anglican cousins against their frequent continental Catholic antagonists. A 'remarkable detestation of the French...prevailed in America until about 1770', one historian has written.[2] Another argued that prior to 1775 the stereotypical image of the French 'suggested an incarnation of the Devil'.[3]

The French–American Alliance against England in 1778, therefore, had marked a critical milestone in the relationship between France and the new American nation. 'The initial reaction to the Alliance', according to one historian, represented 'almost a complete reversal of previous American stereotypes'.[4]

Thus, Americans greeted reports of the French Revolution with 'universal delight'[5] when the news reached the country in 1789. In addition to feeling a sympathetic bond to the country that had come to their aid in 1778,[6] Americans saw the events in France as confirming and validating their own revolution.

Americans had a strong sense of mission about their revolutionary experience and they believed that it had an important role to play in awakening the oppressed peoples of the world. One minister described the establishment of the American republic as 'the primary agent in redemptive history' that would 'wake up and encourage the dormant flame of liberty in all quarters of the earth'.[7]

The French Revolution[8] came at a particularly vulnerable time in the early history of the United States. The new constitution had been ratified only a year earlier and 1789 marked the beginning of a new national government led by George Washington that faced enormous challenges. There was no reason for Americans at that time to be confident that this republican government would survive the decade, much less for more than two hundred years. And while they hoped for the best, fresh in their minds were the struggles of the first American attempt at a national government, which lasted less than a decade.

Thus, the Revolution and subsequent adoption of Republicanism in France reassured Americans that their historic mission was succeeding. For example, the news that all the new state and federal constitutions had been translated into French and circulated in that country was welcome encouragement to Americans that the French were apparently learning lessons from their junior partner in Republicanism.[9]

This optimistic and progressive view of history seemed to mark, as a Boston newspaper rhapsodized, the 'commencement of a Golden Age' that embraced reason, liberty and republicanism – in an age in which despotism and tyranny would be vanquished from the earth. 'Liberty', it was asserted, 'will have another feather in her cap.'[10]

Thomas Jefferson's close collaborator and colleague James Madison stressed the importance of the French Revolution by contending that its enemies were the 'enemies of human nature'.[11] And a correspondent of Madison took up the same theme, prophesying that the 'Fate of human nature' was being decided in France and that European despotism would now 'scarcely survive the 18th century'. The American Revolution had started the process, he argued, for it had 'made the Rent in the great

Curtain that withheld the light from human nature' and as a result 'the Rights of Man became legible and intelligible to... [the] World'.[12]

But along with the enthusiasm and exhilaration that hailed the French Revolution there was also a fear that a failure in France would endanger the fruits of the American Revolution. Madison wrote that America had every reason to pray for the survival of Republicanism in France, 'not only from a general attachment to the liberties of mankind, but from a peculiar regard for our own'. Domestic politics in the United States were closely related to events in France, Madison argued. The political fortunes of the enemies of Republicanism in the United States, he asserted, had 'risen and subsided' in relation to the 'prosperous and adverse accounts from the French revolution'. Any miscarriage in France would thus 'threaten us with the most serious dangers to our present forms and principles of our government'.[13]

Almost immediately after the new federal government under Washington had been installed, the two embryonic proto-political parties, Republicans and Federalists, had begun to emerge. And with this sharp and bitter partisanship, the relationship between the United States and France became the single most polarizing political issue in the last decade of the eighteenth century.

Jefferson in a letter to a friend in France maintained that the histories of both countries were now closely joined and the success of one would strengthen the chances for success in the other. France, he hoped, would be able to establish and maintain a 'firm government, friendly to liberty', for, 'if it does, the world will become inevitably free'. At the same time Jefferson feared that failure in France would increase the number of 'apostles of English despotism' in the United States.[14] A New Yorker opined a similar thought. The 'downfall of nobility in France has operated like an early frost towards killing the germ of it in America', he wrote.[15]

Like many Americans, Jefferson believed that both France and the United States had a common destiny and a historic mission. Reproving an old friend who had expressed some criticism of the unsettling course of events in France, Jefferson asserted that the 'liberty of the whole earth' depended on the success of the French Revolution and asked 'was ever such a prize won with so little innocent blood?' Admitting that some of his close friends had lost their lives to the Terror, Jefferson even went so far as to avow that rather than see the Revolution fail, he 'would have seen half the earth desolated'.[16]

Not all Americans were so sanguine and hopeful, however. Vice-President John Adams expressed his pessimism and concern, declaring that 'From the year 1760 to this hour', he had supported the 'principles' and 'sentiments' of revolution and the creation of republican government. Therefore, he asserted the 'Revolution in France could not...be indifferent to me'. However, he had 'learned by awful experience to rejoice with trembling', and he did not know 'what to make of a republic of thirty million atheists'. 'Too many Frenchmen, like too many Americans,' he warned, 'pant for equality of persons and property. The impracticability of this God Almighty has decreed, and the advocates for liberty who attempt it will surely suffer for it.'[17]

Concern about France intensified beginning in the summer of 1792 when the French Revolution turned more violent. The proclamation of the republic, the execution of Louis XVI and the spread of the European war to England as well as most continental powers by early 1793 had a profound impact on the United States. It aggravated the increasing ideological polarity between the Federalists, who shared English suspicions and hostility about what was happening in France, and their Republican critics who felt a deep attachment to the emerging French republic.

Initially, it was this Republican support of France that was shared by most Americans, who were particularly demonstrative in their affection and interest in events in France. 'American citizens', one historian has contended, engaged in 'the most extraordinary series of celebrations in honor of the achievements of another country which in no way directly concerned them and did not need directly to affect them'.[18]

Beginning in late 1792 a remarkable succession of American public celebrations took place in commemoration of the news that the French revolutionary armies had defeated and driven back the counter-revolutionary forces of European monarchies. These military victories, as well as the fall of the Bastille, were celebrated as public holidays by many Americans in banquets and festivals. Toasts were offered, resolutions were issued and broadsides and newspaper editorials were written. The Philadelphia *Aurora* warned that a victory for the enemies of France would result in extinguishing 'the fire of freedom in every part of the globe'.[19]

Baltimore, New York and Boston held triumphant banquets, and newspapers urged their citizens to don the tricolour in support of France. In Boston, one editor described 'the uncommon joy and satisfaction with which a free people have received the highly animating information' detailing the victories of the French armies. Another Boston newspaper reported 'impatience' in getting more news from France, and, when news arrived that the Prussians were in retreat, 'joy was visible on the countenance of every citizen'.[20]

Some American supporters of France even rejoiced in the execution of the king, despite the fact that he, just a few years earlier, had been celebrated as a critical benefactor of the American Revolution. At a dinner in Philadelphia 'a decapitated roast pig was passed around to represent Louis XVI' after which 'each guest put on the liberty cap, exclaimed, "Tyrant!" and plunged his knife into the pig'.[21]

As time went on the public infatuation with France began to increasingly alarm the Federalists and drove a wedge between them and their Republican critics. Both sides believed that the same drama between revolution and reaction was being played out in the United States as well as Europe.[22] The Republicans alleged that their Federalist opponents were attempting to subvert the constitution and republicanism in an effort to reverse the liberal effects of the American Revolution. The Federalists were convinced that their Republican opponents were no less than agents of radical revolution who were promoting a destabilizing democratic egalitarianism that would be transplanted in American soil and eventually destroy the constitution and republican government. 'Our greatest danger is from the contagion of levelism,' explained one Federalist, for it 'has set the world agog to be all equal to French barbers'. The Republican opponents of the Washington administration were nothing but 'a noisy set of discontented demagogues mak[ing] a rant' while Federalist supporters of the government were composed of 'the great body of men of property' who 'move slowly but move with sure success'.[23]

With the expansion of the European war in the spring of 1793, the Washington Administration resolved that it was critical for the United States to stay out the conflict. The administration thus issued a neutrality proclamation declaring that the country would 'pursue a conduct friendly and impartial towards the belligerent powers'.[24]

A major difficulty with neutrality, however, was that the 1778 alliance between France and the United States had embraced the principle that free ships made free goods and that neutral ships had the right to carry non-contraband goods into ports of belligerents. These were conditions, however, that England, as a great naval power, would never accept. Thus the United States found itself in a real dilemma. To insist upon the neutral rights as stated in the treaty with France would provoke England, while to acquiesce to the English interpretation would alienate France.[25]

In June 1793 the British navy began to enforce their rule that commerce prohibited in time of peace was also prohibited in time of war and began to intercept American vessels engaged in the lucrative Caribbean trade. As the news of captured ships and the confiscation of cargoes and impressment of American seamen began to be reported, there was a groundswell of anti-British public opinion.

How could the United States stay neutral asked critics of the Washington Administration. The 'cause of France is the cause of man, and neutrality is desertion', one newspaper proclaimed. The policy of neutrality was only championed by those who wished 'to draw the cords of connection as tight as possible between the corrupt monarchy of Great Britain and the United States'. Military assistance to France should be given, if requested. America should respond because 'the American mind is indignant, and needs to be but roused a little to go to war with England and assist France'.[26]

Intensifying the controversy over American neutrality was the arrival of the very genial and popular, but very undiplomatic, new French minister to the United States, Edmond Charles Genet or, as he became known, 'Citizen Genet'.[27] Genet arrived with great fanfare in South Carolina in April 1793, and as he travelled to Philadelphia he was greeted and celebrated by adoring American crowds who saw him as an important symbol of the French Revolution.

An enthusiastic correspondent in the *National Gazette* urged that Genet 'should be properly received'. He hoped 'that the true republicans of this country will hoist the three-colored flag, the emblem of patriotism; and to complete the spectacle, that our fair Pennsylvanians will decorate their elegant person and adorn their hair with patriotic ribbands [sic] on the occasion'.[28]

This outpouring of public support for France, however, seriously misled Genet and caused him to overplay his hand. Almost immediately it became obvious that his interpretation of neutrality was much different from that of the United States. He called for the provisions of the 1778 alliance to be enforced, especially those regarding French shipping and commerce. In addition, he sought American help in gaining control of British and Spanish territories in North America. One of his first, albeit covert, actions was to recruit frontier Americans to attack Spanish territory.[29]

Jefferson's first reaction to Genet was extremely favourable, for the French envoy assured the American secretary of state that, although France could, under the Treaty of Alliance, demand American help in protecting the French West Indies, it would not do so. Genet could not have been 'more affectionate, [or] more magnanimous' in what he expected from the United States, Jefferson reported to Madison. Genet and the French, he continued, only wanted the United States to do what was for our own good, and France would do all in its power to promote it. 'Cherish your own peace and prosperity,' he had told Jefferson.[30]

Jefferson was, however, to be quickly disillusioned. Riding the tide of his public popularity and acclaim, Genet pushed American neutrality beyond its limits and began to regard American ports as virtual French naval bases in which seamen could be recruited, privateers armed and equipped, and captured enemy ships outfitted as French privateers and dispatched to fight the British. Jefferson's warnings against these actions were ignored – thus presenting him with a dilemma. Not wanting to alienate the popular Genet, he nonetheless feared that the Frenchman's excesses would ultimately damage, if not destroy, American sympathy for the French Revolution, which, in turn, would severely compromise the embryonic pro-French Republican opposition to the Washington Administration and the Federalists.

In the meantime the Washington Administration was becoming increasingly embattled because of the public hostility to the neutrality proclamation and its seeming betrayal of France. For the first time, even Washington himself was becoming a target with one particularly outrageous poster entitled the 'funeral of George Washington' depicting the president 'placed on a guillotine'. The president was also described by one vociferous critic as being 'buoyed up by official importance' and out of touch with the sentiments of most Americans. The president, he warned should not 'Let... the little buzz of the aristocratic few, and their contemptible minions, or speculators, tories, and British emissaries be mistaken for the exalted and general voice of the American people'. The 'spirit of 1776 is again roused, and soon shall the mushroom lordlings of the day, the enemies of American as well as French liberty, be taught that American whigs of 1776 will not suffer French patriots of 1792 to be vilified with impunity by the common enemies of both'.[31]

The issue came to a head in August 1793, when the Washington Administration by a unanimous vote of the Cabinet requested that the French government recall the headstrong and imprudent Genet. As secretary of state, Jefferson, unbeknownst to Genet, wrote the confidential and private letter to French authorities. In it he carefully tried to distinguish the activities of Genet from the French government by detailing Genet's undiplomatic activities while delicately stressing American support for France.[32]

Washington and Alexander Hamilton, like Jefferson, were angered by Genet's efforts to flagrantly violate American neutrality and sovereignty. However, unlike Jefferson, they were even more concerned that the Frenchman's activities threatened the internal stability and security of the country. Most worrisome to them were Genet's flaunting of authority and threats to appeal directly to the people over the head of the government.[33] Thus Genet's challenge to the control and sovereignty of the United States government reminded Washington and his supporters of the lawlessness of the French Revolution and of the awful possibility that the growing violence and disarray in France might soon contaminate and destroy the civil order of the United States.

John Adams, a number of years later, vividly recalled (although in a somewhat hyperbolic way) the potential for violence in 1793 'when ten thousand people in the streets of Philadelphia day after day *threatened to drag* Washington out of his house and effect a revolution in the government or compel it to declare war in favour of the French Revolution and against England'. It was only after several radical leaders died from yellow fever, he claimed, that the United States was 'saved... from a fatal revolution of government'.[34]

Adding to the alarm and anxiety of the Washington Administration that year was the spontaneous organization of democratic-republican societies. Heirs of the Sons of Liberty and Committees of Correspondence that had been established to enforce support for the American Revolution, these societies quickly grew in number to thirty-five.[35] But while these clubs clearly had American precedents, they were also similar in organization and political purpose to the French revolutionary Jacobin clubs, albeit without the violence. This similarity, along with these societies' countless popular displays of support for the French Revolution and their active engagement in the 'public sphere' of the United States added to the considerable fear among the Federalists and more conservative members of American society.[36]

And the Federalists did have some cause for concern. The societies were formed in response to a growing sense on the part of a number of Americans that the government under Washington was insensitive to their wishes, especially to their support of revolutionary France. A New York democratic-republican society flatly declared that 'he who is an enemy to the French revolution... ought not to be intrusted [sic] with the guidance of any part of the machine of government'.[37] Therefore, it was argued that some type of intermediate institution, like the societies, was needed to educate the public and to collect, shape and articulate the public will.

The continuous extolling of the virtues of the French Revolution and its emissary, Citizen Genet, by these democratic-republican societies both terrified and enraged the Federalists. One in Massachusetts declared the members of these clubs to be 'hot-headed, ignorant or wicked men devoted entirely to the views of France' while another described them as 'born of sin, the impure offspring of Genet'.[38]

Federalists were especially agitated by the news that Genet had been appointed president of a Philadelphia society.[39] 'The history of diplomatic enterprise', Hamilton fulminated, 'affords no parallel to this: We should look in vain for a precedent of a foreign minister, in the country of his mission, becoming the declared head, or even acknowledged member of a *political Association*.'[40]

The popularity of the democratic-republican societies, however, turned out to be short lived. In 1794 they were charged with fomenting a brief but violent western Pennsylvania protest against the federal excise tax on whiskey.

Although there was scant evidence that the societies were directly involved in the so-called Whiskey Rebellion,[41] and most of the societies denounced the violence associated with it, most of the Federalists and many other Americans believed that the democratic-republican societies bore some of the responsibility for the insurrection.

In the late autumn of 1794, President Washington publicly denounced the societies for their alleged support of the whiskey rebels, saying he feared them to be linked to French intrigue 'to sow sedition [and] poison the minds of the people of this country'.[42] His statement reflected the growing concern in the country that the activities of these societies could lead to the same kind of mounting violence and disruption of the civil order that was being experienced in France.

It is impossible to say with any certainty how Genet's imprudent actions and the discrediting of the democratic-republican societies affected the relationship between France and the United States. What *can* be said is that the flourishing of the societies marked the high point in the affection that many Americans had for France during the early republic. And that after that high point the warm relationship between the two countries deteriorated. And by the last half of the decade of the 1790s the formal diplomatic relations between the two countries had worsened to such a point that they were fighting an undeclared naval war.

The Jay Treaty between the United States and England in 1795 was a major factor in accelerating a degenerating relationship between the two allies. The agreement, which represented a failed American effort to get England to accept the United States' position that free ships mean free goods, appeared to many to not only insult France but also to tie America more closely to France's enemy England.

By the time President John Adams took office in March 1797, relations between the two former allies had worsened to the point that France refused to accept a new American envoy. But even more dangerous and ominous was the French declaration that, contrary to the 1778 alliance, they, like England, would no longer abide by the rule that free ships made free goods and would in the future seize neutral ships carrying English goods. In addition the French said that American sailors, if captured while serving on enemy ships, would be treated as pirates.[43]

President Adams, in an effort to repair the relationship with France and stop the undeclared naval war between the two countries, sent a commission to France. The commission, however, was rebuffed and insulted by four unofficial French representatives, later named W, X, Y and Z by President Adams. The Americans were told that in order for official negotiations to begin a bribe and a loan were required. When the American delegation stood their ground, refused to comply and returned home, they were greeted as heroes as an anti-French war fever swept the country. Anticipating war with France, President Adams asked Congress for funds to improve and expand the army and navy as well as to build stronger coastal fortifications to rebuff a possible French invasion.[44]

Alexander Hamilton, who was out of government but was still a powerful force in the governing Federalist administration, took advantage of the war hysteria sweeping the country by seeking to characterize Republicans as having been almost treasonous in their support of France. The Republicans had, he accused, made 'unremitting efforts to justify or excuse the despots of France, to vilify and discredit our own government' and 'to divert ... [the people's] affections from their own [country] to a foreign country'.[45]

Thus, passions in the United States were running high in the spring and summer of 1798 where a pervasive, obsessive, crippling and distorting fear gripped the country. Jefferson reported a riot in Philadelphia between those who wore the black cockade in support of England against those who were mistakenly thought to be wearing the French tricolour cockade. 'A fray ensued' that required 'the light horse being called in, and the city was so filled with confusion from about 6 to 10 O' clock last night that it was dangerous going out'.[46]

And this sort of anti-French frenzy was manipulated and stoked by the Federalists. Jefferson informed his Virginia colleagues that his name was 'running through all the city as detected in criminal correspondence with the French directory'.[47] For instance, after one innocent and naïve Quaker took it upon himself to travel to France in an attempt to settle the dispute between the former allies, the Federalists seized upon the incident. It was a 'secret mission from the Jacobins here to solicit an army from France, [and] instruct them as to their landing etc', they charged.[48]

The culmination of this outpouring of emotion and passion was the passage in the summer of 1798 of the Alien and Sedition Acts by the Federalist-dominated Congress. The Alien Acts, actually three anti-alien Acts, established a registration and surveillance system for foreign nationals and gave the President the power to deport any of these he considered dangerous. These Acts, Jefferson reported, 'so alarmed the French' that they had chartered a ship and 'will sail within about a fortnight for France, with as many as she can carry'.[49]

The Sedition Act that followed, making persons liable for fines and imprisonment for criticizing the government and its officers, represented one of the most repressive and greatest infringements upon the freedom of speech and press in American history. And it did, in fact, lead to the jailing of a number of opposition newspaper editors.[50]

This tumultuous and dangerous period was finally brought to an end when President Adams, who, against the strenuous objections of members of his own Federalist party, decided to send a new diplomatic mission to France in an attempt to end the undeclared naval war between the two countries. And in 1800 an agreement was signed abrogating the 1778 alliance and ending the hostilities. Adams' courageous decision, most likely, was a major factor, however, in causing him to be defeated by Jefferson in the presidential election of 1800.

But while the leaders of the Jeffersonian Republicans began to distance themselves from France at the end of the eighteenth century because of the political liability involved, there were continuing celebrations of French military victories by at least some ordinary Americans up to the end of the decade. And as late as 1800, for instance, French victories in Italy were celebrated by farmers in Fayette County, Kentucky.[51]

By 1800, then, the relationship between the United States and France had been greatly tested. First, it was severely strained because of American disappointment about the course of the French Revolution after 1792–93, and, second, by the outright hostilities between the two countries during the Quasi-War, 1798–1800.

In 1800 John Quincy Adams, son of President Adams and Federalist US senator from Massachusetts from 1803 to 1808,[52] tried to draw lessons from both the American and French Revolutions by praising a book on the American Revolution. This work,[53] he wrote, had rescued the American Revolution 'from the disgraceful imputation of having proceeded from the same principles as that of France'. Adams approvingly noted that this volume had argued that there were 'essential differences' between the two revolutions and those differences were 'between *right* and *wrong*'. The French Revolution with its violence had proceeded in the wrong way, while the American Revolution with its idealism and commitment to Republicanism had been conducted the right way. One historian has said that this 'deradicaliz[ation]' of the American Revolution by Adams has subsequently been part of the creation of the nation's national identity.[54]

Indeed, Americans have been embarrassed by their Revolution and have tried to downplay and forget its radicalism and violence. During the Bicentennial Celebration in 1976, for example, a good part of that commemoration was a paean to commercialism as American companies attempted to draw some connection, as tenuous as it might be, between their businesses and some aspect of the American Revolution. Any serious discussion of the meaning of the American Revolution was drowned out by a chorus of jingoistic nationalism or a preoccupation with meaningless trivia such as a contest sponsored by the National Football League soliciting essays on 'the N.F.L.'s role in American history'.[55]

The Daughters of the American Revolution, a conservative women's organization, in its twentieth-century manual for would-be citizens also reflects this 'deradicalization'. Sanitizing the American Revolution by casting it as a very conservative event, the manual argues that a 'Revolution usually means an attempt to tear down or overturn a government or wreck the existing institutions of a country. The American did none of these things; on the contrary, it was a war fought to PRESERVE the principles of the colonial governments; it was fought to MAINTAIN the liberties of the colonists which George the Third had tried to take away. Americans abhor the kind of revolution which destroys, which murders, loots, and burns.'[56]

Thus, the relationship between France and the United States in the period following the American Revolution was shaped by American self-doubt and fear for the success of their own revolution, republicanism and union. As long as the narrative of the French Revolution seemed to support the narrative of the American Revolution, most Americans could rejoice, since the French experience seemed to be confirming their own experience. But once violence became the story of the French Revolution, more conservative Americans recoiled from any attachment to France. They feared that the chaos, anarchy and violence that seemed to be sweeping France would infect their own country as well.

In the years after 1789 and well into the nineteenth century therefore, as France struggled with political turmoil and instability, Americans watched with considerable apprehension. The seeming inability of the French to maintain republican institutions raised a concern in the United States that their own republic might be short-lived. This became particularly true after 1871 with the establishment of the French Third Republic. As the French republic struggled to survive, Americans saw their own country reflected in the French mirror. After a devastating Civil War ending in 1865, Americans were desperate to be reassured about their own future. By the end of the nineteenth century, the United States like France had become an industrialized and urbanized power. And the critical question in the minds of many Americans was: could Republicanism survive in such an environment where landless workers were crowded into cities and there was a growing economic and social gap between classes? Americans anxiously looked to France for answers.

## Notes

1. Henry Blumenthal (1970) *France and the United States: Their Diplomatic Relations, 1789–1914* (Chapel Hill: University of North Carolina Press), p. 3. Blumenthal has a more negative view. He maintains that 'public opinion in both countries with respect to the other ranged at any given time from admiration to contempt'. I have been influenced and helped in my writing of this essay by a number of sources. Some older books that are still of great importance include: Howard Mumford Jones (1927) *American and French Culture, 1750–1848* (Chapel Hill: University of North Carolina Press) and Charles D. Hazen (1897) *Contemporary American Opinion of the French Revolution* (Baltimore: Johns Hopkins University Press). Some more recent works have been invaluable and include Simon P. Newman (1997) *Parades and the Politics of the Street: Festive Culture in the Early American Republic* (Philadelphia: University of Pennsylvania Press); David Waldstreicher (1997) *In the Midst of Perpetual Fetes: The Making of American Nationalism: 1776–1820* (Chapel Hill: University of North Carolina Press); Jeffrey L. Pasley (2001) *'The Tyranny of the Printers': Newspaper Politics in the Early American Republic* (Charlottesville: University of Virginia Press); and Susan Branson (2001) *These Firey Frenchified Dames: Women and Political Culture in Early National Philadelphia* (Philadelphia: University of Pennsylvania Press). David Brion Davis (1990) *Revolutions: Reflections on American Equality and Foreign Liberations* (Cambridge, Mass.: Harvard University Press) offered a very insightful discussion of the influence of the French Revolution in America and Lloyd S. Kramer (2002) 'The French Revolution and the Creation of American Political Culture', in Joseph Klaits and Michael H. Haltzel (eds), *The Global Ramifications of the French Revolution* (Cambridge: Cambridge University Press) presents a very useful summary. See also James Roger Sharp (1995) *American Politics in the Early Republic: The New Nation in Crisis* (New Haven: Yale University Press).
2. Jones, *American and French Culture*, p. 501.
3. William C. Stinchcombe (1969) *The American Revolution and the French Alliance* (Syracuse, NY: Syracuse University Press), p. 2.
4. Ibid., p. 15.
5. Jones, *American and French Culture*, pp. 530–1.

6. Stinchcombe, *The American Revolution and the French Alliance*, writes that the French–American Alliance was 'a temporary means to a noble end, rather than a long-term commitment to France or European politics'.
7. As quoted in Nathan O. Hatch (1977) *The Sacred Cause of Liberty: Republican Thought and the Millennium in Revolutionary New England* (New Haven: Yale University Press), p. 156.
8. Kramer, 'The French Revolution and the Creation of American Political Culture', argues that the 'French Revolution was the most influential international event in the emergence of a distinctive American political culture during the 1790s and that with the exception of the two world wars, the cold war, and the Vietnam War...no *foreign* event has ever affected American politics and culture as profoundly as the Revolution in France' (see his p. 26).
9. Jones, *American and French Culture*, p. 532.
10. *Boston Gazette*, 7 September 1789, as quoted in Hazen, *Contemporary American Opinion of the French Revolution*, p. 142.
11. Madison to George Nicholas, 15 March 1793, as quoted in Ralph L. Ketcham (1963) 'France and American Politics', *Political Science Quarterly*, LXXVIII (June), 220–1.
12. George Tuberville to Madison, 28 January 1793, Madison Papers, Library of Congress.
13. Madison to George Nichols, 15 March 1793, as quoted in Ketcham, 'France and American Politics', 220–1.
14. Jefferson to Jean Pierre Brissot De Warville, 8 May 1793, in Paul Leicester Ford (ed.) (1892–99) *The Writings of Thomas Jefferson* (New York: Putnam), vol. 6, pp. 248–9.
15. *Boston Gazette and County Register*, 26 September 1791, and *New York Journal and Weekly Register*, 28 January 1792, as quoted by Simon Newman in his 'Principles and not Men': The Political Culture of Leadership in the 1790s', a paper presented to the Philadelphia Center for Early American Studies, 4 May 1990. I am grateful to Professor Newman for sharing this paper with me.
16. Jefferson to William Short, 3 January 1793, in Ford (ed.) *The Writings of Thomas Jefferson*, vol. 6, pp. 153–7. Dumas Malone in his biography of Jefferson attempts to mitigate Jefferson's language by arguing that his response to Short was a flight of hyperbole. However, I think the instinctive and spontaneous response was closer to Jefferson's real feelings. See Dumas Malone (1962) *Jefferson and the Ordeal of Liberty* (Boston: Little, Brown), pp. 45–7.
17. As quoted in Hazen, *Contemporary American Opinion of the French Revolution*, pp. 152–3.
18. Ibid., p. 164.
19. Philip S. Foner (ed.) (1976) *The Democratic-Republican Societies, 1790–1800: A Documentary Sourcebook of Constitutions, Declarations, Addresses, Resolutions, and Toasts* (Westport, Conn.: Greenwood Press), p. 22.
20. Hazen, *Contemporary American Opinion of the French Revolution*, p. 165.
21. Jones, *American and French Culture*, p. 542.
22. See R.R. Palmer (1964) *Age of the Democratic Revolution: A Political History of Europe and America, 1776–1800* (Princeton: Princeton University Press), vol. 2, pp. 518–46, for a discussion of politics in the United States after the 'revolutionizing' of the French Revolution in 1792. See especially p. 525 for a discussion of the Federalist and Republican perception of their

own position in relationship to France. See also Lawrence S. Kaplan (1967) *Jefferson and France: An Essay on Politics and Political Ideas* (New Haven: Yale University Press), Ch. 3; and Alexander De Conde (1958) *Entangling Alliance: Politics and Diplomacy under George Washington* (Durham, NC: Duke University Press), pp. 86–7, for an analysis of the impact of the French Revolution after 1793. Jones, *American and French Culture*, discusses the American reception to various aspects of French culture.
23. Chauncey Goodrich to Oliver Wolcott, 17 February 1793, in George Gibbs (ed.) (1846) *Memoirs of the Administrations of Washington and John Adams* (New York: privately printed), vol. 1, p. 88.
24. The proclamation issued on 22 April 1793, may be found in John C. Fitzpatrick (ed.) (1931–40) *The Writings of Washington* (Washington, DC: Government Printing Office), vol. 32, pp. 430–1.
25. Allan Potofsky (2006) 'The Political Economy of the French–American Debt Debate: The Ideological Uses of American Commerce, 1787–1800', *William & Mary Quarterly*, LXIII, 12. In this excellent piece, Potofsky states that 'George Washington's much-discussed Neutrality Proclamation of April 22, 1793, had the effect of aggravating Franco-American political, diplomatic, and commercial conflicts' and 'helped to discredit the foremost advocates of free exchange among Great Britain, the United States, and France'.
26. *National Gazette*, 15 May and 27 July 1793, as quoted in Claude Milton Newlin (1971) *The Life and Writings of Hugh Henry Brackenridge* (Mamaroneck, NJ: Princeton University Press), pp. 132–3. Also *National Gazette*, 8 May 1793, and *General Advertiser*, 14 December 1793, for similar sentiments.
27. See Harry Ammon (1973) *The Genet Mission* (New York: Norton), pp. 1–31 for Genet's background.
28. As quoted in Hazen, *Contemporary American Opinion of the French Revolution*, p. 175.
29. For a discussion of Genet's arrival in the United States and his instructions, see De Conde, *Entangling Alliance*, pp. 180–5 and 198–201; Charles Marion Thomas (1931) *American Neutrality in 1793: A Study in Cabinet Government* (New York: Columbia University Press), pp. 77–90; Ammon, *The Genet Mission*, pp. 22–9; Malone, *Jefferson and the Ordeal of Liberty*, pp. 90–8; Forrest McDonald (1979) *Hamilton: A Biography* (New York: Norton), p. 272; and Albert Hall Bowman (1974) *The Struggle for Neutrality: Franco-American Diplomacy during the Federalist Era* (Knoxville, Tenn.: University of Tennessee Press), pp. 56–75.
30. Jefferson to Madison, 19 May 1793, in Ford (ed.), *The Writings of Thomas Jefferson*, vol. 6, pp. 259–62.
31. *National Gazette*, 5 and 12 June 1793.
32. Memorandum of Jefferson, 1 and 2 August 1793, in Franklin Sawvel (ed.) (1903) *The Anas of Thomas Jefferson* (New York: Round Table Press), pp. 156–61; Thomas, *American Neutrality in 1793*, pp. 226–32; Ammon, *The Genet Mission*, pp. 101–9; De Conde, *Entangling Alliance*, pp. 206–300; and Malone, *Jefferson and the Ordeal of Liberty*, pp. 124–8.
33. See Jefferson to Monroe, 28 June 1793, in Ford (ed.), *The Writings of Thomas Jefferson*, vol. 6, pp. 321–4.
34. John Adams to Jefferson as quoted in Hazen, *Contemporary American Opinion of the French Revolution*, p. 186.

35. Eugene Perry Link (1942) *Democratic Republican Societies, 1790–1800* (New York: Columbia University Press), pp. 13–15. Michelle Orihel, a graduate student at Syracuse University, is currently working on a dissertation on the democratic-republican societies and has revised the number of societies.
36. Kramer, 'The French Revolution and the Creation of American Political Culture', p. 33, for a discussion of the usefulness of Jürgen Habermas (1989) *The Structural Transformation of the Public Sphere: An Inquiry into a Category of Bourgeois Society* (Cambridge, Mass.: MIT Press) in analysing the development of a new democratic political culture.
37. Foner (ed.), *The Democratic-Republican Societies*, p. 22.
38. As quoted in ibid., p. 23.
39. See Sawvel (ed.), *The Anas of Thomas Jefferson*, p.150, for these rumours.
40. 'No Jacobin NO. VII', in Harold C. Syrett (ed.) (1961–87), *The Papers of Alexander Hamilton* (New York: Columbia University Press), vol. 15, pp. 268–70.
41. See the excellent Thomas Slaughter (1986) *The Whiskey Rebellion: Frontier Epilogue to the American Revolution* (Oxford: Oxford University Press) for the best account of the insurrection.
42. As quoted in Kramer (2002) 'The French Revolution and the Creation of American Political Culture', p. 37.
43. Alexander De Conde (1966) *Quasi-War: The Politics and Diplomacy of the Undeclared War with France 1797–1801* (New York: Charles Scribner & Sons), pp. 16–17.
44. William Stinchcombe (1980) *The XYZ Affair* (Westport, Conn.: Greenwood Press), for an excellent discussion of the XYZ affair.
45. 'Stand No. 1', 30 March 1798, in Syrett (ed.), *The Papers of Alexander Hamilton*, vol. 21, p. 384.
46. Jefferson to Madison, 10 and 17 May 1798 in Ford (ed.), *The Writings of Thomas Jefferson*, vol. 7, pp. 251–4. Jefferson explained to Madison that the French tricolour had been mistaken for the blue and red cockade of the American Revolution.
47. Jefferson to Monroe and Madison, 5 April 1798, in ibid., pp. 230–4.
48. Jefferson to Madison, 21 June 1798, in ibid., pp. 272–5.
49. Jefferson to Madison, 3 May 1798, in ibid., pp. 246–9 and Jefferson to Randolph, 9 May 1798, Jefferson Papers, Library of Congress.
50. For texts of the laws, see James Morton Smith (1956) *Freedom's Fetters: The Alien and Sedition Acts and American Civil Liberties* (Binghamton, NY: Vail-Ballou Press), pp. 435–42.
51. Newman, *Parades and the Politics of the Street*, p. 150.
52. John Quincy Adams later became a Republican and was the only New England Federalist Senator to vote in favour of the Louisiana Purchase.
53. Friedrich von Gentz (1800) *The Origin and Principles of the American Revolution, Compared with the Origin and Principles of the French Revolution* (Philadelphia: Asbury Dickins).
54. Kramer, 'The French Revolution and the Creation of American Political Culture', pp. 42–3.
55. See the *New York Times*, 18 January 1976.
56. Daughters of the American Revolution, *Manual for Citizenship*.

# 11
# The French and North American Revolutions in Comparative Perspective

*Richard Whatmore*

## 1

Over supper on 26 February 1796 President John Adams was said to have commented to Vice-President James Madison 'that there was not a single principle the same in the American and French Revolutions'.[1] The constitutional origins, government and national characters of the two nations were altogether different.[2] During the Terror similar claims were made, epitomized by the unknown translator of Honoré Riouffe's exposé of Jacobin depravities:

> Whatever congeniality in the object or means, a warm passion for liberty may have enabled some men to discover between the American and French revolutions, there was certainly none at this epocha – not more at least than there is between a man and a monkey – a frightful resemblance, from which the man turns with horror and aversion. And this likeness, as well as the partiality for it, must have been occasioned by their viewing the objects through a corrupt medium. But if there be any, who still advocate the terrific system, by which this monster [Robespierre] and his colleagues established their power in France, they are dangerous citizens in this happy country; for nothing is more certain than that, if such men were trusted with power, they would abuse it in the same manner, and wealth and virtue would become equally treasonable in the United States, as they have been in France. A dungeon, a bundle of straw, famine and death, would be the portion of every man, who has the virtue enough to alarm their jealousy, or wealth to tempt their avarice ... Yes, by embracing a philosophy propitious to rapine and murder; and by indulging the lust of power, and the suggestion of avarice, the docile patriots of America

may come to vie with their gallic allies, and the American states equal France in revolutionary horrors.[3]

John Adams' perspective was evident in the writings of his son John Quincy Adams from the early 1790s.[4] It was the younger Adams who discovered that Friedrich Gentz, the Prussian diplomat, had similarly contrasted the colonial fight for liberty with the French revolutionary war on monarchy and Christianity.[5] In such writings, rather than being a proselytizing and outward-looking republican movement, the North American Revolution was portrayed as a local independence struggle which succeeded not because of its republican ideology, but through the support of absolute monarchy via the alliance signed with France in February 1778. France and North America shared only an opposition to British dominion in international politics. They collaborated to establish an alternative that countered self-interested British policy in commerce and politics, famously labelled 'the mercantile system' in Adam Smith's *Wealth of Nations*. Yet North America ultimately followed Britain in erecting a constitution founded on checks and balances, to be contrasted with the unified sovereignty that characterized both Old Regime France and the First French Republic. For many observers unified sovereignty in France ensured the continuity of reason of states politics both domestically and internationally, and this prevented the establishment of a cosmopolitan or republican model in international relations.[6]

Adams' and Gentz's perspective was supported by growing recognition of cultural difference between North America and France despite their initial alliance. An anticipated rapid growth of commerce did not follow the cessation of hostilities with the British. Some projectors continued to envisage Gallo-American trade as a lever to collapse the despised mercantile system, although they acknowledged the continued dominion of British manners, not only in matters of commerce but also with regard to religious ecumenicalism.[7] All parties acknowledged, however, that trade between North America and Britain rose greatly in the years following the Treaty of Paris of 1783, and the argument became commonplace that Britain had lost the war but won the peace.[8] Lack of economic interaction found a counterpart in politics. When Washington declared that North America would be neutral with respect to the wars between republican France and Europe's monarchies in 1793, and when the Jay Treaty was signed in London between Britain and North America in 1794, the distance travelled away from the close links of the 1780s was underscored. Relations then became hostile during the rule of the Directory at Paris, following French interference with American shipping bound for

Britain, and this was compounded by the 'XYZ Affair' and the 'Quasi-War' between 1798 and 1800. Relations were then conducted on the same basis as between any other European state with interests in the Atlantic.[9]

As was the case across Europe, many observers in North America who welcomed the French Revolution in 1789 were equally vocal in subsequently condemning its progress via republicanism, civil war and irreligion.[10] As one commentator put it, '[Americans] considered Christianity itself as being in the greatest danger, and therefore became unfriendly to the French revolution'. By contrast, 'in the constitution of the United States, nothing is said in regard to Religion'.[11] Experience of political life in revolutionary France made General Lafayette rue his statement to George Washington that the 'great monument raised to liberty [in America] should serve as a lesson to the oppressor and an example to the oppressed'.[12] Gouverneur Morris, so prominent at the Constitutional Convention of 1787 and who had become North American ambassador in Paris, was notable for his attempts to subvert the progress of French republicanism through ongoing aid to the court and the king.[13] During the Revolution Talleyrand too affirmed that there was little or no relationship between events in America in the 1770s and 1780s and events in France in the 1790s, arguing that the federal constitution was modelled on Britain, and anticipating Washington as a monarch.[14]

Such commentators were drawing on an established tradition that viewed North America as largely divorced from mainstream European political and economic thought. In older texts America was presented as the 'rêve exotique', in Gilbert Chinard's memorable phrase, and altogether different from Europe because of its lack of inhabitants, abundance of land and limited means of transport, technology and commerce.[15] In the works of Voltaire, Raynal and Crèvecoeur, America was a place of exile from European problems, characterized by Puritan sobriety, religious toleration, civil harmony, agricultural labour and peaceful living.[16] American distinctiveness became the most prominent theme of an extensive literature, with notable contrasts being made between the large slave populations and European social structures.[17] This approach derived the tendency among eighteenth-century observers to explain political difference and formulate rules for political practice by reference to specific and distinct social, political or religious phenomena. Politics and reform strategies in North America had to be different to civilized Europe not simply because of 'backwardness' with respect to commercial development, but also because the American republic was a union of small states. The small state/large state distinction, made famous by Montesquieu but identifiable across the century, enabled contrasts to be made between the refined modes of living in Europe's monarchies and the rudeness of North American politics, trade and morals.

When authors began to call for Europe to follow the North American example, as Diderot famously did with respect to the abolition of ranks and the creation of general assemblies in his contributions to the abbé Raynal's *Histoire philosophique des deux Indes* and in his *Vie de Senèque*, he was unclear about the transition mechanism by which European states might follow America: the practical means of adopting the institutions of another state.[18] Equally, when the Physiocrats lauded North America as the modern state in which land-ownership could most easily be made the foundation of citizenship, there was no sense that the North America conditions, meaning abundant land and a small population, could be mapped onto European life.[19] All the Physiocratic admirers of the new republic acknowledged the different worlds to be found on either side of the Atlantic, with North America allowing a contrast to be drawn with the Machiavellianism of European polities.[20] Condorcet wrote in his *Esquisse d'un tableau historique* that because of events in North America 'it could not be long before the transatlantic revolution must find its imitations in the European quarter of the world'. Despite such a statement, he followed his younger Physiocratic self in going on to explain that the American and French Revolutions had little in common, being the product of different national histories and social and political problems:

> [The French Revolution] was more complete, more entire than that of America, and of consequence was attended with greater convulsions in the interior of the nation, because the Americans, satisfied with the code of civil and criminal legislation which they had derived from England, having no corrupt system of finance to reform, no feudal tyrannies, no hereditary distinctions, no privileges of rich and powerful corporations, no system of religious intolerance to destroy, had only to direct their attention to the establishment of new powers to be substituted in the place of those hitherto exercised over them by the British government. In these innovations there was nothing that extended to the mass of the people, nothing that altered the subsisting of relations formed between individuals: whereas the French revolution, for reasons exactly the reverse, had to embrace the whole economy of society, to change every social relation, to penetrate to the smallest link of the political chain ... The French attacked at once the despotism of kings, the political inequality of constitutions

partially free, the pride and prerogatives of nobility, the domination, intolerance, and rapacity of priests, and the enormity of feudal chains, still respected in almost every nation in Europe ... there appeared on the side of the Gallic revolution the voice only of some enlightened sages.[21]

Prior to the French Revolution much of North America was perceived to be undergoing transition from barbarism to civilization; it made sense that North America had developed forms of politics indebted to the structures and defensive strategies of the Swiss cantons and Dutch federation. The national liberation struggles of these states paralleled North American experience. Direct connection with commercial monarchies seeking empire made much less sense.

## 2

Although Edmund Burke sought to distinguish between events in America he had supported, and those in France he had condemned, the more common view from Britain during the 1790s was to associate the revolutions and attack them.[22] North America was coupled with France as an example to deists, heathens and dissenters of the evils of rebellion and as evidence of God's wrath; alternatively, the 'revolutions in France and North America' were cited as revealing the healthy progress of dissent against Papist or Protestant church establishments.[23] The revolutions were most commonly linked in patriotic rhetoric, abusing Britain's 'natural' enemies and the ideas they expressed. William Cobbett's lampooning Peter Porcupine's statement was characteristic: 'My last breath shall be spent cursing [democrats] like Franklin and Paine, and the French and American revolutions, and republicanism, liberty and equality.'[24] None of this commentary, being polemical, supplied any comparative analysis of France or of North America. It was Thomas Paine, often described by British critics as the founding father of republicanism in each nation, and the most dangerous radical of modern times, who fully enunciated exactly the opposite view to Adams and Gentz.

In all his works Paine declared the identity of North American and French republicanism and called for an age of pacific republics to replace that of king, priest and lord. That France was following North America was the foundational argument in favour of Britain joining the republics in a union sufficiently powerful to challenge the barbarisms of absolute monarchy and institutionalized Christianity, and inaugurate an Age of

Reason in politics, religion, morals and commerce. *The Rights of Man* sought 'the happiness of seeing the New World regenerate the Old', concluding that 'better times are in prospect ... the insulted German and the enslaved Spaniard, the Russ and the Pole, are beginning to think', inspired by a generation living as 'the Adam of a new world'.[25] Paine ranked monarchy 'in scripture as one of the sins of the Jews'. In modern times he held it to have become 'the popery of government'.[26] In addition Paine attacked the aristocracies of Europe as degenerate stock and co-responsible for the decline of their states.[27] Abolishing primogeniture and reforming land tenures, redistributing wealth by tax and insurance measures, removing established churches and instituting civic programmes of republican and moral education were all given roles in the planned transformation. But Paine placed the greatest emphasis upon political representation, which he called the great discovery of the moderns. Representation made the political culture of each republican nation homogeneous and patriotic, while ensuring that the enlightened were called upon to govern. Armed with fervently patriotic citizen soldiers, the resulting state would be impregnable:

> So powerful is the Representative System; first, by combining and consolidating all the parts of a country together, however great the extent; and secondly, by admitting of none but men properly qualified into the government, or dismissing them if they prove to be otherwise, that America was enabled thereby totally to defeat and overthrow all the schemes and projects of the Hereditary Government of England against her.[28]

The premise of Paine's argument was that free states shared a political form and culture, and could be established universally once the two major monarchies of the globe had been transformed into republics. Reform in Britain was vital, not least because Britain under George III was the major impediment to the democratic and cosmopolitan world that Paine envisaged. Yet Paine accepted that much of the momentum for republican reform had arisen because commerce, including corrupt mercantile commerce, was eradicating many of the unique features of polities that had developed across feudal Europe, thereby laying the foundations for global political identities.

Paine's impact was remarkable in Britain, with republicans like John Thelwall seeing themselves as part of an international cosmopolitan movement, and as contributors to a new science of politics with universal applicability. Linkage of the revolutions in France and in America became the cornerstone of Irish radical calls for independence on the basis of 'the spirit of Democracy, and equality of Rights and Privileges'.[29] Democratic revolution could be seen to bring with it great benefits in terms of liberty, equality and wealth. The identification of a growing democratic republican tradition was illustrated by the 'Stanzas on the Anniversary of the American Revolution':

> Ye men of Columbia, Oh! Hail the great day
> Which burst your tyrannical chain
> Which taught the oppress'd how to spurn lawless sway
> And establish'd equality's reign ...
> In your groves ye Colombians, those friends of mankind
> Who courts and court minions despise
> In your groves unmolested, those spirits shall find
> Ev'ry blessing proud Britain denies
> Then would continue a poor drudging thing?
> For tythe-men and tax-men to squeeze?
> When the winds that would bear him from church, peers, and kind
> Would waft him to freedom and ease.[30]

That democratic republics had successfully been established in two states separated geographically and historically challenged older assumptions about political change being determined by particular circumstance. The small state/large state distinction no longer governed political possibilities. Future republics had less to fear concerning the need to adapt reform programmes to national peculiarities. Prospects for defence had also improved, as North America and France had shown that modern republics could stand against commercial monarchies in war.

The foundation of Paine's argument was that France had followed the North American example and in doing so justified republican government the world over. Critics and supporters of Paine acknowledged that both revolutions were linked to general ideas about representation and the abolition of ranks.[31] French interest in the 1780s in North American republican politics and religion had been extensive, and the constitutions of the first republics were widely commented upon.[32] The question was to what extent did the North American example shape French politics in 1789? When things went awry, foreign supporters of the revolution in France could always fall back on the view that a stable republic could only with difficulty be achieved because, unlike America, France had no domestic tradition of reflection about liberty.[33] Other critics speculated whether Paine's political philosophy amounted to much more than the advocacy of representation, and thus questioned what it meant to advocate 'democracy' and 'republicanism' in states like France and North America. John Gillies made this argument in linking Paine to a tradition traceable to Locke and Molyneux, favouring,

> the new unalienable right of all mankind to be fairly represented, a right with which each individual was invested from the commencement of the world, but of which, until very recently, no one knew the name, or had the least notion of the thing.

What Gillies called 'this boasted and specious theory' was:

> begun in the works of our Locke and our Molyneux, continued in those of our Price and our Priestley, and carried to the utmost extravagance in those of (I wish not to say our) Rousseau, Paine, and the innumerable pamphleteers whose writings occasioned or accompanied the American and French revolutions.[34]

For authors like Gillies certain forms of representation were compatible with every political system, but it was a mistake to associate this with republican evangelism. Within France the abbé Sieyes stated that he could not understand why Paine had confounded 'two notions so distinct as those of a representative system and republicanism'. Sieyes was equally sceptical of the practical realization of Paine's advocacy of the abolition of ranks.[35] For Sieyes, any transformation of society rested upon change in popular manners. New laws could alter manners, but the process would always be gradual. For Paine such arguments were counter-revolutionary. Mixed and absolute government prevented human improvement. Britain's monarchy and aristocracy in particular had to be destroyed if the pernicious international influence of the British polity was to end.

## 3

Many historians have followed Paine in linking the Atlantic revolutions. An established historiographical tradition has argued that the French revolutionaries modelled many of their proposals and ideas on the earlier revolution in North America. Contemporaries such as Arthur Young adhered to a view ascribed to Raynal that 'the American Revolution has brought the French one in its train'.[36] A century later John Morley made the point against Hippolyte Taine's *Les origines de la France contemporaine: L'ancien régime* (1875) that in terms of ideas the American and French Revolutions were identical. According to Morley, Taine had 'given an exaggerated importance to the literary and speculative activity of the last half century of the old monarchy':

> Again, we venture to put to M. Taine the following question. If the convulsions of 1789–1794 were due to the revolutionary doctrine, if that doctrine was the poison of the movement, how would he explain the firm, manly, steadfast, unhysterical quality of the American Revolution thirteen years before? It was theoretically based on exactly the same doctrine. Jefferson and Franklin were as well disciplined in the French philosophy of the eighteenth century as Mirabeau or Robespierre. The Declaration of Independence recites the same abstract and unhistoric propositions as the Declaration of the Rights of Man. Why are we to describe the draught which Rousseau and the others had brewed, as a harmless or wholesome prescription for the Americans, and as maddening poison to the French? The answer must be that the quality of the drug is relative to the condition of the patient, and that the vital question for the student of the Old Regime and the circumstances of its fall is what other drug, what better process, could have extricated France on more tranquil terms from her desperate case? The American colonists, in spite of the over-wide formulæ of their Declaration, really never broke with their past in any of its fundamental elements. They had a historic basis of laws and institutions which was still sound and whole, and the political severance from England made no breach in social continuity. If a different result followed in France, it was not because France was the land of the classic spirit, but because her institutions were inadequate, and her ruling classes incompetent to transform them.[37]

The great Cambridge historian Lord Acton rejected Morley's social analysis of the events of the French Revolution in lectures originally given between 1895 and 1899, finding the ultimate origins of 1789 in the critiques of absolutism developed by the sceptical Protestant Pierre Bayle, the Jansenist jurist Jean Domat and the Quietist Archbishop of Cambrai, François de Salignac de la Mothe-Fénelon.[38] Comparative historical analysis led Acton to conclude that the French Revolution was first and foremost about ideology, which alone explained why revolution occurred in France and not elsewhere. But Acton shared with Morley the belief that the ideas of the North American republicans proved the key to the popular rebellion at Paris:

> [John] Adams, after he had been President of the United States [1797–1801], bitterly regretted the Revolution which made them independent, because it had given the example to the French; although he also believed that they had not a single principle in common. Nothing, on the contrary, is more certain than that American principles profoundly influenced France, and determined the course of the Revolution. It is from America that Lafayette derived the saying that created a commotion at the time, that resistance is the most sacred of duties. There also was the theory that political power comes from those over whom it is exercised, and depends upon their will; that every authority not so constituted is illegitimate and precarious; that the past is more a warning than an example; that the earth belongs to those who are upon it, not to those who are underneath. These are characteristics common to both Revolutions.[39]

Recent historians have followed such claims, with Joyce Appleby writing in 1971 that:

> Given the universalist assumptions of eighteenth-century thought, there was nothing incongruous about Frenchmen looking for guidance from a cluster of onetime colonies perched on the edge of a wilderness three thousand miles away. Indeed, to many French reformers the *tabula rasa* of American history was an asset, a return to first principles.[40]

Patrice Higonnet in *Sister Republics* has similarly argued that events in France and North America can be 'similarly stylized' as new political systems 'designed to express the importance of individualism in social life':

> Both revolutions stood for popular sovereignty, nationalism, the rights of man, no taxation without representation, republicanism, and suspicion of established religion. Many Frenchmen were convinced America's achievement was wholly relevant to their own ambitions. Many of the terms and formulations they used were borrowed from America's recent past. Several French institutions and concepts had American precedents, including the Convention, the

Committee of Public Safety, federalism, a written constitution, political clubs, paper money, loyalty oaths, and the Declaration of the Rights of Man.[41]

In this story the sister republics of France and North America are the leading states in a broader movement from Geneva and Holland in the 1780s to the creation of the new republics under the French Directory in Italy, Switzerland and Germany in the late 1790s, forming the 'age of the democratic revolution'.[42] The first global revolutions against feudal and aristocratic forces were followed by a democratic movement inaugurating an age of bourgeois and socialist liberation movements from South America to Russia.[43]

It is significant that Paine, in embracing a universal republican language, was not interested in similarities and differences between France and North America. Despite being equally fascinated by the prospects for global political change, nor were fellow radicals such as David Williams.[44] For liberal-minded critics difference needed to be explained and justified; movements advocating social and political uniformity were suspect. As the latter view predominated, there was little sense in North America of being a 'sister republic' to revolutionary France, although republics like Holland and fellow states of the union were so named.[45] The core problem with linking North America and France in the 1790s was the uncertain identity of the former revolution because of its indebtedness to British traditions. The belief was widespread across Europe that however Anglophobe North Americans were, an ingrained 'Britishness' remained. By contrast, France rejected every aspect of the British model of government, state, church and society. Historians such as Joyce Appleby have sought to define an 'Américaniste' group who followed Turgot's critique of British checks and balances, and included Dupont de Nemours, Lafayette, Target, Sieyes and Roederer. But none of these authors saw themselves to be applying specific ideas of North American origin to France. Dupont de Nemours' expanded edition of John Stevens' *Observations on Government* (1787) may have been as useful as a critique of bicameralism as 'Livingston's' *Examen de gouvernement de l'Angleterre* (1789) but he had opposed Britain's government for some time; the purpose of the work was to warn the Americans against British ideas and the French against democracy.[46] Turgot was more interested in confederations of states as a means to international peace than he was in North America's constitutional example.[47] Roederer was convinced that North America would soon evolve into a mixed monarchy modelled on Britain.[48]

What North American political identity meant in the 1780s was itself uncertain, given the difference between the first state constitutions and the subsequent contested evolution of the polity into a federal state. John Adams became frustrated at the end of the 1790s because of the extent to which ascribed Paineite links between France and the United States masked the stable nature of North American republicanism, developed as it had been from a European small-state republican heritage. By contrast, France saw the genuinely radical revolution in the movement from absolute monarchy to unicameral republic, overthrowing ranks and religion in the process.[49] As the Paineite Charles Piggot wrote in 1795, America was 'a bright and immortal example to all colonies groaning under a foreign yoke' while France was for the peoples of Europe 'their saviour, their deliverer, in having enabled them to purge the earth of their tyrants and oppressors'.[50] In North America the notion became commonplace in the nineteenth century that although 'the republican elements of British self-government found a peculiarly favourable soil in America from the first settlements', the new federal constitution was unique, even when compared with confederated states like Holland and Switzerland:

> the framers of our constitution boldly conceived a federal republic, or the application of the representative principle with its two houses to a confederacy. It was the first instance in history. The Netherlands, which served our fore-fathers as models in many respects, even in the name bestowed on our confederacy, furnished them with no example for this great conception. It is the chief American contribution to the common treasures of political civilization. It is that by which America will influence other parts of the world more than by any other political institution or principle. Already are voices heard in Australia for a representative federal republic like ours. Switzerland, so far as she has of late reformed her federal constitution, has done so in avowed imitation of the federal pact of our Union ... Our frame of government, then, is justly called a federal republic, with one chief magistrate elected by what the Greeks called, in politics, the Koinon, the Whole, with a complete representative government for the whole, a common army, judiciary of the Union, and with the authority of taxing the whole. It is called by no one a league.[51]

## 4

If the Paineite attempt to link the revolutions in France and North America is placed in this broader context the short-lived nature of the democratic republican linkage comes to the fore. For the next generation of French commentators it was obvious that North America was a unique state with only an indirect relationship to mainland European experience. The homogenizing and unifying forces that Paine advocated were no longer necessary elements of every radical platform. In the 1820s and 1830s, when French intellectuals became obsessed with the United States with the visits of Chateaubriand, Édouard de Montulé, Benjamin Saint-Victor, Victor Jacquemont and Achille Murat, the motive forces of the thriving republican confederation were widely seen to be new.[52] This was most clear, of course, from Alexis de Tocqueville's *Democracy in America* (1835 and 1840). North Americans were driven not by Montesquieu's triptych of fear, honour or virtue, but by the twin forces of equality and industry. Equality was not associated with a Spartan absence of wealth but rather with a relative lack of distance between riches and poverty; equality was defined negatively, once more with prevailing conditions on the other side of the Atlantic in mind, as the absence of any legal or informal social hierarchy, at least among North American white males. Numerous observers noted the conjoined spirit of liberty and religion that characterized North American society, the moral temper of its citizens even when labouring in factories, the strength of civil associations and the commitment to moderate politics. Commerce in the north of the union was most often described as a force for social cohesion and societal peace. Individualism was identified in the sense of an all-pervading dedication to self-betterment by industriousness, but did not degenerate into egotism because of the strength of the patriotic covenant perceived to have been entered into by all immigrant pilgrims, and because of the Congregationalist churches that determined mores and monitored behaviour. North America, with its abundance of land, its high wages, and its egalitarian, energetic and zealous populace, was a world away from modern Europe.

Michel Chevalier rose to prominence through his *Lettres sur l'Amérique du Nord*, published in 1836 and translated as *Society, Manners and Politics in the United States*.[53] Chevalier had been employed to report on American commerce by Adolphe Thiers in 1832, then Minister of the Interior in the recently established Orléans monarchy. Like Tocqueville, Chevalier's main sense was the enormity of the divide between the monarchies and republics of Europe and the modes of living, the values and institutional structures that were prominent in North America:

> North America is Europe with its head down and its feet up. European society, in London and Paris as well as at St Petersburg, in the Swiss

republic as well as in the Austrian empire, is aristocratical in this sense that, even after all the great changes of the last fifty years, it is still founded more or less absolutely on the principle of inequality or a difference of ranks. American society is essentially and radically a democracy, not in name merely but in deed. In the United States the democratic spirit is infused into all the national habits, and all the customs of society; it besets and startles at every step the foreigner, who before landing in the country, had no suspicion to what a degree every nerve and fibre had been steeped in aristocracy by a European education. It has effaced all the distinctions, except that of colour; for here a shade in the hue of the skin separates men more widely than in any other country of the world.[54]

At Lowell in Maine Chevalier was astonished at the moral lives of the thousand factory girls who worked in the cotton mills, for whom 'reading is the only recreation', surrounded by 'churches and meeting-houses of every sect, Episcopalian, Baptist, Congretationalist, Methodist, Universalist, Unitarian, &c. and there is also a Roman Catholic chapel'. Despite the latter, Chevalier believed that 'Protestant education, much more than our Catholic discipline, draws round each individual a line over which it is difficult to step.' In consequence there was 'more coldness in the domestic relations' and 'a more or less complete absence of the stronger feelings of the soul', but also a remarkable lack of poverty or degradation, evinced by 'only three cases of illicit connection' among the thousand women, and in every case 'the parties were married immediately, several months before the birth of the child'.[55] Chevalier concluded that 'Anglo-American prudery' was more valuable than French 'ease and freedom of manners'.

Like all French visitors, Chevalier was fascinated by the lessons of North America for Europe. If France wanted to be a great state once again, Chevalier concluded that it had to embrace 'the English pattern' of both government and mores, potentially by becoming Protestant and setting aside both irrational Catholic mysticism and the philosophic irreligious beliefs that had been so common in the previous century.[56] One fact that struck both Chevalier and Tocqueville was that North America was a republic whose citizens lacked any recognizable republican identity, associated with the great republics of Europe's past, with the exception of attitudes to slavery, which was for many the last vestige of classical republicanism. North Americans appeared less interested in the form of their government than by their religion, their inventions and their civil life. While proud of their representative system, and their liberties with respect to the vote, North Americans appeared to be neither warlike nor imperialist.

If North American political language, like so much about their economy and society, was deemed distinctive and novel by Tocqueville, for Chevalier it was an extension of 'Englishness' into a vast, rich and minimally conquered natural environment. Protestantism was intimately associated with the passion for industry for Chevalier, and also with guiding and educating self-interest to make it compatible with the living of peaceful and rational lives:

> Protestantism is republican; Puritanism is absolute self-government in religion, and begets it in politics. The United Provinces were Protestant; the United States are Protestant. Catholicism is essentially monarchical... Under the influence of Protestantism and republicanism, the social progress has been affected by the medium of the spirit of individuality; for protestantism, republicanism, and individuality are all one.[57]

Tocqueville agreed that the mark of the Puritan founding could be seen as a major determinant of North American manners, a force behind the North American Revolution, and the most distinguishable feature of Atlantic republican life.[58] He was equally certain, however, about the compatibility between Protestantism or Catholicism and 'self-interest properly understood', and confident that 'the quiet rule of the majority' would secure for the republic, sometimes by means of unintended consequences, a glorious future in which democracy played a providential role.[59] Chevalier was more circumspect. He was intrigued by the seeds of degeneration discernible within North American life, identified with the inevitable growth of a plutocratic aristocracy and with the imminent entrance of North America into imperial power politics, through the subjugation of Mexico, Canada or other bordering states.

Chevalier was convinced that North America would play a major role in world history and that this entailed a return to well-trodden paths of European history, with aristocracy facing people, competition over resources and with regard to commerce, and between states across the globe when North America became an empire. Although Tocqueville and Chevalier emphasized North American distinctiveness, there was no longer a sense of absolute or ineradicable difference of the kind that had fascinated Enlightenment observers. The time was long past when stages of refinement or distinctions between small and large states determined reform programmes. The end of such perspectives was a Paineite legacy.

Difference was expected but could always be overcome in a world of commerce and empire. Another Paineite continuity could be discerned in the desire to change Europe by the North American example and purge it of British rapacity and imperialism. For Tocqueville such optimism was short-lived. In subsequent decades the militarism and intestine disorders of North American politics led him to the mature view that America was no longer a model for any advocate of liberty.[60] Subsequent commentators did not seek to find new principles or practices in North America that distinguished the republic's politics or ideologies, but rather another history of an aspiring empire facing an all too predictable series of problems, akin to those France had faced in the eighteenth century.[61]

## Notes

1. *The Papers of James Madison*, vol. 17: *31 March 1797–3 March 1801 with a Supplement 22 January 1778–9 August 1795*, ed. D.B. Mattern, J.C.A. Stagg, J.K. Cross and S. Holbrook Perdue, 17 vols (Charlottesville: University of Virginia Press, 1991), Congressional Series, XVII, p. 135.
2. Letter from John Adams to Abigail Adams, 4 December 1796; 'John Adams' autobiography', part 1, 'John Adams', through 1776, sheet 4, p. 3; sheet 9, p. 4: *Adams Family Papers*, http://www.masshist.org/digitaladams/aea/.
3. 'Translator's Preface' to Honoré Riouffe (1796) *Revolutionary Justice Displayed* (Philadelphia), pp. iii–iv.
4. John Quincy Adams (1792) *Observations on Paine's Rights of Man, in a Series of Letters, by Publicola* (Glasgow).
5. Gentz (1801) *Über den Ursprung und Charakter des Knieges gegen die französische Revolution* (Berlin). In 1800 John Quincy Adams translated the book as *The Origin and Principles of the American Revolution Compared with the Origin and Principles of the French Revolution*.
6. John Adams (1787) *A Defence of the Constitutions of Government of the United States of America* (London); compare Jean-Antoine-Nicolas de Caritat marquis de Condorcet (1795) *Outlines of an Historical View of the Progress of the Human Mind* (London), pp. 268–9; see also Graham Jepson (1792) *Letters to Thomas Payne, in Answer to his Late Publication on the Rights of Man* (London), pp. 52–3; Thomas Brooke Clarke (1803) *An Historical and Political View of the Disorganization of Europe* (London).
7. Jacques-Pierre Brissot and Étienne Clavière (1791) *De la France et des États-Unis* (Paris); Brissot (1794) *New Travels in the United States of America*, 2 vols (London), vol. 1, p. 79: 'They will soon be in America in the situation where M. d'Alembert has placed the ministers of Geneva [whom d'Alembert called Socinians in the article 'Genève' in the *Encyclopédie*]. Since the ancient puritan austerity has disappeared, you are no longer surprised to see a game of cards introduced among these good Presbyterians.'
8. John Holroyd, Earl of Sheffield (1783) *Observations on the Commerce of the American States*, 2nd edn (London), pp. 7–37; Dupont de Nemours (1788)

The French and North American Revolutions 235

   *Lettre à la chambre du commerce de Normandie, Sur le Mémoire qu'elle a publié relativement au Traité de Commerce avec l'Angleterre* (Rouen and Paris), p. 248. For the counter-argument see Tench Coxe (1791) *A Brief Examination of Lord Sheffield's Observations on the Commerce of the United States of America* (Philadelphia) and (1795) *A View of the United States of America, in a Series of Papers, Written... between... 1787 and 1794* (Dublin). For the French context of such claims see Antonino De Francesco's Chapter 12, below.
9. Robert Goodloe Harper (1798) *An Abridgement of the Observations on the Dispute between the United States and France* (London: John Stockdale), pp. 2–4: '[France] has formed a plan of aggrandizement at the expense of all her neighbours: that after the example of the Romans, those ferocious and systematic destroyers of mankind, she has resolved to make all Europe, and finally the whole world, bend beneath her yoke; a resolution in the accomplishment whereof she pursues the Roman policy, of dividing to destroy; of bribing on nations with the spoils of another.' See further James Roger Sharp's Chapter 10, above.
10. Joseph Priestley (1794) *Letters Addressed to the Philosophers and Politicians of France, on the Subject of Religion* (Philadelphia); C.D. Hazen (1897) *Contemporary American Opinion of the French Revolution* (Baltimore: Johns Hopkins University Press).
11. Anon. (1798) *An Impartial Review of the Causes and Principles of the French Revolution, by an American* (Boston), p. 40.
12. Lafayette (1825) *Memoirs of General La Fayette, Embracing Details of his Public and Private Life* (New York), pp. 334–94; Anon. (1793) *An Address to the Inhabitants of Great Britain and Ireland; in Reply to the Principles of the Author of the Rights of Man. Written in 1792* (London), p. 36.
13. Gouverneur Morris (1831) *The Life of Gouverneur Morris with Selections from his Correspondence and Miscellaneous Papers*, ed. J. Sparks, 3 vols (New York), vol. 1, pp. 335–87.
14. Talleyrand to Lord Lansdowne, 1 February 1795, in Lord Fitzmaurice (1912) *Life of William Earl of Shelburne*, 2 vols (London: Macmillan), vol. 2, pp. 465–75.
15. G. Chinard (1913) *L'Amérique et le rêve exotique dans la littérature française au XVIIe et XVIIIe siècle* (Paris: Hachette); D. Echeverria (1957) *Mirage in the West: A History of the French Image of American Society to 1815* (Princeton: Princeton University Press).
16. G. Ansart (2008) 'From Voltaire to Raynal and Diderot's *Histoire des deux Indes*: The French *Philosophes* and Colonial America', in A. Craiutu and J.C. Isaac (eds), *America through European Eyes* (University Park: Penn State University Press): I am grateful to Professor Craiutu for allowing me to read this important collection prior to publication.
17. Cornelius de Pauw (1789) *Selections from Les recherches philosophiques sur les Américains* (Bath), p. 99.
18. Diderot (1875) *Essai sur les règnes de Claude et de Néron, et sur les mœurs et les écrits de Sénèque pour servir d'introduction à la lecture de ce philosophe*, in *Œuvres complètes de Diderot*, ed. J. Assézat, 12 vols (Paris), vol. 3, pp. 48, 71, 321–4.
19. Condorcet (1787) *The Life of M. Turgot* (London), pp. 321–2. On this approach see Manuela Albertone's Chapter 6, above.

20. Condorcet (1786) *On the Influence of the American Revolution on Europe* (London).
21. Condorcet (1795) *Outlines of an Historical View of the Progress of the Human Mind* (London), pp. 265–8.
22. Edmund Burke (1791) *An Appeal from the New to the Old Whigs, in Consequence of Some Late Discussions in Parliament, Relative to the Reflections on the French Revolution* (New York), p. 63.
23. William Christie (1791) *An Essay, on Ecclesiastical Establishments in Religion* (Montrose), p. 49; John Baillie (1792) *Two Sermons: The First on the Divinity of Jesus Christ; the Second on Time, Manner, and Means of the Conversion and Universal Restoration of the Jews* (London), p. 70; Joseph Lomas Tower (1796) *Illustrations of Prophecy: In the Course of which are Elucidated Many Predictions, which Occur in Isaiah, or Daniel*, 2 vols (London), vol. 1, p. 286; John Auchincloss (1796) *The Sophistry of Both the First and the Second Part of Mr. Paine's Age of Reason* (Edinburgh), p. 39.
24. William Cobbett (1797) *The Last Confession and Dying Speech of Peter Porcupine, with an Account of his Dissection* (New York), p. 27.
25. Thomas Paine (1791) *Rights of Man: Being an Answer to Mr. Burke's Attack on the French Revolution* (London), Part One, dedication to George Washington.
26. Thomas Paine (1776) *Common Sense: Addressed to the Inhabitants of America* (Philadelphia), p. 11.
27. Paine, *Rights of Man*, Part One, p. 71.
28. Paine (1792) *Fifth Edition of Paine's Letters: Containing a Letter to Mr. Secretary Dundas, in Answer to his Speech on the Late Proclamation* (London), pp. 2–3.
29. Thomas Blaquiere (1797) *General Observations on the State of Affairs in Ireland, and its Defence against an Invasion. By a Country Gentleman* (Dublin), pp. 17–18; William James MacNeven (1799) *An Argument for Independence, in Opposition to an Union. Addressed to all his Countrymen. By an Irish Catholic* (Dublin), pp. 40–1; Anon. (1800) *Irish Independence; or the Policy of Union* (Dublin), p. 13.
30. Anon. (1794) *Liberty Scraps* (n.p.), pp. 12–13. On the development of a tradition of democratic radicalism see Jonathan Israel's Chapter 2, above.
31. Anon. (1791) *Political Dialogues. Number I. On the General Principles of Government* (London), pp. 16–17; Charles Pigott (1792) *The Jockey Club; or a Sketch of the Manners of the Age. Part the Third*, 2nd edn (London), p. 191.
32. H.E. Bourne (1902–3) 'American Constitutional Precedents in the French National Assembly', *American Historical Review*, VIII, 466–86; B. Faÿ (1925) *L'esprit revolutionnaire en France et aux Étas-Unis à la fin du XVIIIe siècle* (Paris: Edouard Champion); G. Chinard (1943) 'Notes on the French Translations of the Forms of Government or Constitutions of the Several United States 1778 and 1783', *American Philosophical Society Year Book* (Philadelphia), pp. 88–106; M. Lahmer (2001), *La constitution américaine dans le débat français: 1795–1848* (Paris: Harmattan).
33. Anon. (1798) *An Impartial Review of the Causes and Principles of the French Revolution, by an American* (Boston), p. 36.
34. John Gillies (1797) *Aristotle's Ethics and Politics, Comprising his Practical Philosophy, Translated from the Greek*, 2 vols (London), vol. 1, pp. 2–7.
35. Sieyes (2003) *Political Writings*, ed. M. Sonenscher (New York: Hackett), pp. 167–9.

36. Arthur Young (1793) *Travels during the Years 1787, 1788 and 1789, Undertaken More Particularly with a View of Ascertaining the Cultivation, Wealth, Resources . . . of France*, 2 vols (Dublin), vol. 1, pp. 190, 375.
37. John Morley (1886) 'France in the Eighteenth Century', *Critical Miscellanies*, 3 vols (London: Chapman and Hall), vol. 3, pp. 288–9.
38. John Emerich Edward Dalberg, Lord Acton (2000) *Lectures on the French Revolution*, ed. J.N. Figgis and R.V. Laurence, with a foreword by S.J. Tonsor (Indiana: Liberty Fund), p. 4.
39. Ibid., p. 38.
40. J. Appleby (1971) 'America as a Model for the Radical French Reformers of 1789', *William & Mary Quarterly*, XXVIII, 268. On the context of such work see Allan Potofsky's Chapter 1, above.
41. P. Higonnet (1988) *Sister Republics: The Origins of French and American Republicanism* (Cambridge, Mass.: Harvard University Press), pp. 1–2; A.A. Fursenko and G.H. McArthur (1976) 'The American and French Revolutions Compared: The View from the U.S.S.R.', *William & Mary Quarterly*, 3rd ser., XXXIII, 481–500; T.K. Murphy (2001) *The Changing Image of America in Europe, 1780–1830* (Lanham, Md.: Lexington Books); M. Bukovansky (2002) *Legitimacy and Power Politics: The American and French Revolutions in International Political Culture* (Princeton: Princeton University Press); S. Dunn (1999) *Sister Revolutions: French Lightning, American Light* (New York: Faber and Faber).
42. R.R. Palmer (1959–64) *The Age of the Democratic Revolution: A Political History of Europe and America, 1760–1800*, 2 vols (Princeton: Princeton University Press), vol. 1, pp. 239–84.
43. J. Godechot (1971) *France and the Atlantic Revolution of the Eighteenth Century, 1770–1799* (London: Macmillan).
44. David Williams (1790) *Lessons to a Young Prince by an Old Statesman, on the Present Disposition of Europe to a General Revolution*, 3rd edn (London), pp. 58–99.
45. Mercy Otis Warren (1994) *History of the Rise, Progress, and Termination of the American Revolution Interspersed with Biographical, Political and Moral Observations*, ed. L.H. Cohen, 2 vols (Indianapolis: Liberty Fund), vol. 2, p. 169; Samuel Miller (1797) *A Discourse, Delivered April 12, 1797, at the Request of and before the New-York Society for Promoting the Manumission of Slaves* (New York), p. 27.
46. Dupont de Nemours (1789) *Examen du gouvernement d'Angleterre, comparé aux constitutions des États-Unis* (London and Paris), p. 38.
47. Condorcet (1787) *The Life of Turgot* (London), pp. 340–8. On Turgot see Maria Luisa Pesante's Chapter 3, above.
48. Roederer (1853–56) 'Cours d'organisation sociale fait au Lycée en 1793', in *Œuvres de Rœderer*, 8 vols (Paris), vol. 8, p. 248.
49. William Cobbett (1796) *The Bloody Buoy Thrown out as a Warning to the Political Pilots of America: or, A Faithful Relation of a Multitude of Acts of Horrid Barbarity, such as the Eye never Witnessed, the Tongue never Expressed, or the Imagination Conceived, until the Commencement of the French Revolution* (Philadelphia), pp. 141–91.
50. Charles Piggot (1795) *A Political Dictionary Explaining the True Meaning of Words* (London), pp. 2, 40.

51. Francis Lieber (1859) *On Civil Liberty and Self Government* (Philadelphia), pp. 262–3.
52. A. Craiutu (2008) 'In Search of Happiness: Victor Jacquemont's Travel in America', *European Legacy*, XIII, 13–33; Craiutu and Isaac (eds), *America through European Eyes*.
53. J. Jennings (2006) 'Democracy before Tocqueville: Michel Chevalier's America', *Review of Politics*, LXVIII, 398–427.
54. Michel Chevalier (1839) *Society, Manners and Politics in the United States* (Boston), p. 187.
55. Ibid., pp. 127–8, 138–9.
56. Ibid., pp. 322–3: 'Place the remains of Voltaire and Montesquieu, of Rousseau and Diderot, in the Pantheon; but on their monuments deposit their works veiled under a shroud. Teach the people to bless their memory; but do not teach it their doctrines.'
57. Ibid., p. 368.
58. Tocqueville (2003) *Democracy in America* (London: Penguin Books), pp. 42–56.
59. Ibid., pp. 336–9, 464–7, 484–5.
60. A. Craiutu and J. Jennings (2004) 'The Third Democracy: Tocqueville's Views of America after 1840', XCVIII, 391–403.
61. J. Portes (2000) *Fascination and Misgivings: The United States in French Opinion, 1870–1914* (Cambridge: Cambridge University Press); S. Brooks (2002) *America Through Foreign Eyes* (Oxford: Oxford University Press); P. Roger (2005) *The American Enemy* (Chicago: Chicago University Press); A. Markovits (2006) *The Uncouth Nation: Why Europe Dislikes America* (Princeton: Princeton University Press).

# 12

## Federalist Obsession and Jacobin Conspiracy: France and the United States in a Time of Revolution, 1789–1794

*Antonino De Francesco*

For a long while, the American and French Revolutions have been seen as essentially different from one another, if not in direct contrast with one another. In the United States, the federalist political model, so the theory goes, ensured that liberty had a firm foundation, because it made it easier for the political parties to recognize each other's respective roles. In France, on the other hand, things went differently, because the fragile equilibrium set up by the 1791 constitution did not stop the violent political infighting, which itself quickly put an end to any notion of liberty. According to this interpretation, the political processes in the two countries soon parted ways, never again to find a point of contact.

However, there is the tendency with this interpretation to underestimate the closeness with which, in both America and France, the political struggle on the other side of the ocean was followed, either because it was held up as an example to be copied or because it was feared as a possible source of contagion. In America, there is no lack of examples which demonstrate this. Genet's mission and the growth of democratic associations are a proof of the enthusiasm aroused in Jefferson and Madison's republicans by the birth of another republic in France. At the same time, the political forces opposing them used the fear created by Jacobinism and the Terror as a powerful tool in the political fight to win support for Hamilton and Adams' federalists.

The same, however, cannot be said for France in this period. There was, it is true, a great deal of interest in the American political model before the Revolution, as is well documented by the debates that took place in the National Constituent Assembly.[1] However, that interest died down once the 1791 constitution had been approved, to vanish almost completely once France became a republic in its turn. What is more, in the summer of 1793, when some of France's provincial cities were protesting against the Convention's decision to expel the Girondins, the Montagnards, who had just come to power, even went so far as to accuse the rebels of federalism, declaring that the rebellious cities' protestations were liable to undermine the unity and indivisibility of the republic.[2] The civil war that ensued and the triumph of the Terror consequently brought an end to any interest in the American model. True, in 1795, when the constitutional debates were taking place in the aftermath of Thermidor, the American constitutional model was acknowledged, but this was really no more than a formal recognition. The two-chamber system introduced by the French constitution of Year III, in fact would be substantially different from that of America.[3]

This strangely contradictory circumstance – in which a group of republicans seemed to studiously ignore the only political system which could have been seen as an example to them – has not, however, been studied in relation to what was happening in America at the same time. As a result, the repercussions of those events on the political debate in France are still virtually unknown, even today. Most importantly of all, we still know very little about just how much interest was aroused in France by the way Madison challenged Hamilton in the period stretching from late 1791 through to 1792. It was the conflict sparked off by this challenge which was to condition the American political landscape up to 1800 and beyond.[4] It is well known, in fact, that Madison was opposed to the idea of consolidating the public debt, the creation of a national bank, governmental support for manufacturing industry and to certain barely concealed sympathies for the British political system. He complained that these would undermine the American constitution, impede the broader participation of the people in the political process and encourage the rise to political power of close-knit financial factions, a process which would inevitably undermine democracy.[5]

Oddly enough, this duel, based entirely on the central importance of public opinion in American politics, has interesting parallels with what was happening in France in the same period. Here, from October 1791 onwards, just after the Legislative Assembly had begun its work, the Jacobins embarked on a struggle for power with the Feuillants, a struggle which was to finish only with the collapse of the French monarchy during the insurrection of 10 August 1792. On this point, it is extremely interesting to notice how, just a few days later, Marie-Joseph Chenier, in the name of the *section* Bibliothèque, asked the Legislative Assembly to grant French citizenship to all those who had fought for the cause of humanity. He identified only three Americans whom he felt fit for this honour – Paine, Priestley and Madison, the third being someone who, he said, had 'développé avec profondeur le système des confédérations'.[6] The Assembly accepted his proposal a few days later, but added to the list the names of Washington and Hamilton.[7] This decision was clearly aimed at demonstrating that the French republic took a balanced view of the American party politics, but it is also worth pointing out how the French ultra-democratic groups considered Madison their political reference point in the United States, even more so than Jefferson, while they did not take Hamilton or Washington into account at all.

This is hardly surprising, as the arguments the Jacobins used in their fight against the Feuillants were remarkably similar to those used by Madison in his battle against Hamilton's Federalists. In March 1792, Étienne Clavière, soon to become Finance Minister in the Dumouriez government, spoke to the Jacobin Club about a plot hatched in certain financial circles close to the court to destroy the value of the assignats and throw the Revolution into social chaos.[8] A few weeks later, in May 1792, first Gensonné and then Brissot told the Legislative Assembly about yet another plot. This was allegedly organized by a *comité autrichien*, which, in agreement with the queen and a number of ministers, apparently wanted to get the constitution changed so that a second chamber could be established, which would then give back to the king many of the prerogatives he had lost and allow the nobles who had emigrated to return to France and take part once more in the political life of the country.[9] Towards the end of June, Billaud-Varenne delivered a speech at the Jacobin Club in which he brought up the argument once again, warning members about a plan which would have allowed the aristocracy to introduce a political system in France based on inequality.[10] Meanwhile, Louvet continued to launch accusations against the Feuillants from the pages of the *Sentinelle*, insisting that they were getting ready to modify the constitution to allow for the creation of a second chamber that would pave the way for the return of the aristocracy and reinstate privilege.[11]

However, the fact that people on both sides of the Atlantic were warning of attempts to bring France and America into line with Great Britain does not mean that recognition by the Republicans of the Jacobin cause (and vice versa) can be dated back to 1792. This is really true only from 1793 onwards.[12] Yet if we were to look at the other side of the political fence, the story would be rather different. There are, in fact, many points of contact between the political line pursued by the Feuillants and the choices made by the Federalist government of the United States. The go-between in this case was the Society of the Cincinnati, which on both sides of the Atlantic supported a constitutional system aimed at limiting the power of public opinion.[13] Among the members of the French society were all the most important representatives of the Feuillants: not only Lafayette, but also both Lameths and, most important of all, François Laborde-Méréville, another ex-member of the Constituent Assembly and son of France's most important banker, who was to promptly supply the Feuillants with all the financial resources they needed for their political initiatives.[14]

One of these initiatives, using as go-between the American ambassador to Paris, William Short, was an attempt to pay off the American war debt by depositing the entire sum owed by Washington's government in the royal coffers in advance. At the same time, the United States would become a debtor to the bankers Hope and Laborde, but at a rate of interest which was lower even than that stipulated for France.[15] This was obviously a case of financial speculation, but it was also clearly politically motivated as well. Given the fact that the assignat was depreciating, the bankers would have made a sizeable profit on their investment, far more than the 4 per cent interest which Washington's government would have guaranteed them. At the same time, however, the Feuillants would have been able to boost the court's finances during its fight against the opposition and in turn come into possession themselves of a considerable sum of money via Laborde-Méréville's own earnings on the deal. Those earnings would then have allowed them to further their own political plans, aimed at the establishment of a second chamber.

The idea for this scheme came from Barnave. Previously, he had been a stern supporter of a single-chamber system, but once the political make-up of the new Legislative Assembly became clear, he changed his mind – so much so that he approached the queen, Marie Antoinette, with the idea of convincing the court to support a plan which would have quickly brought the political situation back on an even keel. The plan was actually fairly simple. First, the crown would have to refuse any political support for the nobles who had emigrated, asking them to return to France immediately. Second, it would publicly declare its desire to preserve constitutional order, but at the same time would underline the fact that the constitution itself would need to be revised. At the same time, it would secretly promise the aristocracy that a second chamber would be formed that would enable them to once again play a leading role in the political life of the country.[16] Even today, it is not clear how much credence Marie Antoinette gave to Barnave's plan. What is sure, though, is that, at least officially, she supported it. She wrote to her brother that she hoped some kind of change in the constitution would help correct it, and, as a reply, obtained from Leopold II his recognition of France as it had emerged from the 1789 revolution.[17]

In this context, it is easier to understand why the court and some of the Feuillants themselves – including Lafayette – were willing to favour the bellicose politics of Brissot. With the onset of war, public opinion would have shifted away from the struggle for power between the executive and the legislature, and this in turn would have made it easier to quickly reform the constitution. In mid-March, Duport and the Lameth brothers – the so-called *triumvirat* – called a meeting to discuss how the new chamber would be made up, but Lafayette rejected the idea of a chamber composed of aristocrats, in which seats would be hereditary, and reiterated that he was only willing to consider a second chamber whose members were elected. The meeting ended without coming to any firm decisions, and this in itself highlighted the fact that there were now two distinct factions forming among the Feuillants.[18] On the one hand there were those who were sympathetic to the British model; on the other, there were those who – like Lafayette – had no intention whatsoever of creating a two-chamber system similar to that of Great Britain.

By the month of May 1792, with war already afoot, the differences between the two groups had become marked indeed. For its part, the *triumvirat* was urging the king to take the initiative and revise the constitution, thereby seeming to come down on the side of the British model. It was opposed, however, by those who had no intention of making a concession of this type to the king, and, taking as their example the American two-chamber system, were asking that Lafayette himself, like Washington, leave the command of the armies on the frontier and take the political situation in hand.[19] This is the sense in which his decision to present himself to the Legislative Assembly and ask for repressive measures against the Jacobins needs to be interpreted, a gesture which allowed him to win over a large number of deputies, who twice refused to vote for the general's impeachment. Despite everything, however, the insurrection that took place in Paris on 10 August against the much-feared *comité autrichien* ended up by sweeping away all the Feuillants and condemning to the oblivion of counter-revolutionary plots a highly original political project which, as late as 1792, looked to the American model as a way of stabilizing France's constitutional crisis.

The Feuillants' debt to the American Federalists is clearly demonstrated by two editorial projects, both from Buisson, and both of which were aimed at making an important contribution to the cause of constitutional reform: the French translations of John Adams' *Defence* and the *Federalist*.[20] Adams' work had been known about in France ever since 1787, when Jefferson, as American ambassador in Paris, thought about having it translated, but quickly changed his mind in the light of the criticisms levelled at Adams' ideas by Condorcet and the other *turgotists*.[21] It seems that interest in the work grew once again at the time of the Constituent Assembly, only to vanish immediately, along with those *monarchiens* who had praised it during the battle to impose a two-chamber system – a battle which they lost.[22] Towards the end of 1791, however, interest in Adams' work revived once more, and a number of Feuillants sponsored the translation of the work into French. What now aroused their passion were Adams' attempts to convince his readers that constitutions that were found to be impracticable in some way should and ought to be revised.[23]

The man entrusted with the translation was Pierre-Bernard Lamare, one of Malesherbes' *protégés*. Lamare already had an important career in the field of letters behind him when, at the beginning of 1789, he entered politics and gradually gravitated towards Lafayette. It was the general himself, in fact, who commissioned the translation, along with the American ambassador Short. Lamare prefaced the work with a long introduction, but preferred, given the rather delicate nature of the argument, simply to append his initials to it.[24] He certainly was not erring on the side of caution here, because in the course of his introduction the author suggested revising the 1791 constitution by establishing a second chamber. From Adams he took the idea that this second chamber would not consist of the aristocracy of the *ancien régime*, but rather an aristocracy that included, as the *sanior pars* of society, landowners and 'men of talent'. This distinction came in useful because it allowed him to link his ideas to the dramatic political events that France was going through at the time. He reminded his readers that the many expatriate nobles were in fact the largest landowners in the country, and sooner or later were sure to return and take their place once more as the most important members of society, a position which their ownership of the land conferred upon them. Lamare launched the idea of reconciling these nobles to the 1789 revolution by allowing them access to a second chamber and a second chamber alone. They would, however, be elected to their seats and the chamber would be renewed every six years. It is for this reason that the translator, whose aim was in any case to protect the constitution from drifting towards democracy, took as his point of reference the American political system, and not the British one.[25] It was a proposal which his editor Buisson, who was rather well known in patriotic circles,[26] was to tone down considerably by asking the best constitutionalist of the time, Jacques-Vincent Delacroix, to add a critical afterword to Adams' work which stressed the importance of the 1791 constitution.[27] The work was published in this form in March 1792, without making too much of a stir,[28] thus allowing the publisher to move on to the translation of another classic of the American political tradition, namely Hamilton, Madison and Jay's *Federalist*.

This appeared in September 1792, just after the collapse of the monarchy, and has all the semblance of an act of homage on the part of French republicans to American political culture. In fact, this translation had been commissioned some time before. Once again, Lamare's linguistic talents were called upon, but this time the work was foreworded by Trudaine de la Sablière, a liberal nobleman who was part of Lafayette's circle. In his introduction, Sablière attempted to show that the French monarchy that had come out of the 1789 revolution was compatible with the American constitutional model.[29]

What these two publications demonstrate is that, from the beginning of 1792 onwards, the Feuillants' plans for constitutional reform were based solely on the American model. It is precisely for this reason that, apart from any kind of nostalgia for the monarchy, their proposals were capable of arousing fear. Not for nothing did their political adversaries attack them on precisely their most original point. The counter-revolutionaries, in fact, accused them directly of wanting to set up a *république fédérative* similar to that of America.[30] The Jacobins, instigated by Brissot, kept their distance from the *Federalist*, which they felt was a work full of contradictions.[31]

These accusations, though, are proof of just how original the Feuillants were. They fought the Jacobins on the Jacobins' own ground, demonstrating that in France the monarchical constitutionalists were in fact politically the most modern of all, and were even better than their adversaries at coming into line with the American revolutionary model. The Jacobins quickly found themselves floundering during this struggle, and retaliated by resorting to traditional plots. Kowtowing to the logic of the political plot typical of the *ancien régime*, they denounced the Feuillants' proposal as the result of the machinations of the *comité autrichien*, relying on the same tool for mobilizing the masses that had given impetus to the Revolution ever since 1789. By so doing, the Jacobins pushed the struggle with their political adversaries into the background. Public opinion, still shocked by the king's flight to Varennes and worried about an economic crisis which the war was exacerbating, was now treated by the Jacobins to a denunciation of the foreign queen and a treacherous court. Ultimately, this is all that 10 August 1792 amounts to – a popular insurrection orchestrated by the Jacobins in an attempt to close accounts with the Feuillants once and for all by involving them in a revolt against the *comité autrichien*. It was a demonstration that any confrontation between political parties would not be allowed to take place simply in parliament, but would have to involve the masses as well.

Hence 10 August annihilated the constitutionalist party and left the Jacobins masters of the field. However, it brought with it the fundamental consequence of shifting the centre of attention for revolutionary activity from America to France. Yet the reasons that had led up to the 'second revolution' deeply influenced the way Jacobin republicanism was to develop. Immediately, the Jacobins moved away from the federalist model from the other side of the Atlantic, because, it seemed to them, it was no safeguard against a pernicious tendency to favour an aristocracy. This is why the ideal of a federal republic rapidly vanished from France, which opted steadfastly for a new, united, indivisible republic instead.[32]

Despite this, American Republicans were enthusiastic over the fall of the monarchy in France. At the beginning of 1793, Thomas Jefferson even pointed to a close connection between his party and the Jacobins, just as, on the other side of the political fence, the Feuillants had hailed a close link with Hamilton's Federalists. This was a move on Jefferson's part that hinted at how he expected the Jacobin victory in France to quickly lead to political repercussions on the other side of the Atlantic, which would allow his republicans to get the better of Hamilton's Federalists.[33] His words, though, were more than a simple expression of hope for future political success. It is, in fact, worth looking at Citizen Genet's well-known mission to the United States in this light, too. Genet, France's plenipotentiary minister to the United States, arrived in the New World in 1793 with explicit instructions to forge a revolutionary alliance between the two countries.[34] His aim was very simple: to stimulate the same revolutionary turn of events in the United States that had led to the overthrow of the monarchy in France. Genet thus wanted to make an appeal to American public opinion in order to exert pressure on the executive. Meanwhile, Jefferson would bring pressure of his own to bear within the executive to overcome Hamilton's hostility and Washington's own resistance to a military alliance with France. This explains Genet's decision to disembark at Charleston and move only very slowly, among the jubilation of the democratic societies, to Philadelphia where, after quickly coming up against the president and his executive, he even went as far as to threaten a direct appeal to Congress.[35]

This affair has often been put down to Genet's lack of understanding of how the American political system worked.[36] However, his republican pedigree and his complete acceptance of the dictates of Brissot's foreign policy seem rather to suggest the opposite. In other words, what the French minister was really doing with all his unscrupulous manoeuvring was to attempt to precipitate an American version of the 10 August uprising in France. This would have led Congress to overrule the president and, as a consequence, the Republicans would get the better of the Federalists inside the American parliament. At a number of points in his correspondence, Genet confirms his belief that the balance of political power in America was similar to that in France prior to the revolution of August 1792. Washington he sees as an aristocrat,[37] Hamilton was able to move with ease within the executive and was aiming to establish good relations, even at an institutional level, with Great Britain, while Jefferson was at the head of a patriotic party that would only be able to form a majority in Congress, and that thanks to the pressure of the patriotic societies.[38] Genet must have been more than impressed by the similarities between the situation in America as he found it and the situation that had obliged the Jacobins to stir up rebellion in France. This explains why he was so fervid in stirring up acts of rebellion – even insurrections – against Great Britain and Spain in the territories of the New World.[39] It was this kind of manoeuvring which impinged on the prerogatives of the American executive, and which eventually would lead to Genet's disgrace. At the beginning of July, Washington had already decided to ask for Genet's recall,[40] and Jefferson did not want to do (or, more likely, could not do) anything to save him. Despite everything, however, Genet's active role in inciting American public opinion, which has become the butt of much easy criticism and facile humour, was practically the only option open to him. For it needs to be borne in mind that he was dispatched to the United States at a time when France was at open war with all the other major colonial powers. Moreover, he had precise orders to bring aid to the colony of Saint-Domingue, where the commissars Sonthonax and Polverel, nominated by the Girondin minister Lebrun, were facing enormous difficulty in restoring order, and were complaining that the English, supported by the American Federalists, were adding much fuel to the flames. The situation as described in the worrying missives from Saint-Domingue[41] were later dramatically confirmed during the summer, when, after a dramatic fight, the two commissars threw the governor, Galbaud, off the island, accusing him of counter-revolutionary activities.[42] Nonetheless, they were unable to stop the English invasion of the island a few weeks later.[43]

Galbaud arrived in New York with thousands of white colonists, ready to denounce Sonthonax and Polverel as the real instigators of the violence committed by the rebellious slaves of the colony.[44] As far as Genet was concerned, this was final proof of a wide-ranging plot against the French, because the English, Hamilton's Federalists and the white slave-owning colonists of Saint-Domingue and the other French colonies were now apparently acting in unison to stop the spread of democracy in the New World. Genet thus sent a final request for help to Jefferson on 30 October. In it, he reminded the secretary of state that the English conquest of Saint-Domingue had been born of a plot set up by the colonists themselves, many of whom had followed Galbaud to America, where they had railed against the way Sonthonax had abolished slavery on the island during August, and where they were warmly welcomed by the federalists, who in turn had never entirely given up on the idea of leading America back to accepting British sovereignty.[45]

Genet's appeal fell on deaf ears. This was partly because Jefferson was now an increasingly isolated member of the executive. The president was becoming less and less neutral and was increasingly moving closer to the position of Hamilton, who openly favoured stronger ties with Britain. Yet it was also due to the fact that, politically speaking, Genet's time was now up. After the Parisian *journées* of 31 May and 2 June 1793, the Girondins had been expelled from the French Convention, and the news of their downfall had now spread throughout America. Not by chance, the accusations launched by Genet at the expatriate colonists of Saint-Domingue were now turned on their head and used against him. At the beginning of November, in precisely those circles closest to the ex-colonists, Genet, Sonthonax and Polverel were accused of being the last remaining representatives of a *brissotinière* which, thankfully, had already been eliminated in France. The ex-colonist Duny, while defending slavery and thanking the Convention, listed the many errors committed by Genet, including not only that of recognizing blacks and half-castes as the legitimate representatives of Saint-Domingue, but also that of wrecking, with his political adventures, the privileged relationship which France and the United States had enjoyed to date.[46]

Duny's point was actually well founded. Washington's ability to stand firm against the challenge launched by Genet allowed Hamilton's Federalists to gain the upper hand in the executive. A short while after, this was to force Jefferson to leave politics altogether, and soon after opposition to the French Revolution began to rise, burgeoning when news of the events surrounding the Terror arrived. Americans started to denounce the French Revolution, and a whole range of violent arguments sprang up which were destined to multiply. For a long time to come, these arguments would condition American political life. Genet's actions, in fact, seemed to confirm the existence of a pro-French faction ready to overthrow the American constitution, a faction nestling in the bosom of the republican societies, which had given much support to the French minister when he decided to challenge Washington.[47]

From this point of view, the Federalists' accusations were not entirely without foundation. The Republicans had become a political party thanks to the foundation of the democratic societies, and when Genet arrived these societies had given a great deal of support to the idea of waging war against Britain alongside republican France. It is for this reason that Federalist propaganda hammered away at the idea of the danger posed by a faction – led by Madison and Jefferson – capable of reducing America to nothing more than a land ripe for conquest by democratic and Jacobin principles. It was the beginning of a new phase in American politics – a phase characterized by hostility to revolutionary France, hostility which even the fall of Robespierre and the arrival in Paris of James Monroe (the American politician closest to the Jacobin tradition) would prove unable to overcome.[48] To the sound of propaganda railing against the atheism and violence of the French Revolution, then, a new era had opened in American politics.[49] The Republican party, in order to weather the storm and somehow find a way to once more take up the fight against the Federalists, was forced to defend itself, and, in the light of its adversaries' aims of setting up a special relationship with Great Britain, fell back on the idea of neutrality in foreign affairs.

Genet's downfall played a major role in the creation of this new era, which would only come to an end in 1800 with a Jeffersonian revolution which, however, conceded nothing to any form of special relationship with France. Any hope of exporting the insurrections of 10 August to the United States, in fact, soon came aground not only on Congress' refusal to rebel against Washington and American neutrality in the war that was being waged in the New World as elsewhere, but above all on the ongoing crisis in Saint-Domingue. What is more, it would drag into the dock the very revolutionary practices which had for so long guaranteed the radicalization of the political process in France. It is not by chance that the first to raise their voices against it were the Montagnards, in an attempt to demonstrate how, below the surface of the Revolution, lurked a plot which aimed at nothing less than the destruction of the Revolution itself. In their political battles against the Girondins, in fact, they used precisely the same arguments as their adversaries. In the summer of 1793, the struggle for power between Girondins and Montagnards in parliament spilled over and invaded the whole of France, adding fuel to the *départements'* complaints that the city of Paris was seeking to establish a hegemony of its own in the country. In the aftermath, there were those who were quick to remind others that the roots of this inevitable counter-revolutionary Girondin plot were to be found in the New World itself. According to Citizen Ducher, the conspiracy originated in London, reached across the Atlantic to Philadelphia, and rebounded off Saint-Domingue. Its aim was to destroy the democratic republic of the United States and establish a hereditary monarchy in the New World which would bring the United States and the English and French possessions there under the direct influence of Great Britain. One of the most important pawns in this game was none other than the minister Genet himself, who had been called upon to provoke the ire of Great Britain and ease the way for the United States to become a French ally. This in turn would have allowed Pitt to present the situation he had planned for with so much forethought to British public opinion as a defensive war.[50]

This interpretation of events was taken up by Robespierre in his well-known speech on the state of military operations to the Convention on 17 November 1793. He, too, gave credence to the idea of a Girondin conspiracy set up in agreement with Pitt to destroy democracy, and pointed to the United States, denouncing Genet and his political adventures there. These, he felt, were aimed at driving a wedge between France and the United States, and concluded that the highly implausible character of his view of events was in itself final proof that the plot actually did exist:

> By a strange contradiction, while in Paris those who had nominated him were persecuting the popular societies and denouncing the republicans who were courageously fighting tyranny as 'anarchists', in Philadelphia Genet was setting himself up as the head of the clubs and continually putting forward and suggesting motions for the government which were as damaging as they were dangerous. This shows how the same faction wanted to reduce the poor to the condition of Helots, place the people under the heel of the aristocracy of the rich and free and arm all the negroes in order to destroy our colonies.[51]

His reasoning is contorted, to be sure, but nonetheless clear. Genet in the United States and Polverel and Sonthonax in Saint-Domingue were the representatives of the Girondins in the New World. They shared the aims of those in France who had distinguished themselves by beating down the patriots and attempting to bend the will of the populace to accept an aristocracy based on wealth. When the federalists rebelled, this faction did not hesitate in joining forces with the counter-revolutionaries, and, as a result, were soon in Pitt's pocket, manoeuvring to ensure that everyone in the New World was opposed to France. Hence, the revolutionary logic that had so fired Genet when he was in the United States was no more than a red herring, because his real aim was to ensure that the British would intervene. The Saint-Domingue commissars had also behaved criminally – they had even gone so far as allowing blacks to take up positions of political power, so that these would have a free hand in the destruction of the colony. To sum up, then, Pitt could rely on the Girondins in France in exactly the same way that he could rely on Hamilton in America, who was also in his pocket. It is for this reason that Robespierre is actually rather cautious when he comes to the subject of the United States. He recalls French generosity at the time of the War of Independence, but in recompense asks for no more than neutrality on the part of the new republic. Morris' presence in Paris, which had alarmed the Montagnards so much, was a clear sign that the Federalists now had the upper hand and were capable of disturbing that fragile equilibrium which Madison and Jefferson, with great difficulty, still managed to maintain.

Robespierre shows that he was a brilliant student of Brissot in the way he reconstructed this counter-revolutionary Girondin plot. Even as early as the 1791 slave revolts on Saint-Domingue, Brissot had insinuated that counter-revolutionary elements were guiding the rebels, making a direct link between the slave-owning colonists, their allies on the American mainland and the Feuillants, who were aiming at constitutional reform in France to prevent the triumph of democracy.[52] Not by chance, the Montagnards picked up on this interpretation of the uprisings, levelling the same accusations at the Girondins that the Girondins had used against the Feuillants little more than a year earlier. This is why the Montagnards denounced the Girondins as federalists in the summer of 1793. By doing this, they wanted to stress the fact that their adversaries' political practices and system of values were in fact taken over from the Feuillants, and that these in turn could be seen reflected in the policies pursued by Hamilton's party, which had always been a kind of British fifth column in the New World. What is more, the Girondins had not restricted themselves to simply creating obstacles to the rise of democracy and fighting the popular societies. They had also followed an economic policy entirely favourable to the merchant classes and tried, as a result, to re-establish an aristocracy in France by rigging the markets and encouraging financial speculation.

All these accusations were part of a global denunciation of federalism as the destroyer of the political unity of the republic, and were the same accusations Madison had used previously in his attacks on Hamilton. It must not be forgotten, then, that the reasons behind the political confrontation in France in 1793 were not so very different from those that were driving the political debate in America at the same time.

Nevertheless, the remarkable similarity between these two political situations has always been passed over, while accusations of federalism, restricted to a political context marked out by the revolutionary government, have been seen merely in terms of an attempt to undermine the unity of the state. The Convention itself is largely responsible for this state of affairs. After the downfall of Robespierre, in fact, it would never have accepted the idea of looking back critically at what it had done in the past. True, the surviving Girondins were reinstated, but the Convention refused in any case to give them the honour due to them. It was a decision which signalled the fact that they had distanced themselves from any kind of contact with the American political model, and the Thermidorians were to hold firm on this. Hence, even if the 1795 constitution introduced a two-chamber system, no claim was ever made of any direct connection to the example given by the United States, apart, of course, from a passing formal tribute to John Adams.

This refusal of any parallel with the American political model would end up by legitimizing the view that the political processes in France and the United States were essentially different from one another. It would do even more by ensuring that the historiographical traditions of the two nations (along with certain other revolutionary movements of the twentieth century) would help create the tendency to contrast the two. Yet this tendency, largely the result of the work of following generations, belies the early years of the Revolution, when the political processes in the United States and France were essentially rather similar. They were both marked, in fact, by the fear that the political conflict between individual parties, in France as in America, may raise its head on both sides of the Atlantic. When the Jacobins described the 'federalist' revolt of 1793 as a bourgeois upheaval aimed at propping up liberal values against democracy, they bombarded their political enemies, the Girondins, with the same political rhetoric the republicans had used in their attacks on the Hamiltonians. In the same way, when the federalists denounced the American democratic societies, they provided the same vivid descriptions of a Jacobin conspiracy against the executive power as the Lafayettistes had previously used in France. The fear of political analogy, in America as well as in France, thus suggests that the two revolutions did not unfold – as is too often suggested – in strikingly different ways. The political crime of federalism in France and, on the other hand, the denunciation of an international Jacobin conspiracy designed to subvert the American government, reveal how close the two revolutions were and how long, in both cases, the road to the two-party system in deeply divided societies was.

## Notes

1. H.E. Bourne (1903) 'American Constitutional Precedents in the French National Assembly', *American Historical Review*, VIII, 466–86; J. Appleby (1971) 'America as a Model for the Radical French Reformers of 1789', *William & Mary Quarterly*, XXVIII, 267–86; E.H. Lemay (1990) 'Lafitau, Démeunier and the Rejection of the American Model at the French National Assembly, 1789–1791', in M.R. Morris (ed.), *Images of America in Revolutionary France* (Washington, DC: Georgetown University Press), pp. 171–84; V. Hunecke (2002) 'Die Niederlage der Gemässigten: Die Debatte über die Franzosische Verfassung im Jahr 1789', *Francia*, XXIX, 75–128.
2. A. De Francesco (1992) *Il governo senza testa: Movimento democratico e federalismo nella Francia rivoluzionaria, 1789–1795* (Naples: Morano); P.R. Hanson (2003) *The Jacobin Republic under Fire: The Federalist Revolt in the French Revolution* (University Park: Pennsylvania State University Press).
3. H. Dippel (2003) 'The Ambiguities of Modern Bicameralism: Input- vs. Output-Oriented Concepts in the American and French Revolutions', *Tijdschrift voor Rechtsgeschiedenis*, LXXI, 409–24; M. Troper (2006) *Terminer la Révolution: La constitution de 1795* (Paris: Fayard).
4. J.R. Sharp (1993) *American Politics in the Early Republic: The New Nation in Crisis* (New Haven: Yale University Press).
5. C. Sheehan (2004) 'Madison v. Hamilton: The Battle over Republicanism and the Role of Public Opinion', *American Political Science Review*, IIC, 405–24.
6. M.J. Chenier (1826) *Œuvres* (Paris: Guillaume), vol. 5, p. 50.
7. J. Guillaume (1889) *Procès-verbaux du Comité d'Instruction publique de l'Assemblée législative* (Paris: Impr. Nationale), p. 116.
8. É. Clavière (1792) *De la conjuration contre les finances et des mesures à prendre pour en arrêter les effets* (Paris: Cercle Social), pp. 8–12.
9. J. Mavidal et al. (eds) (1867–) *Archives parlementaires de 1787 à 1860, recueil complet des débats législatifs et politiques des chambres françaises* (Paris: Impr. Nationale), vol. 64, pp. 33–43. On Brissot's demagoguery and his conspiracy theories, see T. Tackett (2000) 'Conspiracy Obsession in a Time of Revolution: French Elites and the Origins of the Terror, 1789–1792', *American Historical Review*, CV, 690–713. See also M. Hochedlinger (1997) 'La cause de tous les maux de la France: Die Austrophobie im revolutionären Frankreich und der Sturz des Königstums, 1789–1792', *Francia*, XXIV, 73–120; T.E. Kaiser (2000) 'Who's Afraid of Marie-Antoinette? Diplomacy, Austrophobia and the Queen', *French History*, XIV, 241–71 and Kaiser (2003) 'From the Austrian Committee to the Foreign Plot: Marie-Antoinette, Austrophobia and the Terror', *French Historical Studies*, XXVI, 579–617.

10. J.N. Billaud Varenne (1792) *Discours sur notre situation actuelle et quelques mesures à prendre pour assurer le salut public* (Paris: Impr. du Patriote François), p. 7.
11. J.B. Louvet de Couvray (1792) *La Sentinelle* (Paris: Impr. du cercle Social), n. 4.
12. See, for example, the favourable judgements on Jefferson and Madison in J.S. Eustace (1793–94) *Letters on the Crimes of George III, Addressed to Citizen Denis, by an American Officer in the Service of France* (Paris: Impr. des Sans-Culottes), pp. 56–7.
13. M. Myers (1983) *Liberty without Anarchy: A History of the Society of the Cincinnati* (Charlottesville: University Press of Virginia), pp. 162–3 and M. Hünemörder (2006) *The Society of the Cincinnati: Conspiracy and Distrust in Early America* (New York: Berghahn).
14. G. Michon (1924) *Essai sur l'histoire du parti feuillant: Adrien Duport* (Paris: Payot); F. Vermale (1937) 'Barnave et les banquiers Laborde', *Annales historiques de la Révolution Française*, XIV, 48–64. See also, F. d'Ormesson (2002), *Jean-Joseph de Laborde: Banquier de Louis XV, mecène des Lumières* (Paris: Perrin), pp. 250–9.
15. William Short to Alexander Hamilton, 16 June 1792, in A. Hamilton (1966) *The Papers*, ed. H. Syrett (New York: Columbia University Press), vol. 11, pp. 593–5. See also H.E. Sloan (1995) *Principle and Interest: Thomas Jefferson and the Problem of Debt* (New York: Oxford University Press), pp. 45–6.
16. A. Soderhjelm (ed.) (1934) *Marie-Antoinette et Barnave: Correspondance secrete (juillet 1791–janvier 1792)* (Paris: Colin), esp. pp. 50 and 132.
17. A. Ritter von Arneth (ed.) (1866) *Marie-Antoinette, Joseph II und Leopold I: Ihr Briefwechsel* (Leipzig: Köhler), pp. 240 and 282.
18. Pellenc to Lamarck, 15 March 1792, in H. Glagau (1896) *Die Französische Legislative und der Ursprung der Revolutionskriege, 1791–1792* (Berlin: Ebering), pp. 299–301.
19. Pellenc to Lamarck, 2 June 1792, in ibid., pp. 330–2.
20. J. Adams (1792) *Défense des constitutions américaines, ou De la nécessité d'une balance dans les pouvoirs d'un gouvernement libre* (Paris: Buisson); Hamilton, Madisson [sic] and Gay [sic] (1792) *Le Fédéraliste, ou Collection de quelques écrits en faveur de la constitution proposée aux États-Unis de l'Amérique par la Convention convoquée en 1787*... (Paris: Buisson).
21. J. Appleby (1968) 'The Jefferson–Adams Rupture and the First French Translation of John Adams' "*Defence*"', *American Historical Review*, LXXIII, 1084–91; C. Bradley Thompson (1996) 'John Adams and the Coming of the French Revolution', *Journal of the Early Republic*, XVI, 361–87.
22. R. Griffiths (1988) *Le centre perdu: Malouet et les 'monarchiens' dans la Révolution française* (Grenoble: Pug).
23. J.E. Paynter (1996) 'The Rhetorical Design of John Adams' *Defence of the Constitutions of...America*', *Review of Politics*, LVIII, 532–3.
24. 'Lamare knows a great deal about our constitution and about American affairs. He has brought many of their writings to the attention of the French public, especially John Adams' Defence of the American Constitutions, which he translated on request of Lafayette and Short.' See Lamare to Talleyrand, 13 April 1800 in *Archives du Ministère des affaires étrangères, Personnel*, vol. 42, f. 229. See also A. Jainchill (2003) 'The Constitution of the Year

III and the Persistence of Classical Republicanism', *French Historical Studies*, XXVI, 414.
25. Adams, *Défense des constitutions*, vol. 1, pp. xvii–xxiii.
26. C. Hesse (1991) *Publishing and Cultural Politics in Revolutionary Paris, 1789–1810* (Berkeley: University of California Press), pp. 186–7.
27. See Delacroix's remarks in Adams, *Défense des constitutions*, vol. 1, esp. pp. 542–4 and vol. 2, pp. 477–9.
28. See *Moniteur Universel*, no. 86, 26 March 1792, pp. 727–8.
29. On the first French translation of the *Federalist*, see my *The Marvellous History of the First French Translation of the Federalist (Paris: Buisson, 1792)*, forthcoming.
30. See *Lettre du Père éternel à M. de Lameth tant pour lui que pour son frère, MM. Duport, Barnave, Delaborde, le duc d'Aiguillon et consors* (1792) (Paris: n.p.), p. 4.
31. See *Patriote François*, no. 1151, 4 October 1792.
32. De Francesco, *Il governo senza testa*, pp. 173–98.
33. See Th. Jefferson (1950–) *The Papers*, ed. J.P. Boyd, vol. 25 (Princeton: Princeton University Press), pp. 14–15.
34. P. Mantoux (1909–10) 'Le Comité de salut public et la mission de Genet aux États-Unis', *Revue d'Histoire Moderne et Contemporaine*, XIII, 5–35.
35. See especially H. Ammon (1973) *The Genet Mission* (New York: Norton) and A.H. Bowman (1974) *The Struggle for Neutrality: Franco-American Diplomacy during the Federalist Era* (Knoxville: University of Tennessee Press), pp. 39–98.
36. See for example E.R. Sheridan (1994) 'The Recall of Edmond Charles Genet: A Study in Transatlantic Politics and Diplomacy', *Diplomatic History*, XVIII, 467.
37. 'Old Washington, who is rather different from the man who has gone down in history, does not forgive me my successes. He hinders me in a thousand different ways and thus is obliging me to secretly push for Congress to be convened. The majority there, guided by the best minds of the American union, will undoubtedly be on our side.' Genet to Lebrun, 19 June 1793, in C. De Witt (1861) *Thomas Jefferson: Étude historique de la démocratie américaine* (Paris: Didier), pp. 523–4.
38. 'Jefferson is hated by the President and by his other colleagues in the government, despite the fact that he has the weakness of officially sharing their opinions, which he actually condemns. Moreover, we will soon be vendicated. The peoples' representatives are about to meet, and it is they who will let loose the lightning bolts that will destroy our enemies and electrify America.' Genet to Lebrun, 31 July 1793, in ibid., pp. 528–9.
39. F.J. Turner (1898) 'The Origin of Genet's Projected Attack on Louisiana and the Floridas', *American Historical Review*, III, 650–71.
40. Sheridan, 'The Recall of Edmond Charles Genet', p. 474.
41. See Sonthonax to Genet, Port au Prince, 8 May 1793, in Archives nationales, D XXV, d. 44.
42. See R. Stein (1985) 'The Abolition of Slavery in the North, West, and South of Saint-Domingue', *The Americas*, XLI, 47–55 and F. Gauthier (2003) 'The Role of the Saint-Domingue Deputation in the Abolition of the Slavery', in M. Dorigny (ed.), *The Abolitions of Slavery: From L.F. Sonthonax to Victor Schoelcher, 1793, 1794, 1848* (Oxford: Berghahn), pp. 167–79.
43. D.P. Geggus (1982) *Slavery, War and Revolution: The British Occupation of Saint-Domingue* (Oxford: Oxford University Press).

44. See Jefferson, *The Papers*, vol. 27, pp. 32–4, 41–2, 75–8.
45. See Genet to Jefferson, 30 October 1793, in ibid., pp. 284–9.
46. See Duny to Genet, 23 January 1794, in Archives nationales, D XXVI, pièce no. 18.
47. See E.P. Link (1942) *Democratic-Republican Societies, 1790–1800* (New York: Columbia University Press), pp. 175–209. See also A. Koschnik (2001) 'The Democratic Societies of Philadelphia and the Limits of the American Public Sphere, circa 1793–1795', *William & Mary Quarterly*, LVIII, 615–36.
48. A. De Conde (1958) *Entangling Alliance: Politics and Diplomacy under George Washington* (Durham, NC: Duke University Press) and De Conde (1966) *The Quasi-War: The Politics and Diplomacy of the Undeclared War with France, 1797–1801* (New York: Scribner).
49. R.H. Bloch (1988) *Visionary Republic: Millennial Themes in American Thought, 1756–1800* (Cambridge: Cambridge University Press), pp. 186–209.
50. A.-G.-J. Ducher (1793) *Les deux hémisphères* (Paris: Impr. Nationale). See also F.L. Nussbaum (1923) *Commercial Policy in the French Revolution* (Washington, DC: American Historical Association), pp. 205–49.
51. Mavidal et al. (eds) *Archives parlementaires*, vol. 79, p. 380.
52. See Brissot's speech on the revolt of the slaves on 30 October 1791, in ibid., vol. 34, pp. 522–6.

# 13
# In Search of the Atlantic Republic: 1660–1776–1799 in the Mirror
*Pierre Serna*

Fifty years ago Robert Palmer and Jacques Godechot put forward the idea of studying a history of Atlantic revolutions, a history encapsulating the late eighteenth century and its sequence of revolutions, inspired by the same contract-based philosophy of human rights. If this proposition was deemed iconoclastic at the time, today the debate is still open, a proof of the relevance and clairvoyance of this pair of French and American historians.[1]

Historiographical research is today focused, not on the question of the origins of revolutions and their cultural or socio-political foundations, but rather on the problem of their stability and purpose, through the study of the Republican models that emerged from the upheavals. While it is accepted today that, from 1776 to 1799 on the shores of America and Europe, there developed a revolutionary wave which, in different ways, caught up the United States of America, the United Provinces, Switzerland, the Austrian Netherlands, France, Poland, Ireland and Italy, not forgetting Saint-Domingue, England with its string of countless rebellions, the German states or the Spanish colonies of America.

However, to contemporaries, the regimes that brought these violent changes to a close were radically different in nature. All these nations in revolution, after their founding period of trauma and bloody civil war, attempted to build their own model, boasting about its originality and the solidity of its foundations when compared to the aims or apparent difficulties of other newly hatched nation states.

By the end of the eighteenth century, three revolutions had culminated in the creation of well-defined republics: the United States of America, France and, shortly afterwards, Haiti. The situation in France was somewhat unique due to the six sister-republics gravitating around it, all different but united around the constitutional mould of Year III.[2] A careful look at the diplomatic situation shows that these three models of a Republic were in a state of open conflict verging on war. From 1797 on, relations had become suddenly strained between France and the United States, and in early 1802, the French Republic dispatched one of the most violent expeditions of all of France's colonial history to Saint-Domingue, which culminated in a fiasco, and the proclamation of the Haitian Republic in opposition to France. In the light of these considerations, can we still speak of a post-revolutionary Atlantic republic of a specific nature?

The aim here is not to deny the special nature of each of the models emerging from the individual struggles, which themselves were engendered by conditions of conflict often reflecting ancient systems of domination – the fruit of social situations inherent to each kingdom or colony.[3] The aim is also not to succumb to determinism, a renewed form of Montesquieu's thought on the influence of 'climate'. Nor is the aim here to deny the importance of the exchange of ideas and comparisons between republics, or the importance of people's desires to build federal Republican models beyond their own frontiers. The post-1795 period, after the paroxysm of revolutionary conflict brought the first peace treaties between France and kingdoms hostile to it, saw France adopt a new Republican constitution. In this period, France displayed a vast capacity for reflection on the nature of Republican models beyond its own borders and overseas which, while they were different to its own, could certainly be improved upon.

The Directory was an intense period of exchange marked by the opposition of, and sometimes polemical confrontation between, different republican countries. It was a time of travel, writing and translations, and the extensive publication of weighty tomes containing subtle observations on constitutions and erudite research into foreign countries and their pasts. It was a period that certainly does not give the impression of rupture or impermeability between the various republican countries.[4] From statesmen to political figures, writers to enlightened citizens, all were conscious of the emergence of Republican models, which in order to be different drew on the same sources: the ancient republics of Greece and Rome, a classical Republicanism drawn from Machiavelli, and even the modern republics – the ephemeral experience of republican England or the more durable one of the United Provinces. The more astute writers and thinkers looked at the American model, questioning its implacable differences or its possible exportation. Everybody was asking the question of what shape a French Republic in a New Europe ought to take.

Between 1795 and 1804, a general overview of existing republics presents us with a kaleidoscope of different types which is hard to reduce to one national model. Indeed, 1804 closed a period of contrasting stabilization with the end of Jefferson's first mandate in the United States, the proclamation of independence in Haiti and the proclamation of the empire in France, which formally remained a republic, as the *senatus consulte*[5] reminds us. This points to another equally knotty problem: the importance of distinguishing between republic and republicans. The vicissitudes of these troubled times demonstrated, in fact, that republics and republicans were very different entities, and this makes the search for an Atlantic republic much more complex. Depending on the situation, the word 'republic' expresses very different kinds of democratic or authoritarian institutions.[6] There was a whole spectrum of republicans, with a wide range of sensibilities and differences, stretching from Madison to Henri Lee, and Buonarotti to Bonaparte! The intention here is not to generalize out from a single situation, but to look at all the nuances and the political models, as well as the social and cultural models, in the way this heterogeneous community established itself and reflected on itself.

## In the name of Republicanism

With the establishment of the constitution of Year III, everyone was well aware that a new republican era was dawning. France constructed a model in which legislative power was divided into two chambers, and while it did not adopt a fully bicameral system, for the first time since 1789 it opted for a mode of operating reminiscent, in form at least, of the American system and indirectly comparable to the English parliament. There were notable differences of course,[7] even if many imagined the comparisons. Lamare, the translator of Adams' political writings, was asked, in spring 1795, to produce a pamphlet, *l'Equipondérateur*, for the Commission of Eleven, responsible for devising a new constitutional text.[8] Lamare, who was by then very familiar with the American president's theories of the balance of powers, extolled the virtues of balance and institutional buffering.[9] Then, on 5 Messidor Year III, Boissy D'Anglas praised Samuel Adams' system (but made a mistake with 'John' Adams' first name!) and also stressed that the functioning of good government was based on a balance of the three powers.[10] Several weeks after the vote on the constitution, in Fructidor Year III, L. Henry published the works of Harrington and used the preface to deplore the fact that law in the new French constitution was a subject for debate in the Council of

Five Hundred, and not in the Council of Ancients, as had been so wisely suggested by the elderly seventeeth-century English republican's work. In his criticism, he showed there was a continuity in the comparisons that had been made between ancient and recent models, noting that 'The problems of the French Revolution resemble those of the English Revolution too closely for those explorers of the causes of effects not to hasten to foretell the continuation of the others.'[11]

This idea clearly did not shock contemporaries. To them, it was standard intellectual practice to evaluate representative systems according to their respective virtues. It is in this light that we can understand Volney's voyage to America in 1795, a voyage he termed as 'denationalized' in an attempt to immerse himself as best as he could in the new reality he would find on the other side of the Atlantic. Having visited the ruins of the ancient world in the East, the scholar was somewhat disenchanted by his experience of life in a dungeon during the Terror, so he abandoned his teaching post at the École normale supérieure, and set out for the New World to observe the birth of another republic.[12] Volney was not simply re-evoking the spirit of exploration so prevalent since the sixteenth century. His intention was very different. He set out to construct a model of enquiry according to a new method, with the aim of forming an international organization within the Institut in Paris, the beacon of science under the Directory. This new structure would gather the data needed to analyse the social history of different societies in order to create a new branch of republican political science.[13] His correspondence with the Republican Thomas Jefferson, vice-president of the Union, and runner-up in the presidential campaign to the federalist Adams, shows the two men considering the different situations in France and the United States in relation to their identities as sincere republicans, both in their own way representatives of cosmopolitan, humanitarian republics.

On 9 December 1795, in a letter welcoming Volney to the United States, Jefferson reminded the Frenchman of the 'severe revolution' that France had recently undergone, aware that France's future as a republic and the way it would emerge from the Terror could have direct consequences on other countries ('on this will depend the aggravation of the chains of other nations, or their rescue from them'). The vice-president of the United States continued with a presentation of the political differences in his own country: 'our citizens are divided into two political sects, one who fear the people most, the other, the government, from my part I have no fear of a people, well informed'.[14] These few lines are enough to establish the de facto complicity between the two men, from their tacitly accepted yet clear common ground: a shared conception of the republic.

Revolutions since 1776 had invented a form of government based on a clear, self-affirming modernity, which opposed the affluent followers of an authoritative republic and a powerful executive with less wealthy citizens, to whom the republic meant democracy in terms of representation and the pre-eminence of legislative power over the so-called co-active power.[15] The two correspondents sketched out the contours of struggles to come, in the twentieth century and beyond, in the republics emerging from the revolutions of the democratic age, to use Palmer's terms.

For his part, Volney noticed the resemblances between the two countries, despite the inherent differences between a land at peace and a nation at war. These were of little importance: 'If France, due to its situation, must suffer these jolts, it is fortunate to have within the country a second France, a portion of ourselves, that is a peaceful France, while the rest is belligerent and victorious.'[16] At that moment, a fusion, or projection, seemed possible between the two countries, with America playing the role of an ideal France(!). Alas, the two men were soon disillusioned with the state of near-war that broke out between France and the United States following the signing of the Jay Treaty by the Americans. This strengthened the Union's ties with England and provoked anger among French diplomats. In turn, President Adams, horrified by the image he had of France as a secular, atheist republic, did not stand in the way of exception laws against the freedom of expression and foreigners (the Alien and Sedition Acts). These measures completely transformed the atmosphere of Volney's journey, and what he thought would be a calm political exile in the United States. On 12 Floréal Year V, he wrote to Talleyrand, the French foreign affairs minister, whose machinations had fuelled the quarrel between the two countries. Volney made no bones about comparing the United States, not to France, but to England.[17] 'It is no surprise to see a reconciliation with England in a country where the distinctive features of the constitution are marked by such a strong resemblance to the main lines of the English constitution.'[18] Volney pursued this line of thought, shifting to the dichotomy evoked by Jefferson regarding the United States where he identified two groups divided in the 'quarrel of English against French principles. One side wants a monarchy, a king of nobles, and a clergy, while the other wants none of it', proof that the European models were considered a foil, depending on the party. Volney ended up concluding: 'Each party will use foreign influence to prevail as long as is needed, and when needs pass, they shall reject it.' The analysis is shrewd and ultimately debunks the American model's original use of the European model to better affirm its independence in the heat of the debate.[19]

In the meantime, Dr Priestley had published a pamphlet of rare virulence against Volney, the atheist author of *Ruines*. The Alien Bill, voted in during April 1798 on Jefferson's instigation, plunged the country into 'delirium', forcing some to desire to 'septembriser' (*sic*) the French, according to the letter written to Madison on 26 April 1798.[20] Thus the two models switched places, and the United States, so peaceful in 1798, slid towards an emergency regime reminiscent to both men of the Terror, especially because, at that same moment, France was conquering the Mediterranean and seemed to have found peace and prosperity once more, proof that, to its contemporaries, the Directory did not just mean disorder. Somewhat disappointed by his American experience, Volney returned from the land of freedom and plenty – as he had imagined it on his departure – arriving at Bordeaux in early July 1798, and was impressed by the state and prestige of France. Across the Atlantic, Volney had been more than disappointed in the market and mercantile republic led by the fanatically anti-French Adams, guided by self-interest alone, which had brought about the systematic destruction of the American natives. America could not possibly become the Republican model for the Directory, in its endless quest for models from the past or present on which to base its faltering stability. It should also not be forgotten that on both sides of the Atlantic men of good republican sense had avoided the war, as Jefferson said, 'of the cause of Republicanism'.[21]

## The great rebellion that started it all, 1640–1660

A new republic may hide an old republic. The men of the Directory knew very well that there existed political models other than those emerging from the turmoil of 1776. Leaving ancient history aside, French analysts started delving into the past of their favourite enemy, perfidious Albion. The case of Britain was intensely studied, and manipulated according to the particular political conjuncture in France.[22] This marriage of conjuncture and analysis is well illustrated in the debate surrounding the interpretation of the events of 1660 that emerged during spring and summer 1799, at the peak of the Directory's final crisis.[23]

At that moment, to contemporaries of the Directory, it was apparent that two revolutionary cycles at their ends had converged, even if their analyses of this convergence were profoundly different. The interpretation of English events became a fully fledged political issue, because people wanted to know which moment of the English Revolution France was then experiencing in 1799: that of the consolidated republic – referring to the start of the so-called Cromwell Republic around

1650 – or that of imminent military dictatorship, insisting on Cromwell's seizure of power in 1653, after the dissolution of the Rump Parliament? Or perhaps the moment of brutal restoration, born out by the events of 1660? In 1799, ever since the Treaty of Campo Formio in October 1797, the English example was on everyone's lips, preoccupying everybody. It was clear to all that war in Europe would never end until perfidious Albion had been beaten.[24]

From the treaty onwards, a large number of works were published relating to England's tormented history. Multiple accounts of incursions into England since Julius Caesar up to William the Conqueror supposedly presented the weaknesses in the island's defences.[25] Other writings emphasized the faults of the British model. In his own way, Barère criticized the early market-based globalization instigated by the English, whose domination of the seas through its brutal thalassocracy prevented all equitable trade between nations that did not have the military arsenal of the City.[26] Even more revealing were those works expounding how the English political model was running out of steam, having been violently challenged by the riots in the arsenals in 1797, but also by endemic mutiny, which sometimes became virulent, as in Ireland.[27] The country born of the events of 1688 was at the end of the line, on the verge of collapse, and the supposed victories in Egypt would soon put the crown of England at the feet of the republic.[28] Albion was lacklustre and would not last long. A historical cycle was coming to an end. The country that had once been a model was transformed into the foil of a flourishing French Republic, fresh from the revolution of 1789.

However, in spring 1799, when the coalition consolidated by English guineas was taking every bridge it crossed, repelling the French army on the shores of the North Sea and on the Neapolitan coast, it was the republic of the Directory that was seen as traversing a crisis, from which it did not emerge, and which suddenly threw light on the intense debate surrounding the end of the Cromwellian Republic.

It was in this context that an anonymous author announced in the columns of the *Moniteur*, on 14 Thermidor Year VII (1 August 1799), the appearance of a text by Jean-Baptiste Salaville comparing the French and English Revolutions.[29] This account explained the reasons of what had happened, encouraging the former secretary to Mirabeau up until 1791 to reply somewhat curtly to a work that had appeared in Germinal, two months earlier, and that had been widely acknowledged, as two editions had already appeared before Salaville's intervention. The earlier text was signed by Boulay de la Meurthe, a deputy of the Council of Five Hundred.[30] Several days previously, on 23 Messidor (11 July 1799), the *Moniteur* had also announced in a short piece the publication of a work by Benjamin Constant: *Des suites de la contre-révolution de 1660 en Angleterre*[31] ('The Sequel to the Counter-Revolution of 1660 in England'). The three authors were only too aware of the seriousness of the threat to the Year III constitution and its institutions and tried to find in the history of the English Republic reasons for hope or warning signs, each from different perspectives.

The article in the *Moniteur* neglected the work by Benjamin Constant, and focused its attention on the deep-seated disagreement emerging between the works of Boulay and Salaville, while making no attempt to hide its support for the latter. Boulay built his historical thesis on analogy and evoked the disturbing, even worrying, similarities between the events of 1660 and 1799, concluding with the inevitability of a monarchical restoration in the light of the nation's internal crisis and the threat to its borders by troops of the second coalition. Salaville, however, a connoisseur of English history, took the opposing view, maintaining that there was a total lack of resemblance, which meant the two revolutions could not possibly finish in the same way.[32] For Salaville, restoration was impossible in France because those in power guarded their positions too jealously. A return to property transfer through the sale of national goods would be equivalent to fanning the flames of civil war. Furthermore, émigrés had no place in the new society that had abolished feudalism. All these reasons and more made the return of Louis XVIII impossible and any comparison between the two moments in history meaningless.

Boulay de la Meurthe, a forgotten actor of the Revolution, was a key figure during the Directory, from the crisis of 18 Fructidor onwards, in which he played an important role in the republican coup d'état. A year later, on 26 Prairial Year VII (14 June 1799), he demanded the revocation of article 35 of the law of 19 Fructidor which placed newspapers under the jurisdiction of the police inspectorate. It is not so surprising that he supported the events of 30 Prairial, which saw the legislature take up its prerogatives once more by forcing the two directors, Merlin and La Revellière-Lépeaux, to stand down. Through his attitude and his actions, Boulay was one of the main artisans, during the summer of 1799, of the political programme for republican defence and patriotism, in response to the advance of enemy troops on the Dutch, Swiss and Italian fronts. With Roederer and Daunou, Boulay was among those close to Sieyès who were looking for an alternative to the Year III constitution and a remedy for the flaws in the way it functioned. His intended revision was envisaged for a while through a daring rapprochement with the left wing of the Council of Five Hundred, made official on 30 Prairial.[33] This strange alliance between conservative republicans and radical left-wingers was short-lived and the break-up saw the start of the end of the Republic under the Directory.

It was precisely at this moment, during Prairial, that Boulay republished his *Essai d'histoire,* the second edition of which met with great success. At this point, people felt the comparison between the two endangered revolutions, the English and the French, was so important that 20,000 copies were snapped up. Boulay was a shrewd politician, capable of playing to both sides. He went through the motions of an alliance with the left within the assembly chamber of the Council of Five Hundred at least for several weeks, but made his reservations about their programme – he deemed it too daring – in his published history. From the month of Thermidor onwards, Boulay broke off ties with them and came out clearly on the side of the revisionists.

There are three parts to Boulay's work: first, he deals with the causes behind the establishment of the Republic; second, he studied the hidden causes which allowed for the consolidation of the Republic; and finally, he dealt with the 'fall of the Republic'.[34] Like its English 'sister', the still fragile republic was said to be suffering a youthful malady which gravely endangered its life, exposing it to the threat of ultra-revolutionaries and counter-revolutionaries. Boulay distinguished six causes that had brought about the downfall of the republic in England:

1 The division in the Patriotic party between Presbyterians and Independents.
2 The treachery and violence of the Independent party's management plan.
3 The influence and tyranny of the military, and in particular that of Cromwell.
4 The violations of the right to freedom of national representation.
5 The deceitful and Machiavellian conduct of the Royalist party.
6 Finally, the general unrest caused by all the hardships endured by the people during the Republic.

To this first series of explanations Boulay added another argument which, given the political atmosphere in the aftermath of the Germinal Year VII elections, served to fire the debate of June 1799. According to Boulay, when the king had been defeated, 'the Patriotic party split ... a passionate, excessive minority made itself heard through the boldness of their principles and opinions. This was the birth of the Independent party, which differed from the Presbyterian party' (see n. 37 for the use of the word 'excessive' here):

> The Presbyterians, said Clarendon, took decisions only on the basis of what they thought the people would approve; and the Independents took decisions then forced the people to approve their decisions; the result of this difference was that, while the Presbyterians were similarly unappreciated, they were much more patriotic than the Independents, because they were eager to consult the national will in everything.[35]

Who, in the summer of 1799, could not decipher the intention behind this opinion, at a time when the fleeting alliance between democratic and conservative Republicans, formed in opposition to the Directory's encroachments into the prerogatives of legislative power, was at its most fragile? The 'French Presbyterians of 1799', if such an expression is possible, feared the consequences of the circumstantial reconciliation that engendered the day of 30 Prairial (18 June 1799). Naturally, a period of press freedom and patriotic fervour ensued, but also – and this was more worrying for Boulay and his friends – the demands for democracy recalled memories of 1792–93 (with the hostage law and the forced loan law), rendered possible by the dangers on France's borders.[36]

Given the situation, it was up to moderate Republicans, in 1660 as in 1799, to sacrifice and stigmatize the 'excessive' Republicans.[37] Their English predecessors had supported Cromwell's dictatorship and the subsequent regime of terror that ensued. Then, following the death of their Protector, they had plunged the country into anarchy, which Richard, the son of the dictator, had been unable to quell, provoking the restoration, for which they were politically responsible.

In case the reader did not grasp the allusions, rejecting any difference between the two revolutions and the dangers threatening them, Boulay wrote in the conclusion of his essay:

> After the fall of the tyrant, the Royalists formed one of the extremities of the political chain while the Independents or the more extreme section of the Patriotic party were at the other. The Presbyterians occupied the centre ground.

This was a clear indication of the importance to Boulay, in the English Revolution as in the French Revolution, of winning over the centre ground of politics, an essential condition for conserving power for those interested in putting over an image of moderation, restraint and responsibility, even if this meant, once in power, controlling the state with a rod of iron.[38] In this idea, we see the reasons behind the measured comparison and sometimes troubling resemblances between the two republican experiences, which are nearly always dressed up and manipulated by Boulay in his deliberate use of history to describe the immediate crisis of 1799. Boulay produced his work before making his presence felt in the political arena and several days later, on 5 Fructidor Year VII, he was elected president of the Council of Five Hundred, emerging as one of the most important figures of the republican state.[39]

Thus, up to 2 Vendémiaire Year VIII, during the month he presided over the Assembly (from 22 August to 24 September 1799), Boulay played a fundamental role in the definition of the political line to be followed in order to prepare the coup d'état of November.[40]

Salaville was categorically opposed to this use of comparative history. Salaville had been secretary to Mirabeau, and, in 1788, and later in 1789 and 1792, had contributed to the publication of *La théorie de la royauté d'après les Principes de Milton avec sa Défense du peuple par Mirabeau*.[41] The tribune had not anticipated Salaville's initiative, publishing in the second part another text by Milton, written in Latin, seven years after the first, which was summed up as a 'furious denunciation of royalty, based on the defence of the English people'.[42] This same text reappeared in 1792, while discussions on the trial of Louis Capet and the legitimacy of procedure were at the heart of political debate.[43]

Salaville, like Boulay, could claim – albeit in different terms – to represent fervent Republicanism. His interpretation recalls another bold and highly suggestive interpretation of the events of 1660: if there was a restoration in England it was because there had never been a revolution at all! The English Revolution, for example, did not set out to do away with the nobility, who were never categorically abolished. It did not seek to do away with the clergy. Above all, it did not seek to modify the social structure of the country. In France, on the contrary, ever since the summer of 1789, the very structure of the state had changed, which according to Salaville was not the case in England where the two chambers had already existed before the Republic. These conditions made restoration possible in England. In France, however, civil equality at the heart of the political process of the Revolution since 1789 had given rise to citizenship, conferring an identity on citizens as owners of national assets and defenders of the homeland, the bulwark of a republican nation that could no longer accept the monarchy.

In this game of distorted historical comparisons, Salaville had one final parting shot for Boulay. He boldly rejected the parallel between the

English Presbyterians and French conservative Republicans, in which the Presbyterians were presented as the victims of the Independents and merely the supposed forerunners to the democratic Republicans of 1799 who, like them, tended to disrupt public order. On the contrary, the Presbyterians were religious fanatics who shared nothing with the democrats of 1799, whereas the Independents, who were not so opposed to the monarchy, were strong supporters of the splendour of the court of Cromwell. The relatively unknown Salaville, who refused an easy analogy between two periods of revolutionary crisis and did not succumb to the panic so skilfully orchestrated by Sieyès' party during the spring of 1799 – the Republic of order or the chaos of anarchy – achieved more than the writing of history. Through his knowledge of the past, he presented one of the future positions of the indecisive republic describing, through the calculated Presbyterian volte-face before the restoration of 1660, the sometimes disgraceful servility of conservative Republicans before another man who, like William of Orange, turned up to providentially sound the death knell of a constitution, an act they applauded, despite their many avowals to defend the constitution with their own lives.[44]

It must be recognized that the perceived interrelation between French and English history was not exclusive to this generation. The arrival of 18 Brumaire only weeks after the debates mentioned above did little to stem the flow of comparisons between the French and English Revolutions. Bonaparte's rise to power reinvigorated historical research into the question, particularly with regard to his elusive role at the end of the Revolution – dictator, usurper, gravedigger or middleman? The First Consul appealed to the figures of Cromwell, Monck and, more readily, to William, appreciating their merits in different ways. He was also aware of the dangers of comparison with Cromwell and Monck and took the liberticidal measures necessary to control any revisitation of the English Revolution, a process that was never innocent.

## The consul's new clothes and the fortunes of the American Revolution

For a short period, then, the English model was seen as the standard for comparison. However, hostility towards the British Isles was rekindled with the return of Bonaparte, and though the signing of the Amiens Peace Treaty silenced the most Anglophobic elements in France for a while, it soon became clear to all that the uneasy peace it had led to would soon collapse, and that a resumption of the conflict between the two countries[45] was by far the most likely scenario for the near future. Consequently a whole body of literature arose raging against the supposed flaws of the English model and praising the First Consul for seizing control of the Republic. Among this plethora of works is one which is worth dwelling on. It was written by a little-known, second-rate author, Jean Chas. He was no doubt paid for the task, but his work is nonetheless remarkable for the way he attempts to sway public opinion against perfidious Albion by drumming up support for the United States of America, which he considers the only country worthy of comparison with Bonaparte's France. His portrait of Great Britain is, of course, full of vitriol. England, he says, is driven by 'chameleon politics', had imposed an inquisitorial tax system on its subjects, and the whole country had been contaminated by this corruption. The nation is depicted as teetering on the brink of collapse.[46] Its elites lack moral guidance and are only obsessed with the profits of their commerce. The religious tolerance that so impressed Voltaire is but a myth, Chas declares, and hides from view the persecution of the Irish, the English Catholics and the radical Protestant sects. The dishonest ruling elites had purchased their status and were using it to finance wars of destruction throughout the world. He decried England as a land of bandits, who had no respect for any international treaty, a country that had constantly regressed since the revolution of 1688. In a tone recalling the French pamphleteers, Chas proclaims this revolution to be lacking in innovation in any way, as it merely restored old freedoms without inventing any new ones.[47]

The author attempts to cure a section of the enlightened French electorate of an illness inherited from the eighteenth century, called 'Anglomania'. The country is in need of a new revolution. It needs to summon a new William, not the late seventeenth-century William from the shores of Holland, but the earlier William, who came from the beaches of France – William the Conqueror. Jean Chas, the author, lets his imagination roam and gets carried away, while flattering his prestigious reader. His work on the United States, *Le tableau des États-Unis*, published in 1800, however, is much calmer in tone and more interesting.[48] In this work he presents a land of dreams, the product of a wholesome revolution, without violence or excess, in plain language. It is a country without any trace of harmful 'sans-culottisme' or Jacobinism. The revolution in the New World had laid the groundwork for the other wholesome revolution of fin-de-siècle France, that of the 18 Brumaire, a bloodless revolution, the only aims of which were to strengthen the social domination of honest landowners, and to construct the only genuinely worthy Republic where 'everything is done for the people and nothing by the people'. According to the author, only these two Republican models managed to fuse within their structure the construction of public order with respect for religion, which for Chas forms the basis of the social order he champions and defends, an order synonymous with excellent political stability. In this game of somewhat forced comparisons, the author dwells more extensively on the different constitutions of the states, distributing plaudits or criticism. Massachusetts and its constitution with its two chambers and a strengthened executive power is praised by the observer, while the constitution of Connecticut, deemed too democratic, is considered a dangerous, almost anarchist aberrance. Fortunately, beyond the state texts, the federal constitution arrived to erase disparities by according the president a real power of command over the nation.

At root, for the author, the two republics represent two political models that have managed to find a way to construct systems of social conservation that keep democracy at a distance, while integrating the modern lessons of national sovereignty to legitimize power. Chas went further in the comparison of the two countries, and to him, both lands, in their infinite wisdom, had, through the constitutions of 1787 and Year III, managed to found their republics on a government which combined moderate monarchism with conservative Republicanism:

> What can we call the governments of France and the United States, where the First Consul and the President only wield executive power for a limited time? We can call them combined or representative governments, even though the president of the American Congress only has a veto as an observer, and in France the First Consul has the initiative in matters of law. And here we should not confuse constitution and government ... the constitution represents creative power; the government is conservative power. The constitution can be republican, and the government can be a combination. The constitution is republican when it creates a legislative power wielded by the representatives of the nation; the government is combined, or representative, when one sole being in the state wields executive power, and that he sanctions laws or holds the initiative.[49]

This rose-tinted account of the American Revolution allows for a final flattering comparison with the consular Republic. But is this a case of manipulating history? A case of blindness to the profound differences between the two countries? It is also possible that the rapprochement between the two countries is quite sincere, and simply aims at setting landowning citizens at the head of the nation. It could also be an expression of retrospective fear on the part of a conservative author reacting to the excesses of the Terror and the democratic republican character of the Directory. It may also reveal the distant, resolutely French origins of the construction of the myth of the good American Revolution in opposition to the failed, violent French Revolution. All these aspects no doubt feature in Chas' reasoning, alongside a genuine reflection on the construction of Republican models and their future destinies.

In the conclusion to his work, Jean Chas draws a broad outline of the consequences of the invention of the American Republican model, according it a civilizing mission for the future that greatly exceeds the boundaries of the territory of the United States. For him, slavery, a defect of youth, should be gradually abolished, and would indeed soon disappear. Then, within the country itself, Americans, through the excellence of their institutions, would become virtuous and hardworking, 'strengthening federalism, uniting the different states, and reinforcing public freedoms through morality and law':

> The American will sweep through Europe, traversing oceans, sweeping through Japan and the Indies, penetrating into the heart of countries and exploring rivers; with the gold of the south, he will buy the iron of the north; he will unify the west and east. But rest assured, friends of humanity, this amazing revolution will not be achieved through fighting, murdering and burning. America will not imitate the ferocity of Europe. The inhabitants of the New World will be the benefactors, friends and comforters of nations and continents, the land will become the asylum of the fugitive Indian, the oppressed African, the enslaved European, and its inhabitants will revive the virtues of antiquity and the holy laws of nature, abused and forgotten for so many centuries; at this time, all Europe has shown America is murder and execution. The shores of the Atlantic will present the very enactment of peace and virtue, and the comforting tableau of happiness and morality. Thus order will return and nature and providence will be justified.[50]

The point is not whether Jean Chas is a clairvoyant, but how, for the most aware of early nineteenth-century observers, recent events in the United States and the birth of a young federal Republic would change the history of the world. Similarly, France was conferred the mission of peacefully exporting its Republican model throughout Europe, not through a hegemony, but through the firm conviction that the excellence of its

Republican model would guarantee the conditions of sovereignty and freedom necessary for peace and prosperity on the continent. The two republics, on their respective continents, had a moral duty to found republics in line with their own constitutions, as if a Republican model on either side of the ocean could represent the stability of ideals born by the revolutions of the preceding generation. May misfortune befall any country incapable of grasping the republican message! Volney declared to Jefferson. If this is the case the only advice can be, in Volney's words: '4 July 1776!'[51]

## Notes

1. R. Palmer and J. Godechot (1955) 'Le problème de l'Atlantique', in *Comitato internationale di scienze storiche, Xe Congresso internazionale* (Florence: Sansoni), vol. 5, pp. 175–239.
2. J. Godechot (1956) *La Grande Nation, l'expansion révolutionnaire de la France dans le monde 1789–1799* (Paris: Aubier-Montaigne).
3. See M. Albertone (2007) 'Democratic Republicanism: Historical Reflections on the Idea of Republic in the 18th Century', *History of European Ideas*, XXXIII, 108–30.
4. J.G.A. Pocock (1975 and 1997) *Le moment machiavélien* (Paris: Le Félin); see also P. Serna (ed.) (2009) *La république en miroir* (Actes du colloque tenu en Sorbonne les 25 et 26 janvier 2008) (Rennes: Presses universitaires de Rennes).
5. The *senatus consultes* were Acts of the Senate which had the force of law. They covered any areas not foreseen by the articles of the constitution.
6. See J. Livesey (2001) *Making Democracy in the French Revolution* (Cambridge, Mass.: Harvard University Press).
7. M. Troper (2006) *Terminer la Révolution* (Paris: Fayard).
8. J. Adams (1792) *Défense de constitutions américaines ou de la nécessité d'une balance dans les pouvoirs d'un gouvernement libre*, with notes and observations by M. de la Croix (Paris: Buisson). De la Croix was a teacher in public law. A. Jainchill (2003) 'The Constitution of the Year III and the Persistence of Classical Republicanism', *French Historical Studies*, XXVI, 3, 399–435.
9. See John Adams (2004) *Écrits politiques et philosophiques*, 2 vols (Caen: Presses universitaires de Caen), introduction and translation by Jean-Paul Goffinon.
10. Jainchill, 'The Constitution of the Year III'.
11. P.F. Henry (1795) foreword to the *Œuvres de Harrington* (Paris, Year III).
12. G. Chinard (1923) *Volney et l'Amérique, from Unpublished Documents and Correspondence with Jefferson* (Baltimore: Johns Hopkins University Press).
13. See Volney (1795) *Questions de statistique à l'usage des voyageurs* (Paris: éd. de l'imprimerie de la République, Year III).
14. Ibid., letter from T. Jefferson to Volney, p. 35.
15. See G. Wood (1991) *La création de la République américaine, 1776–1787* (Paris: Belin), Ch. X, 'Les vices du système', pp. 455–95.
16. Volney, *Questions*, letter from Volney to Jefferson, 15 January 1797, p. 64.

17. The two countries nearly came to blows because of the 'WXYZ' affair, in which Talleyrand clearly displayed his greed. See William C. Stinchcombe (1977) 'The Diplomacy of the WXYZ Affair', *William & Mary Quarterly*, 3rd ser., XXXIV, 590–617.
18. Volney, *Questions*, letter of the 12 Floréal Year V, p. 83.
19. Ibid., p 84.
20. Ibid., p. 92.
21. Ibid., letter from Jefferson to Madison, 26 April 1798, p. 92.
22. See C. Hill (1977) *The World Turned Upside Down, Le Monde à l'envers: Les idées radicales au cours de la Révolution Anglaise* (Paris: Payot); see also Olivier Lutaud (1978) *Les deux Révolutions d'Angleterre* (Paris: Aubier).
23. On the crisis in the summer of 1799, see P. Serna (1997) *Antonelle: Aristocrate révolutionnaire, 1747–1817* (Paris: Le Félin), pp. 374–88.
24. See M.Belissa (2006) *Repenser l'ordre européen (1795–1802): De la société des rois aux droits des nations* (Paris: Kimé) and N. Hampson (1998) *The Perfidiousy of Albion: French Perceptions of England during the French Revolution* (Basingstoke and New York: Macmillan Press).
25. See J.F Dubroca (1798) *La politique du gouvernement anglais dévoilé, ou Tableau historique de manœuvres que ce gouvernement a employées pour empêcher l'établissement de la liberté en France* (Paris: Dessarts Year VI); Ch. Millon (1798) *Histoire des descentes qui ont eu lieu en Angleterre, Écosse, Irlande, et îles adjacentes depuis Jules César jusqu'à nos jours, suivie d'observations sur le climat* (Paris: L. Prudhomme, Year VI); F. Peyrard (1798) *Précis historique des principales descentes qui ont été faites dans la Grande Bretagne, depuis Jules César jusqu'en l'an V de la République* (Paris: Louis); Anon., *Détail exact des 39 descentes en Angleterre depuis Jules César jusqu'à celle du général Hoche* (Paris: Desseinferjeux).
26. Barère de Vieuzac (1798) *De la liberté des mers, ou le Gouvernement anglais dévoilé* (Paris: Ventôse Year VI), 3 vols in 8, and following editions; J.-A. Mourgue (1797) *De la France, relativement à l'Angleterre et à la maison d'Autriche* (Paris: Desenne, Thermidor Year V).
27. See (1798) *Détails d'une grande insurrection qui a eu lieu en Angleterre* (Paris); *Détails de l'insurrection terrible arrivée en Angleterre, Proclamation de la loi martiale* (Paris Year VI); *Liberté de la presse détails de la grande insurrection qui a éclaté à Londres; Nouvelle qui annonce que cette ville est à feu et à sang et qui porte que Pitt a été pendu* (Paris: Allut); for a recent account, see Harry T. Dickinson (2005) 'L'Irlande à l'époque de la Révolution française', *Annales Historiques de la Révolution française*, LXXVII, 159–83.
28. See (1798) *Sur la situation politique et financière de l'Angleterre, fragments d'un mémoire sur l'Angleterre en général par H.S.P.* (Paris: Imprimerie de Cramer, Year VI).
29. J.B. Salaville (1799) *De la Révolution française comparée à celle de l'Angleterre ou Lettre au représentant du peuple Boulay de la Meurthe, sur la différence de ces deux révolutions pour servir de suite à l'ouvrage publié par ce représentant sur celle de l'Angleterre* ('The French Revolution Compared to the English Revolution, or Letter to the Representative of the People Boulay de la Meurthe on the Difference of these Two Revolutions') (Paris: chez Revol et chez Vatar Year VII).
30. A. Boulay de la Meurthe (1799) *Essai sur les causes qui, en 1649, amenèrent en Angleterre l'établissement de la république; sur celles qui devaient l'y consolider; sur celles qui l'y firent périr*, 2nd edn (Paris: Imprimeur du Corps législatif, Prairial

Year VII Baudoin) ('Essay on the Causes which in 1649 Established the Republic in England; Those Causes that Should Have Consolidated it and those that Made it Perish').
31. B. Constant (1799) *Des suites de la contre-révolution de 1660 en Angleterre*, 2nd edn (Paris: F. Buisson, Year VII).
32. J.B. Salaville (1755–1832). In 1789 he wrote *De l'organisation d'un état monarchique, ou Considérations sur les vices de la monarchie française, et sur la nécessité de lui donner une constituion*, and then went on to work on a number of English texts, in particular those of Sterne, contributing to the translation and publication of the *Œuvres complètes* in 1803.
33. B. Gainot (2001) *1799: Un nouveau jacobinisme?* (Paris: CTHS).
34. B. Gainot (2002) 'Le péril blanc: La restauration monarchique au tournant du Directoire et du Consulat', in *La Révolution française: Idéaux, singularités, influences*, ed. R. Chagny (Grenoble: Presses universitaires de Grenoble).
35. Boulay, *Essai*, part 3/Ch. I: 'Du Parti presbytérien et des Principes et comment il fut exclu de la République', pp. 60–2.
36. On the 30 Prairial crisis and its consequences see J.P. Bertaud (1987) *1799: Bonaparte prend le pouvoir* (Brussels: Éditions Complexes).
37. Boulay uses the French term 'exagéré' (excessive), which was fashionable from the Thermidor Year II backlash onwards to designate by efficient reductionism all Year II actors, indistinctly presented as 'drinkers of blood', who are also said to represent the English Independentists.
38. Boulay, *Essai*, p. 108; see also Pierre Serna (2005) *La république des girouettes: 1789–1815 et au delà . . . Une anomalie politique: La France de l'extrême centre* (Seyssel: Champ-Vallon).
39. See *Le Moniteur*, 5 Fructidor Year VII.
40. On the posterity of Cromwell in the French Revolution, see R. Barny (1993) 'L'image de Cromwell dans la Révolution française', *Dix-huitième Siècle*, XXV, 387–97 and B. Cottret (1992) *Cromwell* (Paris: Fayard).
41. J.-B. Salaville (1791) *Théorie de la royauté d'après les Principes de Milton avec sa Défense du peuple par Mirabeau* (Paris) ('Theory of Royalty according to the Principles of Milton with a Defence of the People by Mirabeau').
42. O. Lutaud (1990) 'Emprunts de la Révolution française à la première Révolution anglaise', *Revue d'Histoire Moderne et Contemporaine*, XXXVII, 597.
43. J.-B. Salaville (1792) *Défense du peuple anglais, sur le jugement et la condamnation de Charles premier, roi d'Angleterre, par Milton. Ouvrage propre à éclairer sur la circonstance actuelle où se trouve la France* (Valence: P. Aurel) (Réimprimé aux frais des administrateurs du Département de la Drôme).
44. See (1800) *Parallèle entre César, Cromwell, Monck et Bonaparte, fragments traduits de l'Anglais* (Paris); P. Serna (2001) 'Gouvernement du lion . . . ou Le règne de l'astre brillant?'; 'Le 18 Brumaire, au regard des historiens contemporains du Premier Consulat (1800–1802)', in J.-P. Jessenne (ed.), *Du Directoire au Consulat: Brumaire dans l'histoire du lien politique de l'état-nation* (Lille: CRHENO), 347–68.
45. C. Millon (1800) *Histoire de la Révolution et de la Contre-Révolution d'Angleterre, contenant les troubles civils sous Charles Ier, le procès de ce prince, sa condamnation à mort et son exécution, l'abolition de la monarchie et l'établissement de la république en 1649, les dilapidations des finances, le protectorat de Cromwell, les différentes institutions, les conspirations, l'anarchie et les factions qui eurent lieu,*

*enfin le renversement de la république et la restauration de Charles II, en 1660, par Monck, avec les suites du rétablissement de la royauté* (Paris: Moutardier, Year VIII).
46. J. Chas (1800) *Tableau historique et politique de la dissolution et du rétablissement de la monarchie anglaise, depuis 1625 jusqu'en 1702* (Paris: chez Pilardeau, Year VIII).
47. J. Chas (n.d.) *Réflexions sur l'Angleterre* (Paris: rue Croix des petits champs).
48. J. Chas et Lebrun (1800) *Histoire politique et philosophique de l'Amérique septentrionale par les citoyens* (Paris: chez Favre, Year X).
49. J. Chas (1800) *Sur Bonaparte premier consul de la république française, par le citoyen Jean Chas de Nismes* (Paris: chez Carteret, Ventose Year VIII), p. 109.
50. Chas, *Histoire politique et philosophique de l'Amérique septentrionale par les citoyens*, p. 455.
51. Volney, *Questions*, 19 Thermidor Year IX, p. 125.

# 14
# The Republican Imagination and Race: The Case of the Haitian Revolution

*Bernard Gainot*

The Saint-Domingue Revolution led to the proclamation, on 1 January 1804, of both Haitian independence and the Republic of Haiti. 'Haiti, the first black Republic'[1] was the opening act of a revolution characterized by extreme violence and inter-ethnic massacre. However, the calls for equality that accompanied the Revolution did not go away in the American tropical zone with its system fashioned on slavery and plantations. Given the context and contradictions of its formation, the new state and its republican form were always going to be ambiguous and short-lived. The great Haitian historian of the nineteenth century, Thomas Madiou, not only described these contradictions and the wide range of repercussions they led to in the short term. He also described the rather picturesque relationship between those contradictions and the 'ceremony of independence' in general.

The generals gave him the title of governor general, which was superior in their minds to general-in-chief, because it was the title Toussaint had taken after publishing his colonial constitution. At that stage, everyone appeared to forget that this title was unsuitable for the head of an independent people, because the idea of governor is associated with that of a higher authority, or a metropolis.[2]

The name of the new state was also symptomatic of this and is an early sign of that desire to form an 'account of origins' which obsessed the elites of colonial societies, then as later. Let us return to Madiou:

> There was an immediate desire to give a new name to this land and its new state. On everybody's lips was the name Haiti, a reminder of the island's aborigines exterminated in the defence of their freedom. It was greeted with enthusiasm and the natives were now called *Haitians*.[3]

Let us highlight in passing that this 'account of origins' refers to an American past, not an African past. The colonial imagination was a Creole imagination, one that transcended the barriers of race. It was shared by whites and former coloured freemen, the new ruling class of the young republic.

In reality, interracial coexistence appeared impossible. The racial exclusiveness that had structured Saint-Domingue society in the eighteenth century was recuperated by the new state and inversed. After a long series of inter-ethnic massacres, the notion of exclusion was pushed to its logical extremes in the declaration of independence. The author of the declaration of independence was Boisrond-Tonnerre, Dessalines' mulatto secretary, who was paradoxically the son of a member of the Council of Five Hundred.[4] According to his implacable logic, there was no place for the white race in Haiti:

> You precious men and intrepid generals, who, insensitive to your own misfortunes, have revived liberty by shedding your own blood, must realize that you have achieved nothing, if you do not set a terrible but just example to other nations of the vengeance a people proud of its freedom and jealous in its defence can exact. Let us warn off all those who dare attempt to deny us liberty again. Let us start with the French ... May they tremble as they approach our coasts, by the memory of the cruelties they committed here, or by our terrible resolution to kill any French-born man who sullies the territory of liberty with his sacrilegious foot.[5]

In the following weeks, up to the start of April, a large majority of whites who did not manage to escape were methodically massacred.

Thus the new republican state was profoundly undermined by the determinism of blood and gender, as the writer René Depestre recently pointed out:

> Independence was lived as a military and political victory that was more 'racial' in nature than national. A Caribbean people of African and French origins created a fantastically mixed-race constitutional charter, with notions of law and civil status based on an amalgamation of 'social' and religious concepts and on foundations both anthropological and ontological that turned out to be absolutely false, mendacious and phantasmagoric.[6]

This political imagination and determinism were for a while counterbalanced by an attempt to graft republican forms of representation onto colonial social formations. In the heat of the racial, social and cultural confrontations, this attempt failed. It was, however, proof of the transatlantic dimension of the political model of this 'age of revolutions'.

## American patriotism

Throughout the eighteenth century, Saint-Domingue's ruling class, made up of white 'inhabitants', was troubled by the calls for autonomy from the metropolis.[7] In their battle for trade freedom and for a distinctly privileged status over other French West Indians, the separatists appealed to a specific 'account of origins', based on the notion of the *independent republic of buccaneers*.

This account is developed in a great many memoirs, some of which are to be found in the Garran-Coulon Commission collection of 1795 to 1799. Here is one such account from 1788:

> Saint-Domingue was not conquered, bought nor subjugated; it belonged to the Spanish, when, in 1630, a group of valiant, independent Frenchmen, inhabitants of the sea who belonged to France in their hearts only and possessed only courage, chased the Spanish and English from this island. This conquest, executed in their own name, with their own might, was their own prize. As Buccaneers, they held it for ten years and were sovereigns of a possession that, although then uncultivated, would assume great importance. As its absolute masters, they were in a position to confer it on the king of Europe they deemed most worthy. By rallying under the protection of France, the Buccaneers received the king's word that their possessions would be defended, their property sustained and their right to govern freely maintained. Alone, they allotted power through the natural representatives of the nation ... through magistrates ... plantation owners to a man, who had sought the suffrage of their compatriots.[8]

The idea of a pact between the buccaneers and the king developed. Hence this proclamation by the Cap-Français lawyer Hilliard d'Auberteuil, one of the most heartfelt spokespeople of Creole independence and the inspiration behind the abbé Raynal's *Histoire philosophique et politique des deux Indes* in 1776:

> We should consider that the settlers' commitments towards the state are as enduring as the sovereign's protection. If this protection ends, the convention also terminates, as it is based on reciprocal utility.[9]

The inspiration here is identical to the inspiration behind the United States of America's Declaration of Independence at the very same moment. Hilliard d'Aubertuil was one of the most fervent partisans of 'American patriotism' in its struggle against metropolitan tyranny.[10]

From here, Hilliard d'Aubertuil developed his contractualist theory, which he opposed to the exclusive relations between the metropolis and its colonies:

> All nations are, to begin with, more warrior in nature than industrious; the Buccaneers were instilled with fervent courage and great passion in response to their multiple necessities. The period of their settlement period in Saint-Domingue forms the colony's first historical age; however, I cannot give this early age direct consideration without a certain digression, and I am right in supposing that all my readers have closely studied the history of the different countries serving their existence or pleasures.
>
> I will thus consider the French colony of Saint-Domingue as a case of French emigration, where the Frenchmen concerned were born after the division of lands within their kingdom and so were not party to this distribution. Frustrated with the lot nature assigned them at birth, and in no position to pay the right to exist within their families, they were forced to leave their country. These unfortunate citizens bore the burden of the state to the extremities of the earth, and the metropolis brought many a convention to bear, which I shall sum up as follows: 'You see these sheer mountains, their peaks enclosed in storms, these swamps robed in saltpetre, these plains from which sulphurous vapours rise, these arid deserts where the bitumen is parched on the burning sand. I offer them to you; they are yours to fertilize. I shall supply the tools and provisions, and we shall share their yield together, and you shall reimburse my outlay.'

This initial contract was totally to the metropolis's advantage:

> The settlers owe much to the goodwill of the monarch and much to their labour. If the hand protecting them ceases to sustain their industry, and if this protection ceases, they will become discouraged. I shall not seek to penetrate their intentions in this state. What might the effect of this powerlessness on their sensibilities be? They express their gratitude through their utility, and if they cease being useful, their gratitude shall also cease.

But the initial pact was concluded between the king of France and the Buccaneers:

> The monarch was interested in extending his domain; the buccaneers were interested in holding out against their irreconcilable enemy, the Spanish. They needed a protector; the king of France was willing, and placed his seal of authority on their conquest.

The respective conventions were determined:

> We swear loyalty, and you shall share our wealth – I accept you as a subject and I protect you; your enemies are my enemies.[11]

The crown's envoys, such as the marquis d'Argenson, noted and regretted this spirit of independence; they had already labelled it 'republican' during the War of the Austrian Succession: 'The inhabitants are rich and republican, and may side with the English at any moment.'[12]

Such a mythical account of origins obviously overlooked, it goes without saying, native Caribbean inhabitants. All colonial mythologies present an insufficient awareness of the lands of settlement, like the mark of a shortfall in native political structure, but this one also overlooked the blacks, the slavery of whom is extensively justified in the same patriotic memories. We would be jumping to conclusions, however, to suppose that this Creole imagination was caused only by the white inhabitants.

In their struggles against the 'colour prejudiced' segregationist system, the free coloureds, and particularly the mulatto owners of the south, adopted this 'account of origins' and reworked it to claim in turn that they were the authentic 'American settlers'. They rightly recalled that the Colbert Edict of 1685, mistakenly called the 'Code noir', bore no trace of racial discrimination, and instead merely defined two groups with antagonistic legal statuses, freemen and slaves, with stipulations for slaves to become freemen. Julien Raimond, spokesperson for the mulatto owners, presented the original population of Saint-Domingue as a population of mixed ethnic origin:

> These first whites – the Buccaneers or their descendants – lived with these African women in a marital state and had children. Some, touched by the care and tenderness of these women, and inspired by paternal love, married their slaves and by freeing them in the Edict of 1685, they legitimized yet further the fruit of their love and customs ... In the early days of the colony, such was the nature of free coloured people.[13]

Julien Raimond's 'account of origins' is a mixed-race version that clearly combines calls for equal race and mixed-race inhabitants. This sexualized imaginary scheme of things did not imply any transgression in gender roles; the imaginary origins instead intensified the reality of the imbalance in favour of males in colonial societies, privileging the relationship between white males and black females. The 'American' character was strongly emphasized; the new class of coloured freemen was made up of genuine American Creoles. Africa was distanced via an implicitly racial logic, which might have initially appeared outmoded by the egalitarian revolution.

In another anonymous memoir dating from the early days of the Revolution, the author significantly claims himself to be an 'American Creole' and 'half-caste':

> The colour of the blacks points to Africa. Solely this colour is subject to taxes from their owners under our laws: its use is well known. The colour of the half-castes points to America; neither the original citizens of this continent nor the constitution of the French monarchy were slaves. It is therefore unjust to confuse us with Negroes; from this injustice is born their extreme insubordination towards us.[14]

The revolution of Saint-Domingue was largely the history of internal confrontation within the economic and social elite – an elite that initially shared a number of common reference points, including the idea of the buccaneer republic, drawn from the works of Oexmoelin and others. Haitian independence saw a violent transference of power from one racial group to another, and the account of origins was temporarily shifted towards the Caribbean people. Note that this still authorized stalemate on the African issue. However, the vast body of farmers, primarily of African origin, became, in the course of the confrontation, actors in their own right in the revolutionary process.

### The 'liberated territories' and the 'maroon republic'

Another myth appeared: the 'maroon republic', which implicitly referred to the mode of government, in 1792, of the 'freed zones', the northern territories administered by Jean-François, Biassou and Toussaint, after the great slave revolt of the Plaine du Cap in August 1791, and the small Platons republic in the south, in the heart of the Hotte Mountains, behind the Les Cayes.

Let us take the example of the Platons, whose insurrection is less well known than that of the northern plain. Its origins are presented in the following way in the *Rapport sur les troubles de Saint-Domingue*, still called the *Garran-Coulon report*, after the name of its author in 1795:[15]

> Definitely the most alarming insurrectionary movement broke out among the Negroes of the south at the start of 1791, more than six months before the uprising of slaves in the north ... in the month of January 1791, two hundred Negroes armed with machetes, sticks, spears and even guns, turned up at the Fabvre home and other homes, from which they removed commanders and various slaves. Other crowds formed in the Plaine du Fond; several of the insurgents were armed with guns, and intent on gathering the Negroes of the workshops to ask their masters for *three free days per week*, which according to them had been *accorded by the king. If whites refused they would be set about and their throats slit.*

After driving back the white troops' first offensive, the insurgents entrenched in the mountains and drew up proposals very similar to the maroon communities of the Caribbean zone in the modern era:

> The Platons Negroes were politically very astute after their victory ... They first demanded freedom for all those who had served with them, while maintaining their demand for three free days in the workshops. They then reduced their demand to four hundred freedmen only, and offered to send the other Negroes back to the workshops, along with nine hundred good rifles as a guarantee of their sincerity ... Negotiations dragged on. The robberies returned; and soon the Negroes returned, demanding *freedom for the whole group and total possession of the Platons.*[16]

These forms of organization showed the type of power attributed to 'African' roots based on charismatic authority, ritual mediations and the maintenance of traditional structures, including domestic slavery. This model is similar to the Quilombos of Brazil and other Spanish *palenques* across the tropical zone from the 'Palmares republic' to Brazil, and the maroons of the Blue Mountains of Jamaica.[17]

The question of territory as 'refuge' is essential in this colonial ecosystem, based on economic yield and strictly divided between 'useful space' and the still wild 'savannah':

> The blacks, under the orders of their own man, Armand, occupied the steep wood-clad hills, riven with deep gorges, which follow the Plaine du Fond.[18]

The Republican Imagination and Race 283

The crucial point lies in maroonage and 'gang' organization. Let us return to Madiou for his eloquent description:

> On the night of 30–31 March 1792, the slaves revolted without any disorderly conduct; not one settler was killed, not one house burned ... This multitude did not even have sixty rifles between them. They were armed with knives hoes, iron-tipped sticks and slings. At three in the morning they attacked the whites in battle formation around the town with tremendous determination. The blacks, driven fanatical by their witchdoctors, met their death with great joy, in the belief that they would be resurrected in Africa. Hyacinthe, armed with a bull's tail, declared to the ranks that it deflected bullets ... Among the insurgents Halaou, Halaou, Bébé Coustard and the coloured Bélisaire particularly distinguished themselves and became famous chiefs. They organized their gangs in an African way: carried at head height, they wore headdresses of roosters and peacock feathers, wielding the right of life and death over their own.[19]

The political and social organization of these 'liberated territories'[20] was based on the model of charismatic authority. The expression is borrowed from Max Weber from his definition of charisma, featuring in many dictionaries:

> A special gift granted by divine favour for the common good; a quality that enables the possessor to hold influence and authority over a group.[21]

If we replace 'divine favour' by 'the staging of a magic power', we arrive at the kind of power the many gang chiefs held over their followers throughout the colonial and revolutionary period, from Macandal to Capoix 'La Mort', via Romaine 'the Prophetess'.

A whole swath of historiography, tinged with ethnography, systematically attempts to interpret the period as a confrontation between the *bossales*, born in Africa, who had recently arrived in the colony and preserved their socio-political and animist culture from their country of origin (if we can speak of a single country of origin – there seems to be an element of fantasy here when we consider the reality of Africa as described in Africanist history), and Creoles, born in the colony and culturally influenced by the European model (again, can we speak of a single model?). The gang, organized around a charismatic chief, therefore operated according to an African/*bossale*/non-hierarchical structure.[22]

It is not our intention here to discuss the relevance of such an interpretation. Let us just say that this phenomenon was not the reserve of the *bossales* (purportedly 'pure Africans'). General Pamphile de Lacroix, another great witness of the Saint-Domingue revolution, portrays a famous gang chief, a coloured freedman close to the Ogé brothers, who organized a gang following the slave revolt in the north:

> They had been brought together from the outset of the insurrection due to contumacy in the Ogé affair, under the orders of a man known as *Candi*, who proved to be as vicious as Jeannot, whose lieutenant he had been ... His name instilled fear in the whites, and his ability to hold his gang together by camping separately in the hills and arguing hatred for the whites, had gained him credit among the blacks.[23]

In these examples, the idea of republic is synonymous with the ideas of counter-revolution (they invoke the king's name, which is not the only paradox of theirs) and above all of independence (the control of a territory); it is also synonymous with the idea of liberty. We find the primitive republican model, of Corsica or Switzerland, in the work of many Enlightenment thinkers such as Rousseau or Marat – in *Les chaînes de l'esclavage*. Independence and frugality are the guarantee of liberty. From here comes the recurrent image of the 'armed Negro' prevalent throughout the period.

## Questions relating to democratic citizenship

The fundamental condition of democratic citizenship is the principle of republican isonomy, that is, that the law is identical in all republics, no matter their location. It is applied indifferently to all citizens, whatever their colour and condition (subject to the usual, not inconsiderable restrictions, which for our purposes apply as much to Europe as to the tropics).

The first official formulation of this principle is to be found in the law of 4 April 1792 that recognized the equality of freedmen, independent of colour. While this first stage undid the segregationist structure, it maintained the colonial edge by maintaining slavery. This is why the second stage, the decree of 16 Pluviôse Year II (4 February 1794) on freedom in general, opened the way to the genuine integration of colonial peoples into the republic. It was this stage that was contained in article 6 of the 1795 constitution: 'French colonies are an integral part of the republic, and are submitted to the same constitutional law.'[24]

But it was in the law of 12 Nivôse Year VI (1 January 1798) that the constitutional principle of isonomy was genuinely applied in the departmentalization of territories that were no longer called 'colonies' but 'overseas departments'. It matters little that, soon afterwards, postrevolutionary events led to the failure of the republic's initial application of the law in the tropics. It is essential to underline today that this law of republican isonomy was the real inspiration behind the thought and action of subsequent colonial reformers, from Bissette to Victor Schoelcher[25] and Aimé Césaire, the young republican Césaire of 1946.

What constitutes this republican isonomy, outlined by Laveaux in 1798? The project first focused on political representation – elected representatives overseas became fully fledged representatives of a single political people under the same conditions as held in a metropolitan territory. It then focused on education. All actors of the 'republican regeneration' of colonial peoples insisted on education as the key to individual and collective improvement. In his declaration on arrival in the Cap in 1796, Sonthonax affirmed education as a priority:[26]

> Education is as useful as work. It is through education that you pass on your rights to your children. It is through education that you learn to fulfil the duties of good family men and citizens. It is through education that you attain the degree of morality that distinguishes the civilized man from the savage, the respectable man from the perverted. Obscurantism harms progress and prevents a people from moving on. People must be educated if we are to combat the harmful influence of selfish ambitious leaders. It is through education that the citizen builds his personality. Education is the faith and duty that leads to evolution. It is the bulwark against exploitation and the guarantee of human rights.

For his part, abbé Grégoire, one of the main figures behind the reformation of the Société des amis des noirs in 1796, devoted much of his time to collecting teaching manuals and pedagogical works, which he entrusted to the constitutional bishop Mauviel, who was sent to Saint-Domingue in 1801. The works were subsequently lost in the crossing and in the tragic upheavals of the Haitian liberation war.[27]

The intentions here were not just pious vows and vain rhetoric doomed to failure. Emancipation, which in this period was called 'regeneration', started to enjoy practical application.[28] A Central School was founded on the Cap, and teachers were sent into all the communes. In the Cap's only town alone, free public education was provided for 800 children.[29]

The most deserving youngsters, or the most representative of the new elite, which now had to include all three colours, were sent to study in metropolitan France at the Institut national des colonies de Paris, founded by General Laveaux and abbé Grégoire. The sons of Toussaint-Louverture were sent there, along with most of the children of Saint-Domingue's coloured officers. These children would naturally have progressed onto the École polytechnique, if the reaction of the consul had not brought a tragic end to the experiment.[30]

This republican project was also very much in evidence at the Société des amis des noirs et des colonies. Dupuch, Guadeloupe's former representative and a member of the second Société des amis des noirs, gave a speech on the subject on 30 Messidor Year VI (18 July 1798):[31]

> In Guadeloupe, the Directory will apply the law of 12 Nivôse last, concerning the constitutional organization of the colonies. It is a fully republican law, which is already quite rightly referred to as the new colony code ... article 85 of the law of 12 Nivôse reads thus: 'The agents of the Directory are charged with organizing forthwith public education in the colonies, according to existing laws.'

One positive point about the 12 Nivôse law is article 86:

> every year in each department of the colonies on 1 Germinal, the day of the festival of youth, six young individuals shall be chosen without distinction of colour, from among the pupils of the Central School, who, at the expense of the nation, shall be transported to France and kept in special schools for the time necessary for their education. Thus the republic equally distributes its great benefits to all its children! It calls them from the furthest reaches of its territory to share education with those at the centre, so that they might take back enlightenment and patriotism to their families. Thus, through ties of gratitude, the legislature brings the colonies into the republic, and the constitution of the republic makes them an integral part of that republic. I invite the Société to promote this salutary institution through all its means, and to sometimes accept into its fold young pupils who shall acquire knowledge useful to their country and who, on returning to their homes, shall remind their fellow citizens of the virtues of the Société's members, to whose work they will have been witness, and of the important service this renders the colonies and humanity.

The third pillar of republican isonomy is political economy. It should enable colonial prosperity to be restored through shared interests on both sides of the exchange; it should allow for the transfer of technology, and possibly the subsequent transfer of qualified European manpower to the tropics; and it should motivate farmers, former slaves and 'new freedmen' to help in the recovery of the plantation economy, spurred on by wage earning or profit sharing. It was on this central question of work that the republican project finally came to grief.[32] It was not through lack of trying to find solutions, often very radical solutions, like those proposed by the public law specialist Édouard Lefebvre, a neo-Jacobin employed at the Ministry of Foreign Affairs, who accorded the colonial question a central role in his plan for the regeneration of the French republic at the end of 1798. In his attempt to reconcile work and liberty, Lefebvre drew up radical agrarian reforms, which were profoundly egalitarian. He went even further. In order to definitively wipe out colour prejudice – the presence of which, he went to great lengths to show, had undermined social relations in the West Indies – he wanted the government to set in motion a policy of voluntary interracial breeding:

> To regenerate this country it is not enough for the government to bring in European peace. It is indispensable for it to destroy the prejudice that has long served to sanction vile tyranny. To this end, it has to encourage, by all the means in its power, marriage between the different classes – white, black, mulatto, half-castes and quadroons, etc. Such marriages will cross species, mingle blood, unite interests and mix colours. Earlier, I proposed that each negro be given a portion of land. Women would also be party to this. With such a dowry, they would easily find husbands among the crowds of sailors, workers and European soldiers who are driven to the colonies by misery or the desire to make their fortune. If needs be, the government could accord a certain portion of land to whites keen on forming such alliances.[33]

In this way, the question of mixed race and interracial marriage became a cornerstone of the republican project. The biological determinism that founded colour prejudice (the indelible 'stain' of the colour black, which passed on the mark of servitude from generation to generation) could only be destroyed by mixing blood through the intermarriage of white men and black women. This obsession with blood and sex that runs through the colonial imagination was also placed at the heart of the regeneration programme. Grégoire gave it special attention.[34] Interracial marriages restored harmony between men and also helped to strengthen the race (Grégoire was in agreement with Buffon on this point); the new race would be better than the two initial races taken separately. The new race would work the soil better and be better placed to learn about advanced agricultural technologies.

These inseparably biological, economic and moral considerations (moral as far as the prospect of civilizing and perfecting the species is concerned) cannot be dissociated from Grégoire's preference for the republic of South Haiti. When commissioned to produce a 'collection of the constitutions of various countries' (the commission probably came from Lanjuinais, who was always close to Grégoire), the abbé Grégoire drew up a 'reasoned table of the constitutions of Haiti'. He showed his undeniable preference for the Southern republic, precisely because 'the form of government we should prefer is indisputably that which ensures property, liberty and equality for all citizens in law. These advantages are right and should be set down and guaranteed in a fundamental pact, and not in the promises and changing will of a leader. For men die, but constitutions live on.'

Remember that in 1806 an uprising led to the assassination of Dessalines and his advisors, and then to the separation of the country into two entities: the kingdom of Christophe I in the north, and the republic of Haiti in the south, of which Alexandre Pétion was the president. According to Grégoire, in the constitution of the republic, 'powers have been wisely distributed and balanced out, while the north has limited itself to establishing a hereditary dynasty, with a Council of State that does not represent the nation'. This monarchic form was seen as an anomaly, a regression, in an 'American' environment that was increasingly being viewed as the 'cradle of the republics':

> We wonder how an absolute monarchy could have been organized next to a republic, a form that sanctions rights, in the vicinity of the American continent where republics are rife, and where some are already in the full radiance of their youth while others, still in the cradle, will develop over the years.

Of course it is possible to object that Grégoire stopped at outward appearances, that his analysis was tainted with legalism, and that the powerful mulatto oligarchy in the south was barely more favourable to equal rights than the black military dictatorship in the north. Grégoire replies to another objection, formulated by those influenced by the abolitionist Thomas Clarkson in particular, who thought that the republic was only possible in the south because the mulattos were more educated in the constitutional forms of representative governments than the black masses in the north, who were still close to their African origins and therefore more inclined to charismatic authority. However, crucially, Grégoire dismissed such cultural determinism:

> The apologists of the north say secondly that a free government is more suitable to the situation in the south-west, where there are predominantly men of colour, because in general civilization and enlightenment are more advanced among them than among the blacks who form the vast majority of the population in the north ... My answer is that, while I have no abundant knowledge of the matter, blacks have enough tact to be able to discern those among them who have more and who by their probity and zeal have acquired public esteem. Journals published in Port-au-Prince show that the republic has enlightened men and good writers. The same is true in the north.[35]

## Conclusion

There is an undeniable polysemy in the use of the term 'republican' in the tropics, as shown in the study of Anne Pérotin-Dumon on Guadeloupe.[36] It temporarily covers and supports racial differentialism, dedicated to American patriotism, as well as ethnic culturalism, to designate, wrongly no doubt, though this remains to be shown, social formations with an absence of self-defining writings, hastily labelled as 'African'.

These unique community-based interests were in competition and soon came into contradiction with a project aimed at bypassing them and even denying them in a certain brutal fashion. The project was one of republican isonomy, or integration. The project had a period of concrete experimentation, albeit partial although not marginal, under the Directory. For four years, unbound equality before the law was the order of the day, and racial differentialism was outlawed. The objection might be that such equality barely touched the surface and that there was a huge gulf between the law and morality. After Napoleon's coup d'état, morality took the ascendancy over law.

Let us return to René Depestre:

> The omnipresence of so-called race and religion options in Haitian mentalities should have been devolved to the state, law, secularization of thought and behaviour, like the free initiative of the market economy. The whole political heritage of the liberation of Haiti was thus frozen, until 2004, into a tragically legendary figure: the first black

republic of modern times, the cradle of history for negritude, which continued, until the faltering 'prophetism' of President Aristide, to create a negative idea that the Haitians have of themselves.[37]

It can therefore be seen that, for the small group of republicans who were not exclusively metropolitan (far from it – I have in mind black representatives like Belley, Thomany or mixed-race representatives like Pétiniaud or Raimond), the task of subverting colour prejudice, legitimized by tropical naturalism and representations of an African past, was huge. Édouard Lefebvre expressed the difficulties of the enterprise in his own way:

> May the government be aware of the truth that, given the current state of the colonies, any stopgap measure would only aggravate the ills of anarchy. There is only one complete system of legislation that can restore them, and this system must emerge from the grand rule of equality, because there is no country in the world today where it is not easier to establish a true democracy without fear of forcing the proportions: thus the establishment of the constitutional regime is the most essential condition for the prosperity of colonies; before this, we need a power that is capable of simultaneously creating men and things, and this power is property.[38]

## Notes

1. Title of the special issue of *Revue Française d'Histoire d'Outre-Mer*, edited by Marcel Dorigny, 2003. The expression also appears in Jacques de Cauna (1987) *Au temps des îles à sucre: Histoire d'une plantation de Saint-Domingue au XVIIIème siècle* (Paris: Karthala); the last chapter is entitled, 'Haiti the First Black Republic in the World'.
2. Thomas Madiou (1803–7) *Histoire d'Haïti* (Port-au-Prince: Courtois) reprint (1987–91) (Port-au-Prince: Henri Deschamps) vol. 3, p. 151. The text of the generals' proclamation mentions Jean-Jacques Dessalines, 'the governor general of Haiti for life'.
3. Ibid., p. 131.
4. Bernard Gainot (2005) 'La députation de Saint-Domingue au Corps Législatif du Directoire', in *Léger-Félicité Sonthonax: La première abolition de l'esclavage: La Révolution française et la Révolution de Saint-Domingue* (Paris: Société française d'histoire d'outre-mer et Association pour l'étude de la colonisation française), pp. 95–110.
5. Quoted in Madiou, *Histoire*, pp. 147–8.
6. René Depestre (April 2004) 'Mon pays d'origine est un appel au secours', *Le Monde diplomatique*, 6 and 7. See also the Unesco conference of the same month, 'Adresse aux Haïtiens d'aujourd'hui': http://www.monde-diplomatique.fr/2004/04/DEPESTRE/11130.

7. Charles Frostin (1975) *Les révoltes blanches à Saint-Domingue, aux XVIIème et XVIIIème siècles (Haïti avant 1789)* (Paris: L'École).
8. *Mémoire instructif adressé à l'Assemblée des notables du royaume par les commissaires de la colonie de Saint-Domingue*, cited by Garran-Coulon (1795) *Rapport sur les troubles de Saint-Domingue, fait au nom de la Commission des colonies, des Comités de Salut Public, de Législation et de Marine, réunis, par J.P. Garran, député par le département du Loiret* (Paris: Imprimerie Nationale), vol. 1, pp. 147–8.
9. Hilliard d'Auberteuil (1776–77) *Considérations sur l'état présent de la colonie française de Saint-Domingue* (Paris: Grange).
10. We might cite in particular *Essais historiques et politiques sur les anglo-américains*, and also *Essais historiques et politiques sur la révolution de l'Amérique septentrionale*, which dates from 1781–82.
11. Hilliard d'Auberteuil, *Considérations*, Livre I, discours premier; 'Des engagements des colons envers l'État', pp. 21–31.
12. R.L. de Voyer de Paulmy, marquis d'Argenson (1859–1867) *Journal et mémoires*, ed. E.J.B. Ratheny (Paris: Société de l'histoire de France), vol. 5, p. 260.
13. Julien Raimond (26 January 1791) *Observations sur l'origine et les progrès du préjugé des colons blancs contre les hommes de couleur, par M. Raymond, homme de couleur de Saint-Domingue* (Paris: Baudouin); Florence Gauthier offers an analysis in (2007) *L'aristocratie de l'épiderme: Le combat de la Société des gens de couleur, 1789–1791* (Paris: CNRS), pp. 226–37.
14. Anon. (1789) *Précis des gémissements des sang mêlés dans les colonies françaises, par J.M.C., américain, sang mêlé* (Paris: Baudouin), repr. in *La Révolution française et l'abolition de l'esclavage* (1968), (Paris: EDHIS), vol. 11, p. 7.
15. Garran-Coulon (1795), vol. 2, pp. 563–4.
16. Ibid., pp. 609–10.
17. For the historical and political problems of maroonage, but not the cultural reconstructions to which the phenomenon gave rise, see the excellent work by Mavis C. Campbell (1988) *The Maroons of Jamaica, 1655–1796: A History of Resistance, Collaboration and Betrayal* (Granby, Mass.: Bergin and Garvey), in particular pp. 209–49.
18. Madiou, *Histoire*, vol. 1, p. 145.
19. Ibid., p. 131.
20. At the risk of anachronism I have borrowed the expression from Yves Bénot (1992), who described the organization of the territories of the north after the great slave revolt: 'Un épisode décisif de l'insurrection: La prise du Dondon (10 septembre 1791)', *Chemins critiques*, II (Port-au-Prince), *Qui a peur de la démocratie en Haïti?*, 97–111. And also (2005) 'Documents sur l'insurrection des esclaves de Saint-Domingue; lettres de Biassou, Fayette ...', *Annales Historiques de la Révolution Française*, LXXVII, 137–50.
21. 'Charisme', *Nouveau Petit Robert*, 1993 edn.
22. Gérard Barthélémy (2000) *Créoles–bossales, conflit en Haïti* (Petit-Bourg à la Guadeloupe: Éditions Ibis Rouge). The author states that the 'first rebel chiefs' were said to have been 'former maroons' (p. 212). They then systematically integrated African-*bossales* and maroon-growers. This led to a cut and dried, and to me very simplified, interpretation in its dualism: 'This pure and simple return to the stage before capture was claimed gradually by all African slaves who led their own struggle through the fifteen years of the independence period' (p. 213). And again: 'These two strategies, one *bossale*,

the other Creole, corresponded fairly well to the two fundamental options of all revolutionary contestation: one that involves adopting the enemy system to turn it against itself, even if it means ultimately reproducing this system (which was the case with the Creole system), and one that involves building a counter-system that is different in every way to the system to be demolished. This strategy set the hierarchy built on slavery with egalitarian democracy' (p. 218).

23. Pamphile de Lacroix (1995) *La Révolution de Haïti* (Paris: Karthala), p. 121.
24. Bernard Gainot (1995) 'La constitutionnalisation de la liberté générale sous le Directoire; 1795–1800', in M. Dorigny (ed.), *Les abolitions de l'esclavage, de Sonthonax à Schoelcher: 1793–1794–1848* (Paris: Presses universitaires de Vincennes and Unesco), pp. 213–29.
25. On this question, see Anne Girollet (2000) *Victor Schoelcher, abolitionniste et républicain* (Paris: Karthala).
26. Cited by Gérard Laurent (2005) 'Sonthonax et sa seconde mission, un réformiste', in *Léger-Félicité Sonthonax: La première abolition de l'esclavage: La Révolution française et la Révolution de Saint-Domingue* (Paris: Publications de la Société française d'histoire d'outre-mer et de l'Association pour l'étude de la colonisation européenne), p. 68.
27. Alyssa Goldstein Sepinwall (2005) *The Abbé Grégoire and the French Revolution: The Making of Modern Universalism* (Berkeley: University of California Press).
28. It is worth remembering today that this republican project has been systematically denigrated in the revisionist undertakings of Sala-Molins and his epigones. See Louis Sala-Molins (2002) *Le Code noir ou le calvaire de Canaan* (Paris: Presses universitaires de France). It is also in good taste in a certain strain of thought, termed 'post-colonial', to talk systematically of the 'colonial Republic' for a more ironic criticism of its integrationist vision.
29. Françoise Bléchet, 'La seconde mission de Sonthonax à Saint-Domingue d'après sa correspondance (mai 1796–août 1797)', in *Léger-Félicité Sonthonax*, pp. 79–93.
30. Bernard Gainot (2000) 'Un projet avorté d'intégration républicaine: L'Institution nationale des colonies (1797–1802)', *Dix-huitième Siècle*, XXXII, 371–401.
31. The full text of the conference is reproduced in Marcel Dorigny and Bernard Gainot (1998) *La Société des amis des noirs, 1789–1799: Contribution à l'histoire de l'abolition de l'esclavage* (Paris: Unesco), pp. 372–7.
32. Our aim here is not to develop this fundamental dimension of the colonial economy and society post-slavery. See my contribution to the debate (2007) 'Quels statuts pour les cultivateurs sous le régime de la liberté générale? (1794–1802) ou Comment peut-on allier, sous la zone torride, l'industrie au bonheur?', in Danielle Bégot (ed.), *La plantation esclavagiste, XVIIe–XIXe siècles* (Paris: CTHS), pp. 23–45. On this subject see also Vertus Saint-Louis (2000) 'Les termes de citoyen et africain pendant la révolution de Saint-Domingue', in Laënnec Hurbon (ed.), *L'insurrection des esclaves de Saint-Domingue, 22–23 août 1791* (Paris: Karthala), pp. 75–95; Carolyn Fick (1990) *The Making of Haïti: The Saint-Domingue Revolution from Below* (Knoxville: University of Tennessee Press); Caroline Oudin-Bastide (2005) *Travail, capitalisme et société esclavagiste: Guadeloupe, Martinique, XVIIe–XIXe siècles* (Paris: La Découverte).

33. Édouard Lefebvre (1796) *Considérations politiques et morales sur la France constituée en République* (Paris: Arthur Bertrand), Year VI, pp. 268–9. The account is found in *La décade philosophique*, no. 3 (30 Vendémiaire Year VII–21 October 1798), in the 'Politique raisonnée' column. Édouard Lefebvre was also a member of the Société libre des sciences, belles-lettres et arts de Paris.
34. See Grégoire (1823) *Considérations sur le mariage et le divorce adressées aux citoyens d'Haïti* (Paris: Baudouin). For a deeper analysis of this question, refer to Sepinwall, *The Abbé Grégoire*, pp. 181–98.
35. *Observations sur la constitution du nord d'Haïti et sur les opinions qu'on s'est formées en France de ce gouvernement*; the manuscript is to be found at the archives of the Arsenal and dates from 1818 (ms 15049/204, folios 1–3, 5, 7); Yves Bénot (2005) places it in its context: 'Grégoire défenseur de la cause des noirs dans les revues de la Restauration', in *Grégoire et la cause des noirs (1789–1831): Combats et projets* (Paris: Société française d'histoire d'outre-mer et Association pour l'étude de la colonisation européenne), pp. 149–62.
36. Anne Pérotin–Dumon (1985) *Être patriote sous les tropiques* (Basse Terre: Société d'histoire de la Guadeloupe).
37. Depestre, 'Mon pays d'origine est un appel au secours'.
38. Lefebvre, *Considérations politiques et morales*, p. 270.

# Index

(Only the works cited as primary sources are listed below)

Acton, John Emerich Edward Dalberg, Lord  227, 237
Adams, John  64, 65, 69, 74–7, 110, 112, 113–14, 119, 203, 205–6, 210, 211–12, 213, 219, 228, 230, 239, 252, 261, 262
   *A Defence of the Constitutions of Government of the United States of America, against the Attack of M. Turgot*  4, 71–2, 73, 74–5, 77, 78, 79, 234
   *A Memorial to their High Mightinesses, the States General of the United Provinces of the Low-Countries*  113, 119
   *Address to the People of the Netherlands*  114
   *Défense des constitutions américaines, ou De la nécessité d'une balance dans les pouvoirs d'un gouvernement libre*  243–4, 254, 272
   *Écrits politiques et philosophiques*  272
Adams, John Quincy  213–14, 218, 220
   *Observations on Paine's Rights of Man, in a Series of Letters, by Publicola*  234
agrarianism  124, 126–7, 129, 136, 189
   degradation of  149
Albertone, Manuela  7, 14, 43, 47, 59, 77–8, 141, 142–4, 272
Aldridge, Alfred O.  143
Alimento, Antonella  78
America
   as agrarian society  124, 126–7, 129
   Alien Acts (1798)  213, 261, 262
   attitude to French Revolution  203–7, 214–15, 221, 246, 248–9
   Bicentennial  214
   Daughters of the American Revolution  214
   Declaration of Independence  24, 124
   Federalists  203, 205, 210–11
   formation of political societies  210–11
   French–American Alliance  203–4
   land-ownership  127–8
   neutrality of  207–9
   republicans  203, 205
   revolutionary history  26–7
   Sedition Acts (1798)  213, 261
   Whiskey Rebellion  211
   worsening relations with France  211–12, 220–1
   *see also* American Revolution
American Civil War  215
American constitution  11, 28, 50, 81, 86, 87, 89–94, 95, 171, 249, 270
American 'revisionism'  35
American Revolution  3, 5, 10, 17–39, 204–5, 214, 225
   origins of  19–20
   'taming' of  27–8
American War of Independence  18, 23, 102–6
   Dutch involvement in  104–5
Amiens Peace Treaty  268
Ammon, Harry  217, 255
*An Address to the Inhabitants of Great Britain and Ireland; in Reply to the Principles of the Author of the Rights of Man*  235
*An Impartial Review of the Causes and Principles of the French Revolution, by an American*  235, 236
Anglo-Dutch Alliance  107, 108

Anglo-Dutch wars 102, 113, 115
Ansart, Guillaume 235
Appleby, Joyce 141, 143, 228–9, 237, 253, 254
Arago, Dominique-François-Jean 143
Arendt, Hannah 33–4, 44
Argenson, René-Louis, marquis d' 280, 291
Armitage, David 13
Atlantic History 31–2
Atlantic republicanism 48, 52
Atlantic revolutions 28–32, 226
  *see also* American Revolution; French Revolution
Auchincloss, John, *The Sophistry of Both the First and the Second Part of Mr. Paine's Age of Reason* 236
Aulard, Alphonse 23–4, 27, 41
Austin, Benjamin 126, 129

Badinter, Robert 98
Baillie, John, *Two Sermons: The First on the Divinity of Jesus Christ; the Second on Time, Manner, and Means of the Conversion and Universal Restoration of the Jews* 236
Bailyn, Bernard 13, 28, 43, 141
Baker, David J. 14
Baker, Keith Michael 35, 40, 43–4, 46, 47, 59, 78, 143
balance of powers 184, 186
Barère de Vieuzac, Bertrand 273
Barlow, Joel 48, 49, 55
Barnave, Antoine-Pierre-Joseph Marie 242
Barny, Roger 274
Barthélémy, Gérard 291
Bartstra, Jan S. 117
Bastid, Paul 177
Baudeau, abbé Nicolas 7
  *Exposition de la loi naturelle* 151–2, 161
Baume, Sandrine 14, 78, 144
Bayle, Pierre 227
Bayly, Christopher A. 14
Bégaud, Stéphane 45
Bégot, Danielle 292
Belissa, Marc 45, 273

Bender, Thomas 14
Bénot, Yves 291, 293
Bergamasco, Lucia 43
Bergasse, Louis 95
Bergasse, Nicolas 5, 81, 85, 94, 96
  *Discours sur la manière dont il convient de limiter le pouvoir législatif et le pouvoir exécutif dans une monarchie* 82–6, 95, 97
Bergh, Albert Ellery 141
Berghahn, Volker 41
Berr, Henri 23
Bertaud, Jean-Paul 274
Bétourné, Olivier 41
Betts, Edwin Morris 142
Biaudet, Jean-Charles 177
Bien, David 33, 44
Billaud-Varenne, Jacques-Nicolas 241, 254
Blaquiere, Thomas, *General Observations on the State of Affairs in Ireland, and its Defence against an Invasion. By a Country Gentleman* 236
Bléchet, Françoise 292
Bloch, Marc 20–1, 23, 40
Bloch, Ruth H. 256
Blumenthal, Henry 215
Boisguilbert, Pierre le Pesant, Sieur de 191
Boisrond-Tonnerre, Louis-Félix-Mathurin 277
Boissy D'Anglas, François-Antoine 259
Bolivar, Simon 20
*Bon hollandais à ses compatriotes* 108–10, 112, 113, 118
Bonaparte, Napoleon 137, 163, 164, 165, 166, 167, 168, 169, 170, 172, 174, 176, 178, 180, 181, 182, 183, 186, 188, 189, 195, 200, 268, 269, 289
Bots, Hans 116
Boulanger, Nicolas-Antoine 48, 55, 56
  *Recherches sur l'origine du despotisme oriental, ouvrage posthume de Mr B.I.D.P.E.C.* 55, 60

Boulay de la Meurthe, Antoine-Jacques-Claude-Joseph, 263, 264–7
*Essai sur les causes qui, en 1649, amenèrent en Angleterre l'établissement de la république; sur celles qui devaient l'y consolider; surcelles qui l'y firent périr* 274
Bourne, Henry E. 236, 253
Bowman, Albert Hall 45, 217, 255
Boyd, Julian P. 141, 255
Braddick, Michael J. 13
Branson, Susan 215
Brewer, John 45
Brinton, Crane 27, 33, 43
Brissot, Jacques-Pierre 32, 46, 49, 50, 55, 234, 241, 243, 245, 247, 251, 253
Brocard, Lucien 161
Brooks, Stephen 238
Brown, Robert 27
Brunet, Pierre 14
Brutus 86–7
Bruun, Geoffrey 42
Bukovansky, Mlada 40, 237
Burgière, André 41
Burke, Edmund 40, 51–2, 223
*An Appeal from the New to the Old Whigs, in Consequence of Some Late Discussions in Parliament, Relative to the Reflections on the French Revolution* 236
*Reflections on the Revolution in France* 17, 165–6, 178
Butel, Paul 45

Cabanis, André 177
Cabanis, George 24
Cain, Julien 25
Campbell, Mavis C. 291
Canny, Nicholas 13
Capellen, Joan Derk van der 106–8, 109, 110–11, 113, 114, 117, 119
Catherine the Great 53, 112, 113, 114
Catholic Church 185, 233
Cauna, Jacques de 290
Cerisier, Antoine-Marie 49, 55, 110, 112, 113, 114

*Le Politique Hollandais* 114
*Onpartydige bedenkingen* 119
*Suite des observations impartiales d'un vrai hollandais* 118, 119
Césaire, Aimé 285
Chagny, Robert 274
Chakrabarty, Dipesh 14
Charles, Loïc 78
Chartier, Roger 43
Chas, Jean 269–72
*Histoire politique et philosophique de l'Amérique septentrionale par les citoyens* 271, 275
*Le tableau des États-Unis* 269, 275
*Réflexions sur l'Angleterre* 269, 275
*Sur Bonaparte premier consul de la république française, par lecitoyen Jean Chas de Nismes* 270, 275
*Tableau historique et politique de la dissolution et du rétablissement de la monarchie anglaise, depuis 1625 jusqu'en 1702* 275
Chateaubriand, François-René de 231
Chaunu, Pierre 45
Cheney, Paul 115
Chenier, Marie-Joseph 240, 253
Chevalier, Michel 231–3, 238
Chinard, Gilbert 24, 27, 34, 42, 144-5, 146, 221, 235–6, 272
Chouillet, Anne-Marie 143
Christie, William, *An Essay, on Ecclesiastical Establishments in Religion* 236
*citoyen fractionnaire* 68
Clarke, Thomas Brooke, *An Historical and Political View of the Disorganization of Europe* 234
Clarkson, Thomas 288
Clavière, Étienne 32, 160, 234, 241, 253
Clemens, Paul G.E. 44
Cloots, Anacharsis 49, 55
Cobbett, William 223
*The Bloody Buoy Thrown out as a Warning to the Political Pilots of America: or, A Faithful Relation of a Multitude of Acts of Horrid Barbarity, such as the Eye never*

*Witnessed, the Tongue never Expressed, or the Imagination Conceived, until the Commencement of the French Revolution* 237
*The Last Confession and Dying Speech of Peter Porcupine, with an Account of his Dissection* 236
*Code noir* 158, 280
Cohen, Lester H. 237
Colbert Edict (1685) 280
Colbert, Jean-Baptiste 189–90, 200
Colbertism 189, 191, 193, 194
Cold War 6, 25, 27, 35
Colenbrander, Herman T. 103, 116, 117
Comte, Auguste 24, 196
Comte, Charles 182, 196
Condillac, Étienne Bonnot de 49
*Le commerce et le gouvernement, considérés relativement l'un à l'autre* 192–3
Condorcet, Marie-Jean-Antoine-Nicolas, Caritat de 4, 7, 8, 26, 46, 49, 55, 64, 69, 71, 76, 79, 131, 134, 144, 148, 160, 244
*De l'influence de la Révolution d'Amérique sur l'Europe* 79, 131–2, 143, 236
*Esquisse d'un tableau historique* 222–3
*Essai sur la constitution et les fonctions des assemblées provinciales* 132, 143, 145
*Lettre à M. le comte de Montmorency* 135, 145
*Lettres d'un bourgeois de New-Heaven à un citoyen de Virginie* 132, 144
'Observations sur le vingt-neuvième livre de *L'esprit des lois*' 133, 177
*Outlines of an Historical View of the Progress of the Human Mind* 234, 236
*Vie de Turgot* 69, 71, 72, 78, 79, 135, 235, 237
Condorcet O'Connor, Arthur 143
Congress of Vienna 181, 185
Constant, Benjamin 8, 163–79, 183
*Acte additionnel aux constitutions de l'empire* 172
*De la Révolution française* 179
*De l'esprit de conquête* 163–4, 166–7, 168, 169, 170, 173, 177, 178, 181–2, 198
*Dernières vues de politique et de finances* 179
*Des suites de la contre-révolution de 1660 en Angleterre* 264, 274
*Discours de la liberté des anciens comparée à celle des modernes* 179
*Du pouvoir exécutif dans les grands états* 179
*Fragments d'un ouvrage abandonné sur la possibilité d'une constitution républicaine dans un grand pays* 170–1, 172–3, 178–9
'Journaux intimes' 179
*Mélanges de littérature et politique* 179
*Mémoire de M. Necker au Roi sur l'établissement des administrations provinciales* 179
*Mémoires sur les Cent-Jours* 177, 178
*Principes de politique* 166, 170, 172, 173, 178, 179
Continental Blockade 8, 38, 137, 169, 181, 193
Cordillot, Michel 26, 42
Corn Laws 170
Cottret, Bernard 274
Courts of Justice 91, 93
Coxe, Tench
*A Brief Examination of Lord Sheffield's Observations on the Commerce of the United States of America* 235
*A View of the United States of America, in a Series of Papers, Written ... between ... 1787 and 1794* 235
Craiutu, Aurelian 235, 238
Crépel, Pierre 143
Crèvecoeur, John Hector St. John de 32, 221
*Letters from an American Farmer* 27, 126
Cromwell, Oliver 262–3, 265, 266, 268
Cross, Jeanne K. 234
Crouzet, François 45, 178
Curtis, Eugen N. 42

Daire, Eugène 198
Dam, Fred van 118–19
Davis, David B. 10, 14, 215
Davis, Natalie Z. 40
De Conde, Alexander 217–18, 256
De Francesco, Antonino 11, 253, 255
Deism 4
Delacroix, Jacques-Vincent 244, 272
Delmas, Bernard 143
Demals, Thierry 143
Depestre, René 277, 289–90
Dessalines, Jean-Jacques 277, 288, 290
Destutt de Tracy, Antoine-Louis-Claude 7, 139
  *A Commentary and Review of Montesquieu's Spirit of Laws* 138, 146
  *A Treatise on Political Economy* 143
  *Commentaire sur L'esprit de lois de Montesquieu suivi d'Observations inédites ... de Condorcet* 133, 138, 177
  *Traité de la volonté* 130
*Détail exact des 39 descentes en Angleterre depuis Jules César jusqu'à celle du général Hoche* 273
*Détails d'une grande insurrection qui a eu lieu en Angleterre* 273
*Détails de l'insurrection terrible arrivée en Angleterre, Proclamation de la loi martiale* 273
Dickens, Charles
  *A Tale of Two Cities* 42
Dickinson, Harry T. 273
Diderot, Denis 46, 48, 49, 50, 53, 55, 56, 57, 58, 147, 192, 222
  *Essai sur les règnes de Claude et de Néron, et sur les moeurs et les écrits de Sénèque pour servir d'introduction à la lecture de ce philosophe* 235
Dilthey, Wilhelm 26
Dippel, Horst 253
Domat, Jean 227
Dorigny, Marcel 7, 8, 162, 255, 290, 292
Drury, Victor 26
Dubroca, Jean-François, *La politique du gouvernement anglais dévoilé, ou Tableau historique de manoeuvres que ce gouvernement a employées pour empêcher l'établissement de la liberté en France* 273
Ducher, Gaspard-Joseph-Amand 250, 256
Duchet, Michèle 31, 43
Dumas, Charles-William-Frédéric 110, 111
Dunn, John 21, 41, 141, 177
Dunn, Susan 237
Dunoyer, Charles 182, 196
Dupont de Nemours, Pierre-Samuel 7, 24, 64, 130, 131, 132, 136–41, 145, 156, 158, 229
  *Examen du gouvernement d'Angleterre, comparé aux constitutions des États-Unis* 237
  *Examen du livre de M. Malthus sur le Principe de Population* 137, 139, 145
  *Lettre à la chambre du commerce de Normandie, Sur le Mémoire qu'elle a publié relativement au Traité de Commerce avec l'Angleterre* 235
  *Mémoire sur les municipalités* 132
  *Observations sommaires sur l'utilité des encouragemens è donner aux manufactures américaines* 140
  *Sur l'agriculture et les manufactures aux États-Unis* 139–40, 146
Dutch Patriots 105, 110
Dutch republic *see* Netherlands

Eagen, James Michael 42
Echeverria, Durand 31, 43, 143, 235
Edelstein, Melvin 33
Edler, Friedrich 116, 119
Egron, Adrien 180
Elliot, Jonathan 98
Elliott, John H. 13
Ellis, Richard E. 142
Eltkins, Stanley 34, 44
Emmer, Pieter 38–9, 45
English Revolution 262–4, 266, 267
enlightened despotism 157

Erlick, E.-M. 99
Eustace, John S., *Letters on the Crimes of George III, Addressed to Citizen Denis, by an American Officer in the Service of France* 254

Fabius, Arnoldus Nicolaas Jacobus 116
Fabre, Jean 179
Faccarello, Gilbert 199
Fairchilds, Cissie 45
Farrand, Max 98
Faÿ, Bernard 24–5, 34, 42, 236
Febvre, Lucien 23
federalism 3, 123–4, 203, 205, 210–11
  consensus and legitimacy 173–7
  decentralization 170–3
  denunciation of 251–2
Fénelon, François de Salignac de la Mothe 227
feudalism 195
Fick, Caralyn 292–3
Figgis, John N. 237
Fink, Beatrice 163, 177
Fitzmaurice, Edmond 235
Fitzpatrick, John C. 217
Fling, Frederick M. 23, 41
Flynn, Dennis O. 45
Foner, Eric 43
Foner, Philip 40, 216
Fontana, Biancamaria 8, 14, 78, 144, 177–8
Forbonnais, François Veron de 192
Ford, Paul L. 144, 216
Fourquet, François 199
France
  1814 Charter 180, 197
  *ancien régime* 48, 85, 194, 244, 245
  *comité autrichien* 241, 243, 245, 246
  Directory period 258, 262, 263, 264, 265, 271
  Estates General 18
  Feuillants 11, 240, 241, 242, 243–4, 245–6, 251
  Girondins 240, 248, 249–52
  Jacobins 11, 164, 219, 240, 241, 243, 245–6, 247, 252

Louis XIV 182, 183
Louis XVIII 180, 197
mercantilism 190–1
Montagnards 149, 240, 249, 251
National Constituent Assembly 239–40
*royaume agricole* 190–2
Thermidorians 252
*triumvirat* 243
Franco-American Treaty of Amity (1778) 100–1
Franklin, Benjamin 18, 23, 111, 131, 160, 179, 227
French–American Alliance 203–4
French constitution 86, 90, 172, 180–1, 239, 240, 241, 242–3, 244–5, 251, 252, 258, 259, 264, 270, 284
French Revolution 2, 3, 17–39, 47–8, 182, 203, 213–14, 222–3
  American attitude to 203–7
  Committee of Public Safety 26
  neo-Tocquevellian interpretation 35
  social interpretation 32–4
  Terror 18, 26, 239, 240, 248, 260, 271
Frostin, Charles 291
Fuchs, Barbara 14
Furet, François 6, 35, 40, 44
Fursenko, A.A. 237

Gagnebin, Bernard 179
Gainot, Bernard 8, 12, 14, 162, 274, 290, 292
Galbaud, François-Thomas 247–8
Galiani, Ferdinando 100
  *Correspondance avec Mme d'Epinay, Mme Necker, Mme Geoffrin, &c. Diderot, Grimm, d'Alembert, De Sartine, d'Holbach, &c.* 115
Garran-Coulon, Jean-Philippe, *Rapport sur les troubles de Saint-Domingue* 282, 291–2
Gauchet, Marcel 35, 177, 179
Gauthier, Florence 255, 291
Geggus, David P. 255
Gem, Richard 134–5, 144
Genet, Edmond Charles 208–11, 239, 246–9, 250, 251

Gentz, Friedrich von 220
　*The Origin and Principles of the American Revolution, Compared with the Origin and Principles of the French Revolution* 218, 234
Gibbs, George 217
Gillies, John 226, 236
Giraldez, Arturo 45
Girollet, Anne 292
Glagau, Hans 254
Godechot, Jacques 10, 20, 28–32, 33, 36, 43–4, 178–9, 237, 257, 272
Goens, Rijklof Michaël van 112–13, 119
Goffinon, Jean-Paul 272
Gottschalk, Louis 26
Gouhier, Henrix 198–9
Grampp, William D. 142
Grange, Henri 178–9
Graslin, Jean-Joseph 192
Greene, Jack 27
Greer, Donald 26, 42
Grégoire, abbé Baptiste-Henri 285, 286, 287–9
　*Considérations sur le mariage et le divorce adressées aux citoyens d'Haïti* 293
Gregor, Mary 60
Griffiths, Robert 254
Gueniffey, Patrice 35
Guillaume, James 253

Habermas, Jürgen 29, 43, 218
Haiti (Saint-Domingue) 12, 20, 30, 247–8, 250–1, 257, 258, 259, 276–93
　account of origins 276, 277, 278–80
　American patriotism 278–81
　maroon republic 281–4
　Platons 281–2
Haitsma Mulier, Eco O.G. 116
Halevy, Ran 35
Halpérin, Jean Louis 97
Haltzel, Michael H. 14, 215
Hamilton, Alexander 5, 7, 11, 81, 82, 86–7, 89–94, 99, 137, 203, 209, 211, 212, 239, 240, 241, 246, 247, 248, 251, 252, 254
　*Le Fédéraliste, ou Collection de quelques écrits en faveur de la constitution proposée aux États-Unis de l'Amérique par la Convention convoquée en 1787* (the *Federalist*) 243, 245, 254
　*Report on Manufactures* 123, 129, 141
Hampson, Norman 273
Hancock, David 44
Hanson, Paul R. 253
Harouel, Jean-Louis 20, 40
Harper, Robert Goodloe,
　*An Abridgement of the Observations on the Dispute between the United States and France* 235
Harrington, James 71–3, 259
Hartig, Aglaia 41
Hartz, Louis 27
Harvey, John 41
Hatch, Nathan O. 216
Hazen, Charles D. 215–17, 235
Helvétius, Claude-Adrien 46, 49, 53–4, 56
　*De l'homme: De ses facultés intellectuelles et de son éducation* 60
Herlitz, Lars 199
Herrenschwand, Johann Friedrich de, *De l'économie politique moderne: Discours fondamental sur la population* 153–4, 162
Hesse, Carla 255
Higham, John 43
Higonnet, Patrice 228–9, 237
Hill, Christopher 273
Hill, Peter P. 37, 45
Hilliard d'Auberteuil, Michel-René 278–80
　*Considérations sur l'état présent de la colonie française de Saint-Domingue* 278–80, 291
　*Essais historiques et politiques sur la révolution de l'Amérique septentrionale* 291
　*Essais historiques et politiques sur les anglo-américains* 291

Hochedlinger, Michael 253
Hofmann, Etienne 177, 178–9
Hofstadter, Richard 27
Holbach, Paul-Henri Dietrich, baron d' 46, 48, 49, 52–3, 54, 55, 56, 57, 58, 59, 60
Holmes, Steven 98
Holroyd, John, Earl of Sheffield, *Observations on the Commerce of the American States* 234
Hont, Istvan 14, 77, 178
House of Orange 6, 102, 104, 107, 114, 268
Hulliung, Mark 78
Hume, David 22, 41, 49, 50, 52, 53, 54, 55, 58
*Of National Characters* 41
Hunecke, Volker 253
Hünemörder, Markus 254
Hunt, Lynn 41, 44
Hunter, Brooke 44
Hurbon, Laënnec 292

Ignatieff, Michael 77
industrialism 187, 189–90, 196
*Irish Independence; or the Policy of Union* 236
Irhoven van Dam, Willem van 49, 55
Isaac, Jeffrey C. 235, 238
Israel, Jonathan 3, 4, 14, 59, 60, 116

Jacob, Margaret C. 116
Jacquemont, Victor 231
Jainchill, Andrew 254–5, 272
Janssen, Antoon Edmond Maria 116
Jay Treaty 211, 220, 261
Jebb, John 49, 55
Jefferson, Thomas 4, 7, 23, 24, 32, 38, 123–41, 142, 143, 145, 160, 179, 203, 204, 208–9, 212, 213, 216, 218, 227, 239, 241, 244, 246, 247, 248, 249, 251, 255, 259, 260–2
 agrarianism 124, 126–7, 129, 136
 *Commonplace Book* 132–3
 *Farm Book* 127
 *Garden Book* 127
 land-ownership 127–8
 *Notes on the State of Virginia* 125–6, 129, 141
 Physiocracy 128–33
 public debt 133–4
 republicanism of 123–4
Jennings, Jeremy 238
Jepson, Graham, *Letters to Thomas Payne, in Answer to his Late Publication on the Rights of Man* 234
Jessenne, Jean-Pierre 274
Jones, Colin 42
Jones, Howard Mumford 215
Jones, John Paul 104, 105
Jourdain, Annie 20, 40
judicial power 80–94

Kaiser, Thomas E. 253
Kant, Immanuel 55–6, 60
Kaplan, Lawrence S. 217
Kaplow, Jeffrey 33
Katz, Stanley N. 142
Kerber, Linda K. 43
Ketcham, Ralph 98, 216
Keynes, John Maynard 189
King, Norman 178
Klaits, Joseph 14, 215
Klein, Stephan Robert Edward 116
Klooke, Kurt 177
Knuttel, W.P.C. 117
Koch, Adrienne 144
Koschnik, Albrecht 256
Kossmann, Ernst Heinrich 116
Kramer, Lloyd 10, 14, 215–16
Kramnick, Isaac 141
Kwass, Michael 44

Laborde de Méréville, François 242
Laboulaye, Edouard 22
Labrouquère, André 162
Lacroix, Pamphile de 284, 292
Lafayette, Marie-Joseph-Paul-Yves-Roch-Gilbert du Motier, marquis de 18, 23, 24, 26, 131, 221, 228, 229, 235, 242, 243, 244, 245

Lagrave, Jean-Paul de  42
Lahmer, Marc  236
Lamare, Pierre-Bernard  244–5, 259
    *l'Equipondérateur*  259
Lameth, Alexandre-Theodore-Victor  242, 243
Lameth, Charles-Malo-François  242, 243
Larkin, Edward  40
Larrère, Catherine  14
Laslett, Peter  142
Laurence, Reginald V.  237
Laurens, Henry  104, 105, 112
Laurent, Gérard  292
Le Mercier de la Rivière, Pierre-François-Joachim-Henri  7, 155, 159–60, 162
    *Canevas d'un code constitutionnel, pour servir de suite à l'ouvrage intitulé: 'Les voeux d'un François'*  145
    *L'ordre naturel et essentiel des sociétés politiques*  68, 78, 192
Le Trosne, Guillaume-François  158
    *De l'ordre social*  152, 161
League of Armed Neutrality  112, 113, 115, 119
Lee, Arthur  111
Lee, Henri  259
Lee, William  111
Leeb, Isidore Leonard  116
Lefebvre, Édouard  29, 287
    *Considérations politiques et morales sur la France constituée en République*  290, 293
Lefebvre, Georges  29
legislative power, division of  80–94
Legros, Charles-François  48
    *Analyse et examen de l'Antiquité devoilée, du despotisme oriental, et du christianisme devoilé, ouvrages posthumes de Boullanger*  48, 59
Lemay, Edna H.  253
*Lettre du Père éternel à M. de Lameth tant pour lui que pour son frère, MM. Duport, Barnave, Delaborde, le duc d'Aiguillon et consors*  255
*Liberté de la presse détails de la grande insurrection qui a éclaté à Londres;*

*Nouvelle qui annonce que cette ville est à feu et à sang et qui porte que Pitt a été pendu*  273
*Liberty Scraps*  236
Lichtenberg, Georg Christoph  50
Lieber, Francis  238
Link, Eugene Perry  218, 256
Lipscomb, Andrew A.  141
Livesey, James  272
Locke, John  52, 59, 124, 127, 135, 226
    *Two Treatises of Government*  95, 142
Lodge, Henry Cabot  141
Logan, George  127, 129–30, 136
Longhitano, Gino  8–9
Louvet de Couvray, Jean-Baptiste  241, 254
Lutaud, Oliver  273–4
Luther, Martin  183, 186
Luzac, Elie  105, 106

Mably, Gabriel Bonnot de  55, 56, 72
    *Observations sur les Romains*  60
McArthur, G.H.  237
McCoy, Drew R.  141
McDonagh, Josephine  42
McDonald, Forrest  40, 142, 217
McDonald, Michelle Craig  44
Mackintosh, Robert  178
Mackintosh, Sir James  169, 170, 178
    *Vindiciae Gallicae: A Defence of the French Revolution 1791*  178
McKitrick, Erick  34, 44
MacNeven, William James, *An Argument for Independence, in Opposition to an Union. Addressed to all his Countrymen. By an Irish Catholic*  236
Madiou, Thomas  276, 283, 290
Madison, James  11, 19, 28, 84, 86–9, 90, 93, 95, 97, 98, 133, 134, 135, 139, 203, 204–5, 219, 239, 240, 241, 249, 251, 252, 259
Magrin, Gabriele  79
Maier, Charles  41
Malcolm, Janet  42
Malone, Dumas  143, 216–17

Malthus, Thomas   138, 140, 170
  *Essay on the Principle of Population*
    137, 145
  *The Grounds of an Opinion on the
    Policy of Restricting the Importation
    of Foreign Corn*   178
Mandelblatt, Bertie   44
Mantoux, Paul   255
Marbois, François de   125
Maréchal, Sylvain   49
Marienstras, Elise   41–2
Markovits, Andrei   238
Marongiu, Antonio   95
Martellone, Anna Maria   77
Marx, Karl   196
Marx, Leo   142
Marzagalli, Silvia   44
Mathiez, Albert   24, 26, 29
Matson, Cathy D.   141
Mattern, David B.   234
Mavidal, Jerome   253
May, Louis Philippe   162
Mazzei, Filippo   64
  *Recherches historiques et politiques sur
    les États-Unis de l'Amérique
    septentrionale*   79, 144
Meadows, R. Darrell   45
Mee, Jon   42
Melon, Jean-François   157–8, 181
  *Essai politique sur le commerce*   162
Mélonio, Françoise   22, 41
*Mémoire instructif adressé à l'Assemblée
  des notables du royaume par les
  commissaries de la colonie de
  Saint-Domingue*   291
Meyer, Jean   45
Michon, Georges   254
Mijnhardt, Wijnand W.   116
Miller, Augustus C.   142
Miller, James   60
Miller, Melanie Randolph   40
Miller, Samuel, *A Discourse, Delivered
  April 12, 1797, at the Request of
  and before the New-York Society for
  Promoting the Manumission of
  Slaves*   237
Millon, Charles

*Histoire de la Révolution et de la
  Contre-Révolution d'Angleterre*
  274–5
*Histoire des descentes qui ont eu lieu
  en Angleterre, Écosse, Irlande, et îles
  adjacentes depuis Jules César jusqu'à
  nos jours, suivie d'observations sur
  le climat*   273
Mirabeau, Honoré-Gabriel de Riquetti,
  comte de   46, 49, 55, 110
  *Considérations sur l'ordre de
    Cincinnatus*   60
Mirabeau, Victor de Riquetti, marquis
  de   7, 154–5, 158, 159
  *L'ami des hommes ou Traité de la
    population*   148–51, 161
  *Philosophie rurale, ou économie
    générale et politique de l'agriculture
    pour servir de suite à l'ami des
    hommes*   154, 157, 162
Miranda, Francisco de   20
Molho, Anthony   41
Molyneux, William   226
Monroe, James   249
Montesquieu, Charles de Secondat,
  baron de   4, 17, 50, 52, 54, 55,
    80, 85, 89, 132–3, 147, 171, 173,
    222, 231
  *De l'esprit des lois*   84, 133, 165, 177
Montulé, Édouard de   231
Moore, Barrington   34
Morgan, Edmund   27
Morgan, Kenneth   44
Morley, John   227, 237
Morris, Gouverneur   18, 221, 235
Morris, Michèle R.   253
Morris, Robert   37
Moulier-Boutang, Yann   161–2
Mourgue, Jacques A., *De la France,
  relativement à l'Angleterre et à la
  maison d'Autriche*   273
Murat, Achille   231
Murphy, Thomas K.   237
Myers, Minor   254

Naigeon, Jacques-André   49
Napoleon *see* Bonaparte, Napoleon
Necker, Jacques   171–2, 192

Nefontaine, Luc  42
neo-Whigs  27, 28
Netherlands (Dutch republic)  100–19
  downfall of the republic  110–15
  international role  104
  lending of Scotch brigade to Britain  104, 106
  neutrality  100, 103, 106–10
  loss of  104–5, 110–15
  Patriot Revolt/*Patriottenbeweging*  47, 105
  Stadtholders  103
  William V  106, 114
  trade  105, 108, 110–11
  American–Dutch  111–12
  Anglo–Dutch  107, 108, 111
Newlin, Claude Milton  217
Newman, Simon P.  215–16
Nijenhuis, Ida  118
Nordholt, Schulte  115–17, 119
Nussbaum, Frederick L.  256

O'Brien, Conor Cruise  177
*Observations sur la constitution du nord d'Haïti et sur les opinions qu'on s'est formées en France de ce gouvernement*  293
O'Leary, Patrick  178
Olivero, Isabelle  41
Onouf, Peter S.  141
*Onpartydige bedenkingen van een welmeenend Hollander*  118
Orangists  108–10
Ormesson, François d'  254
O'Rourke, Kevin  45
Oudin-Bastide, Caroline  293
Ozouf, Mona  35, 40, 44

Paape, Gerrit  49, 55, 59
Pagden, Anthony  13
Paine, Thomas  10, 11, 17–18, 19, 24, 32, 46, 48, 49, 55, 56, 179, 223–6, 229, 231, 241
  *Common Sense: Addressed to the Inhabitants of America*  236
  *Rights of Man*  17, 40, 136, 145, 224, 236

Palmer, Robert R.  9, 10, 13, 14, 20, 24, 26–7, 28–32, 33, 41, 43–4, 216–17, 237, 257, 261, 272
Pappas, John N.  60
*Parallèle entre César, Cromwell, Monck et Bonaparte, fragments traduits de l'Anglais*  274
Parrington, Vernon L.  142
Pasley, Jeffrey L.  215
Pasquet, Denis  23, 41
Pasquino, Pasquale  5, 95, 99
Pauw, Cornelius de, *Selections from Les recherches philosophiques sur les Américains*  235
Paynter, John E.  254
Peden, William  144
Perdue, S. Holbrook  234
Pérotin-Dumon, Anne  289, 293
Pesante, Maria Luisa  4
Peterson, Merrill D.  141
Pétion, Alexandre Sabès  288
Peyrard, François, *Précis historique des principales descentes qui ont été faites dans la Grande Bretagne, depuis Jules César jusqu'en l'an V de la République*  273
Philadelphia constitution  87, 88
*philosophes*  17, 24, 25, 47, 48, 49, 53, 57, 58
Physiocrats  7–9, 17, 66, 67–8, 69, 76, 123, 190–3, 222
  economic/political heritage  128–33
  and slavery  147–61
Pietschmann, Horst  45
Piggot, Charles  230
  *A Political Dictionary Explaining the True Meaning of Words*  230, 237
  *The Jockey Club; or a Sketch of the Manners of the Age. Part the Third*  236
Pinto, Isaac de  105, 107–8, 110, 118
  *Examen impartial des intérêts actuels de la République par rapport à une alliance*  119
  *Lettre de mr. \*\*\*\*\* a mr. S.B. ... au sujet des troubles qui agitent actuellement toute l'Amérique Septentrionale*  118

*Réponse de mr. J. de Pinto, aux observations d'un homme impartial, sur sa lettre à mr. S.B. ... au sujet des troubles qui agitent actuellement toute l'Amérique Septentrionale* 118
*Seconde lettre de M. de Pinto, à l'occasion des troubles des colonies, contenant des réflexions politiques sur ... l'etat actuel de l'Angleterre* 118
*Tribut Patriotique* 107–8
Pocock, John G.A. 4, 13–14, 28, 61–3, 64, 72, 73, 76, 77, 79, 141, 272
*Political Dialogues. Number I. On the General Principles of Government* 236
Polverel, Étienne 247, 248, 250, 251
Popkin, Jeremy 41
Porter, Roy 45
Portes, Jacques 238
Potier, Jean-Pierre 143
Potofsky, Allan 6, 9–10, 40–1, 44, 115, 217
*Précis des gémissements des sang mêlés dans les colonies françaises, par J.M.C., américain, sang mêlé* 281, 291
Price, Jacob Munro 37, 45
Price, Richard 40, 49, 55, 64, 65–6, 117
*A Discourse on the Love of Our Country* 40
*Additional Observations on the Nature and Value of Civil Liberty, and the War with America* 78
*Observations on the Importance of the American Revolution* 77
Priestley, Joseph 40, 49, 51–2, 53, 55, 117, 241, 262
*Letters Addressed to the Philosophers and Politicians of France, on the Subject of Religion* 235
*Letters to the Right Honourable Edmund Burke* 40, 50–1, 60
public debt 133–4

Quasi-War 213, 221

Quesnay, François 7, 18, 130, 144, 148, 153, 157, 159, 191, 194

Radical Enlightenment 3, 46–59
Raimond, Julien 280–1
*Observations sur l'origine et les progrès du préjugé des colons blancs contre les hommes de couleur, par M. Raymond, homme de couleur de Saint-Domingue* 280, 291
Rakove, Jack 98, 99
Rawls, John 99
Raymond, Marcel 179
Raynal, Guillaume-Thomas-François 17, 31, 147, 221, 226
*Histoire philosophique et politique des deux Indes* 50, 222, 278
Rearick, Charles 41
Renaut, Francis P. 116
representation 224
  decentralization of 170–3, 174
republicanism 4, 61–2, 71, 73, 259–62
revolution of the mind 46, 49, 56
Ricardo, David 193
Riouffe, Honoré 219
*Revolutionary Justice Displayed* 219–20, 234
Ritter von Arneth, Alfred 254
Robertson, John 14
Robespierre, Maximilien 30, 56, 180, 182, 188, 200, 219, 227, 249, 250, 251, 252
Roche, Daniel 44
Roche, John P. 27
Roederer, Pierre Louis, comte 229, 237, 264
Røge, Pernille 162
Roger, Philippe 238
Rosanvallon, Pierre 199
Rossiter, Clinton 28, 43
Roulin, Alfred 179
Rousseau, Jean-Jacques 17, 47, 48, 53, 55, 56, 62, 147, 176, 226, 227, 284
*Considérations sur le gouvernement de Pologne* 179
Royer, Jean-Pierre 96

Sagnac, Philippe   23–4, 27, 41
Saint-Domingue *see* Haiti
Saint-Louis, Vertus   292
Saint-Simon, Henri de   8, 9, 183, 193–7, 199
  *Considérations sur les mesures à prendre pour terminer la Révolution*   199–200
  *De la réorganisation de la société européenne*   180, 183–7, 198
  *L'industrie*   182, 187–9, 195–6, 198–9
  *Mémoire sur la science de l'homme*   197–8
  *Travail sur la gravitation*   198
Saint-Victor, Benjamin   231
Sala-Molins, Louis   292
Salaville, Jean-Baptiste   263, 264, 267–8
  *De la Révolution française comparée à celle de l'Angleterre*   273
  *De l'organisation d'un état monarchique, ou Considérations sur les vices de la monarchie française, et sur la nécessité de lui donner une constitution*   274
  *Défense du peuple anglais, sur le jugement et la condamnation de Charles premier, roi d'Angleterre, par Milton. Ouvrage propre à éclairer sur la circonstance actuelle où se trouve la France*   274
  *Théorie de la royauté d'après les Principes de Milton avec sa Défense du peuple par Mirabeau*   267, 274
Sas, Nicolaas Cornelis Ferdinand van   116
Sawvel, Franklin B.   217
Say, Jean-Baptiste   7, 24, 125, 128, 139, 141, 143, 160, 182, 189, 193, 194, 196
  *Traité d'économie politique*   137
Schapiro, Jacob S.   42
Schelle, Gustave   78, 162
Schmidt, Nelly   161
Schmitt, Carl   94, 95, 99
Schoelcher, Victor   285
Scott, Jonathan   43
separation of powers   80–94

Sepinwall, Alyssa Goldstein   292
Serna, Pierre   11–12, 14, 272–4
Seven Years War   29, 104, 105
Sharp, James Roger   10, 215, 253
Sheehan, Colleen A.   253
Sheridan, Eugene R.   255
Short, William   242, 244
Shorto, Russell   116
Sieyes, Emmanuel-Joseph, abbé   226, 229, 236, 264, 268
Silvestri, Gaetano   95
Skocpol, Theda   34, 44
Slaughter, Thomas   218
slavery   7–8, 147–61, 271
  economic inefficiency of   152–5
  ending of   156–61
  as violation of human rights   148–52
Sloan, Herbert E.   144, 254
Smart, William   178
Smith, Adam   50, 59, 128, 158, 193, 194, 196, 198
  *The Theory of Moral Sentiments*   59
  *The Wealth of Nations*   193, 220
Smith, James Morton   218
Smith, Melancton   86
Société des amis des noirs   158, 285, 286
Soderhjelm, Alma   254
Sofka, James   115
Somos, Mark   115
Sonenscher, Michael   14, 178, 236
Sonthonax, Léger Félicité   247, 248, 250, 251, 285
Sowerby, E. Millicent   143
Spang, Rebecca   40
Sparks, Jared   235
Staël Anne-Louise-Germaine Necker, madame de   180
  *Considérations sur la Révolution française*   170, 178
Stagg, John C.A.   234
Stapelbroek, Koen   5, 115–16
Stein, Robert   255
Steiner, Philippe   14, 78, 143, 199
Stern, Joseph P.   59
Stevens, John   64
  *Observations on Government*   229

Stinchcombe, William C. 215–16, 218, 273
Stone, Bailey 20, 40
*Sur la situation politique et financière de l'Angleterre, fragments d'un mémoire sur l'Angleterre en général par H.S.P.* 273
Sweet, Alec Stone 94, 99
Syrett, Harold C. 218, 254

Tackett, Timothy 253
Taine, Hippolyte 227
Talleyrand, Charles-Maurice de 221, 261, 273
Tarrade, Jean 36–7, 45
Taylor, George 35, 44
Taylor, John 127
Temple, William 113
 *Observations upon the United Provinces of the Netherlands* 116
Thelwall, John 224
Thierry, Augustin 8, 9, 182, 183, 189, 193–7, 199
 *Considérations sur l'histoire de France* 182
 *De la réorganisation de la société européenne* 180, 183–7, 198
 *Essai sur l'histoire de la formation et des progrès du Tiers État* 182, 200
 *Histoire de la conquête de l'Angleterre par les Normands* 182
 *L'industrie* 182, 187–9, 195–6, 198–9
 *Vues sur les révolutions d'Angleterre* 182
Thiers, Adolphe 231
Thomas, Charles Marion 217
Thompson, C. Bradley 254
Tilly, Charles 34
Tiran, André 142–3
Tocqueville, Alexis de 21–3, 41, 182–3, 231, 232–3, 234, 238
Todd, Stephen C. 97
Tonsor, Steven J. 237
Tortarolo, Edoardo 14
Tower, Joseph Lomas, *Illustrations of Prophecy: In the Course of which are Elucidated Many Predictions, which Occur in Isaiah, or Daniel* 236
Treaty of Breda (1667) 108
Treaty of Campo Formio 263
Treaty of Paris 220
Treaty of Westphalia 184
Troper, Michel 78, 253, 272
Trudaine de la Sablière, Charles-Michel 245
Turgot, Anne-Robert-Jacques 18, 49, 53, 64–5, 68–72, 75–7, 153, 156–7, 158, 160, 192, 229
 *Lettre au docteur Price* 4, 65, 67, 68, 77, 78, 79
 *Mémoire sur les municipalités* 66, 67, 68, 70–2, 78
 *Réflexions rédigées à l'occasion d'un mémoire remis par Mr de Vergenne au Roi sur la manière dont la France et l'Espagne doivent envisager les suites de la querelle entre la Grande-Bretagne et ses colonies* 65, 77
Turner, Frederick Jackson 255

Unitarianism 4
United Provinces *see* Netherlands
United States *see* America
Urbinati, Nadia 144

Vauguyon, Paul-François de La 103, 105
Venturi, Franco 4, 14, 61–2, 63, 64, 76, 77
Vergennes, Charles Gravier, comte de 18, 113
Vermale, François 254
Vezzosi, Elisabetta 77
Vidal, Cécile 42
Vile, Maurice John C. 94
Villiers, Patrick 45
Visser, Joseph 45
Vollenhoven, Cornelis van 115, 119
Volney, Constantin-François Chassebœuf, comte de 24, 46, 49, 55, 260–2, 272
 *Les Ruines, ou méditations sur les révolutions des empires* 262
 *Questions de statistique à l'usage des voyageurs* 272

Voltaire, François-Marie Arouet 17, 49, 50, 52, 53, 54, 55, 58–9, 133, 147, 192, 221, 269
  *Lettres de Memmius* 58
Vossler, Otto 143
Vovelle, Michel 42
Vreede, Pieter 55

Waldstreicher, David 215
Wallerstein, Immanuel 34
Walsh, Robert, *A Letter on the Genius and Disposition of the French Government, including a View of the Taxation of the French Empire* 178
Warren, Mercy Otis 237
Washington, George 37, 123, 141, 203, 204, 205, 207, 209–10, 211, 220, 221, 236, 241, 243, 246, 247, 248, 255
Weber, Max 283
Weymouth, Lally 142
Whatmore, Richard 6, 10–11
Whiskey Rebellion 211
White, Morton G. 141
Wijk, Frederik Willem van 116–17, 119
Wilkie, Everett C. 43
Williams, David 229
  *Lessons to a Young Prince by an Old Statesman, on the Present Disposition of Europe to a General Revolution* 237

Williamson, Jeffrey G. 45
Wills, Garry 141
Witt, Cornélis Henri de 255
Woloch, Isser 33, 44
Womersley, David 79
Wood, Dennis 177
Wood, Gordon 19, 28, 40–1, 273
Wootton, David 79
Wright, Benjamin 27
Wright, Johnson Kent 60
Wulf, Naomi 41–2
(W)XYZ Affair 212, 221, 273

Yorke, Joseph 103, 105, 112, 117, 118
Young, Arthur 226–7
  *Travels during the Years 1787, 1788 and 1789, Undertaken More Particularly with a View of Ascertaining the Cultivation, Wealth, Resources ... of France* 237

Zagrebelsky, Gustavo 96, 97
Zizek, Joseph 43
Zoller, Elisabeth 90